I Tatti Research Series
7

GLOBAL GOLD

Aesthetics, Material Desires, Economies in the Late Medieval and Early Modern World

edited by
Thomas B.F. Cummins

I TATTI

I TATTI

I Tatti – The Harvard University Center
for Italian Renaissance Studies
Via di Vincigliata, 26
50135 Florence – Italy
itatti.harvard.edu

Project coordinator: Thomas Gruber and Mary Doyno
Cover design: Juliet Strachan

Published and distributed in Italy by

OFFICINA
LIBRARIA

Officina Libraria
Via dei Villini, 10
00161 Rome – Italy
officinalibraria.net

Publisher and project coordinator: Marco Jellinek
Art director: Paola Gallerani
Layout: Elisabetta Mancini
Copyediting: Wendy Keebler
Index: Matteo Bonanomi
Color separation: Giorgio Canesin, Cernusco sul Naviglio (Milano)
Printed and bound by Esperia, Lavis (Trento)

Publication of this volume has been made possible by

The Myron and Sheila Gilmore Publication Fund at I Tatti
The Robert Lehman Endowment Fund
The Jean-François Malle Scholarly Programs and Publications Fund
The Andrew W. Mellon Foundation Fund for Scholarly Programs and Publications
The Barbara and Craig Smyth Fund for Scholarly Programs and Publications
The Lila Wallace-Reader's Digest Endowment Fund
The Malcolm Wiener Fund for Scholarly Programs and Publications

Worldwide distribution by Harvard University Press

Italian distribution by Officina Libraria

ISBN 978-06-742-961-76 (Harvard University Press)
ISBN 978-88-3367-222-9 (Officina Libraria)

CONTENTS

Introduction

Thomas B.F. Cummins[1]

One might ask: why a set of essays on gold and why in this historical period? After all, there have been several recent books and exhibitions on gold as a natural material, a valued commodity, and an unequaled substance to fashion things of great beauty throughout the world.[2] However, from the late fifteenth century to the mid seventeenth century the world was increasingly opened up to an international mercantile economy. Gold was a major lubricant in the machinations of merchants' interactions, and it was a word that was used by the Venetians as "an all-inclusive term for 'riches.'"[3] For the Jesuits in Cartagena de las Indias, God became the great merchant who gathered souls by the means of gold.[4] Gold as the medium par excellence for mercantile transactions also became the material for the creation and destruction of things of beauty, as detailed in the essays of Dunlop, Frosinini, and Lippit. It was, moreover, an object of extreme desire for political expansions, for evangelization, and for acts of inhumane degradation in various forms. As analyzed in the essays presented here, gold in all its diverse cultural values, suddenly became a global good with a certain enforced universal value—a legacy to which we still all adhere, whether we like it or not.

The words of Francesco Carletti (1573–1636), a Florentine merchant under the protection of Ferdinando I de' Medici, Grand Duke of Tuscany, to whom he addresses his chronicle, tell us of the role of gold as an international medium of exchange as he traveled around the world, bargaining from port to port. He begins, however with the foulest, most dehumanizing act of mercantile capitalism that still haunts the world today by describing the degrading transactions of his purchase of African people in the Cape Verde Islands to sell in America. [5] There he bought seventy-five men and women (paying dearly, in his words), so as to transport them as cargo to sell in Cartagena de las Indias, which he did. The proceeds of his sale were immediately reinvested in merchandise from Spain which he transported to Peru to sell at a profit. As we shall see, like gold ingots these African individuals were marked, branded with their owners' marks, reduced to commodities in a global market.[6]

Regarding this mercantile transaction of gold for humans, Carletti writes: "This thing ... causes me much sadness and confusion of conscience because truly, Most Serene Highness, it seems to me an inhuman traffic unworthy of a professed and pious Christian. ... this business never pleases me."[7] One can therefore not imagine a set of essays about gold's place in the world without Africa and Africans and the centrality of gold within Western culture, whether as a metaphor of wealth, a sign of power, or an instrument of discord. Suzanne Blier's essay "Blood Money" is fundamental to our volume, as she details these relationships and how they come to fore in the marketplace of the coast and the world. Such a market cannot exist, however, without a structure of accounting and reconciliation. Carlo Taviani's essay focuses on a microcosm of the mercantile reckoning of gold and trade as the networks of trade expanded exponentially from the mid fifteenth century to the mid sixteenth century. In fact, Italian gold as a medium of exchange, the ducat, was recognized by Charles V in 1524 when he declared the Venetian ducat the standard in his ever-growing Holy Roman Empire. However, only by fine-grained research, as Taviani's essay demonstrates, can the role of gold in the economies of the world be understood.

As we shall see in my chapter and Kris Lane's chapter, which focus on America and the desire for gold, Christian monarchs, citizens, and artists transformed the gold used in this new global market to create pious works and express everlasting devotion in Europe. Within the Western Christian context, gold is therefore both pernicious and esteemed.[8] Gold's Manichean quality also has resonance in Asante (see Blier's essay) and Mexica (Aztec) mytho-histories,[9] just as it does in Judeo-Christian mytho-histories. In both cases it is transformed symbolically as European trade and invasion invest gold with alien values.

Gold nonetheless has certain universal characteristics. While the forms it takes in objects are mutable, the metal itself is almost indestructible and therefore reusable, as we shall witness in the crucible of world conquest in the sixteenth century by Europeans and others. Its brilliance, scarcity, malleability, color, and incorruptibility are culturally transcendent qualities, and they are a constant reference in the essays here, whether investigating the economics of gold in Europe or considering its use in Italian painting, Spanish sculpture, or Japanese architecture. However, the values that are attributed to the properties of gold and how they are deployed culturally are not the same.

Thus, what can be considered as a golden idol can be recast to be a devotional image; or, in the case of Asante coronation, older golden images and objects are recast to re-energize them to be new but in concert with the past.

The intersection of different histories and cultures after 1492 led to the moment when gold became a universal. In what was to become America, "the purity of gold" as related to "the exchange value of gold" did not necessarily have the same valence for the Taino, Muisca, Inca, Aztec, and others, as the Spaniards were quick to learn, because gold was not always refined to be as pure as possible but was combined with copper for various reasons.[10] The essays presented in this volume concentrate on different cultures (Asante, Italian, Islamic, Hapsburg, Japan, Inca, Mexica) and places (Europe, America, Africa, and Asia) to create a broad framework of how gold as a material entered into so many differing elements of beliefs, artistic and architectural practices, mining exploration and techniques, and economies of trade and accounting.

If we return to Carletti, the Florentine merchant, who was returning from India in 1604 with pearls, diamonds, and 1600 ounces of musk, among other riches, we find a description of him aboard the Portuguese ship the *San Jacopo* (*São Jago*), loaded with all his goods and riches. The events that unfolded and the narrative elements give us a glimpse into the microcosm of the different places and issues that structure the essays in this book. After eight years circumnavigating the world, trading up at each port, the *São Jago* neared the island of Saint Helena, where it was attacked, boarded, and looted by the crews of two Dutch vessels, the *Zeelandia* and the *Langebarke*, which belonged to the forerunner of the Dutch East India Company (VOC). Carletti describes the Dutch barbarity toward the slaves and servants aboard the São *Jago*, who could not be ransomed or sold in Holland. As these men and women had no mercantile value for the Dutch sailors, they were thrown into sea from the deck of the *São Jago* to drown, so as to make room for the cargo that could not be taken aboard the *Zeelandia* and the *Langebarke* to be sold in the Dutch marketplace. Carletti tells his reader (Ferdinando I de' Medici) that his own Korean "servant"

> played a trick on them [the Dutch], notwithstanding the fact he did not know how to swim yet knowing that they were not taking aboard servants or slaves like himself: he put two of my little pictures around his neck, on one of which was painted a crucified Christ, and on the other an *Ecce Homo*, and both of them on copper, which were dear to me as they were made in Japan with great artistry. Wearing them my servant threw himself into the sea and he was im-

> mediately retrieved by the [Dutch] sailors, who thought that he had something of great value to them. Seeing what they were they gave them back to him and as he was already in the longboat they left him and took him to the ship. ... I have the little paintings as most of them [the sailors] are Calvinists and they do not want paintings of the saints or the crucifixion.[11]

This small incident in Carletti's account underscores the almost immediate world trade and its concomitant terror, beginning with the purchase and sale of humans using gold to acquire them, to the final traumatic event in his journey.[12] He is overwhelmed by the theft of his gold and other riches for the market, the sinking of his ship, and the killing of slaves and servants.[13] The copper images made in Japan with Christian iconography that saved the life of his Korean servant in the waters off Saint Helena—as their metallic brilliance sparkled as if something of material value—make clear the tangible interrelationship between Italy and Holland, India and Japan.

Yukio Lippit's essay brings this relationship into focus in terms of gold in the imagination of others, such as Marco Polo or the Chinese. The Kinkakuji, "Temple of the Golden Pavilion," was as closely involved in the politics of Japan as it was in Buddhism; as he notes, "gold served as the material of choice for the gilded face of Japanese diplomacy," even though Japan had "relatively paltry production of gold." The gilding of the exterior of the Kinkakuji was at one level like the gilding in gold plates of the Inca temple of the *coricancha* ("golden enclosure" in Quechua). However, unlike the *coricancha*, which was stripped of its cladding by foreigners for its gold, the Kinkakuji "was experienced within a discursive environment in which overseas visitors were prepared and even expected to encounter aurelian manifestations of abundance." The overseas visitors were Chinese, and someone like Carletti would never have seen it. Certainly, the Japanese Christian convert who produced the painted copper images of Christ and sold them to Carletti in Nagasaki would not have seen the exterior of the Kinkakuji either. The image of the sacrificed man-god was what he worshipped. These Japanese paintings did not need to be of gold to radiate. However, to the Dutch sailors, for a passing moment they shimmered like gold worn around the neck of a man meant to be drowned but who was saved, not by the grace of God but by the brilliance of a gilded reflection.

China, as a partner in the exchange of global gold, was also represented on the *São Jago*. A significant part of the cargo on the Portuguese ship had been purchased with American gold and silver. This precious cargo was Chinese export porcelain (mostly made in Jingdezhen), purchased in Macao and

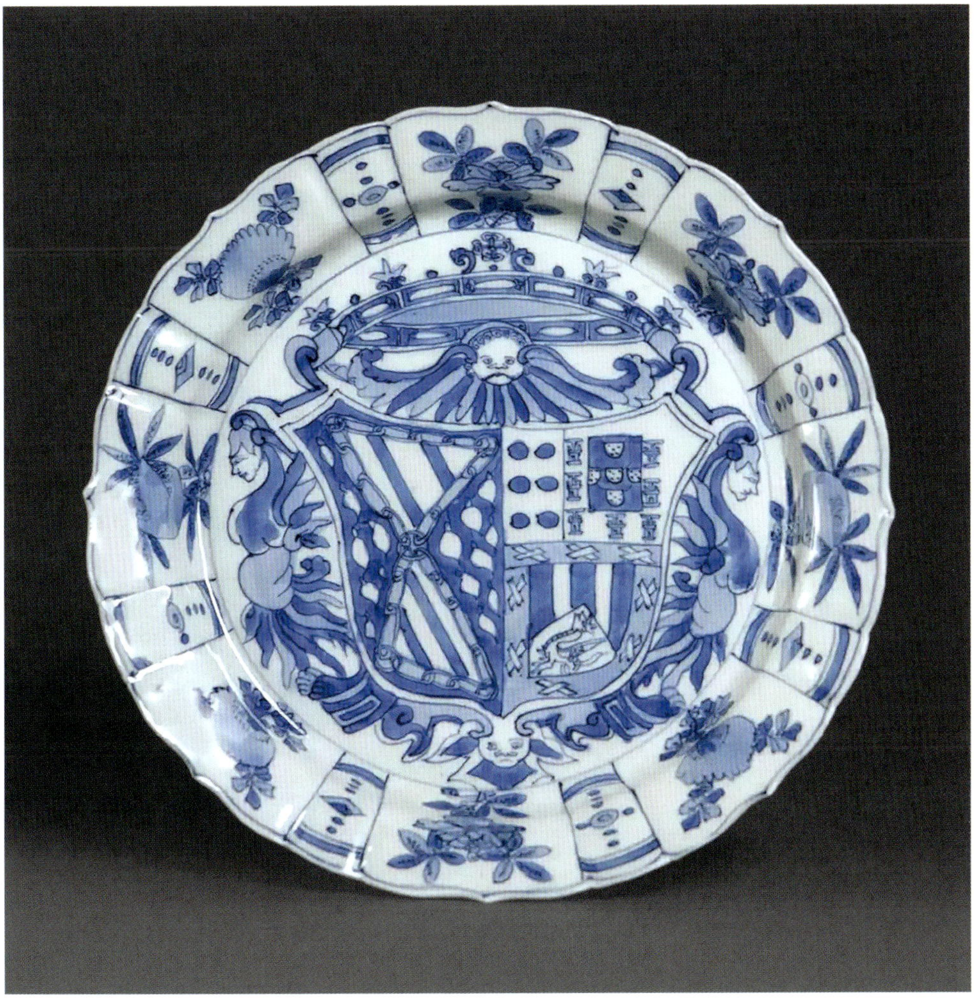

Fig. 1. Plate with the coats of arms of Viceroy García de Mendoza y Manrique and his wife, Teresa de Castro y de la Cueva, Jingdezhen, China, ca. 1590, porcelain. Thomas Lurie collection

destined for Lisbon. American gold and silver were already being used to acquire porcelain worldwide, including from Peru, where the Viceroy García de Mendoza y Manrique had commissioned a set of plates with his coat of arms alongside that of his wife, Teresa de Castro y de la Cueva, which were placed at the center of the plates and were produced in Jingdezhen between 1590 and 1593 (fig. 1).[14]

When the two Dutch ships, the *Zeelandia* and the *Langebarke*, returned to Middelburg with Carletti aboard, the company auctioned off the booty, the greater part of which consisted of this newish commodity of porcelain. The

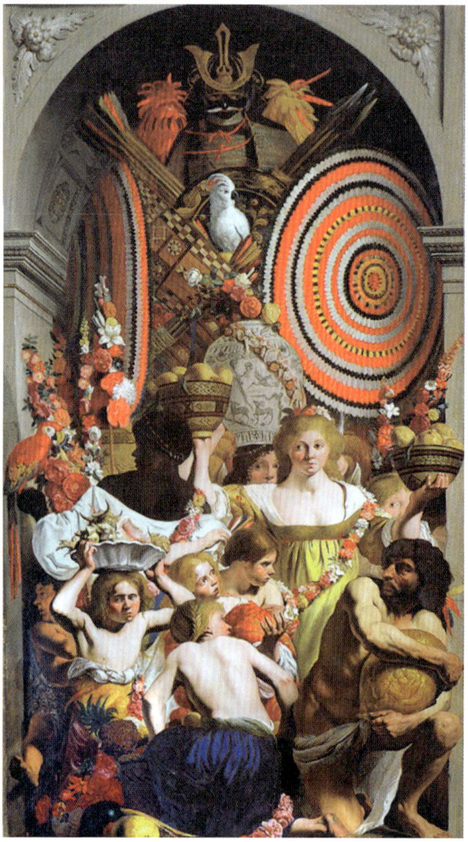

Fig. 2. Jacob van Campen, *Triumphal Procession with Presents from the East and West*, 1648–52, oil on canvas, 308 × 205 cm. The Hague, Paleis Huis ten Bosch, Oranjezaal

profits were so high from the auction that the newly formed VOC decided to develop a regular trade in porcelain, thus setting off an ever-increasing demand. It was so extensive that by 1657 more than three million pieces had been sold in the Netherlands, and by 1682 that number had increased to twelve million pieces, such that porcelain lost most of its value and was no longer worth selling at auction and was in daily use in Dutch orphanages.[15]

Through this global expansion—whether by trade, war, or piracy—abundance became a defining character of early modern Dutch culture.[16] The VOC was mirrored for a short period by Dutch investment in America, with the formation of the West India Company, in order to increase this expansive wealth yet further. Brazil in particular became an object of desire and commerce for the West India Company, and Holland took control of northern coastal Brazil from 1624 to 1654, most notably under its governor Johan Maurits van Nassau-Siegen, who among other things had a set of remarkable paintings of people, fauna, and landscapes produced for him by Albert Eckhout and Frans Post.

These East and West Company interests were brought together in the Dutch royal imaginary some forty-one years after the Dutch captured the *São Jago*, when the cornerstone of the Huis ten Bosch palace was laid. It was a summer residence for Prince Frederik Hendrik and his wife, Princess Amalia, who converted it into a memorial for her husband, who died in 1647. She commissioned the central room known as the Oranjezaal, which was dedicated to the prince's life and work. Designed and partially painted by Jacob van Campen, the room is an allegorical tribute to the prince's many successes. Gold abounds in terms of both the room's gilded architectural ornament and the painted subjects, such as Jacob Jordeans's *The Triumph of Fredrick Henry*. However, Van Campen reserved for himself the most literal and allegorical subject of all—the riches of the world and Dutch possessions—in an oil-on-canvas painting entitled *Triumphal Procession with Presents from the East and West* (fig. 2). It is a very busy composition, stuffed with people and things pressed forward that more or less coalesce into an extravagant display of the familiar, the foreign, and riches framed by but spilling out of a *trompe-l'oeil* architectural niche.

In the upper half of the canvas are representations of actual objects, while in the lower half are allegorical figures, some of which are, however, based on portraits of real people. In the right corner a classicized kneeling Michelangelo-like figure grasps a golden vessel. The style shifts to more contemporary reference in the central figure that embodies the familiar, the foreign, and riches. Placed in the near foreground is a buxom, rosy-cheeked, blonde young woman wearing a golden silk dress. She is the familiar, a Dutch beauty in the fullness of youth. However, she holds aloft two woven reed baskets filled with fruit, one in each hand, and through this gesture and the objects held it becomes clear that she is also a pastiche of two portraits painted by Albert Eckhout in Brazil in 1641.[17] One is a full-length portrait of an African mother and child from the Gold Coast and the other is a full-length portrait of a *mameluca* (offspring of a European and a Native American) from Brazil (figs. 3 and 4).[18]

Like Eckhout's *mameluca* figure, van Campen's looks slightly to her left, but she has the same forceful frontal stance of the African figure. Not only are poses seen in Eckhhout's paintings obviously copied here, but the woven designs of the basket that van Campen's figure holds in her right hand is almost identical to the one held aloft in Eckhout's portrait of the woman from the Gold Coast.[19] The racial switch in this frontally arresting figure by van Campen is complemented by the African woman placed in counterpoint next to her. The latter is the black to the white, with her back to the viewer and her head turned in silhouetted profile, in contrast to the white woman's frontal outward gaze. She too, however, has her hand held upward, supporting an American parrot that also comes from Eckhout's sketches. These sources by Eckhout are of course obvious and they are meant to be, as they are important visual cues that mark

Following pages

Fig. 3. Albert Eckhout, *Portrait of an African Woman and Child in Brazil*, 1641, oil on canvas, 282 × 189 cm. Copenhagen, Nationalmuseet

Fig. 4. Albert Eckhout, *Portrait of a Mameluca*, 1641, oil on canvas, 171 × 170 cm. Copenhagen, Nationalmuseet

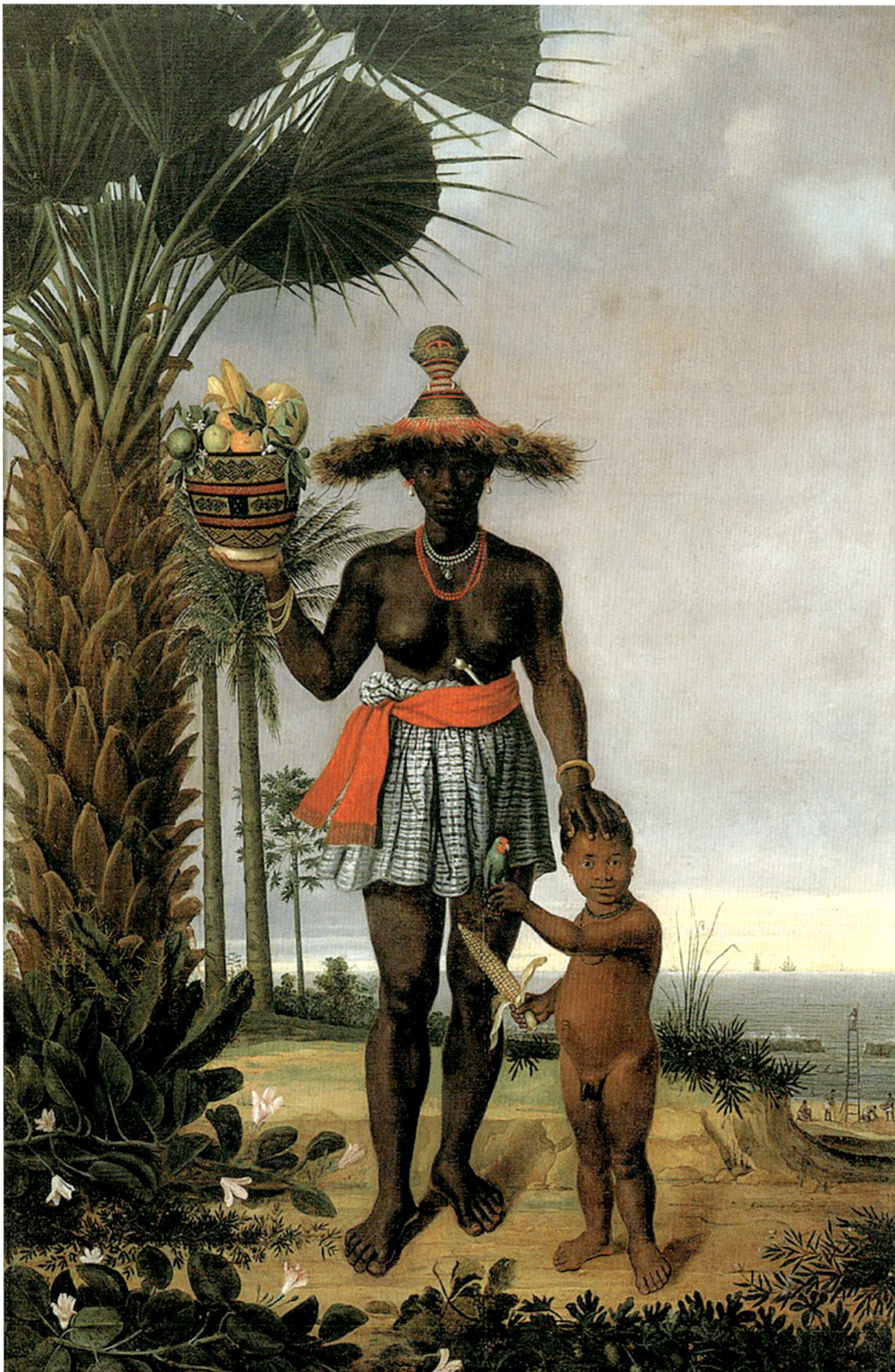

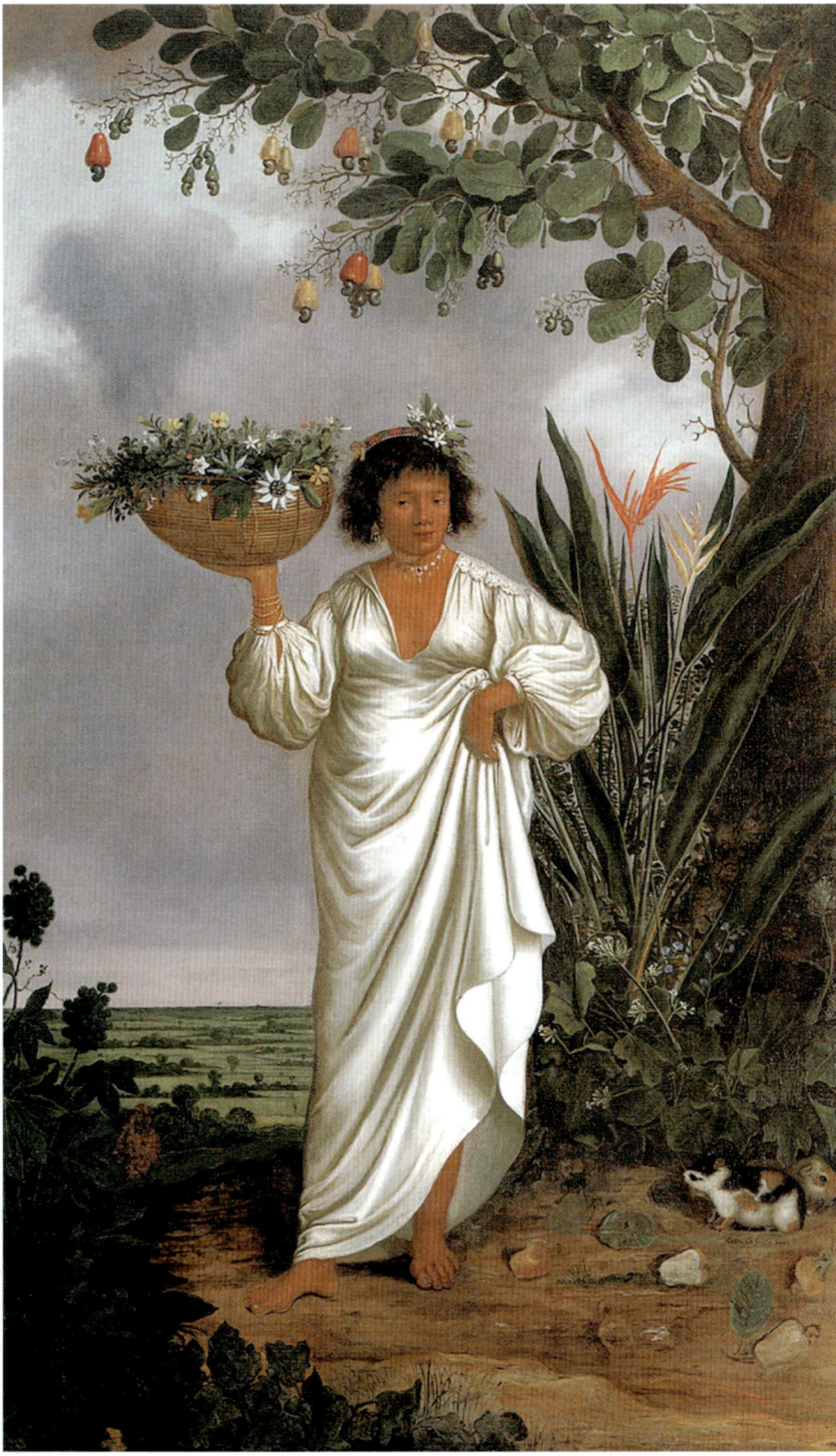

not only the artistic presence of the Dutch project in Brazil but its "exotic" treasures.

The riches of China and the VOC are figured by the porcelain jar born on the head of a dark-haired figure whose face is just visible behind the blonde, fair-skinned girl, turning to look at the viewer as she carries the jar from left to right of the image. She has a slightly a darker, reddish complexion. Above, we see the magnificent feather shields and arrows of the Tupinambá, separated by an Inca *uncu* (tunic) replete with woven *tocapu* (abstract geometric) designs. The latter expresses wish fulfillment, as the Dutch had launched an attempt to capture Peru and its natural wealth.[20] Finally, Japan appears at the apex of the composition, where there is a complete set of Samurai armor flanked by the hoods of Tupinambá feathered capes. This, then, is not a painting of a cabinet of curiosities but the allegorical depiction of the wealth of a mercantile nation expressed in objects—a wealth oiled by global gold.

Notes

1. I thank Thomas Gruber, Leonardo López Luján, Cocó Acalá, Mary Seo, Joseph Connors, Byron Hamann, and an anonymous reviewer, among others, for all their help in composing this essay. Any faults, omissions, and other things gone or gotten wrong are solely my fault, but so be it in the years 2020–22. I would also like to thank Lauren Toman for all her editorial efforts to bring this volume to completion.

2. For example, see the essays in *El oro y la plata de las Indias en la época de los Austrias* (Madrid: Fundación ICO, 1999); Jeffery Quilter and John Hoopes, eds., *Gold and Power in Ancient Costa Rica, Panama, and Colombia* (Washington, DC: Dumbarton Oaks Research Library and Collection, 2003); Elisenda Vila Llonch, *Beyond El Dorado: Power and Gold in Ancient Colombia* (London: British Museum, 2013); Rebecca Zorach and Michael Philips Jr., *Gold: Nature and Culture* (London: Reaktion Books, 2016); Joanne Pillsbury, Timothy Potts, and Kim Richter, eds., *Golden Kingdoms: Luxury Art in Ancient America* (Los Angeles: J. Paul Getty Museum, 2017); Kathleen Bickford Berzock, *Caravans of Gold, Fragments in Time: Art, Culture, and Exchange Across Medieval Saharan Africa* (Princeton: Princeton University Press, 2019).

3. Federica Ambrosini, "Venetian Diplomacy, Spanish Gold, and the New World in the Sixteenth Century," in *The New World in Early Modern Italy, 1492–1750*, edited by Elizabeth Hororowich and Lia Markey (Cambridge: Cambridge University Press, 2017), 47.

4. Alonso de Sandoval, *De instauranda Aethiopum salute. El mundo de la esclavitud negra en América* (Bogotá: Biblioteca de la Presidencia de Colombia, 1956). See also M. E. Beers, "Alonso de Sandoval: Seventeenth-Century Merchant of the Gospel," accessed June 20, 2022, https://web.archive.org/web/20180726181004/http://www.kislakfoundation.org/prize/199702.html.

5. A version of Carletti's chronicle, written after his return to Florence 1606, was published in 1701 as *Ragionamenti di Francesco Carletti Fiorentino sopra le cose da lui vedute ne'suoi viaggi si dell'Indie Occidentali, e Orientali come d'altri paesi* (Florence: Stamperìa di G. Manni, per il Carlieri, 1701); however, none of his text concerning the shame of buying or selling slaves appears in that publication: see pages 17–20, which were removed by the editor, Jacopo Carlieri. I have used the *Ragionamenti del mio viaggio intorno al mondo*, edited by Adele Dei (Milan: Mursia, 1987), which is based on the manuscript 'Ragionamenti' in the Biblioteca Angelica, Rome, Codice 1331 (T.3.22).

6. For an analysis of Carletti's text in relation to the Jesuit artistic programs directed toward newly arrived Africans at the slave market in Cartagena, see Thomas B.F. Cummins, "'Me parece un negocio inhumano': el Barroco Negro y la misericordia de dios en Nueva Granada y Peru," keynote speech, *Congreso de Arte Virreinal: El futuro del arte del pasado, Lima, July 19, 2019; an expanded version is in La Imagen como testigo Bogotá (in press).*

7. "Cosa vertamente, ch'a ricordarni di fatta per comomandamento di chi poteva in me, mi causa, una certa tristeza e confusion di conscientia, perché vertiermente, Serebenissimo Signore, questo mi parve sempre un traffic inumano et indigno della proessione et pietá cristiana, non é dubbio alcuno, che si viene a fare incetta d'uomini o, per dire piú propriamente, di carene e sangue unmano, e tanto piú vergona essendo battezzai, che se bene sono differenti nel color e nella fortuna del mondo, nulladimeno hanno quella medisima anima formatali, dall'istesso Fattore che formó le nostre." Carletti, *Ragionamenti del mio viaggio intorno al mondo*, 38.

8. The pernicious aspect of gold within the Judeo-Christian cosmos is, of course, rooted in idolatry and the worship and destruction of the Golden Calf, as told in Exodus. Idolization through a golden image continues into the twenty-first century as demonstrated by the pseudo-golden likeness of Donald Trump and the adoration it received at the 2021 meeting of the Republican Conservative Political Action Conference. Yet gold can be redeemed: after Moses destroys the Golden Calf and makes the Israelites drink it, the gold is used to build the ark of the covenant, as described in Exodus 25:10–22: "They shall make an ark of acacia wood, two and a half cubits long, a cubit and a half wide, and a cubit and a half high. ... Overlay it with pure gold—overlay it inside and out—and make upon it a gold molding round about."

9. For an understanding of the Zemi (Cemi) in Taino culture, see José Oliver, *Caciques and Cemi: The Web Spun by Taino Rulers Between Hispanola and Puerto Rico* (Tuscaloosa: University of Alabama Press, 2009), 59–116.

10. Heather Lechtman, "Andean Value Systems and the Development of Pre-Hispanic Metallurgy," *Technology and Culture* 25 (1984): 1–36.

11. "Ma un mio servitore di nationale Corea fece loro una burla, no ostatante che non sapese notare et che sapeva che non ricevevano servitori né schiavi, como esso era: si mise al collo due mia quadretti, uno dove era dipinto un Chisto crocifisso et nell'altro un Ecce Huomo, ambi sopra rame, quali sono appresso di me et li stimo assai, sí perché sono fatti nel Giappone da buono artifice, come per questo caso che seguí di questo mio servitore. Con li quali si gettò al mare e su subito racolto da quelli marinari, che si pensorno avesse qualche gran cosa di lor utile, et visto quello erano glie ne resero et giá che era nel battello lo lassorno stare e condussero nella lor nave, dove mi salvò detti quadretti con poca difficultà, perché questi, come che sieno eretici calvinistici la maggior parte, non vogliono verdere pitture di Sante né dell'istresso Iddio crocifisso." Carletti, *Ragionamenti del mio viaggio intorno al mondo*, 198.

12. The intellectual conflation of an immediate transactional relationship between gold and slavery within the Spanish mercantile value system is demonstrated by the structure of the chapters in José de Veita Linaje, *Norte de la contratacion de las Indias Occidentales* (Seville: Juan Francisco de Blas, 1672). The book narrates and compiles the laws, rules, and regulations governing the commerce as well as navigation between Spain and America. The rules assaying and determining the value of gold and silver are given in chapters XXXIII and XXXIV, which are followed by the compilation of the history and value of enslaved African people in America in chapter XXXV, entitled "De los esclavos negros que se llevan á las indias y forma de los asientos que suelen hazerse dellos." In fact, these three chapters are written in concert, as their subjects formed the basis of all American commerce.

13. The ongoing antagonisms between differing peoples and cultures who were brought together by this new global mercantile economy is reduced to a near suicidal and absurd moment in the narrative of travel aboard a ship voyaging between Japan and China. The crew was composed of Japanese and Portuguese, who began to quarrel. This was based on not understanding each other and the actions and words that were received as great insults because the Portuguese did not understand the culture of the Japanese ("un certo un fastidioso Portughese, non sapendo forse la natura e conditione delli Giapponesi, che non solamente non sofferiscono alcuna spetie d'ingiuria"). The two groups of about sixty each gathered at either end of the ship ready to fight to the death. "E ne sarebbe seguito del male non poco, se non vi provvedeva la miserocodia di Dios per mezzo di quelli reloigiosi della Compagnia di Gesú che venivano nel vascello, li quali con loro destrezza cominciorno a persuadere con buone parole quelli Giapponesi cristiani, cche sarebbono causa della rovina e morte di tutti e di loro ancora, e insieme della perdita di quell vascello, del qual giánon viera ci tenesse conto, restando abbandonato il governo del Timone e conseguentemente quello delle vele" (It would have gone from bad to worse if it weren't for the mercy of God ... the Jesuits aboard persuaded those Japanese Christians that they might become the cause of the ruin and death of everyone, themselves included, together with the loss of the vessel, which at the time no one was taking any care of ...). Carletti, *Ragionamenti del mio viaggio intorno al mondo*, 126–27. This is an almost comical but deadly situation that seems straight out of an Eugène Ionesco play or a Monty Python skit, except that it was very real.

14. Dennis Carr, ed., *Made in the Americas: The New World Discovers Asia* (Boston: MFA Publications/ Museum of Fine Arts, Boston, 2015), 40.

15. Jan Veenendaal, *Asian Art and Dutch Taste* (Zwolle: Waanders/Gemeentemussen Den Haag, 2014), 15.

16. See Simon Schama, *The Embarrassment of Riches: An Interpretation of Dutch Culture in the Golden Age* (New York: Alfred A. Knopf, 1987).

17. Whether Eckhout painted these portraits in Brazil is debated, but this debate is of no importance for the discussion as a source for van Campen. See Rebecca Parker Brienen, *Visions of Savage Paradise: Albert Eckhout, Court Painter in Colonial Dutch Brazil* (Amsterdam: Amsterdam University Press, 2006), 172–74.

18. These portraits of women are each part of a pendant series of man and wife that depict racial types of Native Americans and Africans and their intermarriage, as well as marriage with Europeans, and the ethnogenesis of peoples such as mulattos and mamelukes. Eckhout's paintings (often euphemistically called ethnographic portraits) anticipate the Mexican *casta* genre series. For *casta* paintings, see Ilona Katzew, *Casta Painting: Images of Race in Eighteenth-Century Mexico* (New Haven: Yale University Press, 2005).

19. Eckhout's work as van Campen's source for this figure is clearly demonstrated by the basket shape and woven design. These are a direct citation from Eckhout's painting and they cannot not be from the watercolor-on-paper copies made by Zacharias Wagener for his *Theirbuch*, ca. 1641, as they are rather different. For a discussion of the relationship of Wagener to Eckhout, see Brienen, *Visions of Savage Paradise*, 131–69.

20. It is unclear how or where van Campen saw the Inca (colonial?) textile. It may have been in Johan Maurits's or Eckhout's possession, gathered while in Brazil, as an expeditionary force was organized in Brazil to attack Chile and turn the people there against the Spaniards. That force was led by Henrick Brouwer who had already been appointed to the Supreme Council of Brazil and he "accepted command for an expedition to Chile which, it was hoped, would alleviate the Company's burden of debt by means of trade and bring riches from the country's gold mine. ... Brouwer was instructed to spread the reformed religion among the barbarians and to liberate them into the clear light of truth. He was to overcome paganism with the help of Christianity, and while searching for gold show the truth path for salvation of those in error. We did not want to appear as though looking for riches only, but also as showing compassion for those who wander in error." Caspar van Baerle, *The History of Brazil under the Governorship of Count Johan Maurits of Nassau, 1636–1644*, trans. Blanche T. van Berckel-Ebeling Koning (Gainsville: University of Florida Press, 2011; original published 1647), 251–54.

Bibliography

Ambrosini, Federica. "Venetian Diplomacy, Spanish Gold and the New World in the Sixteenth Century." In *The New World in Early Modern Italy, 1492–1750*, edited by Elizabeth Hororowich and Lia Markey, 47–60. Cambridge: Cambridge University Press, 2017.

Baerle, Caspar van. *The History of Brazil under the Governorship of Count Johan Maurits of Nassau, 1636–1644*. Translated by Blanche T. van Berckel-Ebeling Koning. Gainsville: University of Florida Press, 2011. Original published 1647.

Beers, M. E. "Alonso de Sandoval: Seventeenth-Century Merchant of the Gospel." Accessed June 20, 2022. https://web.archive.org/web/20180726181004/http://www.kislakfoundation.org/prize/199702.html.

Berzock, Kathleen Bickford. Caravans of Gold, Fragments in Time: Art, Culture, and Exchange Across Medieval Saharan Africa. Princeton: Princeton University Press, 2019.

Brienen, Rebecca Parker. *Visions of Savage Paradise: Albert Eckhout, Court Painter in Colonial Dutch Brazil*. Amsterdam: Amsterdam University Press, 2006.

Carletti, Francesco, *Ragionamenti del mio viaggio intorno al mondo*. Edited by Adele Dei. Milan: Mursia, 1987.

Carletti, Francesco. *Ragionamenti di Francesco Carletti Fiorentino sopra le cose da lui vedute ne'suoi viaggi si dell'Indie Occidentali, e Orientali come d'altri paesi*. Edited by Jacopo Carlieri. Florence: Stamperìa di G. Manni, per il Carlieri, 1701.

Carr, Dennis, ed. Made in the Americas: The New World Discovers Asia. Boston: MFA Publications/ Museum of Fine Arts, Boston, 2015.

Cummins, Thomas B.F. "'Me parece un negocio inhumano': el Barroco Negro y la misericordia de dios en Nueva Granada y Peru." Keynote speech, *Congreso de Arte Virreinal: El futuro del arte del pasado. Lima, July 19, 2019.*

Katzew, Ilona. *Casta Painting: Images of Race in Eighteenth-Century Mexico*. New Haven: Yale University Press, 2005.

Lechtman, Heather. "Andean Value Systems and the Development of Pre-Hispanic Metallurgy." *Technology and Culture* 25 (1984): 1–36.

Oliver, José. *Caciques and Cemi: The Web Spun by Taino Rulers Between Hispanola and Puerto Rico*. Tuscaloosa: University of Alabama Press, 2009.

El oro y la plata de las Indias en la época de los Austrias. Madrid: Fundación ICO, 1999.

Pillsbury, Joanne, Timothy Potts, and Kim Richter, eds. *Golden Kingdoms: Luxury Art in Ancient America*. Los Angeles: J. Paul Getty Museum, 2017.

Quilter, Jeffery, and John Hoopes, eds. *Gold and Power in Ancient Costa Rica, Panama, and Colombia*. Washington, DC: Dumbarton Oaks Research Library and Collection, 2003.

Sandoval, Alonso de. *De instauranda Aethiopum salute. El mundo de la esclavitud negra en América*. Bogotá: Biblioteca de la Presidencia de Colombia, 1956.

Schama, Simon. *The Embarrassment of Riches: An Interpretation of Dutch Culture in the Golden Age*. New York: Alfred A. Knopf, 1987.

Veenendaal, Jan. *Asian Art and Dutch Taste*. Zwolle: Waanders/Gemeentemussen Den Haag, 2014.

Veita Linaje, José de. *Norte de la contratacion de las Indias Occidentales*. Seville: Juan Francisco de Blas, 1672.

Vila Llonch, Elisenda. *Beyond El Dorado: Power and Gold in Ancient Colombia*. London: British Museum, 2013.

Zorach, Rebecca, and Michael Philips Jr. *Gold: Nature and Culture*. London: Reaktion Books, 2016.

PART I

The Making of Gold and Aesthetics

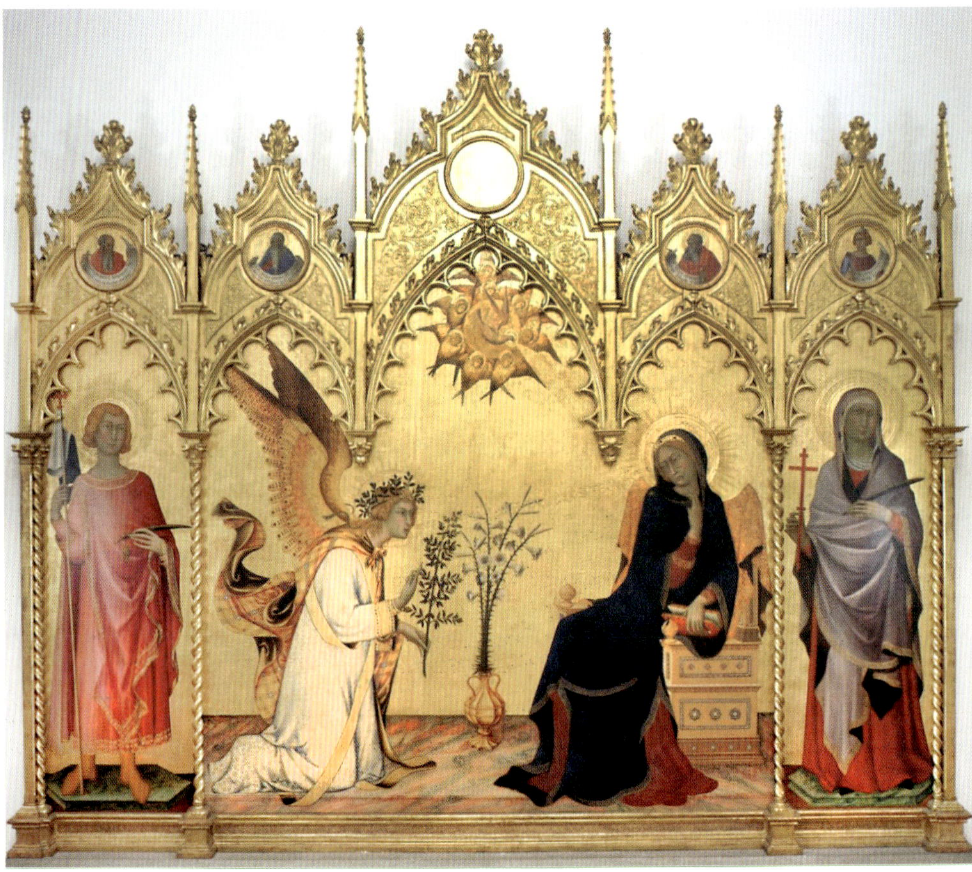

Fig. 1. Simone Martini and Lippo Memmi, *Altarpiece of the Annunciation with Saints Ansanus and Margaret*, 1333, tempera and gold on panel, 184 × 114 cm (center panel); 105 × 48 cm (side panels). Florence, Gallerie degli Uffizi

On Gold and Gold-Backs in Early Italian Art

Anne Dunlop

In the field of Italian painting, the presence or absence of gold has been historiographically determinant: it is taken to divide the medieval from the modern. Although the term is a little old-fashioned, the works of the thirteenth to fifteenth centuries are still occasionally called gold-back or gold-ground painting, and studies of the period often reference gold in their very titles.[1] Looking at a famous example like Simone Martini and Lippo Memmi's 1333 *Annunciation*, done for one of the main altars of the Cathedral of Siena, it is easy to see why. The work is almost two meters high and more than two meters wide, and almost the entire surface is covered in gold, including the elaborate frame (fig. 1).[2] Gold leaf has been laid down and burnished to form the space and setting for the drama between the two figures, and gold is also used as a kind of pigment. To create the Angel Gabriel's startling clothes and wings, for instance, egg tempera was laid over a layer of the metal, and then scratched away and finished with more translucent varnishes to create effects of depth and color. A similar technique produced the cluster of angels around the dove of the Holy Spirit (fig. 2). Gold models Mary's figure at the edges of her robe, and has even been shaped into the words that she and Gabriel exchange against the flat gold ground. Almost a century later, Gentile da Fabriano made use of some of the same effects: in a fragmentary *Madonna and Child* in the Berenson Collection, much of the composition has been painted over a layer of gold leaf that was then

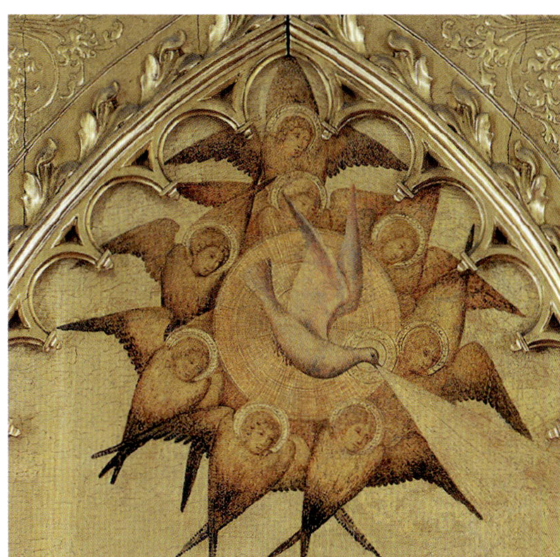

Fig. 2. *Altarpiece of the Annunciation*, detail of the dove of the Holy Spirit

scratched, scored, and punched to create forms, fabrics, and patterns (fig. 3).[3]

Early Italian painting may be the only subfield of art history where the working and tooling of gold has even served as a mode of authorial authentication. The punches on such works were handmade and unique, and they can sometimes be traced from father to son and shop to shop; some scholars have argued that attributions and filiations can therefore be made from this evidence.[4] Conversely, a number of paintings have been linked to the modern artist, restorer, and forger Icilio Federico Joni (1865/66–1946) because the gold has been worked in his characteristic fashion.[5]

Yet a turn away from gold was coming: less than twenty years after Gentile da Fabriano's work, Leon Battista Alberti would declare in his *De pictura* that paint, not gold itself, should be used to create gold in painting, and that the artist's hand added value to the metal, not the other way around.[6] Michael Baxandall's fundamental study *Painting and Experience in Fifteenth-Century Italy* famously argued that the use of gold and precious pigments was supplanted by a stress on the artist's skill and handiwork—"from gold to 'brush'", as he terms it—over the course of the quattrocento; he could point to humanists like Lorenzo Valla (ca. 1407–57), who ridiculed earlier scholars and theorists for their defense of gold as the noblest form of color.[7] This same gold-ground production is also sometimes called Italian *primitive* art, linking it to a first stage of artistic evolution or a kind of childhood, and it is easy to tie the profusion of gold to an idea of unsophisticated excess, just as Sigmund Freud famously linked the retention of feces by the anal-stage child to the hoarding of gold by the adult misers those children would become – an idea given contemporary form in works like Maurizio Cattelan's *America*, a solid-gold toilet first installed for admiration and public use at the Guggenheim Museum.[8] Nor is the linking of gold and waste, human or otherwise, a new idea, if we take sublimation to be its core: it is easy to recall the medieval Abbot Suger of Saint-Denis describing his glittering gold treasures, which led his mind from the excrement of the mundane to heaven, or so at least he claimed.[9]

Yet gold is the most polyvalent and powerful of signifiers. In sixteenth-century France, for instance, it was caught up in everything from debates on inflation to the very question of if, and how, value might be added to God's creation, the natural world, through human work.[10] In recent years, a re-evaluation of the role of gold in early Italian art has begun, and what follows here is intended as a contribution to this work.[11] It will pick up on the linking of gold and the autograph, pushing, however, against the distinction between material and skill, gold and brush. I will suggest that early artists staged skill and process

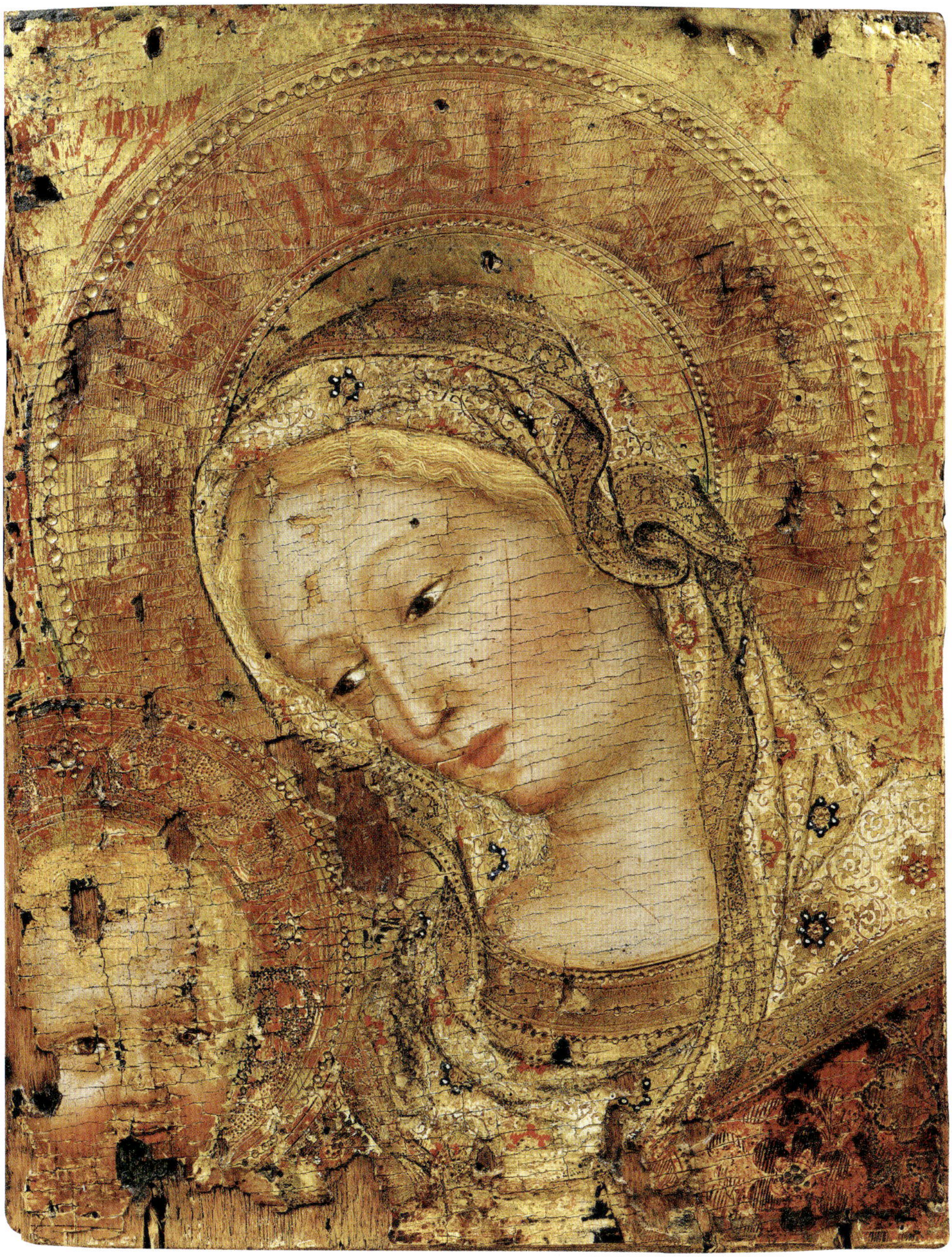

Fig. 3. Gentile da Fabriano, *Madonna and Child*, ca. 1418–19, tempera and gold on panel, cut down, 24.8 × 19 cm. Florence, Villa I Tatti, Berenson Collection

most clearly and importantly in their manipulation of gold; the associations and properties of the metal allowed an inchoate notion of art-making as process to be made manifest, in a medium, tempera, with relatively few affordances for such marking. What follows will therefore trace some of the fundamental ideas of gold in this period, including its sources in far-away West Africa, and the metal's associations with time and process very different from normal human life; it concludes with a single but representative case study.

The gold of Italian gold-backs has its own particular history. Gold is one of the rarer metals: the crust of the Earth holds approximately 2.5 grams of gold for every 1000 tonnes of rock.[12] Yet medieval Europe was particularly gold-poor.[13] Gold had been extensively mined in Spain and elsewhere throughout the Roman period, and some memory of antiquity's lost riches remained: in fourteenth-century Rome, for instance, rental contracts normally had a clause to cover ownership of any treasure found on the property, and at least one Roman convent was swindled out of 50 gold ducats in an effort to find a greater haul.[14] But medieval mining production was mostly silver, concentrated in Germany and the Kingdom of Hungary. The first major post-antique European mine, in what is now Serbia, opened only in 1252; gold volumes did not significantly increase until after the rise of the mine at Kremnica (now Slovakia) in the 1320s; and they continued to wax and wane well into the fifteenth century.[15]

An early fourteenth-century Venetian merchant's book known as the *Zibaldone da Canal* noted that the bankers of Venice bought silver from Germany and Hungary and refined it, and that the mint would pay merchants for gold but refused anything that was less than 23.5 carats in purity. Yet the same book also recorded that gold came from Tunis.[16] Most gold reached medieval Europe from Africa, in a trans-Saharan trade for silver, copper, and salt. West African gold was a very old commodity in the Islamic world: "Ghana the land of gold" is mentioned as early as the end of the eighth century by a geographer, al-Fazārī, in faraway Bagdad; and, in a study of North African gold coins minted between 1070 to 1250, almost all used metal from these Western mines.[17] Gold was ferried across the Sahara by Berber camel caravans, running north via Awdaghost (modern Tegdaoust) or Taghaza to Sijilmasa (near modern Rissani, Morocco). The trade was encouraged by successive states in the Magreb, as the minting of gold coinage was a traditional sign of political sovereignty within the Islamic world.[18]

As the Ghanaian state weakened in the late twelfth century, and fell for good in the 1220s, it was replaced and much surpassed by the rising kingdom of Mali on the Niger River. The result was a partial shifting of the gold trade from the far west of Africa toward the center of the continent, with a terminus now in modern Tunisia, under the Hafsids of Tunis.[19] The Hafsids signed trade treaties with Pisa, Venice, Genoa, and Sicily in the 1230s.[20] By the same era Italian merchant ships had increased in size, and no longer had to use Sicily as a way station. Thus gold was ferried into Europe on Italian and especially Genoese ships. As a result of this new source and to finance the concomitant expansion of trade, in 1252 both Florence and Genoa began to mint gold coins—the florin and the *genovino*—as money of record. Within a century, all the major Italian states were doing so.

Something of the horror of this trans-Saharan trade can be gleaned from the account of Abu Abdallah ibn Battuta of Tangier, known as Ibn Battuta (1304–68/9), a jurist from Morocco who followed this trade route on one of his journeys.[21] In 1352, he left Fez and traveled as far south as Sijilmasa. He then pushed south to Taghaza, which took a further twenty-five days. The town disgusted him: it was situated on a dry salt lake, and infested with the worst flies he had ever seen. The buildings were miserable, made out of salt slabs with camelskin roofs, and inhabited by starving slaves who carved out huge blocks of salt crystal to be transported on the backs of camels. But Taghaza had many traders: men who came from the south to trade their gold for salt. Ibn Battuta set out with a caravan party ferrying this salt across the Sahara. It took almost two months to make the 1600-km trip. The lice were so bad that travelers wore small bags of mercury at their necks; a member of the party left the main group, and was never seen again, although they came upon the bones of another traveler. Further south the heat was so intense they could only travel at night. And then there were the snakes: one man lost a finger to snakebite. The shine of Italian gold-backs is less bright if one thinks about the human misery of this African trade.

There were probably few contemporary Italians who thought of Africa when they made or looked at paintings. Gold reached artists at second and third hand. In some cases, used objects made of gold were collected and melted down to provide gold for art: the artist Gentile da Fabriano, for instance, seems to have used such recycled sources.[22] Most gold leaf was derived from gold coins, the *ducati*, *fiorini*, and *genovini*, beaten into micro-thin sheets, from 100 to 150 per coin, at rates set by statute and law. The major Italian cities, especially those with cloth manufacturing, had goldbeater specialists called *battiloro* or *battifoglia*. They are first recorded in the thirteenth century, and the bulk of their work was to provide the gold threads that were used in luxury textiles.[23]

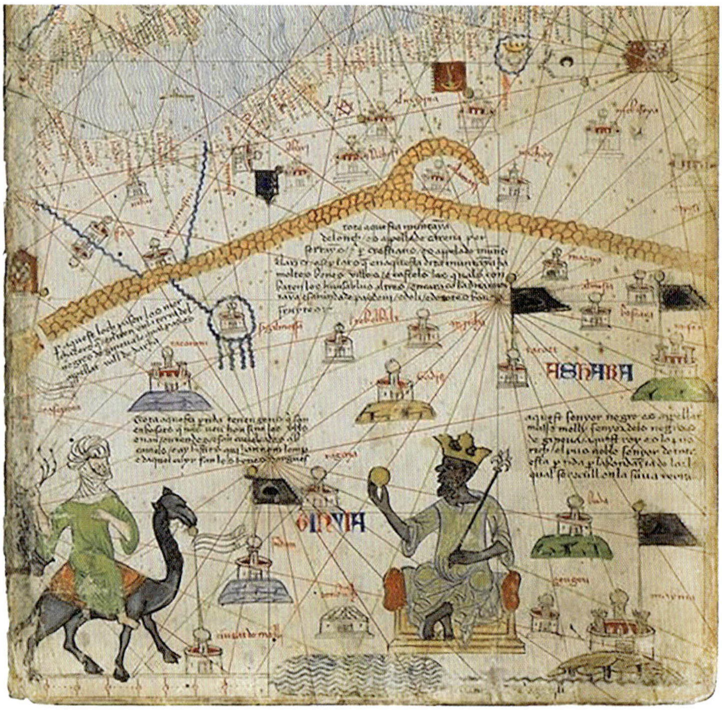

Fig. 4. Abraham Cresques, *Catalan Atlas*, ca. 1375, colored inks on parchment; 64.5 × 25 cm (full leaf), detail of western Africa with Mansa Musa I. Paris, Bibliothèque nationale de France, MS Espagnol 30

There were also specialists who applied gold leaf, at least for occasional large commissions: in 1353, a man called Filippo di Lazzaro was paid "per metere l'oro in nella taula" (to put the gold on the panel) of a work by the Florentine artist Taddeo Gaddi.[24] Gold was big business in Italy. In Florence between 1371 and 1444 there were thirteen *battiloro* registered in the Guild of the *Medici e speziali*; there are no fewer than 130 goldsmiths recorded in fourteenth-century Siena alone; and there were about 100 each in Lucca and Bologna. These are very large numbers if it is correct that by 1400 Siena's population was perhaps no more than 15,000 people.[25]

Yet some classes of makers, patrons, and viewers probably did make the connection to gold's faraway origins. One of the only things that elite Europeans knew about Africa beyond the Mediterranean basin was that it was full of gold. The 1376 *Catalan Atlas*, a summum of contemporary European knowledge of the world, includes the ruler of Mali.[26] He is correctly positioned near Taghaza and Gao, with gold crown and orb; the text explains that "This black lord is called Musa Meli, Lord of the blacks of Guinea. So abundant is the gold which is found in his country that he is the richest and most noble king in all the land" (fig. 4). The reference is to the Mansa Musa I, who ruled from about 1312 to 1337 and who became famous for his gold after passing through Cairo on a pilgrimage to Mecca in 1324. It was claimed that he and his retinue spent and gave away so much gold that the metal was devalued.[27]

Similarly, an anonymous Spanish Franciscan writing in the mid-trecento narrates an imaginary journey, clearly following a map like the Catalan Atlas. In a perfect inversion of actual trade, he claims that, in Africa, he "went by the ZAHARA with some Moors who were taking gold to the King of Guinea on camels."[28] He namechecks Sijilmasa on the way to the country of the River of Gold, which he claimed was one of the four rivers of Paradise; the reference is to Genesis 2:11, where the Phison River is said to come from the region "where gold groweth." Beyond this lay the Mountains of Gold, where, he tells us, "they collect ... the gold in the ant hills which the ants make on the river banks. The ants are as big as cats, and dig out much earth." It is a story that can be traced back to Herodotus (*Histories*, Book 3), who, however, placed the ants in India beyond Persia, not in western Africa.

These fantastic origin stories and the link to God and Paradise suggest the most basic aspect of premodern gold: it was not only exotic but also uncanny, to use a modern term, particularly in its relation to creation, decay, and time. Gold was the heaviest metal then known, and, according to authorities like the thirteenth-century scholar Albertus Magnus, it was also the purest metal because it held the greatest heat with minimal imperfection.[29] This was why it was shining and yellow, like the sun, and also why it was unreactive in our terms: being already perfected, it was not subject to change. The quality was easy to allegorize. According to Alexander Neckham's early thirteenth-century *De naturis rerum*, "Gold is correctly compared with wisdom, because it is not weakened in the long duration of time."[30]

There was a further aspect: gold could concretely alter the effects of time and decay in the secular time of human bodies. As such, it was the rich person's medical panacea. According to an herbal produced in mid-fourteenth-century southern France, gold "is a metal that is hot and dry, and more temperate than any other. And it is (formed) in veins of earth, and it comforts all the members of the body and it conserves youth, etc."[31] This is illustrated by a king with golden crown, orb, and scepter, flanked by a golden sun (fig. 5). Albertus Magnus noted that gold was prescribed for almost anything from dementia to the common cold: "tremors of the heart and for black bile which causes melancholy, especially for [the disorder] that makes a man talk to himself when he is alone. It is prescribed for these afflictions either ground up with other things having the same power, or taken by itself as a powder."[32] A treatise on diet by the most famous doctor of quattrocento Italy, Michele Savonarola, dedicated to the ruler of Ferrara around 1450, concludes with a medicine intended to extend life and cure everything from paralysis to leprosy; gold is the first and major ingredient.[33] Gold was widely ingested, at least by those who could afford it: Alexander Neckham noted that it was a great help to digestion, among its other virtues.[34] At a banquet in Ferrara held by the ruler Niccolò II d'Este (d. 1388), everything served over three days, including bread, was covered in gold leaf; the same thing was true at a banquet held in 1368 to celebrate the marriage of Violante Visconti, daughter of the ruler of Milan, and Lionel, Duke of Clarence, second son of King Edward III of England. Almost everything served in the eighteen courses had an outer covering of gilding. Possibly this is part of the reason that, after months of these festivities, Lionel died in October of that same year.[35]

Gold was also drunk, in a concoction known as *aurum potabile* (literally "drinkable gold"). This brew could involve highly corrosive substances—nitric acid, for instance—or caustics like urine, alcohol, or vinegar.[36] Early in the twenty-first century, it was determined that the fabled Diane de Poitiers (1499–1566), mistress of King Henri II, was poisoned because of a daily dose of *aurum potabile*, in this case gold chloride and diethyl ether. Although this kept her hair fine and her face as white as snow (anemia is one side effect), it also ate away her teeth and bones.[37] Arguably, then, when Albertus Magnus claimed a skull had been found in his own time with gold in the sutures of the skull bones, he was pointing not only to the continuity of all things made by God, but also to the incommensurability of human time and gold's own endurance.[38] There was seemingly no end to the ways in which gold was imagined to suspend the normal bodily processes: a fifteenth-century manuscript from the Veneto (Newberry Case MS 25) has among its eighty-nine recipes a potion, made with gold, described as *aqua ad deodorandum*—that is, a deodorant rinse.[39]

At this point and to conclude, we can return to gold-back paintings, and a single and most famous example. In the 1420s, when Palla Strozzi created a family chapel and sacristy at the church of Santa Trinita in Florence, he commissioned Gentile da Fabriano to create the main altarpiece (fig. 6). The subject, Epiphany or the Adoration of the Magi, was a popular one in fifteenth-century Florence, and allowed displays of exotic figures and imported wealth. Strozzi was then the richest man in the city, and one of its most important and erudite patrons, and in Gentile he chose one of the most innovative artists of the Renaissance period.[40] Most of Gentile's fresco work is lost, but the work in tempera is almost unbelievably technically complicated. Egg tempera is an unforgiving medium and its properties are almost the opposite of oil paint. It does

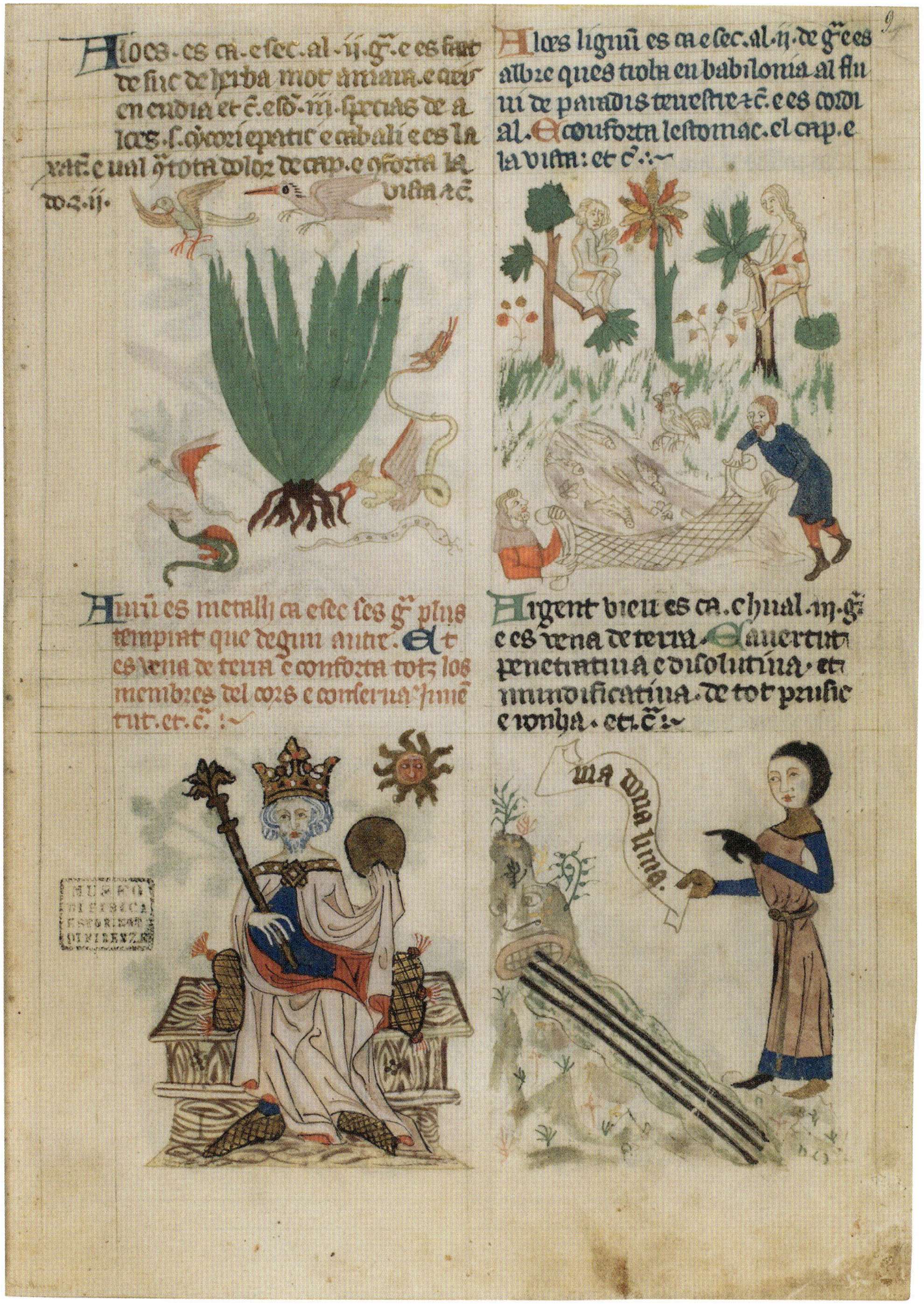

Fig. 5. *Aurum*, southern France, mid-fourteenth century. Florence, Biblioteca Nazionale Centrale, MS Palatino 586, fol. 9

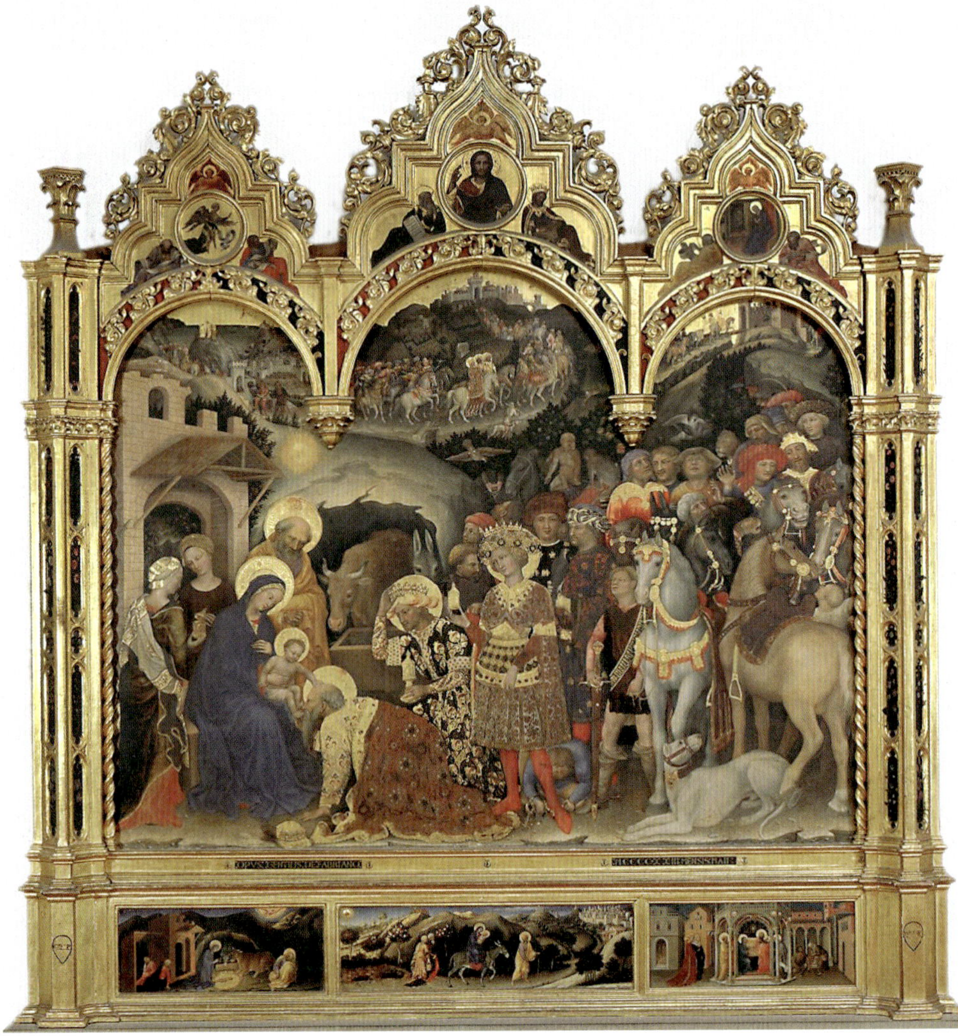

Fig. 6. Gentile da Fabriano, *Adoration of the Magi* (*Strozzi Altarpiece*), 1423, tempera, gold, and silver on panel, 300 × 282 cm. Florence, Galleria degli Uffizi

not blend well, and it dries to a hard and matte surface rather than a glossy shine. Many pigments in tempera have good covering power, but there can be little translucency. There is also little room for gestures of the brush, meaning that the medium is typically marked by saturated areas of juxtaposed colors, and depth of impasto cannot be used to vary effects. In the Strozzi altarpiece, Gentile pushed these characteristics to a kind of limit, experimenting with the inherent properties of his pigments; within this practice, gold is the medium for the most unexpected and imaginative experiments and effects.

Gentile da Fabriano had by this date developed a technique of fast and alternately loose and tight small strokes, something a little like a horizontal impasto, so that the matte tempera almost shimmers and shimmies. In an inversion of what might be expected, he tended to use materials with good opaque coverage in oil binders to create glazes, and those with greater transparency to cover ground. The effect can be seen in the tiny detail of a stag at the center of the panel, or in the horses' skins and bridles that are themselves worked in *sgraffito*. Gold is used to reinforce this effect through sheen and refraction. Gentile creates folds by clustering and spacing out small gold dots; in the predella *Nativity*, for instance, this technique is used to catch attention and to suggest scattered light. What is even more extraordinary, however, is that gold is used here to create other textures and colors, in an exact inversion of the process Alberti would later recommend. The hairnet on one midwife is delicately traced in gold while the other's headdress is of silver with gold layered onto it. The red doublet of one attendant—by no means a major figure—was built up by gold scratched in tiny shimmering strokes, and then covered in a red lake that is thinned out as the color comes forward into the notional light (fig. 7).[41] *Pastiglia* is used in the front center, to draw the eye, in clumps at the closest plane that further destabilize space and light. Gold ground hovers only at the tops of the spandrels and the limits of the horizon.

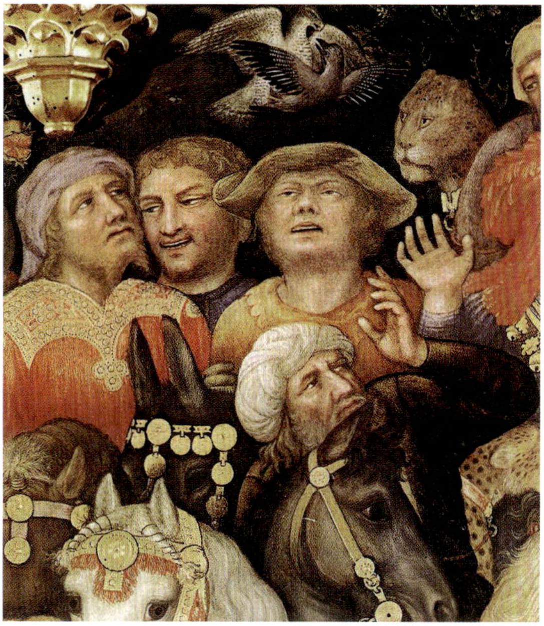

Fig. 7. *Strozzi Altarpiece*, detail of attendants

Within the overall display of skill and mastery, then, gold is singled out here as a privileged medium for artistic claims. This exotic, least tractable, and most perfected substance is being used to make something else, and to further rather than to undermine representation. No contemporary viewer could have missed the artistic stakes here—the artist's hand, through sheer skill, making one thing into another. This last phrase echoes Cennino Cennini's famous definition of art around 1400: "to discover things not seen, hiding under the shadow of natural objects, and to fix them with the hand." His theory of art is emphatically process-based;

the phrase "operazione di mano" comes up no fewer than three times in the few hundred words of his preface.[42] In the working of gold both within and against its own notional properties, such works come as close to self-consciously time-layered and gestural painting as tempera can get. As such, we might fruitfully think of painting like this as engaged in the problems of staging and the relation to time that haunted so much of early European art. It is a strategy to mark self-consciousness about the act of representing, in a medium with only very limited resources for doing so.

Notes

This material was first presented at the 2016 *Gold* conference. I am grateful to Tom Cummins and Alina Payne for the invitation, to Rebecca Zorach and Evelyn Lincoln, and to all the conference participants for their suggestions and comments.

1. Two examples: Antonio Natali et al., eds., *Bagliori dorati. il gotico internazionale a Firenze 1375–1440* (Florence: Giunti, 2012); Stefan Weppelmann, *Geschichten auf Gold. Bilderzählungen in der frühen italienischen Malerei* (Berlin: Staatliche Museen/Dumont, 2005).

2. Andrea De Marchi, "Oro come luce, luce come oro: l'operazione delle lamine metalliche da Simone Martini a Pisanello, fra mimesi e anagogia," in *Medioevo, natura e figura*, ed. by Arturo Carlo Quintavalle (Milan: Skira/AISAME, 2015), 701–15; Cathleen S. Hoeniger, "Cloth of Gold and Silver: Simone Martini's Techniques for Representing Luxury Textiles," *Gesta* 30, no. 2 (1991): 154–62. The current frame is a nineteenth-century replacement, presumed to have been modeled on an earlier design.

3. Carl Brandon Strehlke and Machtelt Brüggen Israëls, *The Bernard and Mary Berenson Collection of European Paintings at I Tatti* (Florence: Villa I Tatti in collaboration with Officina Libraria, 2015), 289–92.

4. Erling S. Skaug, "Painters, Punchers, Gilders or Goldbeaters? A Critical Survey Report of Discussions in Recent Literature about Early Italian Panel Painting," *Zeitschrift* für *Kunstgeschichte* 71, no. 4 (2008): 571–82; Erling S. Skaug, *Punch Marks from Giotto to Fra Angelico: Attribution, Chronology and Workshop Relationships in Tuscan Panel Painting*, 2 vols. (Oslo: IIC Nordic Group, 1994); Mojmír J. Frinta, "The Quest for a Restorer's Shop of Beguiling Invention: Restorations and Forgeries in Italian Panel Painting," *Art Bulletin* 60, no. 1 (1978): 7–23; Mojmír J. Frinta, "An Investigation of the Punched Decoration of Mediaeval Italian and Non-Italian Panel Paintings," *Art Bulletin* 47, no. 2 (1965): 261–65.

5. Gianni Mazzoni, ed., *Falsi d'autore. Icilio Joni e la cultura del falso tra Otto e Novecento* (Siena: Protagon, 2004); see also Strehlke and Israëls, *Berenson Collection*, 627–29, 638–42, 654–56.

6. Leon Battista Alberti, *On Painting and On Sculpture: The Latin Texts of* De Pictura *and* De Statua, ed. and trans. Cecil Grayson (London: Phaidon, 1972), 60–61 and 92–93.

7. Michael Baxandall, *Painting and Experience in Fifteenth-Century Italy: A Primer in the Social History of Art*, 2nd ed. (Oxford: Oxford University Press, 1988), 14–23, 84–85, 169–70.

8. Sigmund Freud, "Character and Anal Eroticism (1908)," in *The Standard Edition of the Complete Psychological Works of Sigmund Freud, volume 9: Jensen's* Gradiva *and Other Works*, ed. by James Strachey with Anna Freud et al. (London: Hogarth Press and the Institute of Psycho-analysis, 1959), 167–80; "Maurizio Catellan: 'America'," https://www.guggenheim.org/exhibition/maurizio-cattelan-america, accessed June 12, 2017.

9. *Abbot Suger on the Abbey Church of St.-Denis and Its Art Treasures*, ed. and trans. Erwin Panofsky and Gerda Panofsky-Soergel, 2nd ed. (Princeton: Princeton University Press, 1979), 63–65.

10. Rebecca Zorach, *Blood, Milk, Ink, Gold: Abundance and Excess in the French Renaissance* (Chicago: University of Chicago Press, 2005), 189–235; and Rebecca Zorach and Michael W. Phillips Jr., *Gold: Nature and Culture* (London: Reaktion Books, 2016).

11. See, for instance, Stephen J. Campbell, ed., *Ornament and Illusion: Carlo Crivelli of Venice* (Boston: Isabella Stewart Gardner Museum and Holberton, 2015), esp. Alison Wright, "Crivelli's Divine Materials," 56–77; and Cristina Guarnieri and Andrea De Marchi, eds., "Rabeschi d'oro: pittura e oreficeria a Venezia in età gotica," *Arte Veneta* 71 (2014).

12. Philip Ball, *The Elements: A Very Short Introduction* (Oxford: Oxford University Press, 2002), 45.

13. Gold production has soared since the nineteenth century, with new discoveries and mines, and new procedures for extraction developed in the 1890s. It is estimated that all the gold mined by the early sixteenth century was about 8 cubic meters; by 1908 that volume had reached 1000 cubic meters: Ball, *The Elements*, 48, 50; and more broadly Zorach and Phillips, *Gold*, 173–97.

14. Anne Dunlop, "The Dominicans and Cloistered Women: The Convent of Sant'Aurea in Rome," *Early Modern Women* 2 (2007): 60.

15. Martin Stefánik, "Italian Involvement in Metal Mining in the Central Slovakian Region, from the Thirteenth Century to the Reign of King Sigismund of Hungary," *I Tatti Studies in the Italian Renaissance* 14/15 (2011–2012): 11–46; Ian Blanchard, *Mining, Metallurgy and Minting in the Middle Ages, Vol. III: Continuing Afro-European Supremacy, 1250–1450* (Stuttgart: Franz Steiner Verlag, 2005), 924–1063; Louise Robbert, "Monetary Flows: Venice 1150 to 1400," in *Precious Metals in the Later Medieval and Early Modern Worlds*, ed. by J. F. Richards (Durham, NC: Carolina Academic Press, 1983), 53–77.

16. The anonymous manuscript (Yale, Beinecke Library, MS 327) was named *Zibaldone da Canal* after a later owner. For an edition, see *Merchant Culture in Fourteenth Century Venice: The Zibaldone da Canal*, ed. and trans. by John E. Dotson (Binghamton, NY: Medieval and Renaissance Texts and Studies, 1994), here at 32 and 83.

17. Nehemia Levtzion, *Ancient Ghana and Mali* (London: Methuen and Co, 1973), 3 (for al-Fazārī). More generally, see Philip D. Curtin, "Africa and the Wider Monetary World, 1250–1850," in Richards, *Precious Metals*, 231–68, esp. 233–41. See also Blanchard, *Mining, Metallurgy and Minting*, 1111–1217; Thomas Walker, "The Italian Gold Revolution of 1252: Shifting Currents in the Pan-Mediterranean Flow of Gold," in Richards, *Precious Metals*, 29–52; Andrew M. Watson, "Back to Gold – and Silver," *Economic History Review* 20 (1967): 1–34; Robert S. Lopez, "Back to Gold, 1252," *Economic History Review* 9 (1956): 219–40.

18. Levtzion, *Ancient Ghana and Mali*, 124–52.

19. Walker, "Italian Gold Revolution," 37.

20. Ibid., 50.

21. Said Hamdun and Noël King, eds., *Ibn Battuta in Black Africa* (Princeton: Markus Wiener, 2004), 29–75. There is a debate whether Ibn Battuta completed all the travel he claimed to have undertaken: see Roxanne L. Euben, "Liars, Travelers, Theorists: Herodotus and Ibn Battuta," in *Journeys to the Other Shore: Muslim and Western Travelers in Search of Knowledge* (Princeton: Princeton University Press, 2006), 46–89, esp. 47–52. I thank Suzanne Preston Blier for telling me about these debates.

22. Roberto Bellucci and Cecilia Frosinini, "Tecnica e stile: appunti su Gentile da Fabriano," in *Gentile da Fabriano. Studi e ricerche*, ed. by Andrea De Marchi, Laura Laureati, and Lorenza Mochi Onori (Milan: Electa, 2006), 61–62.

23. Susan Mosher Stuard, *Gilding the Market: Luxury and Fashion in Fourteenth-Century Italy* (Philadelphia: University of Pennsylvania Press, 2006), 146–81; Alessandro Guidotti, "Battiloro e dipintori a Firenze fra Tre e Quattrocento: Bastiano di Giovanni e la sua clientela (dal Catasto del 1427)," in *Scritti di storia dell'arte in onore di Roberto Salvini* (Florence: Sansoni, 1984), 239–49. For the link to textiles, a sector that became more specialized from the fifteenth century, see Bruno Dini, "I battiloro fiorentini nel Quattrocento," in *Medioevo mezzogiorno mediterraneo. Studi in onore di Mario Del Trappo*, ed. by Gabriella Rossetti and Giovanni Vitolo, 2 vols. (Naples: Liguori, 2000), 2.139–61.

24. Irma Passeri, "Tecniche di lavorazione delle foglie metalliche nei dipinti su tavola e organizzazione del mestiere tra XIII–XV secolo: proposte circa i metodi di pulitura" (tesi di diploma, Scuola di Restauro, Opificio delle Pietre Dure, Florence, 1998), 30. The painting was ordered for San Giovanni

Fuoricivitas in Pistoia. I thank Dottoressa Passeri for allowing me to read her work.

25. Ibid., 28 (for Florence); Stuard, *Gilding the Market*, 158, 166.

26. Georges Grosjean, *Mapamundi. The Catalan Atlas of the Year 1375* (Zurich: Urs Graf Verlag, 1978); "L'Atlas Catalan," http://expositions.bnf.fr/marine/albums/catalan/index.htm, accessed August 1, 2017.

27. Warren Schultz, "Mansa Musa's Gold in Mamluk Cairo: A Reappraisal of a World Civilizations Anecdote," in *History and Historiography of Post-Mongol Central Asia and the Middle East: Studies in Honor of John E. Woods*, ed. by Judith Pfeiffer and Sholeh A. Quinn with Ernest Tucker (Wiesbaden: Harrassowitz Verlag, 2006), 428–47.

28. Marcos Jiménez de la Espada, ed., *Book of the Knowledge of All the Kingdoms, Lands, and Lordships That Are in the World, and the Arms and Devices of Each Land and Lordship, or of the Kings and Lords Who Possess Them. Written by a Spanish Franciscan in the Middle of the XIV Century*, ed. and trans. by Sir Clements Markham (London: Hakluyt Society, 1912), 28–34.

29. Albertus Magnus, *Book of Minerals*, trans. Dorothy Wyckoff (Oxford: Clarendon Press, 1967), 198, 226. For a more detailed discussion of the associations of artists' pigments, see Anne Dunlop, "On the Origins of European Painting Materials, Real and Imagined," in *The Matter of Art: Materials, Practices, Cultural Logics, c. 1250–1750*, ed. by Christy Anderson, Anne Dunlop, and Pamela H. Smith (Manchester: Manchester University Press, 2014), 68–87.

30. Alexander Neckham, *De naturis rerum, libri duo*, ed. by Thomas Wright (London: Longman, Green, Longman, Roberts, and Green, 1863), 162: "Recte igitur comparatur aurum sapientiae, quae temporis vetustati non est obnoxia."

31. "Aurum es metalli caut e sec ses & plus temprat que negun autre. Et es vena de terra e conforta totz los membres del cors e conserva Iuventut et c." On the manuscript, see Matteo Milani, "Aloes es caut e sec ...: edizione di un erbario occitano (Firenze, Biblioteca nazionale centrale, Palatino 586)," *La Parola del Testo* 8, no. 2 (2004): 369–91. The manuscript has been digitized: see https://teca.bncf.firenze.sbn.it/ImageViewer/servlet/ImageViewer?idr=BNCF0002979162#, accessed January 4, 2017.

32. Albertus Magnus, *Book of Minerals*, 229.

33. Michele Savonarola, *Libreto de tutte le cosse che se magnano. Un'opera di dietetica del sec. XV*, ed. by Jane Nystedt (Stockholm: Almqvist & Wiksell International, 1988), 193.

34. Neckham, *De naturis rerum*, 162: "in cibariis suptum virtutum virtuti cooperatur digestivae. Confortativum est, et consumptionem non reformidat. Situ non ducit rubiginem, nec vetustatis longaevae perhorrescit invidiam. Ignis non pertimescit edacitatem, sed et absque sui detriment vertitur in liquorem."

35. Claudio Benporat, *Feste e banchetti. Convivialità italiana fra Tre e Quattrocento* (Florence: Leo S. Olschki, 2001), 129–34. For the menu of the Milan banquet, see John Larner, *Italy in the Age of Dante and Petrarch, 1216–1380* (London: Longman, 1980), 211–13.

36. Jacqueline Proust, "*L'aurum potabile* au temps de la Renaissance en France et en Angleterre," in *L'or au temps de la Renaissance. Du mythe à l'économie*, ed. by M. T. Jones-Davies (Paris: Université Paris-Sorbonne, 1978), 15–26; Ball, *Elements*, 60–61.

37. Henry Samuel, "French King's Mistress Poisoned by Gold Elixir," *The Telegraph*, December 22, 2009, https://www.telegraph.co.uk/news/worldnews/europe/france/6865939/French-kings-mistress-poisoned-by-gold-elixir.html.

38. Albertus Magnus, *Book of Minerals*, 232.

39. D. Bommarito, "Il ms. 25 della Newberry Library: la tradizione dei ricettari e trattati sui colori nel Medioevo e Rinascimento veneto e toscano," *La Bibliofilia* 87 (1985): 1–38.

40. On Gentile's technique in these years, see Andrea De Marchi, *Gentile da Fabriano. Un viaggio nella pittura italiana alle fine del gotico* (Milan: Federico Motta, 2006), 161–225; Cecilia Frosinini, "L'Intercessione: il 'nuovo' politico di Gentile da Fabriano ritrovato," in Marco Ciatti and Cecilia Frosinini with Roberto Bellucci, *Il Gentile risorto. Il "Polittico dell'Intercessione" di Gentile da Fabriano. Studi e restauro* (Florence: Edifir, 2006), 17–38; Bellucci and Frosinini, "Tecnica e stile," 54–65; Laura Laureati and Lorenza Mochi Onori, eds., *Gentile da Fabriano and the Other Renaissance* (Milan: Electa, 2006). The analysis that follows here is indebted to this work.

41. De Marchi, *Gentile da Fabriano*.

42. Cennino Cennini, *Il libro dell'arte*, ed. by Fabio Frezzato (Vicenza: Neri Pozza, 2008), 62: after noting that science is the most noble work, he continues, "seghuitò alchune discendentii da quella, la quale conviene avere fondamento di quella, chon operazione di mano; e quest'è un'arte che ssi chiama dipignere, che conviene avera fantasia e hoperazione di mano, di trovare cose non vedute chacciandosi sotto ombra di naturali, e fermarle con la mano, dando a dimostrare quello che nonne sia." He concludes his first chapter by noting that he is passing on what he has learned from his master and tested with his own hands, "quello che con mia mano ò provato." For the translation, see Cennino d'Andrea Cennini, *The Craftsman's Handbook: "Il Libro dell'Arte"*, trans. by Daniel V. Thompson Jr. (New York: Dover, 1960), 1: "man pursued some [ie occupations] related to the one which calls for a basis of that [i.e. theory, *scienza*], coupled with skill of hand: and this is an occupation known as painting, which calls for imagination, and skill of hand, in order to discover things not seen, hiding themselves under the shadow of natural objects, and to fix them with the hand, presenting to plain sight what does not actually exist."

Bibliography

Alberti, Leon Battista. *On Painting and On Sculpture: The Latin Texts of* De Pictura *and* De Statua. Edited and translated by Cecil Grayson. London: Phaidon, 1972.

Albertus Magnus, *Book of Minerals*. Translated by Dorothy Wyckoff. Oxford: Clarendon Press, 1967.

"L'Atlas Catalan." Accessed August 1, 2017. http://expositions.bnf.fr/marine/albums/catalan/index.htm.

Ball, Philip. *The Elements: A Very Short Introduction*. Oxford: Oxford University Press, 2002.

Baxandall, Michael. *Painting and Experience in Fifteenth-Century Italy: A Primer in the Social History of Art*. 2nd ed. Oxford: Oxford University Press, 1988.

Bellucci, Roberto, and Cecilia Frosinini. "Tecnica e stile: appunti su Gentile da Fabriano." In *Gentile da Fabriano. Studi e ricerche*, edited by Andrea De Marchi, Laura Laureati, and Lorenza Mochi Onori, 54–67. Milan: Electa, 2006.

Benporat, Claudio. *Feste e banchetti. Convivialità italiana fra Tre e Quattrocento*. Florence: Leo S. Olschki, 2001.

Blanchard, Ian. *Mining, Metallurgy and Minting in the Middle Ages, Vol. III: Continuing Afro-European Supremacy, 1250–1450*. Stuttgart: Franz Steiner Verlag, 2005.

Bommarito, D. "Il ms. 25 della Newberry Library: la tradizione dei ricettari e trattati sui colori nel Medioevo e Rinascimento veneto e Toscano." *La Bibliofilia* 87 (1985): 1–38.

Campbell, Stephen J. ed. *Ornament and Illusion: Carlo Crivelli of Venice*. Boston: Isabella Stewart Gardner Museum and Holberton, 2015.

Cennini, Cennino. *Il libro dell'arte*. Edited by Fabio Frezzato. Vicenza: Neri Pozza, 2008.

Cennini, Cennino d'Andrea. *The Craftsman's Handbook: "Il Libro dell'Arte."* Translated by Daniel V. Thompson Jr. New York: Dover, 1960.

Curtin, Philip D. "Africa and the Wider Monetary World, 1250–1850." In *Precious Metals in the Later Medieval and Early Modern Worlds*, edited by J. F. Richards, 231–68. Durham, NC: Carolina Academic Press, 1983.

De Marchi, Andrea. *Gentile da Fabriano. Un viaggio nella pittura italiana alle fine del gotico*. Milan: Federico Motta, 2006.

De Marchi, Andrea. "Oro come luce, luce come oro: l'operazione delle lamine metalliche da Simone Martini a Pisanello, fra mimesi e anagogia." In *Medioevo, natura e figura*, edited by Arturo Carlo Quintavalle, 701-15. Milan: Skira/ AISAME, 2015.

Dini, Bruno. "I battiloro fiorentini nel Quattrocento." In *Medioevo mezzogiorno mediterraneo. Studi in onore di Mario Del Trappo*, edited by Gabriella Rossetti and Giovanni Vitolo, 2.139–61. 2 vols. Naples: Liguori, 2000.

Dotson, John E., ed. and trans. *Merchant Culture in Fourteenth Century Venice: The Zibaldone da Canal*. Binghamton, NY: Medieval and Renaissance Texts and Studies.

Dunlop, Anne. "The Dominicans and Cloistered Women: The Convent of Sant'Aurea in Rome." *Early Modern Women* 2 (2007): 43–71.

Dunlop, Anne. "On the Origins of European Painting Materials, Real and Imagined." In *The Matter of Art: Materials, Practices, Cultural Logics, c. 1250–1750*, edited by Christy Anderson, Anne Dunlop, and Pamela H. Smith, 68–87. Manchester: Manchester University Press, 2014.

Espada, Marcos Jiménez de la, ed. *Book of the Knowledge of All the Kingdoms, Lands, and Lordships That Are in the World, and the Arms and Devices of Each Land and Lordship, or of the Kings and Lords Who Possess Them. Written by a Spanish Franciscan in the Middle of the XIV Century*. Edited and translated by Sir Clements Markham. London: Hakluyt Society, 1912.

Euben, Roxanne L. "Liars, Travelers, Theorists: Herodotus and Ibn Battuta." In *Journeys to the Other Shore: Muslim and Western Travelers in Search of Knowledge*, 46–89. Princeton: Princeton University Press, 2006.

Freud, Sigmund. "Character and Anal Eroticism (1908)." In *The Standard Edition of the Complete Psychological Works of Sigmund Freud, volume 9: Jensen's* Gradiva *and Other Works*, edited by James Strachey with Anna Freud et al., 167–80. London: Hogarth Press and the Institute of Psycho-analysis, 1959.

Frinta, Mojmír J. "An Investigation of the Punched Decoration of Mediaeval Italian and Non-Italian Panel Paintings." *Art Bulletin* 47, no. 2 (1965): 261–65.

Frinta, Mojmír J. "The Quest for a Restorer's Shop of Beguiling Invention: Restorations and Forgeries in Italian Panel Painting." *Art Bulletin* 60, no. 1 (1978): 7–23.

Frosinini, Cecilia. "L'Intercessione: il 'nuovo' politico di Gentile da Fabriano ritrovato." In Marco Ciatti and Cecilia Frosinini with Roberto Bellucci, *Il Gentile risorto. Il "Polittico dell'Intercessione" di Gentile da Fabriano. Studi e restauro*, 17–38. Florence: Edifir, 2006.

Grosjean, Georges. *Mapamundi. The Catalan Atlas of the Year 1375*. Zurich: Urs Graf Verlag, 1978.

Guarnieri, Cristina, and Andrea De Marchi, eds. "Rabeschi d'oro: pittura e oreficeria a Venezia in età gotica." Special issue, *Arte Veneta* 71 (2014).

Guidotti, Alessandro. "Battiloro e dipintori a Firenze fra Tre e Quattrocento: Bastiano di Giovanni e la sua clientela (dal Catasto del 1427)." In *Scritti di storia dell'arte in onore di Roberto Salvini*, 239–49. Florence: Sansoni, 1984.

Hamdun, Said, and Noël King, eds. *Ibn Battuta in Black Africa*. Princeton: Markus Wiener, 2004.

Hoeniger, Cathleen S. "Cloth of Gold and Silver: Simone Martini's Techniques for Representing Luxury Textiles." *Gesta* 30, no. 2 (1991): 154–62.

Larner, John. *Italy in the Age of Dante and Petrarch, 1216–1380*. London: Longman, 1980.

Laureati, Laura, and Lorenza Mochi Onori, eds. *Gentile da Fabriano and the Other Renaissance*. Milan: Electa, 2006.

Levtzion, Nehemia. *Ancient Ghana and Mali*. London: Methuen and Co, 1973.

Lopez, Robert S. "Back to Gold, 1252," *Economic History Review* 9 (1956): 219–40.

"Maurizio Catellan: 'America'." Accessed June 12, 2017. https://www.guggenheim.org/exhibition/maurizio-cattelan-america.

Mazzoni, Gianni, ed. *Falsi d'autore. Icilio Joni e la cultura del falso tra Otto e Novecento*. Siena: Protagon, 2004.

Milani, Matteo. "Aloes es caut e sec ...: edizione di un erbario occitano (Firenze, Biblioteca nazionale centrale, Palatino 586)." *La Parola del Testo* 8, no. 2 (2004): 369–91.

Natali, Antonio, et al., eds. *Bagliori dorati. Il gotico internazionale a Firenze 1375–1440*. Florence: Giunti, 2012.

Neckham, Alexander. *De naturis rerum, libri duo*. Edited by Thomas Wright. London: Longman, Green, Longman, Roberts, and Green, 1863.

Panofsky, Erwin, and Gerda Panofsky-Soergel, eds. and trans. *Abbot Suger on the Abbey Church of St.-Denis and Its Art Treasures*. 2nd ed. Princeton: Princeton University Press, 1979.

Passeri, Irma. "Tecniche di lavorazione delle foglie metalliche nei dipinti su tavola e organizzazione del mestiere tra XIII–XV secolo: proposte circa i metodi di pulitura." Tesi di diploma, Scuola di Restauro, Opificio delle Pietre Dure, Florence, 1998.

Proust, Jacqueline. "*L'aurum potabile* au temps de la Renaissance en France et en Angleterre." In *L'or au temps de la Renaissance. Du mythe à l'économie*, edited by M. T. Jones-Davies, 15–26. Paris: Université Paris-Sorbonne, 1978.

Robbert, Louise. "Monetary Flows: Venice 1150 to 1400." In *Precious Metals in the Later Medieval and Early Modern Worlds*, edited by J. F. Richards, 53–77. Durham, NC: Carolina Academic Press, 1983.

Samuel, Henry. "French King's Mistress Poisoned by Gold Elixir." *The Telegraph*. December 22, 2009. https://www.telegraph.co.uk/news/worldnews/europe/france/6865939/French-kings-mistress-poisoned-by-gold-elixir.html.

Savonarola, Michele. *Libreto de tutte le cosse che se magnano; un'opera di dietetica del sec. XV.* Edited by Jane Nystedt. Stockholm: Almqvist & Wiksell International, 1988.

Schultz, Warren. "Mansa Musa's Gold in Mamluk Cairo: A Reappraisal of a World Civilizations Anecdote." In *History and Historiography of Post-Mongol Central Asia and the Middle East: Studies in Honor of John E. Woods*, edited by Judith Pfeiffer and Sholeh A. Quinn with Ernest Tucker, 428–47. Wiesbaden: Harrassowitz Verlag, 2006.

Skaug, Erling S. "Painters, Punchers, Gilders or Goldbeaters? A Critical Survey Report of Discussions in Recent Literature about Early Italian Panel Painting." *Zeitschrift* für *Kunstgeschichte* 71, no. 4 (2008): 571–82.

Skaug, Erling S. *Punch Marks from Giotto to Fra Angelico: Attribution, Chronology and Workshop Relationships in Tuscan Panel Painting.* 2 vols. Oslo: IIC Nordic Group, 1994.

Stefánik, Martin. "Italian Involvement in Metal Mining in the Central Slovakian Region, from the Thirteenth Century to the Reign of King Sigismund of Hungary." *I Tatti Studies in the Italian Renaissance* 14/15 (2011–2012): 11–46.

Strehlke, Carl Brandon, and Machtelt Brüggen Israëls. *The Bernard and Mary Berenson Collection of European Paintings at I Tatti.* Florence: Villa I Tatti in collaboration with Officina Libraria, 2015.

Stuard, Susan Mosher. *Gilding the Market: Luxury and Fashion in Fourteenth-Century Italy.* Philadelphia: University of Pennsylvania Press, 2006.

Walker, Thomas. "The Italian Gold Revolution of 1252: Shifting Currents in the Pan-Mediterranean Flow of Gold." In *Precious Metals in the Later Medieval and Early Modern Worlds*, edited by J. F. Richards, 29–52. Durham, NC: Carolina Academic Press, 1983.

Watson, Andrew M. "Back to Gold – and Silver," *Economic History Review* 20 (1967): 1–34.

Weppelmann, Stefan. *Geschichten auf Gold. Bilderzählungen in der frühen italienischen Malerei.* Berlin: Staatliche Museen/Dumont, 2005.

Zorach, Rebecca. *Blood, Milk, Ink, Gold: Abundance and Excess in the French Renaissance.* Chicago: University of Chicago Press, 2005.

Zorach, Rebecca, and Michael W. Phillips Jr. *Gold: Nature and Culture.* London: Reaktion Books, 2016.

Since the essay was completed and submitted, there have been a number of important new studies of medieval gold and of gold-ground painting. Some of the notable English-language additions would include:

Kathleen Bickford Berzock, ed., *Caravans of Gold, Fragments in Time: Art, Culture, and Exchange across Medieval Saharan Africa* (Chicago: Block Museum of Art in association with Princeton University Pres2, 2019).

Lauren Jacobi, "Reconsidering the World-system: the Agency and Material Geography of Gold," in *The Globalization of Renaissance Art*, ed. Daniel Savoy (Leiden and Boston: Brill, 2017), 131-157.

David Young Kim, "Points on a Field: Gentile da Fabriano and Gold Ground," *Journal of Early Modern History* 23/1-2 (2019): 191-226; and now *Groundwork: A History of the Renaissance Picture* (Princeton and Oxford: Princeton University Press, 2022), 56-81 and nts.

and one older addition:

Michael Viktor Schwarz, "The Gold Ground in the Middle Ages. 'Don't ask for the meaning, ask for the use!'," in *Gold: Artists in Gold, Tradition and Today*, eds. Agnes Husslein-Arco and Thomas Zaunschirm (Munich: Hirmer Verlag in association with University of Chicago Press, 2012); 28-37.

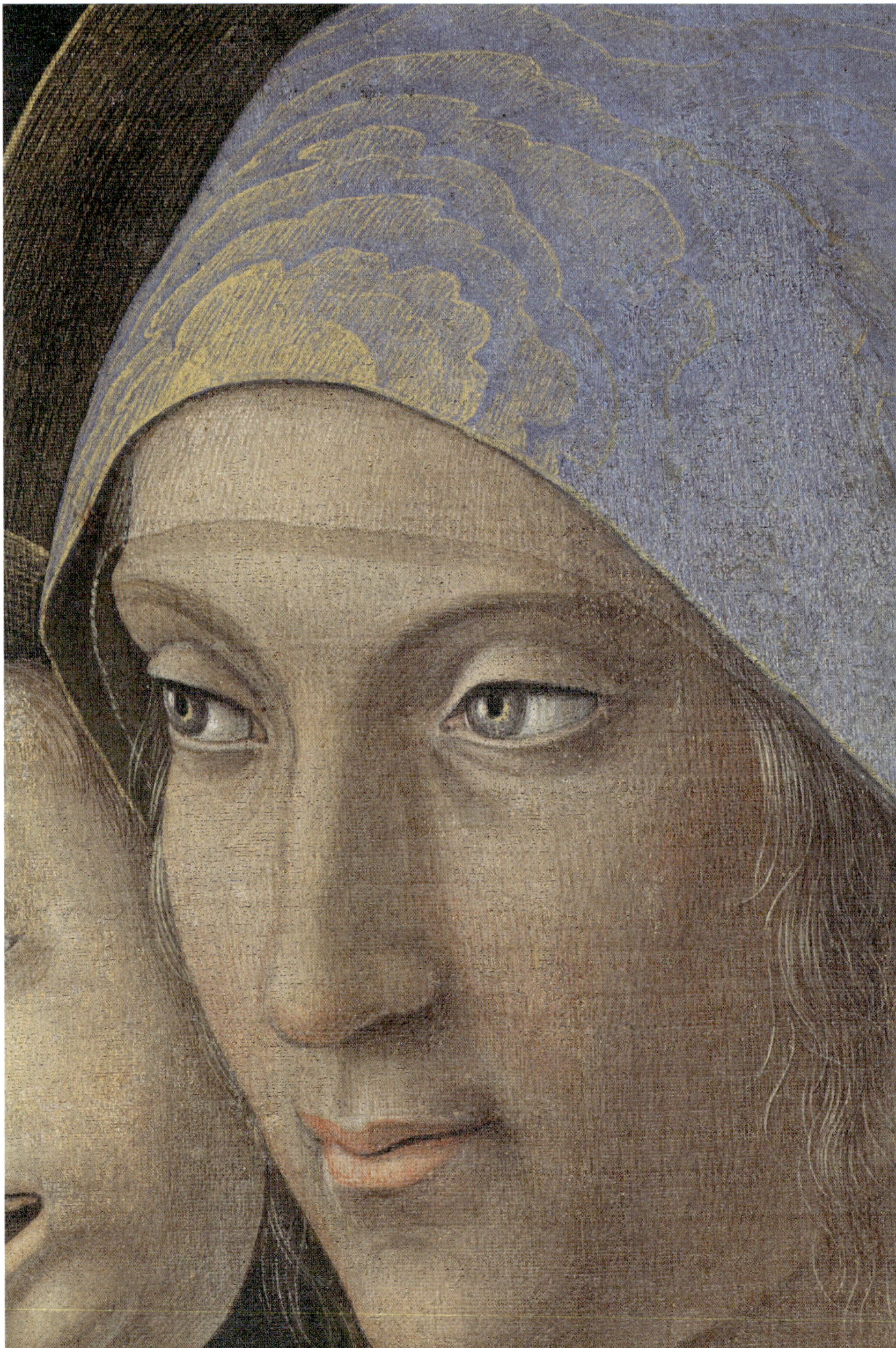

The Gold Experience in Art and in Italian Artisan Tradition between the Middle Ages and the Renaissance

Cecilia Frosinini[1]

Gold: Symbol and Substance

The creation of sacred space in the medieval church was aimed at the restitution of the "metaphysics of light," which saw the world as an emanation of God—the supreme light—thus giving light not only a spiritual and mystical value but also an aesthetic dimension.[2] Thomas Aquinas, first, and later Bonaventure and Robert Grosseteste, summarized the Platonic and Aristotelian conceptions that light is composed of the materiality of bodies, "which must be in a truer and more dignified way in the grades of beings according to the greater or lesser participation in it."[3] In this metaphysics of light, the main concept, or the first divine attribute, is not existence or truth or good, but light.

The theological idea of God transmitted through light combines with the desire to recreate the eternal light of God inside a church: this was precisely the function of liturgical furnishings and, in particular, the altarpiece, whose main purpose was to evoke a vision of God and to encourage veneration. The use of gold is most likely rooted here, in this inseparable link with light, rather than connoting the wealth that surrounds the ruler or the king, which was typical of many pre-Christian pagan religions. The appreciation for materials that reflect and magnify light, for gold and gems, seems to be a particular constant in medieval thought, as it is a symbolic manifestation of divine light.[4]

There is no doubt that the metaphysical concept of light as a divine emanation, and therefore the expression of God on earth, should be considered one of the cornerstones of medieval aesthetic philosophy. With regard to panel painting, the preciousness and the brightness of the material shines forth mainly in the gold backgrounds: the gold leaf forms an area of rich, abstract purity whose effect was amplified in the half-light of candlelit churches.

Andrea Mantegna, *Madonna and Child*, end of the 1470s, distemper on canvas, 44 × 32 cm, detail of Virgin. Bergamo, Accademia Carrara

Art Treatises

Just as gold took on a symbolic value and its reflected light became an emanation of the divine, so technological knowledge was developed for goldsmithing, but also for using gold in textiles, on altarpieces, and, albeit to a lesser extent, on frescoed walls. Not only were there craft practices but there were also bodies which grouped and socially and legally organized the artisans engaged in this production. Essentially, the documentary and technical written sources on the subject seem to point toward two main groups of workers: those who melted the gold and worked it from a metallurgical point of view, preparing alloys and specific measurements, thicknesses, and derivatives suitable for each procedure (goldsmiths and goldbeaters); and those who made the finished product or applied the gold that had been reduced to leaf or very thin laminates (the gilders).

The history of goldworking dates back to very ancient times and many historic artifacts prove the long-established ability of craftsmen to reduce the metal into leaf and very thin laminates.[5] The presence of craftsmen skilled in beating metal leaves is first documented in a papyrus kept in the British Museum in London, in which a certain Neferronpet is mentioned: he lived around 1300 BC and appears in the text with the appellation of "head of the makers of thin gold."[6] In ancient Rome, the presence of goldbeaters and gilders is attested to by bas reliefs, epigraphs, and inscriptions on tombstones. In fact, a dedicatory inscription engraved on the marble base of the statue of Concordia in the Gallery of the Candelabra in the Vatican palace reports that, in imperial Rome, goldbeaters and gilders were grouped in a *collegium*. In Book 33 of Pliny's *Natural History*, in a chapter on gold and silver, the Romans are described as being very familiar with the art of shaping metals for various purposes, ranging from the artistic to the medicinal. Pliny provides information about the supply and the amounts of gold and silver present in antiquity and about the methods used for metal purification and working. He also praises the aesthetic, physical, and mechanical properties of gold, saying: "Nor is there any material more malleable than this, none that admits of a more extended division, seeing that a single ounce of it admits of being beaten out into seven hundred and fifty leaves, or more, four fingers in length by the same in breadth."[7] The texts handing down goldworking techniques, from ancient times to the Middle Ages,[8] reveal a continuity of knowledge: from Dioscorides (first century AD),[9] to *Compositiones ad tingenda musiva*, commonly known as the Lucca Manuscript, written by an anonymous author of the ninth century,[10] and to *Schedula diversarum atrium*, by Theophilus, from the twelfth century.[11]

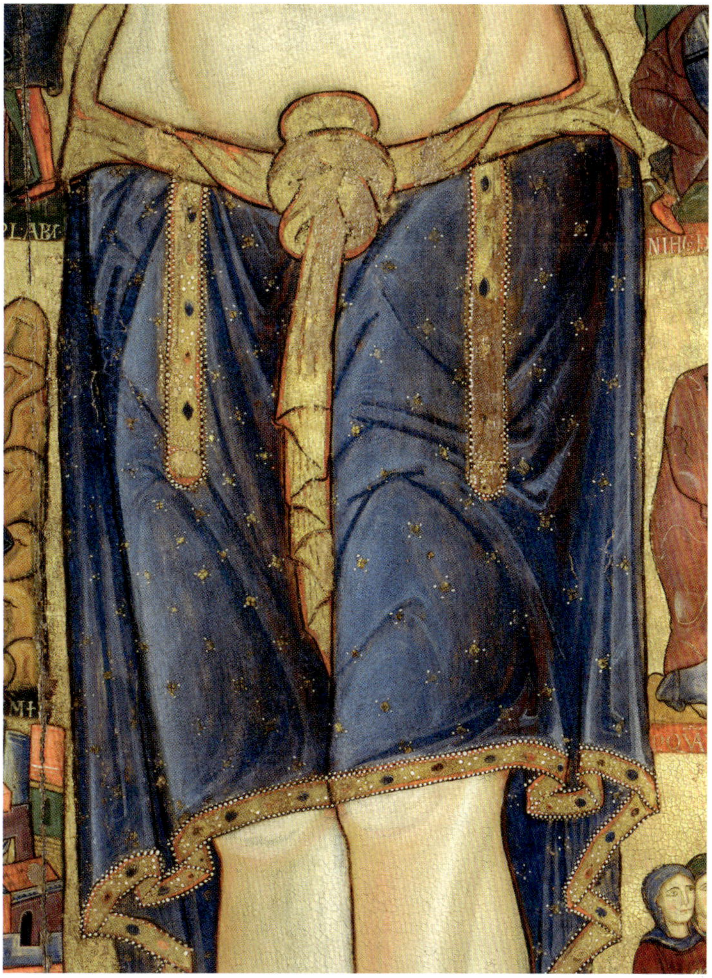

Fig 1. *Croce di Rosano*, ca. 12th century, tempera on wood panel, 445 × 370 cm, detail. Rignano sull'Arno (Florence), Abbey of Santa Maria di Rosano

In Theophilus's treatise *Schedula diversarum atrium*, the technical procedure described for the production of metal leaf proves to be surprisingly similar to modern techniques of beating gold and silver. Although the author puts these complex instructions in the chapter on painting techniques, simply because of the link between the metal leaf and its use in panel painting and illumination, he must have been aware that the production of the leaf implied great technical skill and knowledge of the craft which, in all probability, were possessed only by the goldbeaters or those craftsmen who handled metals extensively. Even the working tools quoted by Theophilus, such as the hammer, the bench with the precise surface for beating, the parchment bag, and the small scissors made specifically to cut the gold leaf, do not seem to belong to a painter's studio, but more to a goldbeater's or a goldsmith's workshop.[12]

Theophilus also provides the first extant description of how to make a punch, a tool that is called *ferrus punctorius* in the treatise. In chapter 73 of Book 3 the monk first presents the procedure required to make the most basic versions of the tools and then explains the graining process.[13] These instructions appear in the book on trades in the metallurgical field and lead us to the conclusion that it was blacksmiths, and not painters, who made punches. The fact that, centuries later, Cennino Cennini did not devote a single passage in his work to the methods of making these tools seems to confirm that punches were forged by craftsmen who worked metal, but it also leads us to consider the diversity of the crafts then existing.

De coloribus et artibus Romanorum, known as the Heraclius treatise, includes the method used to gild tin.[14] *De coloribus faciendis* by Peter of Saint Audemar explains the technique used to apply gold leaf to walls.[15] *De arte illuminandi*, a treatise almost exclusively dedicated to miniatures, mentions gold powder, derived from grinding the leaf, preferably on a porphyry surface, for chrysography; and mosaic gold, a chemical preparation to be used instead of gold for backgrounds and coloring.[16] As gold is a soft and ductile metal, pounding it in the mortar tended to join the particles together rather than break them apart. Heraclius recommends working it in wine, while Theophilus provides a description of a tool for grinding the gold leaf in water. Egg white, gum, honey, and vegetable juices were used to apply the gold leaf to manuscript parchment; they were called "water mordants"—water-soluble substances that "bit," or rather attached, the gold. The gold leaf was then smoothed or burnished by rubbing the surface with a hard-tipped tool to give it a reflecting metallic splendor. A rounded stone or a tooth was often used: Heraclius says, "let it be made very shiny using a wild bear's tooth."

Cennino Cennini's *Libro dell'arte*, which is a more detailed and systematic text on artistic techniques, devotes large sections to the gilding techniques used for panel painting, while giving an account of the Florentine post-Giottesque tradition on the eve of the Renaissance.[17] In chapters 134–39 Cennini describes in great detail the technique for the correct application of gold leaf, from the preparation of the ground to advice about handling leaf and some tricks for obtaining the best results.[18] In chapter 123 he describes marking out the areas to be painted, outlining them with an incised line, so that the remaining background could be gilded accurately and precisely.[19] This is a very important chapter, albeit minimal in terms of length, as it discloses some information about the division of the phases of work among different professions, which are discussed in detail in the subsequent text. Incised outlines were necessary whenever the master of the workshop established the composition as a whole, but then wished to delegate the application and tooling of the gold to others. Moreover, the aspects relating to the most suitable timing for the various phases of the gilding, which Cennini covers in chapters 134–39, indicate that, very often, the paintings were executed in distinct phases that were far apart in time (and perhaps also carried out in different workshops), based on technical necessities. We need to adopt a medieval artisan's mentality and to understand the social circumstances of the time, which were so alien to our own. Ours have been undergoing rapid change, especially since the eighteenth century, with the advent of mechanized processing, industrialization, and computerization having revolutionized them to the point that it is difficult for us even to imagine a world based on seasonal and natural rhythms.[20]

Chapters 131–33 deal with the different kinds of preparatory layers and adhesives for gold, that is, Armenian bole (a red clay) and the rarer preparation in green earth.[21] In chapters 140–43 and then 160, Cennini talks about how to gild to create special effects, especially in decoration: for instance, in graining or decorative incisions (for which mechanical instruments were used); the simpler methods of burnishing (which, as we have seen, had a long tradition); and modifications such as glazing or toning (*campeggiatura* and *palliatura*), obtained with layers of semi-transparent colors, such as resins and oils.[22]

The Sienese painters were masters of these techniques. This was particularly true of Simone Martini, to the extent that it was thought that he had invented them or at least had introduced them to Italy from elsewhere.[23] Essentially, the techniques involve painting on the gold leaf, applying color either opaquely or with transparent glazes that allow the gold to show through, and then scratching through the paint to create damask patterns. The use of glazes was a key characteristic of the elegance of Martini's painting, who promulgated it during his stay in Avignon, paving the way for the great late Gothic painting of the fifteenth century.

In the chapters directly dedicated to painting, Cennini often speaks of the use of gold as a color, employed to give brilliant effects to some details such as the regal drapery of the Virgin or other holy figures. These are the techniques of mordant gilding or painting with "shell" gold (so called because the valves of shells were where powdered colors were mixed with a binder, prior to being applied).[24] In chapter 155, rather surprisingly, Cennini advises us to refrain from varnishing gold.[25] Finally, chapters 157–59 are devoted to gilding for manuscripts; chapters 95–101 to gilding wall paintings; chapters 128 and 174 to gilding stone; and chapter 165 to how to apply gold to canvas.[26]

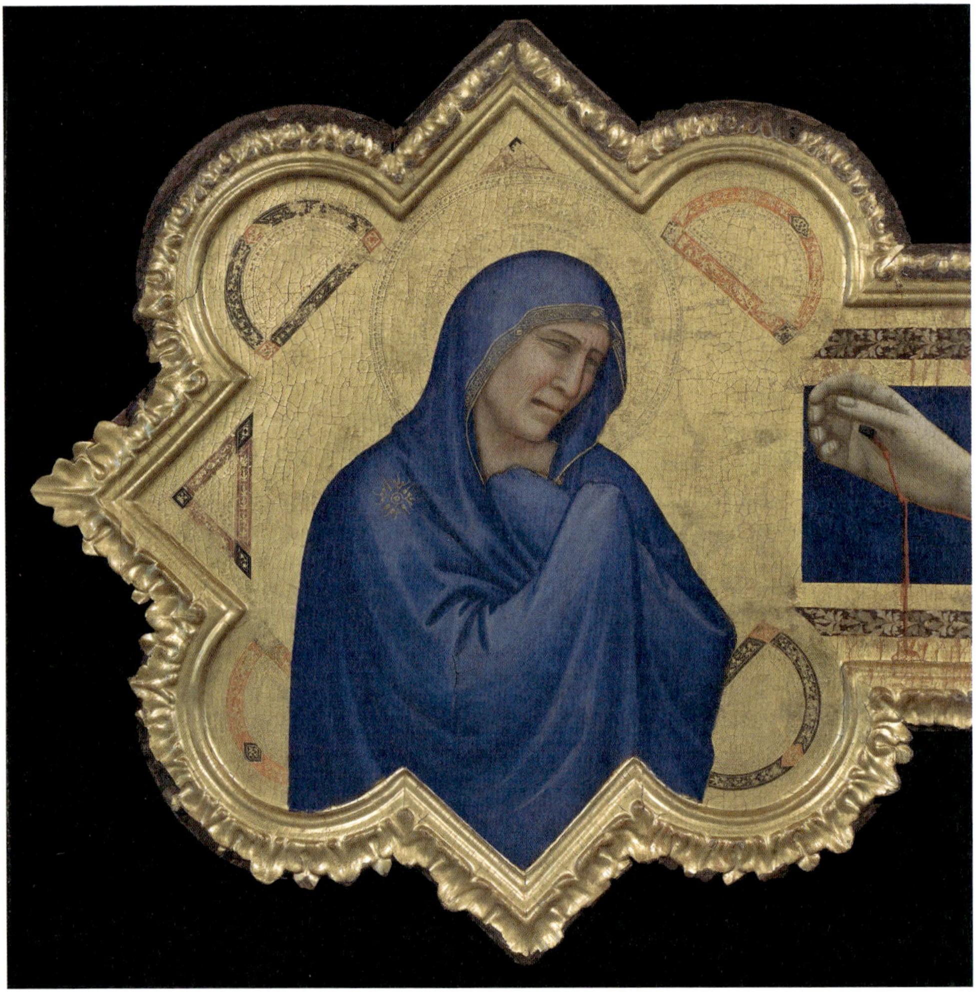

Fig. 2. Giotto, *Croce di Ognissanti*, ca. 1315, tempera and gold on wood panel, 468 × 375 cm, detail of the weeping Virgin. Florence, Church of Ognissanti

With his light and expressive prose, Cennini makes a number of observations that broaden our understanding of what the use of gold must have meant for art at that time. For example, in a chapter dedicated to lapis lazuli blue, a highly valued and sought-after pigment, he says: "And let some of that color, combined with gold, which adorns all the works of our profession, whether on wall or on panel, shine forth in every object."[27]

For the true Renaissance period, in which the application of gold continued for at least most of the fifteenth century, contemporary sources which thoroughly describe the goldbeater's art are not so readily found. By the middle of

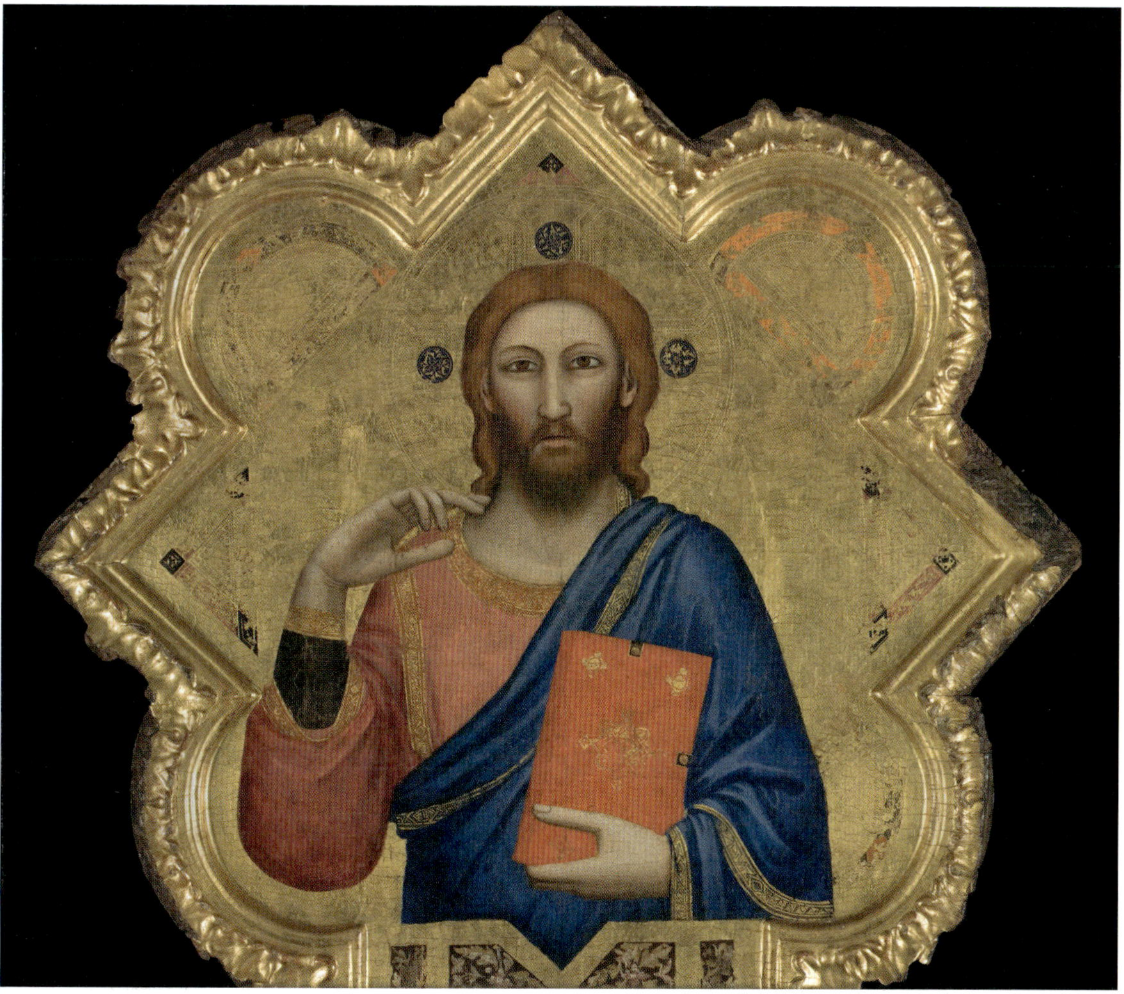

Fig. 3. Giotto, *Croce di Ognissanti*, ca. 1315, tempera and gold on wood panel, 468 × 375 cm, detail of God the Father blessing. Florence, Church of Ognissanti

the sixteenth century it was evidently an art in decline, though Vasari praises it, saying: "It was a beautiful secret and a sophisticated investigation that found a way to beat gold into such thin sheets that for every thousand beaten pieces, one-eighth of a *braccio* on each side, the value of only six scudi was enough for the artifice and the gold."[28]

The Social Organization of the Craft

In addition to recipe books and treatises on artistic technique, which were important but difficult to use, the statutory and legislative written sources are very important.[29] Their strength lies in the fact that they are not works of literature but they nevertheless provide a social and political framework for the society to which they refer.[30]

All guilds had a statute to manage relationships among the individual guild members and to legislate on the organization of labor within workshops and on the quality of their production. The main purpose of the guilds was to defend the exercise of the individual crafts, making sure they were practiced exclusively by guild members. The stipulated conditions for enrollment consisted in a public oath before the entire guild and the payment of a fee. But many people avoided the obligations imposed by the statutes: they did not enroll in the guild but preferred to be employed by a guild member who performed the same craft. This limited their professional activity, as it did not allow them to have a workshop in their own name or undertake contracts, and it did not allow them to have a public or political career.

One of the external prerogatives of a guild was to ensure the quality of the products that came from its workshops and discourage the influx of "foreign" workers into the city, carrying out the same craft. This detailed prohibitionist policy was implemented by means of strict regulations regarding the production and use of materials, as a guarantee for the buyer. In addition to the aforesaid conditions, the guild required all those who wished to practice a craft to undergo a long period of apprenticeship, the *discepolato*, which ranged in length according to the training requirements of each job. In this connection, it is interesting to note that a relative of a person enrolled in the guild did not have to pay the enrollment fee, because a family apprenticeship was considered a further guarantee of the quality of the product he would make.

Guild statutes that regulated artistic production begin, in chronological order, with the Statute of Painters of the city of Florence, dated 1315 document. This opens with a decree listing the activities that characterize the guild members. It is worth quoting the whole sentence, and then examining it thoroughly:

> These are certain provisions, statutes and ordinances made, drawn up and compiled by the consuls of the said art, by authority and bail granted to them by the aforesaid art, pertaining to the members of those apothecaries, who buy, sell, and work gold and silver and beaten tin, glue [color, i.e., diluted with glue], white lead, azure, cinnabar [i.e., vermillion red], and other colors, and they make others relating to and pertaining to the members named above.[31]

The guild was defined as "an association among craftsmen of related or affiliated activities."[32] Indeed, the Arte dei Medici e Speziali (Guild of Physicians and Pharmacists) incorporated the category of painters in 1315, as they were considered related to pharmacists (the second branch of the main guild) because they sold (*vendunt*) and used (*operantur*) essential materials for their activity, such as "aurum et argentiim et stangnum battutum, collam, biaccham, azzurrum, cinabrium et alios colores." Note that the word *operantur*, also (and perhaps more often) has the meaning of "setting to work" rather than "working on."

This list of materials defining the scope of the guild includes "aurum et argentum et stagnum." Precious metals were thus granted a paratactic association with painting; hence all those who devoted themselves to working the metals used by painters were allowed to join the guild.[33] Goldbeaters (*battiloro*), tinbeaters (*battistagno*), and tinsel makers (*orpellai*) were therefore partnered with painters in the same guild, favoring trade relations and even leading to the possibility of setting up a corporation.[34]

Goldworkers could also enroll as members of the Arte di Por Santa Maria or Arte della Seta (Por Santa Maria Guild or Silk Guild), through the same kind of connection to the specialized work being carried out. Only goldsmiths enrolled in this guild;[35] however, as early as 1375 there are mentions of goldbeaters as metal workers who worked gold into thread for weaving. It can easily be seen that these particular craft associations (goldbeaters with painters, goldbeaters with weavers, and goldbeaters with goldsmiths) depended on a strict association between the material produced and its specific artistic use in order to make economic transactions easier.

In the painters' statute of 1349, the *battiloro* are defined in the twenty-third column as: "makers, sellers, or beaters of tin, tinsel, gold, silver or similar materials."[36] In the statutory reform of 1378, it is said that "painters, goldbeaters, tinsel makers and furniture painters" were part of a single branch of the guild. The reform dated 1403 gives for the first time the measurements of the gold, silver, and gold-silver laminate (*oro di metà*) leaves,[37] which are also drawn at the end of Codex C.[38] It is obvious that precisely specifying the size of the leaves meant regulating the goldbeaters' activity to prevent fraud to the detriment of both painters and clients.

In many fourteenth-century documents, it is said that gold leaf was obtained from beating gold coins. While no mention of this is made in the statutory regulations of the Arte dei Medici e Speziali, the statutes of the guild of goldsmiths do mention gold for coin-making.[39] Many commission contracts certify the use of the florin for the production of metallic leaves, so it was easy to find the metal; at the same time, the producer, the consumer, and the client were guaranteed the use of pure gold. Indeed, the production of gold and silver coins was strictly controlled by the mints, which ensured that a high-quality currency was released into the market. Quality control did not only occur during the production phases but also on the circulating coins. For example, the assayer was responsible for verifying the weight of florins by means of a test: all those that did not meet the set standard were marked and removed from circulation.[40]

Cennini's *Libro dell'arte* explains in chapter 139 that one hundred leaves could be obtained from the beating of a single coin: "[As for] the gold that is put into leaves, know that one would not want to get more than a hundred pieces out of a ducat."[41] An interesting passage from the same chapter instructs the painter on how to recognize good-quality metal leaf: "And look, when you want to know gold, when you buy it, take it from someone who is a good *battiloro* [literarily, goldbeater(s); defined as 'makers, sellers, or beaters of tin, tinsel, gold, silver or similar materials' in the painters' statute of 1349, page 9, footnote 35]. And look at the gold, because if you see it billowing and brisk, as if made from parchment, then consider it good."[42] Here Cennino also informs us about the provenance of the leaf and about the number of leaves to be obtained from the beating of one gold coin, but notes that gilding a panel requires a thicker leaf, because the gold "for the panel wants to be rather dull." He regrets that sometimes the ducat yields 145 leaves (rather than 100), which were clearly thinner, "oro sottilissimo e ragnato" (gold marked by microfractures or characterized by excessive and uneven transparency), a kind he recommended using for carvings or frames.[43] Using metal leaf of different thicknesses depending on the application areas was mainly a function of practical, aesthetic, and economic factors: the thicker leaf was better placed on a flat surface, creating the effect of a compact metal surface, which was typical of medieval gilding; thinner ones were suited to the profiles of wavy, discontinuous, and uneven surfaces, where a thicker leaf might break up or dull the carving.

All goldbeaters who did not meet the regulations set by the statutes were severely punished. The control of the Florentine production of metal leaf was performed by specific investigators called *cercatori*, who made sure that no one put non-regulation products on the market.[44] If in the Arte dei Medici e Speziali all members were admonished not to deceive painters by selling *oro di metà* as pure gold, the same warning was addressed to painters, who were not to deceive customers by using *oro di metà* or toned silver as gold, as already explicitly established in the statues in 1315.[45] The same kind of prohibition is found in the regulations of the guilds of Siena[46] and Perugia.[47] The strict regulations

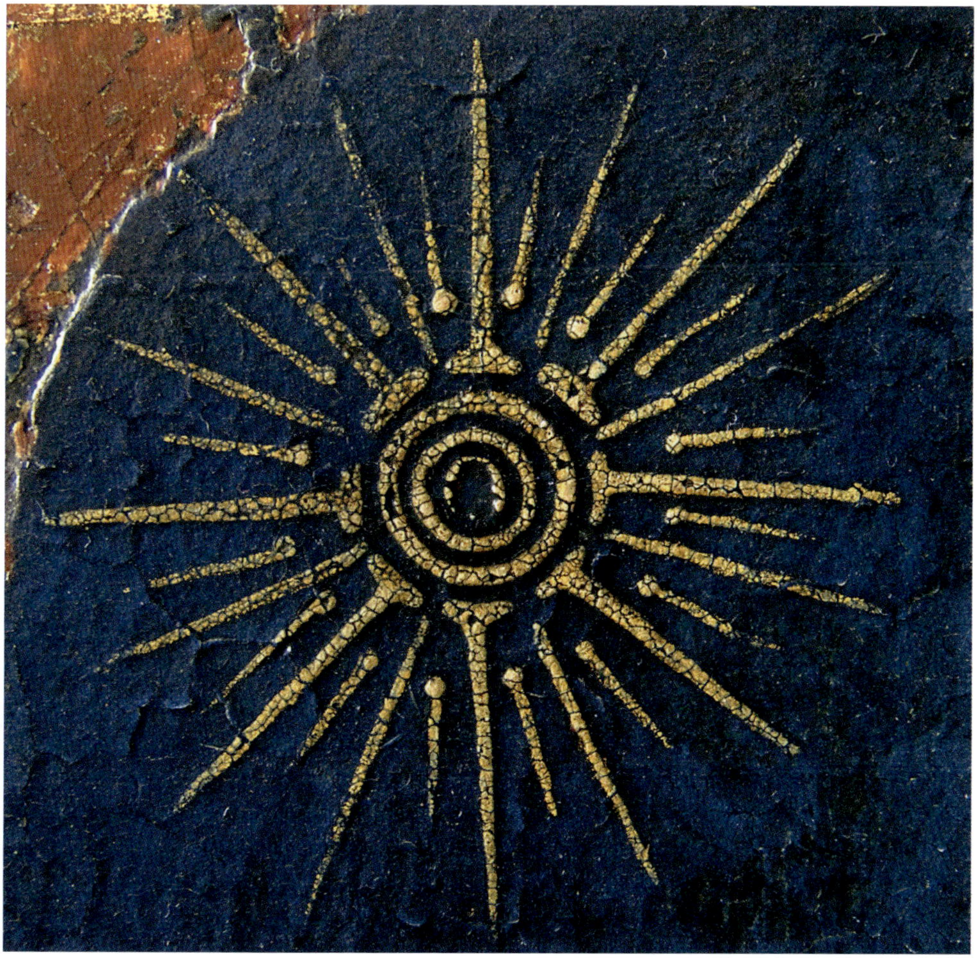

Fig. 4. Stefano di Giovanni di Consolo, known as il Sassetta, *Madonna and Child with Angels, St. Anthony of Padua, St. John the Evangelist*, tempera and gold on poplar wood, 207 × 118 cm, detail. Paris, Musée du Louvre

of the three statutes were the result of a long and complex development by a single Trecento organization that supervised and watched over the work of its artisans, with the aim of converting the products of their crafts into one of the clearest, most visible examples of the economic wealth and cultural sophistication of their city.

The Debate: Painters and Goldbeaters – Who Did What?

Despite the many studies, the organization and interrelationship of artistic professions in late medieval society is still not understood in full—not so much as regards matters occurring within the same workshop, but rather in terms of the collaboration among several workshops with different specialties, all contributing to a single finished product. Such knowledge would enable us not only to clarify the relationships among artists or artisans of different crafts, but would also allow art historians to have a greater understanding of the specific and complex economic administration and distribution of labor in Trecento and Quattrocento society. This collaboration did not always have a hierarchical nature, but was often based on equal and, in part, self-governing relationships: parallel specializations that were essentially tied to specific working techniques and materials.[48]

The focused specialization of artisans and consequent divisions of labor were mainly due to economic and practical considerations. The division into sectors of activity allowed savings in terms of both time and materials: different processes could be made in dedicated locations, with the minimum investment of materials and space by the head of the workshop who undertook the task. The few surviving inventories of such workshops (for example, from the documents of the Pupilli in the Florence State Archives[49]) and a general analysis of the tax records of the properties where the craft and commercial activities were performed show that the workshops were extremely small and equipped with specific and dedicated materials and tools. Rarely were many workers employed, and the labor organization appears to have been partitioned and specific. In a society where specialization was considered an important virtue serving to protect artisan traditions, we should not be surprised by the specific role played by some craftsmen and merchants, who established preferential relationships of collaboration with the world of painting.[50]

Among the activities directly related to the painter's craft there was that of the goldbeater. Although there are several goldbeaters' names enrolled in the lists of the Arte dei Medici e Speziali and in those of the religious confraternity of Saint Luke (a lay association that included the Florentine painters), little has been done to understand their specific area of artistic accomplishment, which is usually considered to have been exclusively the task of reducing gold bars to leaf. It is interesting to investigate the possibility that goldbeaters directly contributing to further working on the gold: that is, in particular, by punching the backgrounds and halos – maybe not always, but for the richest and most important commissions, in which precision and symbolism would have had a significant role and importance.[51]

The historical identity of only two Florentine master goldbeaters has been reconstructed, Bastiano di Giovanni di Nardo and Piero di Francesco, allowing us to delineate, at least in part, their activity and customers.[52] In an attempt at a broader examination of the social phenomenon, it is interesting to note that from 1371 to 1444 there were thirteen goldbeaters and two tinbeaters enrolled in the Arte dei Medici e Speziali among the painters.[53] There are no extant registration lists from 1446 to 1490. The context of the period may be integrated, in part, with data from the painter Neri di Bicci's *Le ricordanze*, which covers precisely the period of time from 1453 to 1475. It is a kind of diary, which gives the reader a wonderful cross section of the complex work relationships mentioned previously and which, here, revolve around Neri. In the *Ricordanze*, seven goldbeaters are mentioned.[54] Other names have been obtained from the lists of the Company of Saint Luke, the lay confraternity dedicated to painters, whose members also included the two aforementioned goldbeaters, Bastiano di Giovanni and Piero di Francesco.[55] This brief and certainly incomplete list of goldbeaters active in Florence from the mid-fourteenth century until late in the fifteenth century allows us to insert these representative examples into a professional landscape characterized by a large group of producers and sellers of metal leaf, upon which many artists working in Florence depended.

One question that has been raised is how a goldbeater was defined. Were goldbeaters limited to producing gold leaf or did they also apply it and decorate it?[56] As well as helping to broaden the view of trade in the artisan society of the time, this question addresses many discrepancies and technical characteristics, known to those who closely examine paintings with gilded backgrounds. The evidence seems to show that the various working phases belonged to different craftsmen. The need to use incisions to delimit the areas to be gilded and distinguish them from the areas to be left for the application of paint could alone indicate that, following this phase, a number of different craftsmen took over the work, and that these may not have been aware of the conception and planning steps. In contrast, the absence of incisions in the gilding of Piero della Francesca's *Polyptych of the Misericordia*, characterized nevertheless by the precision of the contours, has led to the hypothesis that the gold was directly laid and worked by the artist.[57]

Moreover, how can one explain, within the corpus of the same author, both refined punching and hasty punching, or even ugly or mistaken punching, if not through the employment of different hands? This is, for example, the case for Masaccio and Masolino, in whose Florentine works one can see punched decoration of high quality, while the Polyptych of Santa Maria Maggiore in Rome, a work designed for an extraordinary destination and commissioned by the Colonna family, is of a much lower quality. This could be explained by the use of Roman workers, who were surely less specialized. How can errors of planning be explained – changes made during the process of punching, where the marks go beyond the desired boundary or modify a contour?

There is even a body of documentary records concerning works gilded and painted by different hands: that is, works in which a master entrusted a specialized artist with the task of decorating the gilding. These cases of multiple hands at work include Pietro Lorenzetti's Arezzo Polyptych, there is the painting done by Spinello Aretino for the church of Santa Maria Nuova in Rome, "nella quale fece Spinello in campo d'oro un numero infinito di figure, fra piccole e grandi, con molto giudizio" (in which Spinello painted an infinite number of figures, from small to large, in a field of gold, with great judgment), entrusting a certain master Gabriel Seracini with the work of gilding in Lucca.[58] Seracini is documented as enrolled in the Arte dei Pittori Senesi (Guild of the Painters of Siena) in 1356 and 1389.[59]

A document found by Andrew Ladis records a master Stefano who was paid to *granare* (embellish with graining) a panel of the Virgin, painted by others.[60] There is a chest for the Palazzo Pubblico in Siena, painted by Luca di Tommè and gilded by Niccolò di Luccio.[61] There is a document recording Lippo Memmi being paid as much as 70 florins "per l'adoramento dele cholone civori e cercini della tavola di Santo Sano" (for the gilding of the columns, ciboria, and hoops of the panel of St Ansanus), that is, the *Annunciation* painted by Simone Martini (today in the Uffizi).[62] Then there is the case of Sano di Pietro: there is a mention of a panel (now lost) that Sano received already gessoed and gilded, which he painted between 1467 and 1475 for the altar of Maddalena di Matteo da Campriano in San Domenico.[63] And the case of the Sienese painter-gilders, circulating in early Renaissance Siena, has been brought to light with a wealth of documents and an astute interpretation by Machtelt Israëls.[64]

Furthermore, there are cases of artists specifically enrolled in the Florentine guilds as *pittore-battiloro* or painter-goldbeaters. Antonio di Stefano, lived at the end of the fifteenth century and beginning of the sixteenth. He belonged to a family of goldbeaters, which included his grandfather Antonio di Stefano di Francesco, who was enrolled in the Arte dei Medici e Speziali, his father, Stefano d'Antonio, and his uncle Giovanni Gualberto.[65] In his *catasto* tax records for 1480, Antonio's father says that he does not have his own workshop but works for a certain "Domenico, the painter-goldbeater." This documents the presence of other painter-goldbeaters active in Florence in the second half of the Quattrocento.

Finally, in concluding this list of examples, which is illustrative and certainly not complete, mention must be made of the case of the painter-gilders

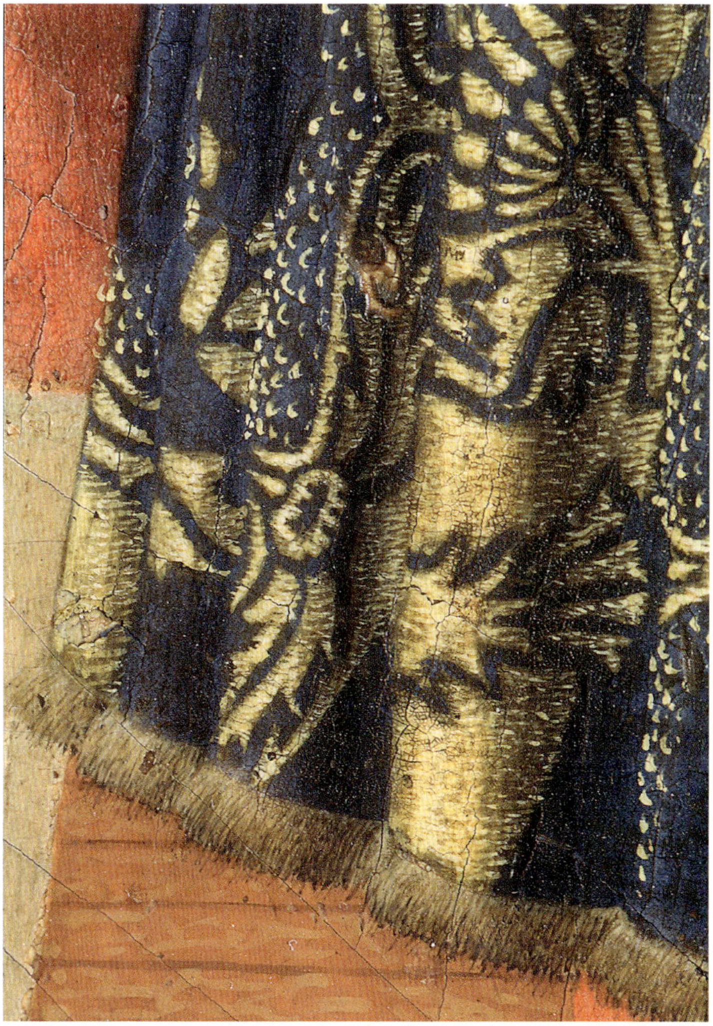

Fig 5. Piero della Francesca, *Flagellation*, ca. 1459-1460, tempera on wood panel, 67.5 × 91 cm, detail. Urbino, Galleria Nazionale delle Marche

(*pittore-mettiloro*), who are documented beginning in the mid-Trecento. A certain Filippo di Lazzaro was entrusted with gilding Taddeo Gaddi's polyptych for the church of San Giovanni Fuorcivitas in Pistoia in 1353: "per metere l'oro in nella taula," (to lay in the gold on the wood panel) gilding for which the leaf had been purchased in Florence.[66] For the same project, Filippo di Lazzaro was paid for a certain amount of tin which was to be used to finish the staff of the curtain rod on which the painting hung: "A Filipo di Lazzaro per istagnio che puose à ferri della chortina sol. III."[67] Filippo di Lazzaro is also mentioned as a painter for the commission of an altarpiece for the church of Santa Maria in Grignano.[68] So he was not only the gilder of a polyptych painted by the major artist Taddeo Gaddi but was also a painter in his own right.

In the Trecento and Quattrocento, the fact that goldbeaters engaged with painters confirms the interdisciplinary nature of artistic activities and broadens our understanding of the role of goldbeaters whose workshops included artisans specialized in gilding and metal leaf tooling.[69] In a world dominated by specializations, the assumption that every painter punched his own panels and owned his own set of punches seems less and less obvious. Many workshop inventories never mention the presence of punches and instead we find them listed in those of the goldbeaters.[70] In his *Libro dell'arte*, Cennini himself does not speak about the use of punches, but about the use of tools for the techniques of graining and sgraffito, techniques closely related to the representational effects that gold could take on in connection with the image and that justified a direct execution by the painters.

Another interesting document bears witness to the presence of goldbeaters, gilders, and toolers (*stampatori*) in the city of Siena: it is the "Aggiunta al Breve dell'Arte de' Pittori Senesi," where it is said that, on Saint Luke's day, masters, boys, and subjects both of the city and of the surrounding area had to offer "un cero di valuta soldi dieci," (a candle of the value of 10 soldi) and among those who had to carry out this task, there are "Tutti li mettitori d'oro, d'argento a pennello o in qual si vogli cosa, escetto a fuoco," (All who put gold and silver by brush or whatever you want, except by fire) "Tutti i battelori, battestagni, e simili" (All the goldbeaters, tinbeaters, and the like) and "Tutti li stampatori d'ogni cosa, escetto li stampatori di libri (All printers of everything except book printers)."[71] (The term *stampatori* probably means those who created patterns *a stampo*, by imprinting or punching, almost certainly on the areas decorated in gold, as they are counted along with goldbeaters and gilders. These *a stampo* imprinted patterns recall the gold graining and tooling mentioned by Cennini.)

Despite the obvious gaps, the perspective that this collection of documents helps to assemble speaks of a flexible and diversified division of work, a craft world where painters knew how to apply metal leaf onto their paintings especially when they were small, but one where painters turned to specialized artisans for bigger and more important commissions. Neri di Bicci himself mentions many times in his *Ricordanze* that he was engaged in some commissions exclusively as a gilder—that is, to "mettere d'oro"—as, for example, in the wood tabernacle made by Giuliano da Maiano, painted and gilded by Neri, which showed a glazed Madonna by Luca della Robbia; or for the *Viti di Vangelo* made by Zanobi di Domenico and gilded by Neri; or for the terracotta head of Saint Catherine whose creator is not mentioned but whose polychromy and gilding were passed to Neri.[72] These examples also supply us with documentary evidence regarding the number of different artists who could take part in a single work. Colnaghi's *Dictionary of Florentine Painters* notes Bernardo di Iacopo as a painter-gilder whose life straddled the fifteenth and sixteenth centuries, and he reports "The Gilders were included among the painters and were, occasionally, painters as well as gilders."[73]

It seems no coincidence that the use of gold in paintings gradually disappeared, not only through the progress of artistic evolution and the changing furnishing of churches, but also due to the profound social changes occurring from the middle of the fifteenth century onwards. The guild statutes were overtaken by the rules of the market; painters, acquiring a higher social role and a greater awareness of their own status, began to be valued more for these reasons than for the quality of the materials used. The less important role of gold in paintings was part of a general trend—occurring throughout western Europe at the time—towards a kind of selective restriction of ostentation, which manifested itself in many other sorts of behavior, as pointed out by Baxandall.[74] It was equally evident in the client's clothes, where the gilded fabrics and gaudy colors were abandoned in favor of the more serious Burgundy black. This fashion was accompanied by sumptuary laws and the premonitory signs of strong moral restrictions.

The representation of realistic, illusionistic, and architectural space also burst into paintings including religious subjects, replacing the empyrean implication of light that the gold ground provided. For a few more decades we witness the struggle of traditionalist requests by patrons, who sought to capture, as if in a gilded cage, innovative artists such as Masaccio and Piero della Francesca. The Virgin of the *Polyptych of the Misericordia* is sculptural and compact, almost like an ivory tower. She stands out on a golden ground which Piero manages to turn into radiant light through the physica reflection of gold, as if the Madonna were lit from behind.

However, for other purposes, art theorists—for example, Leon Battista Alberti in *Della pittura*—urged painters to represent even golden objects not by using gold itself but through the skillful application of yellow and white. But about fifty years later, Botticelli made wide use of this metal, braiding his goddess's hair with gold in the *Birth of Venus* and scattering it among the leaves of the trees behind her.[75] According to advice from a strong Cennini tradition, a spray of gold mixed with green could evoke the idea that "some trees seemed to be trees from heaven."

Thereafter, the splendor and symbolism of gold lost its religious and theological significance, becoming a manifestation of a world of luxury and of pagan aesthetic games. Nevertheless, altarpieces with gold grounds continued to be created for settings far from major cities, in traditional or, frankly, provincial centers, almost as if taking a stand against change, remaining firmly harnessed to times past—either awaiting a desired revival or through a profound inability to be pervaded by Dante's sky of *oriental zaffiro*, which becomes atmospheric and distinctly colored.

Notes

*This essay was completed in December 2018; therefore, the author did not take in consideration publications printed after that date.

1. This research would not have been possible without the contributions of Roberto Bellucci and Ciro Castelli, with whom I have shared work and study experiences on a daily basis. These two experts have been sources of profound material, technical, and historical knowledge for many long years now. In particular, I would also like to thank Carl Brandon Strehlke, Machtelt Bruggen Israëls, Irma Passeri, and Giovanni Pagliarulo for our many conversations on the topic, for their suggestions, as well as, for their friendship and aid. A special acknowledgment is due to Giulia Scarpone, the author of an important work of doctoral research on the gold grounds and gilded decoration of Duccio di Buoninsegna's panel paintings (Università di Firenze, under the guidance of Andrea De Marchi, Sonia Chiodo and Cecilia Frosinini), the publication of which is eagerly awaited. I thank Adele Leccia and Jason Di Resta for bringing bibliographic sources to my attention. The present essay was finished in December 2018, and therefore does not include citations or bibliography from after this date.

2. The expression "metaphysics of light" (*Lichtmetaphysik*) was coined at the beginning of the twentieth century by Clemens Baeumker (C. Baeumker, *Witelo. Ein Philosoph und Naturforscher des XIII. Jahrhunderts* (Münster: Aschendorffsche Buchhandlung, 1908), 372–422) to show the tendency of third- and fourth-century authors in particular to develop physical and metaphysical doctrines focusing on the category of light.

3. "Che hanno l'essere in modo più vero e più degno nei gradi degli enti secondo la maggiore o minore partecipazione ad essa." Roberto di Grassatesta, *Metafisica della Luce*, introduction, translation and notes by Paolo Rossi, (Milan: Rusconi 1986), 113–23.

4. G. Duby, *Saint Bernard. L'art cistercien* (Paris: Flammarion, 1979) (Italian translation *San Bernardo e l'arte cistercense* (Turin: Einaudi, 1982)); R. Assunto, *Die Theorie des Schönen im Mittelalter* (Cologne: DuMont Schauberg, 1963); U. Eco, "Sviluppo dell'estetica medioevale," in *Momenti e problemi di storia dell'estetica, I. Dall'antichità classica al barocco* (Milan: Marzorati, 1959), 115–229; A. Grabar, *Les origines de l'esthétique médiévale* (Paris: Macula, 1992); S. Pedone, "La passione aurea: il colore dell'oro a Bisanzio," in *In corso d'opera. Ricerche dei dottorandi in storia dell'arte della Sapienza, 1*, ed. by Michele Nicolaci, Matteo Piccioni, and Lorenzo Riccardi (Rome: Campisano, 2015), 15–22.

5. For this and the following examination of the craft through documentary sources, see I. Passeri, "Gold Coins and Gold Leaf in Early Italian Paintings," in *The Matter of Art: Materials, Practices, Cultural Logistics, c. 1250–1650*, ed. by Christy Anderson, Anne Dunlop, and Pamela Smith (Manchester: Manchester University Press, 2015), 97–115.

6. For goldbeaters in the Egyptian age, see T. G. H. James, "Gold Technology in Ancient Egypt," *Gold Bulletin* 5, no. 2 (1972): 38–42; E. D. Nicholson, "The Ancient Craft of Gold Beating," *Gold Bulletin* 12, no. 4 (1974): 161–66.

7. Pliny the Elder, *Natural History*, ed. and trans. by J. Bostock and H. T. Riley (London: Henry G. Bohn, 1855), 33.19.

8. C. R. Dodwell, "Gold Metallurgy in the Twelfth Century," *Gold Bulletin* 4, no. 3 (1971): 51–55.

9. Dioscorides, *De materia medica*, ed. by T. Osbaldeson and R. P. A. Wood (Johannesburg: IBIDIS, 2000).

10. H. Hedfors, *Compositiones ad Tingenda Musiva* (Uppsala, 1932). The passage is also quoted by C. Merzenich, "Dorature *e policromie delle parti architettoniche nelle tavole d'altare toscane nel Tre-Quattrocento: Piero di Francesco battiloro, l'oro fine, l'oro di metà, l'argento e lo stagno dorato," Kermes* 26 (1996): 54.

11. Theophilus, *On Divers Arts: The Foremost Medieval Treatise on Painting, Glassmaking and Metalwork*, ed. and trans. by J. G. Hawthorne and C. Stanley Smith (Chicago: University of Chicago Press, 1963).

12. Ibid., 81–87.

13. Ibid., 149.

14. S. M. Alexander, "Medieval Recipes Describing the Use of Metals in Manuscripts," *Marsyas* 12 (1967): 34–51, para. 45.

15. Ibid., para. 190.

16. C. Pasqualetti, *Il Libellus ad faciendum colores dell'archivio di stato dell'Aquila. Origine, contesto e restituzione del "De arte illuminandi"* (Florence: SISMEL edizioni del Galluzzo, 2011), 230–31.

17. Regarding the interpretation, dating, and provenance of Cennino Cennini's *Libro dell'arte* there have recently been several positions and proposals, which are not compatible one with another. However, these have had the merit of reopening a question which had apparently already been settled regarding a Paduan milieu and the very nature of the text as a kind of manual for an artist's workshop. See S. Baroni and S. B. Tosatti, "Sul *Libro dell'arte* di Cennino Cennini," *Acme* 51, no. 1 (1998): 51–72; R. Bellucci and C. Frosinini, "Working Together: Technique and Innovation in Masolino's and Masaccio's Panel Paintings," in *The Panel Paintings of Masolino and Masaccio: The Role of Technique*, ed. by C. B. Strehlke and C. Frosinini (Milan: 5 Continents, 2002), 29–67; S. Baroni, "Il *Libro dell'arte* di Cennino Cennini," in S. B. Tosatti et al., *I trattati di tecniche artistiche medievali con accenni sull'antichità e l'età moderna. Storia delle tecniche artistiche* (Milan: CUSL, 2002), 101–14; F. Frezzato, foreword in C. Cennini, *Il libro dell'arte*, ed. by F. Frezzato (Vicenza: Pozza, 2003); W.-D. Löhr and S. Weppelmann, eds., *Fantasie und Handwerk. Cennino Cennini und die Tradition der toskanischen Malerei von Giotto bis Lorenzo Monaco* (Berlin: SMB, Gemäldegalerie Staatliche Museen zu Berlin, 2008); E. Skaug, "More Cenniniana: Technical Notes on the Origin and Purpose of *Il libro dell'arte*," *Arte Cristiana* 98, no. 857 (2010): 81–88 (in particular vis polemic); T. Burns, "Cennino Cennini's *Il libro dell'arte*: A Historiographical Review," *Studies in Conservation* 56 (2011): 1–13. Recently Bellucci and Frosinini's proposal was reiterated and supported by A. Monciatti, review of "*L'officina di Giotto. Il restauro della Croce di Ognissanti*, by M. Ciatti," *Arte Medievale*, 4th ser., 2 (2012): 304–9.

18. C. Cennini, *The Craftsman's Handbook: The Italian "Il Libro dell'Arte,"* trans. by D. V. Thompson, Jr. (New York: Dover, 1960), 80–85, chaps. 134–39.

19. Ibid., 76, chap. 123.

20. By way of example, see J. Le Goff, *Tempo della chiesa e tempo del mercante* (Turin: Einaudi, 2000); R. Bordone, *Uno stato d'animo. Memoria del tempo e comportamenti urbani nel mondo comunale italiano* (Florence: Firenze University Press, 2002); R. Capasso and P. Piccari, eds., *Il tempo nel Medioevo. Rappresentazioni storiche e concezioni filosofiche* (Rome: Società italiana di demodossalogia, 2000).

21. Cennini, *Craftman's Handbook*, 79–80, chaps. 131–33. Regarding the different ways of preparing the gold leaf, see J. Nadolny, "The Techniques and Use of Gilded Relief Decoration by Northern European Painters, c. 1200–1500" (PhD diss., Courtauld Institute of Art, University of London, 2001); J. Nadolny, "All That's Burnished Isn't Bole: Reflections on Medieval Water Gilding – Part 1: Early Medieval to 1300," in *Medieval Painting in Northern Europe: Techniques, Analysis, Art History*, ed. by J. Nadolny et al. (London: Archeotype, 2006), 148–62; C. Frosinini, entry on St. Stephen from the Museo Horne, in *Giotto e compagni*, ed. by D. Thiebaud (Milan: Officina Libraria, 2013), 139–40.

22. Cennini, *Craftman's Handbook*, 85–89, 102, chaps. 140–43, 160.

23. C. S. Hoeniger, "Cloth of Gold and Silver: Simone Martini's Techniques for Representing Luxury Textiles," *Gesta* 30 (1991): 154–62; A. De Marchi, "Oro come luce, luce come oro: l'operazione delle lamine metalliche da Simone Martini a Pisanello, fra mimesi e anagogia," in *Medioevo natura e figura*, ed. by A. C. Quintavalle (Milan: Skira 2015), 701–16.

24. Cennini, *Craftman's Handbook*, 91–93, 95–98, chaps. 145–46, 150–53. The evidence of shells as containers of pigments dates back to antiquity (see A. Hauptmann et al., "On the Making and Provenancing of Pigments from the Early Dynastic Royal Tombs of Ur, Mesopotamia," *Metalla* 22, no. 1 (2016): 41–74. The use persisted in time, and was still attested in the eighteenth-century *Encyclopédie* of Diderot et d'Alembert (1751–65).

25. Cennini, *Craftman's Handbook*, 91–93, chap. 145.

26. Ibid., 100–2, chaps. 157–59; 61–63, chaps. 95–101; 78, 118–19, chaps. 128, 174; 103–7, chaps. 162–66.

27. Ibid., 36, chap. 62.

28. G. Vasari, *Le vite de' più eccellenti pittori, scultori e architettori*, ed. by P. Barocchi and R. Bettarini (Firenze, Sansoni, 1966-1987, 11 vols.), 1.147. *Della pittura*, chap. 28. See also A. Citolini, *Tipocosmia* (Venice, 1561), 402–3; T. Garzoni, *Piazza universale di tutte le professioni del mondo nobili et ignobili* (Venice, 1587; 1st ed. 1585), 905. Even though they offer an accurate description of the goldbeater's craft, they do not record every technical process, but they do include a detailed and noteworthy list of tools.

29. On recipe books and treatises on technique, and purely by way of example, see S. Bordini, *Materia e immagine. Fonti sulle techniche della pittura* (Rome: Leonardo-DeLuca, 1991); V. Gheroldi, "Ricette, ricettari," in *Ricette e ricettari. Tre fonti per la storia delle tecniche delle arti alla Biblioteca Queriniana di Brescia (sec. XVI–XVII)* (Brescia: Musei Civici, 1995), 13–88; S. Baroni, "I ricettari medievali per la preparazione dei colori e la loro trasmissione," in *Il colore nel Medioevo. Arte, simbolo, tecnica*, ed. by F. Dell'Acqua and R. Silva (Lucca: Istituto storico lucchese, 1996), 117–44; S. B. Tosatti, *Trattati medievali di tecniche artistiche* (Milan: Jaca Book, 2007); S. Eyb-Green et al., eds., *The Artist's Process: Technology and Interpretation* (London: Archetype, 2012).

30. See, in general, A. Zorzi, "Le fonti normative a Florence nel tardo Medioevo: un bilancio delle edizioni e degli studi," in *Statuti della Repubblica Fiorentina*, ed. by R. Caggese, new ed. by G. Pinto, F. Salvestrini, and A. Zorzi, 2 vols. (Florence: Olschki, 1999), 1.liii–ci.

31. "Hee sunt quedam provisiones, statuta et ordinamenta facta, hedita et compilata per consules ditte artis, ex auctoritate et balia eisdem concessa per artem predictam, pertinentia ad membrum illorum spetiariorum, qui emunt, vendunt et operantur aurum et argentiim et stangnum battutum, collam, biaccham, azzurrum, cinabrium et alios colores, et alia faciunt, spectanfia et pertinentia ad membrum siiperius nominatiim." In S. La Sorsa, *Gli statuti degli orefici e sellai Fiorentini al principio del secolo XIV* (Florence: Galileiana, 1901). This was the first publication of this source; it was revised by R. Ciasca in *Gli statuti dell'Arte dei Medici e Speziali* (Florence: Galletti e Cocci, 1922). In 1901 La Sorsa had incorrectly assigned this statute to the goldsmiths stating that "The name goldsmiths means several persons following various trades." This misinterpretation probably arose from the general custom of considering goldsmiths the masters par excellence in metalworking.

32. U. Procacci, *Studio sul Catasto Fiorentino* (Florence: Olschki, 1996).

33. A. Guidotti, "Battiloro e dipintori a Firenze fra Tre e Quattrocento: Bastiano di Giovanni e la sua clientela (dal Catasto del 1427)," in *Scritti di Storia dell'Arte in onore di Roberto Salvini* (Florence: Sansoni, 1984), 239–49. The *orpellaio* reduced base metals to leaf using several processes, giving them the semblance of a noble metal, to be used for the decoration of leather, fur, paintings, or wooden objects such as large chests.

34. In general for trade and statutory rules, see A. Guidotti and M. De Marco, "Examination and Elaboration of Documentation Concerning Florentine Studios and Workplaces," *Bollettino d'informazioni del Centro di elaborazione automatica di dati* 6 (1985): 169–213; A. Guidotti, "Il mestiere del 'dipintore' nell'Italia due-trecentesca," in *La pittura in Italia. Il Duecento e il Trecento* (Milan: Electa, 1986), 529–40; A. Guidotti, "Pubblico e privato, committenza e clientela: botteghe e produzione artistica a Florence tra XV e XVI secolo," *Ricerche storiche* 16 (1986): 535–50; L. Indrio, "Firenze nel '400: divisione e organizzazione del lavoro nelle botteghe," *Ricerche di storia dell'arte* 38 (1989): 61–70; A. Bernacchioni, "Le botteghe di pittura: luoghi, strutture, attività," in *Maestri e botteghe. Pittura a Florence alla fine del Quattrocento*, by M. Gregori, A. Paolucci, and C. A. Luchinat (Milan: Silvana, 1992), 23–33; A. Thomas, *The Painter's Practice in Renaissance Tuscany* (Cambridge: Cambridge University Press, 1995); W. Jacobsen, *Die Maler von Florenz* (Munich: Deutscher Kunstverlag, 2001), 109–50.

35. U. Dorini, *Statuti dell'Arte di Por Santa Maria del tempo della Repubblica* (Florence: Olschki, 1934), 791.

36. Ciasca, *Gli statuti dell'Arte dei Medici e Speziali*, 131–35, Statute 1349, col. 23: "Che dicti e ciascuno esercitanti della arte giurino all'arte predetta, e siano sottoposti a consoli della detta arte." (That the said art's practitioners individually swear by the aforesaid art, and be subjected to the consuls of the said art.).

37. Ibid., 371, Reform dated 1403, col. 4: "Misura dell'oro e dell'argento battuto. Detta misura è disegnata in questo libro" (The dimension of beaten gold and silver. This dimension is drawn in this book); the drawing is given on 377.

38. "che ogni pezzo d'oro puro o vero fine debba essere ... è più nona parte e meno octava parte d'un braccio alla misura di Florence, e ogni pezzo d'oro di metà e d'argento debba essere e sia di misura e a misura l'altra maggiore pè detti consoli ordinata, maggiore cioè l'octava parte e minore la settima parte del braccio sopra detto ...." (That every piece of pure (i.e., refined) gold must be ... more than the ninth and less than the eighth part of a Florentine fathom, and every half-gold-and-half-silver piece should and shall be of the measure ordained by the said consuls, that is, greater [than] the eighth and lesser [than] the seventh part of the aforesaid fathom). The surface of the leaf was then set between 1⁄9 and 1⁄8 of a Florentine *braccio*, which corresponds to about 6.5–7.3 cm per side. Although this rule was only introduced in 1403, it is very likely that it was meant to define a current and already pre-existing practice that, not by chance, corresponded to that recorded in classical times by Pliny.

39. Guild statutes of Por Santa Maria dated 1335, col. "De deaurandis rebus infrascripto modo," chap. 21, in Dorini, *Statuti dell'Arte di Por Santa Maria*, 147. Before 1252, the year of the introduction of the florin, the gold circulating was low-percentage gold, mentioned in the sources as *paiola* or *pagliola* gold from northwest Africa, which reached the Italian coast by several routes. For a closer understanding of the circulation of gold in the early Middle Ages, see the essential text P. Spufford, *Money and Its Use in Medieval Europe* (Cambridge: Cambridge University Press, 1988); R. Bellucci, "La Croce di Sarzana tra materia e immagine," in *Pinxit Guillielmus. Il restauro della Croce di Sarzana*, ed. by M. Ciatti (Florence: Edifir, 2001), 41–54; Passeri, "Gold Coins and Gold Leaf."

40. M. Bernocchi, *Le monete della Repubblica Fiorentina, III. Documentazione* (Florence: Olschki, 1976), 1–14; for the control of the florins already in circulation, see in particular p. 9.

41. Cennini, *Craftman's Handbook*, 84–85. The original text reads "Sappi che l'oro che si mette in piani non se ne vorrebbe trarre del ducato altro che cento pezzi." The fact that Cennini refers to the ducat and not to the florin is explained simply by his prolonged stay in Padua. In any case, the florin, the *genovino*, and the ducat all had an almost identical weight and title. See D. Bomford et al., *Art in the Making: Italian Painting before 1400* (London: National Gallery, 1989), 22; Merzenich, "Dorature *e policromie,*" 57 and n.46. In the books of accounts of expenditure for altarpieces it is often said that the amount of one hundred laminates per florin was quite a widespread standard. For example, the contract signed on April 17, 1320 by Pietro Lorenzetti for the Arezzo polyptych reads: "Laboranbo in campis et spatiis ipsarum figurarum de optimo auro de C. folis pro floreno." So, among the expenses met for the polyptych of the high altar of San Pier Maggiore in Florence by Jacopo di Cione, dated 1371 (today at the National Gallery, London), there are three payments linked to the purchase of gold leaf: the first "per cento pezzi d'oro per li fregi e drappi d'oro delle fighure, d'agosto, fior. I d'oro"; the second "per cento pezzi d'oro per lì fregi e drappi delle fighure, a dì 2 settembre, fior. I d'oro"; the third "per cento pezzi d'oro per drappare il colmo di mezzo a dì 10 settembre fior. I." See Bomford et al., *Art in the Making*, 197 and 199 n.9.

42. "E guarda, quando vuoi conoscere l'oro, quando li comperi, toglilo da persona che sia buon battiloro. E guarda l'oro; che se 'l vedi mareggiante e tosto, come di carta di cavretto, allora tiello buono."

43. Many documents attest that, from the fourteenth century to the first half of the fifteenth century, the number of leaves beaten from a florin increased by 25% compared to the initial 100 leaves. One example is given by the payment made by Lorenzo Monaco for gold leaf used in the polyptych of the high altar of the Church of Sant'Egidio, where it is stated: "E a dì 31 d'ottobre 1420, fiorini 8 lire 1 per pezzi M [= mille] d'oro da Pietro di Francesco battiloro." That is 125, in comparison with the 100 leaves per florin that was the ratio suggested by Cennini.

44. "Et che e consoli le dette misure per loro ordinate, continuamente debbino espresso a loro o presso al notaio della dett'arte tenere marchiata del loro marchio, et le dette misure così marchiate dare a cercatori che anno a cercare delle cose divietate tra gli artefici della dett'arte, e per essi cercatori far cercare colla detta misura e investigare se le predette cose s'osservano; e trovati i colpevoli, punire e condempnare secondo la forma del presente ordinamento." (And that the consuls must keep the said [standard] measures ordained by them either with them, or with the notary of the said art, marked with their seal, and must give the said measures thus marked to the seekers who have to seek forbidden items among the artisans of the said art, and must make the seekers search with the said measure and investigate whether the aforesaid things are observed; and having found the guilty, punish and condemn according to the form of the present ordinance). Ciasca, *Gli statuti dell'Arte dei Medici e Speziali*, 371, and see above, note 40, for individuals responsible for controlling florins.

45. "Item, quod nullus de dicta arte possit, ancent, vel presummat commitere aliquam fraudem aucent, in arte predicta, in mittendo vel ponendo argentum pro auro, aurum di metà pro auro fini, et azzurum de Alemania pro ultramarino, nee similia, unde opus aliquod dapnum recipiat, sub pena soldorum quadraginta f.p., et quotiens, et at restituendum daptum quod reciperetur ex malatia supradicti, sen sequeretur exinde." (Also, that no one of the aforesaid art is able to commit or presume to commit any fraud, in the aforesaid art, in sending or placing silver for gold, half gold for pure gold, and azure from Germany [i.e., a pigment made by crushing azurite] for ultramarine azure [i.e., a pigment made by crushing lapis lazuli], nor the like, from which the work may receive some loss, under penalty of forty sous of little pennies of Florence, and as many times, and to restore the loss which was received from the malice of the aforesaid, or that would follow from there). Ciasca, *Gli statuti dell'Arte dei Medici e Speziali*, 82, col. 12.

46. In the Sienese statute titled "Breve dell'Arte dei Pittori Senesi," dated 1355, there is a requirement "Di non mettere uno oro per uno altro, o uno colore per altro": chap. 14, "Ancho ordiniamo, che nullo de' l arte de' dipintori ardisca over presuma di mettere ne' lavorii che facesse altro oro o ariento o colori che avesse promesso, sì come oro di metà, per oro fino, e stagno per argento, azzurro de la Magna per azurro oltremarino, ...; e chi contrafacesse per le predette cose sia punito et condannato per ogni volta in X libr." "Breve dell'Arte de' Pittori Senesi," (Not to put one gold for another, or one color for another / We also order that none of the art of painters dares or presumes to put in the works that he makes other gold or silver or colors than [those that] he had promised, such as half gold for pure gold, and tin for silver, azure from Germany [i.e., a pigment made by crushing azurite] for ultramarine azure [i.e., a pigment made by crushing lapis lazuli], ...; and whoever counterfeited the aforesaid things is to be punished by and condemned to, for each time, [a fine of] 10 pounds [i.e., 2,400 of Florence]. In *Documenti per la storia dell'arte senese*, ed. by G. Milanesi, 3 vols. (Siena, 1854), 1.7. See also A. Fehm Jr., "Notes on the Statutes of the Sienese Painters Guild," *Art Bulletin* 54 (1972): 198–200.

47. In "Odinamenta Hominus Artis Pictorum civitatis Perusi" chap. 3: "Item dicimus et ordinamus quod quiquicunque de dicta arte promittet dare alicui aurum finum in aliquo opere et dabit argentum superauratum, nomine pene. C. sold. den. solvere teneatur", and chap. 4: "Item dicimus et ordinamus quod quicunque promictet alicui dare argentum finum et dabit stangnum pro argento, nomine pene. XL. sold. den. solvere teneatur." (*The Ordainments of the Men of the Art of the Painters of the City of Perugia*. Ch. 3: Also, we say and order that whoever of the said art promises to give someone pure gold in a certain work, and will give gilded silver, he will be bound to pay a fine of 100 sous of pennies [of Florence]. Ch 4: Also, we say and order that whoever promises to give someone pure silver and will give tin for silver, he will be bound to pay a fine of 40 sous of pennies [of Florence]. In L. Manzoni, *Statuti e matricole dei pittori delle città di Florence, Perugia e Siena nei testi originali del secolo XIV* (Rome: Loescher, 1904), 159.

48. For example, see the constant cooperation between Neri di Bicci and Giuliano da Maiano, in N. di Bicci, *Le ricordanze (1453–1475)*, ed. by B. Santi (Pisa: Edizioni Marlin, 1976). For a more general understanding of the phenomenon, see A. Guidotti, "Indagini su botteghe di cartolai e miniatori a Florence nel XV secolo," in *La miniatura italiana tra Gotico e Rinascimento*, ed. by E. Sesti (Florence: Olschki, 1985), 473–507.

49. A. Guidotti, "Gli inventari del magistrato fiorentino dei pupilli come fonti lessicali," in *Convegno nazionale sui lessici tecnici delle arti e dei mestieri*, ed. by M. Fileti (Florence: Eurografica, 1979), 231–85.

50. One example is the apothecary Bonifacio di Donato di Bonifacio: included in his cadastral records dated May 31, 1433 are many credit and debt transactions, obviously made for commercial reasons, with the category of painters. Two other specialized tradesmen are Antonio di Dino d'Agnolo, in the community of Sant'Ambrogio, and Michele di Ramondo, in the community of San Michele Visdomini, who are recorded in book G of the registrations of the Physicians and Apothecaries: the first, on October 2, 1428, as "merciarius qui facit tabulas gessatas" (merchant who makes gessoed panels [i.e., prepares wooden panels for painting by applying a plaster preparation]); the second, on December 22, 1432, as "qui laborat de azzurro" (who works with blue). See Guidotti, "Battiloro e dipintori a Firenze," 239–40; Bellucci and Frosinini, "Working Together," 30.

51. Regarding the study of punches in the decoration of gold backgrounds, their artistic context, and attribution issues, see M. Frinta's historically important contribution "An Investigation of the Punched Decoration of Medieval Italian and Non-Italian Panel Paintings," *Art Bulletin* 47 (1965): 261–65; and the monumental catalogue of E. Skaug, *Punch* Marks from Giotto to Fra Angelico: Attribution, Chronology, and Workshop Relationships in Tuscan Panel Painting c. 1330–1430 (Oslo: IIC, Nordic Group, 1994); M. Frinta, "Deletions from the Oeuvre of Pietro Lorenzetti and Related Works by the Master of the Beata Umilta, Mino Parcis da Siena, and Jacopo di Mino del Pellicciaio," *Mitteilungen des Kunsthistorischen Institutes in Florenz* 20, no. 3 (1976): 271–300, and J. Dunkerton, "Tooling and Punching," in Bomford et al., *Art in the Making*, 24–27, interpret the repetition and application of punches within the artists' oeuvre as proof of reciprocal relations, through apprenticeship, collaboration, and hereditary passage of the punches during the artist's life. Skaug remains more cautious on attribution issues, admitting the possibility that the punches were transferred from one studio to another during the life of an artist. However, he remains committed to the identification of a punch as a unique specimen and, consequently, to its traceability and affinity with the output of a painter's studio. For other critical contributions, see J. Polzer, "Observations on Known Paintings and a New Altarpiece by Francesco Traini," *Pantheon* 29 (1971): 379–89; A. Tartuferi, "Note in margine a un trattato sulla decorazione punzonata dei dipinti trecenteschi," *Arte Cristiana* 83 (1995): 478–82.

52. Between 1415 and January 1416 many payments were made to Piero di Francesco and Bastiano di Giovanni, goldbeaters in the Piazza San Giovanni in Florence, in connection with the altarpiece by Mariotto di Nardo for the Spedale degli Uomini in Florence. The large sum paid was to be used not only as payment for the metal leaf but also perhaps for its application and tooling. U. Procacci, "Documenti e ricerche sopra Masaccio e la sua famiglia," *Rivista d'arte* 14–17 (1935): 91–111; Guidotti, "Battiloro e dipintori a Firenze"; Merzenich, "Dorature e policromie."

53. From the list of the goldbeaters registered in the Arte dei Medici e Speziali. From 1371 to 1378 there were four goldbeaters: Michele di Giovanni Palmieri (registered 1371), Antonio di Puccinello (registered 1373), Sandro di Alamanno (registered 1376, to be identified with his namesake who enrolled in 1372 as a goldbeater in the Arte di Por Santa Maria), Maffio di Giovanni Palmieri (registered 1378); added to these is Biagio di Niccolò, tinbeater (registered 1363). From 1386 to 1408 there were five: Giovanni di Jacopo (registered 1393), Iacopo di Puccino (registered 1393), Guasparre di Filippo (registered 1393), Biagio d'Andrea di Berto (registered 1399), Bastiano di Giovanni di Nardo (registered 1407–8); these five dates are reported by M. Haines, "A Reconstruction of the Lost Books of the Registrations in the Arte dei Medici e Speziali in Florence from 1353 to 1408," *Rivista d'arte* 41 (1989): 173–207. Niccolò di Biagio di Niccolò, son of Biagio Battistagno, registered in 1399. From 1423 to 1444 there were another four: Niccolò di Giovanni di Niccolò (registered 1423, of the community of Cristoforo), Antonio di Stefano di Francesco (registered 1440, of the community of San Lorenzo).

54. Their names are: Gabriello in Porta Rossa, mentioned in the year 1462 (Bicci, *Le ricordanze*, 185); Romolo di Andrea di Nofri mentioned in the years 1463–64 (ibid., 239); Antonio di Mariano, Sandro Botticelli's brother, mentioned together with his "companions" in 1467 (ibid., 293–94); Piero D'Antonio, registered with the confraternity of Saint Luke in 1424 (ibid., 213). Bruno di ser Benedetto da Staggia is also mentioned (ibid., 151–59, 278, 343), in the year 1469, for whom Neri di Bicci commits himself to paying a monthly salary, guaranteeing stable continuity of work ("Ricordo chome questo presente dì, a' prieghi e chontenprazione di Benedetto di Domenicho dipintore, el quale istà mecho a botegha, prometto a Bruno di ser Benedetto Stag[i]a battiloro, per.llo sopradetto Benedetto, paghare ogni mese l.3 di parte del suo salaro" [I put on record that this present day, because of the prayers and insistence of Benedetto (son) of Domenico, painter, who works in my workshop, I promise Bruno son of ser Benedetto Stagia, *battiloro* (literarily, goldbeater; defined as 'maker, seller, or beater of tin, tinsel, gold, silver or similar materials in the painters' statute of 1349, page 9, footnote 35), for the aforementioned Benedetto, to pay 3 pounds (of Florence) every month as part of his wage]); Domenico di Bartolomeo, mentioned from 1464 to 1474, registered with the Confraternity of Saint Luke in 1460 (ibid., 237); Domenico (no further name), mentioned in the year 1474.

55. The names and registration dates are taken from Manzoni, *Statuti e matricole dei pittori*, 123–31: Antonio di Mazzano, registered in 1350; Bernardo di Francesco, registered in 1350; Iacopo di Puccino, registered in 1393; Giovanni di Gherardo, registered in 1402; Andrea d'Alessio, registered in 1405; Maffio di Giovanni Palmieri, registered in 1405; Antonio Salesso, registered in 1408; Niccolò D'Antonio, registered in 1408; Giovanni di Jacopo, registered in 1410; Bastiano di Giovanni, registered in 1424; Matteo D'Antonio registered in 1424; Piero D'Antonio, registered in 1424; Piero di Francesco, registered in 1424; Antonio di Stefano, registered in 1435; Domenico di Bartolomeo, registered in 1460; and Giovanni D'Antonio di Domenico and Taddeo di Francesco, whose registration date I could not find. On Bastiano di Giovanni and Piero di Francesco, see Procacci, "Documenti e ricerche sopra Masaccio," 108–11; Merzenich, "Dorature *e policromie,*" 66–67. The name Piero di Francesco is often mentioned in important contracts, such as that drawn up for the altarpiece of Sant'Egidio made by Lorenzo Monaco and identified with the *Adoration of the Magi* of the Uffizi, dated 1420–21, to confirm the importance of his studio.

56. On the assumption that the activity of the goldbeaters is not solely related to reducing the golden florins to leaf, but also connected with their application and punching, see Bellucci and Frosinini, "Working Together," 56, n.3; C. B. Strehlke, "The Case for Studying Masolino's and Masaccio's Panel Paintings in the Laboratory," in Strehlke and Frosinini, *Panel Paintings of Masolino and Masaccio*, 13–27. Recently E. Skaug reaffirmed his opposing position, with a polemical attitude worthy of a better cause and little consideration of the substantial continuity of craft practices from the centuries of the late Middle Ages to modern times (E. Skaug, "Painters, Punchers, Gilders or Goldbeaters? A Critical Survey Report of Discussions in Recent Literature about Early Italian Painting," *Zeitschrift für Kunstgeschichte* 71 (2008): 571–82). A. De Marchi refers repeatedly to the painters' role in gold tooling (*Gentile da Fabriano. Un viaggio nella pittura italiana alle fine del gotico* (Milan: Federico Motta, 2006); "Geometria e naturalezza, modulo e ritmo: un'opera fondativa alle origini del concetto illusionistico del polittico gotico," in *Giotto. Il restauro del Polittico di Badia*, ed. by A. Tartuferi, (Florence: Mandragora, 2012), 31–51).

57. R. Bellucci and C. Frosinini, "La pianificazione dell'opera e il disegno preparatorio nel Polittico della Misericordia," in *Ripensando Piero della Francesca, il polittico della Misericordia di Sansepolcro. Storia, studi e indagini tecnico-scientifiche*, ed. by M. Betti, C. Frosinini, and P. Refice (Florence: Edifir, 2010), 189–202.

58. U. Procacci, "La creduta tavola di Monteoliveto dipinta da Spinello Aretino," *II Vasari* 2 (1928–29): 35–48.

59. Milanesi, *Documenti per la storia dell'arte senese*, 1.35, no. 6.

60. A. Tartuferi, "Note in margine a un trattato sulla decorazione punzonata," 480. On the specific *granatura* technique, see B. Eclercy, "*Granare*: zur historischen Terminologie des Goldgrund-Dekors im Traktat des Cennino Cennini," *Mitteilungen des Kunsthistorischen Institutes in Florenz* 51 (2007): 539–54.

61. G. Chelazzi Dini, ed., *Il gotico a Siena. Miniature, pitture, oreficerie, oggetti d'arte* (Florence: Centro Di, 1982), 328–31 (I thank Machtelt Bruggen Israëls for the suggestion).

62. A. Cecchi, *Simone Martini e l'Annunciazione degli Uffizi* (Milan: Silvana, 2001); A. De Marchi, "La parte di Simone e la parte di Lippo," *Nuovi Studi* 11 (2007): 8 n.10.

63. State Archives of Siena, Patrimonio Resti 2204, fol. 80r: "Maestro Sano di Pietro, dipintore, die avere addi per insino 26 d'aprile 1467 lire cento vinti per una tavola da dipignare già da altri innorata, pell'altare di Matheo da Campriano, posto drieto ala porta dala nostra chiesa." (Maestro Sano [son] of Pietro, painter, must have today until 26 April 1467 one hundred and twenty pounds [of Florence] for a panel to be painted, already gilded by others, for the altar of Matteo da Campriano, placed behind the door of our church). Cited in P. A. Riedl and M. Seidel, eds., *Die Kirchen von Siena: Oratorio della Carità - S. Domenico*, 4 vols. (Munich: Deutscher Kunstverlag, 1985–2006), vol. 2.2, 738, no. 18 (I thank Machtelt Bruggen Israëls for the information).

64. M. B. Israëls, "Ludovico di Luca pittore ornatista del primo Rinascimento senese," in *Sano di Pietro. Qualità, devozione e pratica nella pittura senese del Quattrocento*, ed. by G. Fattorini (Milan: Silvana, 2012), 95–127.

65. C. Filippini, "Il pittore battiloro Antonio di Stefano, compagno di bottega dell'Indaco," in *La Toscana al tempo di Lorenzo il Magnifico. Politica, economia cultura, arte* (Pisa: Pacini, 1992), 305–11. Stefano and Giovanni were registered with the confraternity of St. Luke; their father should have been registered in the Arte dei Medici e Speziali if his son enrolled in 1520 without paying the enrollment fee, in accordance with practices at the time. Their father's enrollment was not found, and is probably in the lost books, but the grandfather's enrollment, in 1439, does appear: see above, n.52.

66. However, Taddeo Gaddi is recorded in another commission as a painter and a gilder: in the decoration of the crypt of San Miniato al Monte in Florence, he is paid for gilding the capitals of some columns and for executing a painting for the choir ("dipingne e mettere a oro i capitelli delle colonne"). Bomford et al., *Art in the Making*, 26.

67. Merzenich, "Dorature *e policromie,"* 60.

68. D. Colnaghi et al., *A Dictionary of Florentine Painters from the 13th to the 17th Centuries* (London: John Lane, 1938), 144.

69. Regarding the inner organization of the workshops of goldbeaters who supplied metal leaf to painters, a study of goldbeaters active in manufacturing for the textile industry may be of help: here there was a precocious sharing of work among individuals who specialized in only one phase of the long process of production. These are indicated in the manufacturing records with very specific names: the stretcher (*stenditore*), who carried out the first phase of beating the bars; the leaf master (*maestro di foglia*), who reduced the previously beaten metal to thin leaves; the boys (*garzoni*), who helped in the first two phases; the scissormen (*forbiciai*), who sharpened scissors and cut the leaves into thin strips; and the spinners (*filatrici*). On this topic, see B. Dini, "Una manifattura di battiloro nel Quattrocento," in *Tecnica e società nell'Italia dei secoli XII–XVI* (Pistoia: Centro Italiano di Studi di Storia e d'Arte, 1987), 83–111, which takes into account Tommaso Luigi Ridolfi's craftsmanship; also Dorini, *Statuti dell'Arte di Por Santa Maria*, 791.

70. On the topic of workshop inventories, see F. Melis, "La scrittura contabile alla fonte della storia economica," (1950), now in *L'azienda nel Medioevo*, ed. by M. Spallanzani, 3–44 (Florence: LeMonnier, 1991); C. Bartoletti, "Le botteghe a Firenze: arredi," in *Lorenzo Ghiberti. Materia e ragionamenti* (Florence: CentroDi, 1978), 275–76; B. Conti, "Botteghe di artigiani e artisti negli inventari dei Pupilli avanti il principato, 1400–1479: arredi e arnesi" (MA diss., University of Florence, 1981–82); Guidotti, "Pubblico e privato"; G. Cantini Guidotti, *Orafi in Toscana tra XV e XVIII secolo. Storie di uomini, di cose e di parole* (Florence: Presso l'Accademia, 1994); Bellucci and Frosinini, "Working Together," 56–57.

71. Milanesi, "Breve dell'Arte de' Pittori Senesi," "Aggiunta al Breve dell'Arte de' Pittori Senesi," 1.52–56, chap. 64; Bomford et al., *Art in the Making*, 26.

72. Bicci, *Le ricordanze*, 224, 362, 59.

73. Colnaghi et al., *Dictionary of Florentine Painters*, 39.

74. M. Baxandall, *Pittura ed esperienze sociali nell'Italia del Quattrocento* (Turin: Einaudi, 1978), 19–23. See also A. De Marchi, "Aureole e aura: la materia che cattura la luce e ne è trasfigurata, sperimenti nella pittura tardo-medioevale," in *Trasparenze ed epifanie. Quando la luce diventa letteratura, arte, storia, scienza*, ed. by M. Graziani (Florence: Firenze University Press, 2016), 153–73.

75. R. Bellucci et al., "La tecnica pittorica del Botticelli: un'analisi comparata," in *L'incoronazione della Vergine del Botticelli*, ed. by A. Paolucci (Florence: Edifir, 1990), 85–109.

Bibliography

Alexander, S. M. "Medieval Recipes Describing the Use of Metals in Manuscripts." *Marsyas* 12 (1967): 34–51.

Assunto, R. *Die Theorie des Schönen im Mittelalter.* Cologne: DuMont Schauberg, 1963.

Baeumker, C. Witelo. *Ein Philosoph und Naturforscher des XIII. Jahrhunderts.* Münster: Aschendorffsche Buchhandlung, 1908.

Baroni, S. "Il Libro dell'arte di Cennino Cennini." *In I trattati di tecniche artistiche medievali con accenni sull'antichità e l'età moderna. Storia delle tecniche artistiche*, by S. B. Tosatti, S. Baroni, M. Bellaria, D. Bertani, M. Pugliese, C. Mori, and I. Mangili, 101–14. Milan: CUSL, 2002.

Baroni, S. "I ricettari medievali per la preparazione dei colori e la loro trasmissione." In *Il colore nel Medioevo. Arte, simbolo, tecnica*, edited by F. Dell'Acqua and R. Silva, 117–44. Lucca: Istituto storico lucchese, 1996.

Baroni, S., and S. B. Tosatti. "Sul Libro dell'arte di Cennino Cennini." *Acme* 51, no. 1 (1998): 51–72.

Bartoletti, C. "Le botteghe a Firenze: arredi." In *Lorenzo Ghiberti. Materia e ragionamenti*, 275–76. Florence: CentroDi, 1978.

Baxandall, M. *Pittura ed esperienze sociali nell'Italia del Quattrocento.* Turin: Einaudi, 1978.

Bellucci, R. "La Croce di Sarzana tra materia e immagine." In *Pinxit Guillielmus. Il restauro della Croce di Sarzana*, edited by M. Ciatti, 41–54. Florence: Edifir, 2001.

Bellucci, R., and C. Frosinini. "La pianificazione dell'opera e il disegno preparatorio nel Polittico della Misericordia." In *Ripensando Piero della Francesca, il polittico della Misericordia di Sansepolcro. Storia, studi e indagini tecnico-scientifiche*, edited by M. Betti, C. Frosinini, and P. Refice, 189–202. Florence: Edifir, 2010.

Bellucci, R., and C. Frosinini. "Working Together: Technique and Innovation in Masolino's and Masaccio's Panel Paintings." In *The Panel Paintings of Masolino and Masaccio: The Role of Technique*, edited by C. B. Strehlke and C. Frosinini, 29–67. Milan: 5 Continents, 2002.

Bellucci, R. et al., "La tecnica pittorica del Botticelli: un'analisi comparata." In *L'incoronazione della Vergine del Botticelli*, edited by A. Paolucci, 85–109. Florence: Edifir, 1990.

Bernacchioni, A. "Le botteghe di pittura: luoghi, strutture, attività." In *Maestri e botteghe. Pittura a Florence alla fine del Quattrocento*, by M. Gregori, A. Paolucci, and C. A. Luchinat, 23–33. Milan: Silvana, 1992.

Bernocchi, M. *Le monete della Repubblica Fiorentina, III. Documentazione.* Florence: Olschki, 1976.

Bicci, N. di. *Le ricordanze (1453–1475)*, edited by B. Santi. Pisa: Edizioni Marlin, 1976.

Bomford, D., J. Dunkerton, D. Gordon, and A. Roy. *Art in the Making: Italian Painting before 1400.* London: National Gallery, 1989. Exhibition catalog.

Bordini, S. *Materia e immagine. Fonti sulle techniche della pittura. Rome: Leonardo-DeLuca*, 1991.

Bordone, R. *Uno stato d'animo. Memoria del tempo e comportamenti urbani nel mondo comunale italiano.* Florence: Firenze University Press, 2002.

Burns, T. "Cennino Cennini's Il libro dell'arte: A Historiographical Review." *Studies in Conservation* 56 (2011): 1–13.

Cantini Guidotti, G. *Orafi in Toscana tra XV e XVIII secolo. Storie di uomini, di cose e di parole.* Florence: Presso l'Accademia, 1994.

Capasso, R., and P. Piccari, eds. *Il tempo nel Medioevo. Rappresentazioni storiche e concezioni filosofiche.* Rome: Società italiana di demodossalogia, 2000.

Cecchi, A. *Simone Martini e l'Annunciazione degli Uffizi.* Milan: Silvana, 2001.

Cennini, C. *The Craftsman's Handbook: The Italian "Il Libro dell'Arte."* Translated by D. V. Thompson, Jr. New York: Dover, 1960.

Cennini, C. *Il libro dell'arte*, edited by F. Frezzato. Vicenza: Pozza, 2003

Chelazzi Dini, G., ed. *Il gotico a Siena. Miniature, pitture, oreficerie, oggetti d'arte.* Florence: Centro Di, 1982. Exhibition catalog.

Ciasca, R. *Gli statuti dell'Arte dei Medici e Speziali.* Florence: Galletti e Cocci, 1922.

Citolini, A. *Tipocosmia.* Venice, 1561

Colnaghi, D. *A Dictionary of Florentine Painters from the 13th to the 17th Centuries*, edited by S. Brinton and P. G. Konody. London: John Lane, 1938.

Conti, B. "Botteghe di artigiani e artisti negli inventari dei Pupilli avanti il principato, 1400–1479: arredi e arnesi." MA diss., University of Florence, 1981–82.
De Marchi, A. "Aureole e aura: la materia che cattura la luce e ne è trasfigurata, sperimenti nella pittura tardo-medioevale." In *Trasparenze ed epifanie. Quando la luce diventa letteratura, arte, storia, scienza*, edited by M. Graziani, 153–73. Florence: Firenze University Press, 2016.
De Marchi, A. *Gentile da Fabriano. Un viaggio nella pittura italiana alle fine del gotico.* Milan: Federico Motta, 2006.
De Marci, A. "Geometria e naturalezza, modulo e ritmo: un'opera fondativa alle origini del concetto illusionistico del polittico gotico." In *Giotto. Il restauro del Polittico di Badia*, edited by A. Tartuferi, 31–51. Florence: Mandragora, 2012.
De Marchi, A. "Oro come luce, luce come oro: l'operazione delle lamine metalliche da Simone Martini a Pisanello, fra mimesi e anagogia." In *Medioevo natura e figura*, edited by A. C. Quintavalle, 701–16. Milan: Skira 2015.
De Marchi, A. "La parte di Simone e la parte di Lippo." *Nuovi Studi* 11 (2007): 5–24.
Dini, B. "Una manifattura di battiloro nel Quattrocento." In *Tecnica e società nell'Italia dei secoli XII–XVI*, 83–111. Pistoia: Centro Italiano di Studi di Storia e d'Arte, 1987.
Dioscorides. *De materia medica*, edited by T. Osbaldeson and R. P. A. Wood. Johannesburg: IBIDIS, 2000.
Dodwell, C. R. "Gold Metallurgy in the Twelfth Century." *Gold Bulletin* 4, no. 3 (1971): 51–55.
Dorini, U. *Statuti dell'Arte di Por Santa Maria del tempo della Repubblica.* Florence: Olschki, 1934.
Duby, G. *Saint Bernard. L'art cistercien.* Paris: Flammarion, 1979.
Duby, G. *San Bernardo e l'arte cistercense.* Turin: Einaudi, 1982.
Dunkerton, J. "Tooling and Punching." In *Art in the Making: Italian Painting before 1400*, by D. Bomford, J. Dunkerton, D. Gordon, and A. Roy, 24–27. London: National Gallery, 1989.
Eclercy, B. "Granare: zur historischen Terminologie des Goldgrund-Dekors im Traktat des Cennino Cennini." *Mitteilungen des Kunsthistorischen Institutes in Florenz* 51 (2007): 539–54.
Eco, U. "Sviluppo dell'estetica medioevale." In *Momenti e problemi di storia dell'estetica, I. Dall'antichità classica al barocco*, 115–229. Milan: Marzorati, 1959.
Eyb-Green, S., J. H. Townsend, M. Clarke, J. Nadolny, and S. Kroustallis, eds. *The Artist's Process: Technology and Interpretation.* London: Archetype, 2012.
Fehm, A. Jr. "Notes on the Statutes of the Sienese Painters Guild." *Art Bulletin* 54 (1972): 198–200.
Filippini, C. "Il pittore battiloro Antonio di Stefano, compagno di bottega dell'Indaco." In *La Toscana al tempo di Lorenzo il Magnifico. Politica, economia cultura, arte*, 305–11. Pisa: Pacini, 1992.
Frinta, M. "Deletions from the Oeuvre of Pietro Lorenzetti and Related Works by the Master of the Beata Umilta, Mino Parcis da Siena, and Jacopo di Mino del Pellicciaio." *Mitteilungen des Kunsthistorischen Institutes in Florenz* 20, no. 3 (1976): 271–300.
Frinta, M. "An Investigation of the Punched Decoration of Medieval Italian and Non-Italian Panel Paintings." *Art Bulletin* 47 (1965): 261–65.
Garzoni, T. *Piazza universale di tutte le professioni del mondo nobili et ignobili.* Venice, 1587; 1st ed. 1585.
Gheroldi, V. "Ricette, ricettari." In *Ricette e ricettari. Tre fonti per la storia delle tecniche delle arti alla Biblioteca Queriniana di Brescia (sec. XVI–XVII)*, 13–88. Brescia: Musei Civici, 1995.
Grabar, A. *Les origines de l'esthétique médiévale.* Paris: Macula, 1992.
Guidotti, A. "Battiloro e dipintori a Firenze fra Tre e Quattrocento: Bastiano di Giovanni e la sua clientela (dal Catasto del 1427)." In *Scritti di Storia dell'Arte in onore di Roberto Salvini*, 239–49. Florence: Sansoni, 1984.
Guidotti, A. "Indagini su botteghe di cartolai e miniatori a Florence nel XV secolo." In *La miniatura italiana tra Gotico e Rinascimento*, edited by E. Sesti, 473–507. Florence: Olschki, 1985.
Guidotti, A. "Gli inventari del magistrato fiorentino dei pupilli come fonti lessicali." In *Convegno nazionale sui lessici tecnici delle arti e dei mestieri*, edited by M. Fileti, 231–85. Florence: Eurografica, 1979.
Guidotti, A. "Il mestiere del 'dipintore' nell'Italia due-trecentesca." In *La pittura in Italia. Il Duecento e il Trecento*, 529–40. Milan: Electa, 1986.
Guidotti, A. "Pubblico e privato, committenza e clientela: botteghe e produzione artistica a Florence tra XV e XVI secolo." *Ricerche storiche* 16 (1986): 535–50.
Guidotti, A., and M. De Marco. "Examination and Elaboration of Documentation Concerning Florentine Studios and Workplaces." *Bollettino d'informazioni del Centro di elaborazione automatica di dati*

6 (1985): 169–213.
Haines, M. "A Reconstruction of the Lost Books of the Registrations in the Arte dei Medici e Speziali in Florence from 1353 to 1408." *Rivista d'arte* 41 (1989): 173–207.
Hauptmann, A., S. Klein, R. Zettler, U. Baumer, and P. Dietemann. "On the Making and Provenancing of Pigments from the Early Dynastic Royal Tombs of Ur, Mesopotamia." *Metalla* 22, no. 1 (2016): 41–74.
Hedfors, H. Compositiones ad Tingenda Musiva. Uppsala, 1932.
Hoeniger, C. S. "Cloth of Gold and Silver: Simone Martini's Techniques for Representing Luxury Textiles." *Gesta* 30 (1991): 154–62.
Indrio, L. "Firenze nel '400: divisione e organizzazione del lavoro nelle botteghe." *Ricerche di storia dell'arte* 38 (1989): 61–70
Israëls, M. B. "Ludovico di Luca pittore ornatista del primo Rinascimento senese." In *Sano di Pietro. Qualità, devozione e pratica nella pittura senese del Quattrocento*, edited by G. Fattorini, 95–127. Milan: Silvana, 2012.
Jacobsen, W. *Die Maler von Florenz*. Munich: Deutscher Kunstverlag, 2001.
James, T. G. H. "Gold Technology in Ancient Egypt." *Gold Bulletin* 5, no. 2 (1972): 38–42.
La Sorsa, S. *Gli statuti degli orefici e sellai Fiorentini al principio del secolo XIV*. Florence: Galileiana, 1901.
Le Goff, J. *Tempo della chiesa e tempo del mercante*. Turin: Einaudi, 2000.
Löhr, W.-D., and S. Weppelmann, eds. *Fantasie und Handwerk. Cennino Cennini und die Tradition der toskanischen Malerei von Giotto bis Lorenzo Monaco*. Berlin: SMB, Gemäldegalerie Staatliche Museen zu Berlin, 2008.
Manzoni, L. *Statuti e matricole dei pittori delle città di Florence, Perugia e Siena nei testi originali del secolo XIV*. Rome: Loescher, 1904.
Melis, F. "La scrittura contabile alla fonte della storia economica." In *L'azienda nel Medioevo*, edited by M. Spallanzani, 3–44. Florence: LeMonnier, 1991
Merzenich, C. "Dorature e policromie delle parti architettoniche nelle tavole d'altare toscane nel Tre-Quattrocento: Piero di Francesco battiloro, l'oro fine, l'oro di metà, l'argento e lo stagno dorato." *Kermes* 26 (1996): 51–71.
Milanesi, G. *Documenti per la storia dell'arte senese*. 3 vols. (Siena, 1854).
Monciatti, A. Review of "L'officina di Giotto. Il restauro della Croce di Ognissanti, by M. Ciatti." *Arte Medievale*, 4th ser., 2 (2012): 304–9.
Nadolny, J. "All That's Burnished Isn't Bole: Reflections on Medieval Water Gilding – Part 1: Early Medieval to 1300." In *Medieval Painting in Northern Europe: Techniques, Analysis, Art History*, edited by J. Nadolny, with K. Kollandsrud, M. L. Sauerberg, and T. Frøysaker, 148–62. London: Archeotype, 2006.
Nadolny, J. "The Techniques and Use of Gilded Relief Decoration by Northern European Painters, c. 1200–1500." PhD diss., Courtauld Institute of Art, University of London, 2001
Nicholson, E. D. "The Ancient Craft of Gold Beating." *Gold Bulletin* 12, no. 4 (1974): 161–66.
Pasqualetti, C. *Il Libellus ad faciendum colores dell'archivio di stato dell'Aquila. Origine, contesto e restituzione del "De arte illuminandi."* Florence: SISMEL edizioni del Galluzzo, 2011.
Passeri, I. "Gold Coins and Gold Leaf in Early Italian Paintings." In *The Matter of Art: Materials, Practices, Cultural Logistics*, c. 1250–1650, edited by Christy Anderson, Anne Dunlop, and Pamela Smith, 97–115. Manchester: Manchester University Press, 2015.
Pedone, S. "La passione aurea: il colore dell'oro a Bisanzio." In *In corso d'opera. Ricerche dei dottorandi in storia dell'arte della Sapienza*, 1, edited by Michele Nicolaci, Matteo Piccioni, and Lorenzo Riccardi, 15–22. Rome: Campisano, 2015.
Pliny the Elder. *Natural History*. Translated and edited by J. Bostock and H. T. Riley. London: Henry G. Bohn, 1855.
Polzer, J. "Observations on Known Paintings and a New Altarpiece by Francesco Traini." *Pantheon* 29 (1971): 379–89.
Procacci, U. "La creduta tavola di Monteoliveto dipinta da Spinello Aretino." *II Vasari* 2 (1928–29): 35–48.
Procacci, U. "Documenti e ricerche sopra Masaccio e la sua famiglia." *Rivista d'arte* 14–17 (1935): 91–111.
Procacci, U. *Studio sul Catasto Fiorentino*. Florence: Olschki, 1996.

Riedl, P. A., and M. Seidel, eds. *Die Kirchen von Siena: Oratorio della Carità – S. Domenico.* 4 vols. Munich: Deutscher Kunstverlag, 1985–2006.
Skaug, E. "More Cenniniana: Technical Notes on the Origin and Purpose of Il libro dell'arte." *Arte Cristiana* 98, no. 857 (2010): 81–88.
Skaug, E. "Painters, Punchers, Gilders or Goldbeaters? A Critical Survey Report of Discussions in Recent Literature about Early Italian Painting." *Zeitschrift für Kunstgeschichte* 71 (2008): 571–82.
Skaug, E. *Punch Marks from Giotto to Fra Angelico: Attribution, Chronology, and Workshop Relationships in Tuscan Panel Painting c. 1330–1430.* Oslo: IIC, Nordic Group, 1994
Spufford, P. *Money and Its Use in Medieval Europe.* Cambridge: Cambridge University Press, 1988.
Strehlke, C. B. "The Case for Studying Masolino's and Masaccio's Panel Paintings in the Laboratory." In *The Panel Paintings of Masolino and Masaccio: The Role of Technique*, edited by C. B. Strehlke and C. Frosinini, 13–27. Milan: 5 Continents, 2002
Tartuferi, A. "Note in margine a un trattato sulla decorazione punzonata dei dipinti trecenteschi." *Arte Cristiana* 83 (1995): 478–82.
Theophilus. *On Divers Arts: The Foremost Medieval Treatise on Painting, Glassmaking and Metalwork.* Edited and translated by J. G. Hawthorne and C. Stanley Smith. Chicago: University of Chicago Press, 1963.
Thiebaud, D., ed. *Giotto e compagni.* Milan: Officina Libraria, 2013. Exhibition catalog.
Thomas, A. *The Painter's Practice in Renaissance Tuscany.* Cambridge: Cambridge University Press, 1995.
Tosatti, S. B. *Trattati medievali di tecniche artistiche.* Milan: Jaca Book, 2007.
Vasari, G. *Le vite de' più eccellenti pittori, scultori e architetti.* Edited by P. Barocchi and R. Bettarini, 11 vols. Florence: Sansoni and S.P.E.S., 1966-1987.
Zorzi, A. "Le fonti normative a Florence nel tardo Medioevo: un bilancio delle edizioni e degli studi." In *Statuti della Repubblica Fiorentina*, edited by R. Caggese, new ed. by G. Pinto, F. Salvestrini, and A. Zorzi, 1.liii–ci. 2 vols. Florence: Olschki, 1999.

The Temple of the Golden Pavilion

Yukio Lippit

No Kyoto landmark is more popular than Kinkakuji, "Temple of the Golden Pavilion" (fig. 1), nestled at the base of the Kitayama Mountains in the northern part of Japan's ancient capital. Built by medieval Japan's most powerful shogun, Ashikaga Yoshimitsu (1358–1408), in 1397, Kinkakuji was originally one of the featured structures of his retirement palace, the Kitayama Villa. The three-story building faces an expansive lake within a beautifully designed garden setting, offering a striking silhouette against its forested, mountainous backdrop. More than anything, what has fascinated its onlookers throughout the centuries and still brings throngs of visitors to the site every year is the gold foil covering all of the walls and timber components of its upper two floors. Thus gilded, Kinkakuji glows brilliantly under the sun and softly under the moon, posing a singular and surreal spectacle within the surrounding landscape. In an architectural tradition associated with a lack of ornamentation and subdued coloration, it represents a striking anomaly indeed.

Fig. 1. Kinkakuji (Temple of the Golden Pavilion), 1397 (original structure), reconstructed 1950–55. Kyoto, Rokuonji Temple

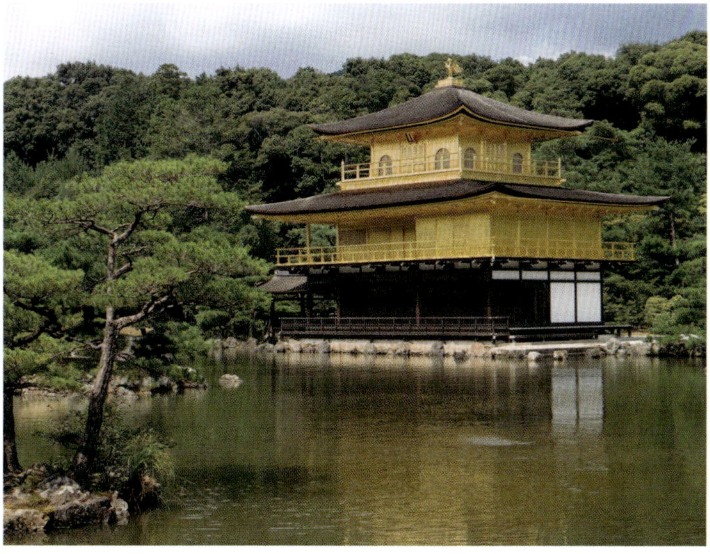

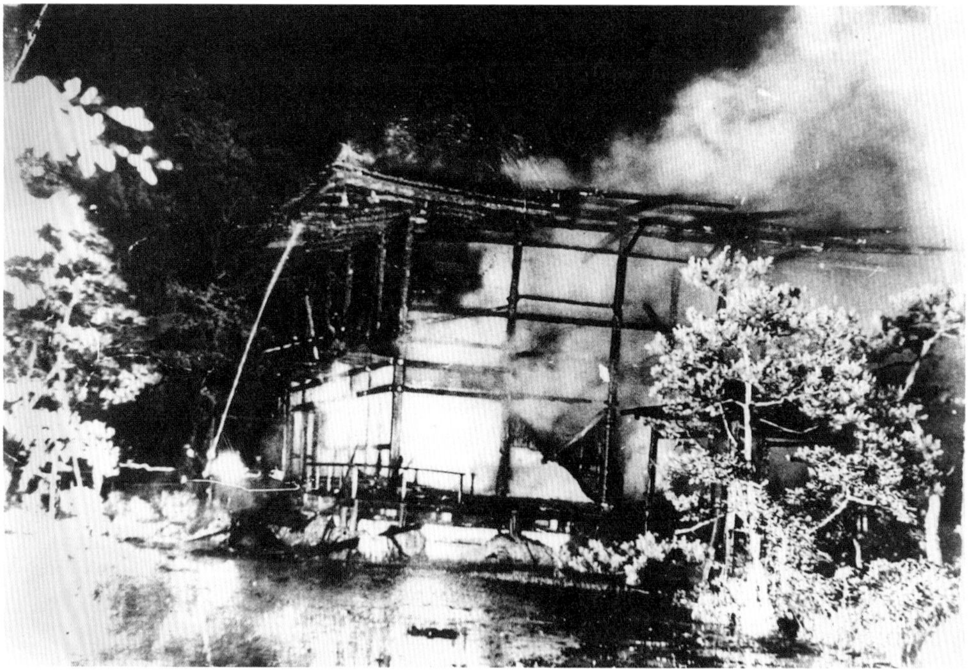

Fig. 2. Kinkakuji burning

Kinkakuji is also notable for falling victim to the most infamous case of arson in Japan's modern history. In the early morning of July 2, 1950, a young, mentally disturbed priest by the name of Hayashi Yōken set fire to the temple before attempting suicide (fig. 2). The resulting conflagration left it in ruins, with only the charred remains of its wooden skeleton left standing (fig. 3). The incident caused an immediate sensation. Among other things, it inspired Yukio Mishima's novel *The Temple of the Golden Pavilion* (*Kinkakuji*, 1956), as well as Ichikawa Kon's film *Conflagration* (*Enjō*, 1958), based upon Mishima's novel. The trauma of Kinkakuji's burning would last into the next decade, reappearing in Mizukami Tsutomu's fictional account of the incident, *The Pavilion of the Evening Mist at Gobanchō* (*Gobanchō yūgirirō*, 1963), also followed by a movie version.[1]

Soon after Kinkakuji was reduced to ashes, a national campaign commenced to rebuild the landmark. Previously, from 1904 to 1906, the architects Takeda Goichi (1872–1938) and Matsumuro Shigemitsu (1873–1937) had overseen a thorough conservation of the structure, and their report served as a basis for Kinkakuji's reconstruction. From 1952 onward, the architectural historian Murata Jirō (1895–1985) led a team of government officials and master

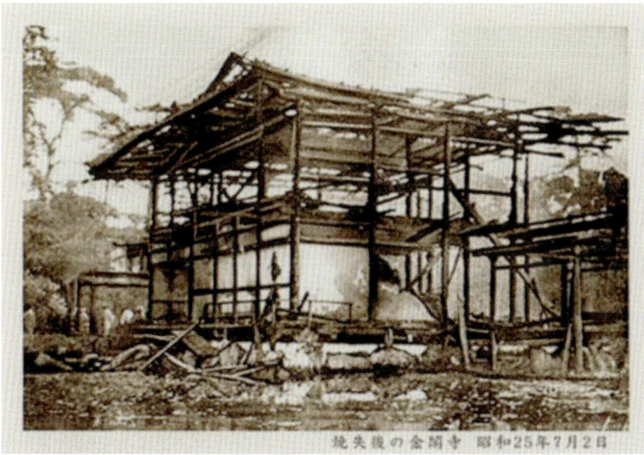

Fig. 3. Kinkakuji in ruins

carpenters to restore the temple to its former glory.[2] After several years, much like the phoenix-shaped finial that is one of its most famous attributes, a new Kinkakuji rose from the ashes and was consecrated on October 10, 1955. It is this rebuilt version that is visited by throngs of tourists today.

Ironically, the reconstruction of Kinkakuji has served as an impediment to its scholarly study. Although designated as a National Treasure in 1929 the temple was never redesignated as a cultural property after its reconstruction; nor has it ever been acknowledged as a structure worthy of serious historical investigation by specialists. And while Murata's reconstruction was based upon the detailed renderings of the earlier conservation report, a number of commentators have questioned important aspects of the rebuilding, including the degree to which gold foil was sheathed over the surfaces of the building's second story.[3] In the absence of the original physical structure, Kinkakuji has proven to be an awkward subject for scholarly study and interpretation. This relative scarcity of commentary extends to perhaps the most obvious question surrounding the building: why its upper floors were encased in gold foil to begin with.

Given the extreme rarity of such gilding in Japanese architecture, Kinkakuji's golden exterior constitutes the primary impetus for the present essay. Although its flamboyant brilliance might simply be attributed to the shogun Yoshimitsu's taste for extravagance, the temple's setting, structure, and usage suggest a more complex horizon of interpretation. In this regard, it is crucial that the Golden Pavilion be resituated within the context of the statecraft carried out at the Kitayama Villa and the ever-evolving geopolitical landscape of Japan and East Asia in the decades before and after 1400. Doing so makes clear that Kinkakuji's profile is closely tied to the complex and multifaceted nature of Yoshimitsu's kingship.

Lives and Afterlives

The origins of the Kitayama Villa can be traced back to the grand estate of the Saionji family, a branch of the aristocratic Fujiwara clan that held a powerful position in thirteenth-century politics through providing the official liaison between the Kyoto nobility and the warrior shoguns based in the eastern city of Kamakura. The establishment of the Saionji estate at the base of Mount Kinugasa north of Kyoto followed the siting practices of the aristocracy during the Heian period (794–1185), when it became common for regents and retired emperors to situate their villas outside the confines of the traditional grid plan of Heian (Kyoto). As Matthew Stavros has discussed, they did so in order to take advantage of the unbuilt natural landscape, but also to avoid the highly regulated urbanism of the capital city. This was also the case for the grand temple complexes of the retired emperors of the eleventh and twelfth centuries.[4]

The Saionji estate was consecrated under Fujiwara Kintsune (1171–1244) in 1222, and its praises were sung by numerous visitors during the following decades, including the poet Fujiwara no Teika (1162–1241), who used an abundance of superlatives in his journal *Record of the Clear Moon* (*Meigetsuki*). The most extensive description of the Saionji temple complex is found in *The Clear Mirror* (*Masukagami*), a fourteenth-century historical chronicle that details the structures and landscaped gardens of the estate.[5] Numerous emperors were welcomed as guests well into the fourteenth century. With the fall of the Kamakura shogunate in 1333, however, the Saionji family's fortunes declined, and the estate became more and more dilapidated, as noted in *The Clear Mirror*.

By the time that the Ashikaga shoguns based themselves in Kyoto from the mid-fourteenth century onward, the Saionji estate was largely in ruins, but it was situated in an area with considerable locational pedigree.[6] While early Ashikaga palaces were located within Kyoto proper, it was natural for Yoshimitsu to seek to situate his retirement villa beyond the borders of the capital. Accordingly, he purchased the Saionji estate from Saionji Kanenaga (1377–1431). The timing of the villa's construction was not accidental, and came at the culmination of a heady period in Yoshimitsu's rule. In the tenth month of 1392, he succeeded in uniting the imperial lineage, which had been split for over five decades into rival lineages referred to as the Northern and Southern Courts. Several months earlier, he had constructed the monastery Shōkokuji, which served as the administrative head of the entire Gozan or "Five Mountains" system of officially sponsored Zen monasteries in Kyoto, and which was where the Registrar of Monks (Sōrokushi) was located. In 1394 Yoshimitsu retired from his shogunal seat and was appointed Grand Minister of State (Dajō daijin); the following year he took Buddhist vows. This brings us to 1397, the year he purchased the Saionji estate; the ridgepole ceremony consecrating the Golden Pavilion took place in the fourth month of that year. Despite Yoshimitsu's nominal retirement, his emeritus status gave him more freedom to govern, and he held the de facto reins of power until his death in 1408. Indeed, during his final decade he was more active as a sovereign than ever, and the Kitayama Villa served as the site of his energetic statecraft.

The primary structures on the premises were three residences in the *shinden* style common for the nobility. The primary residence was inhabited by Yoshimitsu, with secondary residences for his wife, Hino Yasuko, and her mother. *Shinden* palaces were designed specifically for conducting state rituals under the Ritsuryō Codes, and are a clear reflection of the status of the Kitayama Villa as the center of shogunal politics. Numerous other buildings were spread across the estate, including a Hall of Nobility (Kuge no ma), Fire Ritual Hall (Gomadō), Ablution Hall (Hōsu-in), Fountain Hall (Izumidono), Snow-Viewing Lodge (Kansetsu-tei), and Penitentiary Hall (Zanpōdō). At the time, Kinkakuji—often understood as a later appellation originating in the Edo period (1615–1868)—was referred to as the Reliquary Hall (Shariden). It was joined to a remarkable two-story reception hall (*kaisho*) named Pavilion of the Mirror of Heaven (Tenkyōkaku) by a two-story covered bridge, a most unusual feature whose traversal would be likened by later visitors to "walking on air" or "a long rainbow across the sky."[7]

The siting of Kinkakuji was based upon a Heian-period building type known as a "fishing pavilion" (*tsuridono*)—a lakeside structure that was a part of *shinden* complexes and used among other things for boating outings and other amusements—found on the Saionji estate. As with the earlier structure, Kinkakuji served among other things as an extension of the main space for entertaining visitors at Yoshimitsu's palace estate. In the case of the Kitayama Villa, the pond by the structure was reduced in size, and the Golden Pavilion was situated on newly filled-in land in such a way that it appeared to be standing in the water itself.[8] However, while its position by the water followed aristocratic precedent, in terms of architectural style only the first floor was construed in the *shinden* mode. Its multistory profile followed the precedent of Chinese Chan monastic architecture, domesticated in Japan during the previous century. In the case of Kinkakuji, the most immediate example was the Saihōji temple in Kyoto, reconstructed from 1339 onward by Musō Soseki (1275–1351), a religious master to the early Ashikaga shoguns. Yoshimitsu is known to have admired Saihōji, and he visited its precincts in 1382 to practice seated

Zen meditation.[9] Kinkakuji emulated the Emerald Hall (Ruriden) at Saihōji, a three-story structure that Musō named after a famous Zen *kōan*.[10]

After the construction of the Golden Pavilion in 1397, the surrounding complex continued to be elaborated, most notably with the assembly of the monumental seven-story octagonal pagoda in 1404, a structure that had formerly been located on the premises of Shōkokuji monastery. Kitayama Villa became the site where esoteric rituals of state were conducted, foreign diplomats from China and Korea received, and lavish entertainments organized.[11] In 1408, Yoshimitsu invited Emperor Go-Komatsu for an extravagant imperial visitation at the Kitayama Villa, the first in which a sitting emperor was hosted by a warrior leader. The twenty-day affair included boat trips, *bugaku* court dance and popular *sarugaku* theater, linked-verse and *waka* poetry gatherings, and performances by female court dancers (*shirabyōshi*). There was also a remarkable display of Chinese luxury objects (*karamono*), assembled by Yoshimitsu in the Reception Hall and Golden Pavilion.[12] The emperor rowed a boat onto the pond from Kinkakuji, and the entertainments culminated in a poetry reading held on the second floor of the Golden Pavilion. Poems of the time likened the structure to a "Tower of the Immortals" (*senkaku*).[13]

Yoshimitsu's death in 1408, however, sent the prospects of the Kitayama Villa into a downward spiral. His son and successor, Ashikaga Yoshimochi, lived briefly in the palace but soon began construction of his own residence at Sanjō-bōmondono. Buildings from the estate were raided for their timber components, or given to other monastic campuses in Kyoto.[14] In 1420 the villa was renamed Rokuonji, and now served solely as a mortuary temple for Yoshimitsu, consisting of Kinkakuji, the Fire Ritual Hall (Gomadō), and the Ablution Hall (Hōsu-in). After the Zen monk Zuikei Shūhō visited the site in 1448, he noted in his diary many of the changes that had taken place in the decades since Yoshimitsu's passing. These included the donation of a number of buildings to other temples in Kyoto, such as the Penintentiary Hall (Zenpōdō) to Tōjiji, the Hall of Nobility (Kuge no ma) to serve as the abbot's quarters (Hōjō) at Kenninji, and similarly the Reception Hall to serve as the abbot's quarters of Nanzenji.[15] During the Onin War (1467–77) that devastated over half of Kyoto, the grounds of Rokuonji were used as an encampment for the Western Army, and its remaining buildings were damaged, with the exception of Kinkakuji. The courtier Sanjōnishi Sanetaka reports in his diary that the Fire Ritual Hall (Gomadō) burned down completely in 1485, and that the Fudō statue that had been rescued from the building was relocated to the Relic Hall.[16] By the sixteenth century, the Golden Pavilion appears to have been the

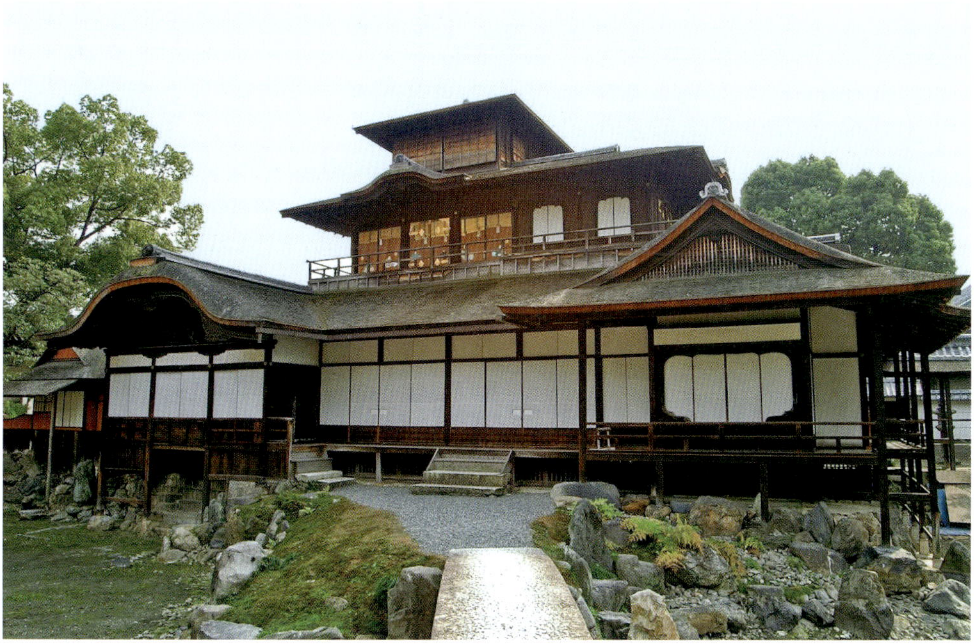

Fig. 4. Hiunkaku, Nishi Honganji. Kyoto

only original building to have survived from the once-glorious estate.

Due to its association with Yoshimitsu and a developing poetics of ruin, Kinkakuji's reputation grew among a small coterie of cultural figures, first and foremost Ashikaga Yoshimasa. The eighth Muromachi shogun visited the premises numerous times, and famously modeled the Kannon Hall of his Higashiyama Villa after the structure.[17] Ashikaga Yoshihisa was also a visitor, and a 1488 entry in the *Daily Record of the Inryōken* (*Inryōken nichiroku*) chronicles an outing to the estate by Zen monks, who rode a boat around the pond and recited Chinese poetry.[18] Slowly but surely, the renown of Kinkakuji continued to spread. During the late sixteenth century the Jesuit missionary Luis Frois visited and left a lengthy description of the building, which mentions that the second floor contained a portrait of Yoshimitsu and Musō. Some have argued that the *tenshu* keeps built by the warlord Oda Nobunaga at Gifu and Azuchi castles were inspired by Kinkakuji.[19] The Golden Pavilion may also have inspired the famous Pavilion of Flying Clouds (Hiunkaku) at Nishi Honganji Temple in Kyoto (fig. 4). Indeed, Kinkakuji's imprint on the architectural history of early modern Japan was considerable and merits greater study.

It was not until the early seventeenth century that serious attempts were made to restore Kinkakuji to its former glory. The shogun Tokugawa Ieyasu visited the grounds in 1605 and appointed the monk Saishō Jōtai to serve as abbot of Rokuonji, charging him with its revival. His energetic successor, Hōrin Jōshō (1593–1668), detailed this restoration in his journal *Kakumeiki*.[20] Hōrin took an interest in Kinkakuji and led numerous visitors to the site, as well as overseeing a restoration in 1649. As a result of this heightened interest, sometime during the Kan'ei era (1624–44) the tea master Kanamori Sōwa constructed the teahouse Sekkatei near the temple. Kinkakuji was increasingly the destination of aristocratic gatherings and pleasure outings. It was also frequently depicted in screen paintings of Kyoto known as "Scenes In and Around the Capital" (Rakuchū rakugai zu).[21] By the late Edo period, Kinkakuji was firmly established as a major landmark of the imperial capital, a fixture in guidebooks and city literature.

With the Meiji Restoration of 1868, the fortunes of Rokuonji changed, as they did for many other temples throughout the Kansai region. The persecution of Buddhist institutions known as *haibutsu kishaku* ("Abolish Buddhism and Destroy Shakyamuni") devastated many architectural structures and forced monasteries to sell their cultural treasures in order to continue their existence. Fortunately Kinkakuji was spared a similar fate, and in 1894 the Golden Pavilion and its gardens were opened to the public for a fee, thus generating income for daily operations. Three years later, in 1897, Kinkakuji was designated a "Special Protection Building" (*tokubetsu hogo kenzōbutsu*) by the government, and eventually, in 1929, a National Treasure.

A Closer Look

The structure of Kinkakuji is unusual because of its eclecticism. An initial glance suggests that it is a three-story building facing south onto Mirror Pond (Kyōkochi), with a pyramidal roof sheathed with wooden shingles (*kokera-buki*) and crowned with a gilt bronze phoenix finial. Because there is no roofline between the first and second floors, the exterior profile is a somewhat deceptive; while its double roof suggests a two-story structure, in fact the building has three stories. The first floor consists of unpainted wood and plaster, but the second and third stories are covered entirely in gold foil, right down to the banister railings and even the flooring inside the third floor. The first and second floors have the same rectangular floor plan and are five by four bays wide, whereas the third floor is a smaller square plan measuring three by three bays. There are no walls between the south-facing pillars of the first floor, or for a portion of the second floor, resulting in a dynamic and asymmetrical façade that offers an ever-changing profile of the building as it is encircled.

Closer examination reveals that all three floors of the building are constructed in different architectural vocabularies that draw upon distinct traditions of building in Japan. The ground floor (fig. 5), referred to as the Ablution Hall (Hōsu-in), is constructed in the *shinden* style of aristocratic residential architecture, characterized by thin unpainted wooden pillars, earthen walls, wooden boards, and reticulated shutters (*shitomido*) for partitioning. A small arbor with a gabled roof extends westward from the first floor onto the water; it has seating and is used for mooring boats. The second floor is a temple hall in the traditional Japanese *wayō* style, with non-penetrating tie beams (*nageshi*), wooden boarding (*mairado*), and latticed window partitions (*kōshimado*). With a plaque reading "Tide Sound Cavern" ("Chō'ondō") overhead, a sculpture of the Bodhisattva Kannon is installed inside, surrounded by the Four Heavenly Kings.[22] The walls and floor of the interior are covered with black lacquer, while the ceiling is decorated with paintings of flying *apsaras* (*hiten*) on the interior and phoenixes on the exterior, with all four walls surrounded by a veranda and railing. The third floor (fig. 6) is a temple hall in the Zen style, with wooden shutters (*sankarado*) and floriated windows (*katōmado*) for partitions. The veranda railing is also distinguished from that of the second story. While the floors of the interior and exterior are black lacquer, the entirety of the walls, ceiling, and banisters are covered in gold. The plaque on the third floor reads "Pinnacle of the Realm of Perfection" ("Kyukyōchō"), implying that it had been intended as a precinct for Buddha relics.[23]

Certain details of the 1952–55 reconstruction have been challenged. This reconstruction made a number of changes to the 1904–6 restoration, including the elimination of latticed windows (*renjimado*) on the east and west walls of the second floor, as well as inserting a plaster wall on the north side of the first floor. Although a range of details have been questioned, two aspects loom above others in significance. The first is the idea that, in contrast to the current configuration of the third floor, which is centered directly over the second floor, originally the top floor was situated over the western side of the second floor in a dynamically off-center arrangement.[24] In this configuration, Kinkakuji would have resembled more closely later structures such as the Pavilion of the Flying Cloud at Nishi Honganji Temple, which showcases a multistory, asymmetrical design.[25]

The second aspect of the mid-century reconstruction that has generated debate is the use of gold foil on the second floor of the Golden Pavilion. It is difficult to determine precisely which areas of the temple's exterior surface were covered with gold during the premodern period, as pictorial representations of

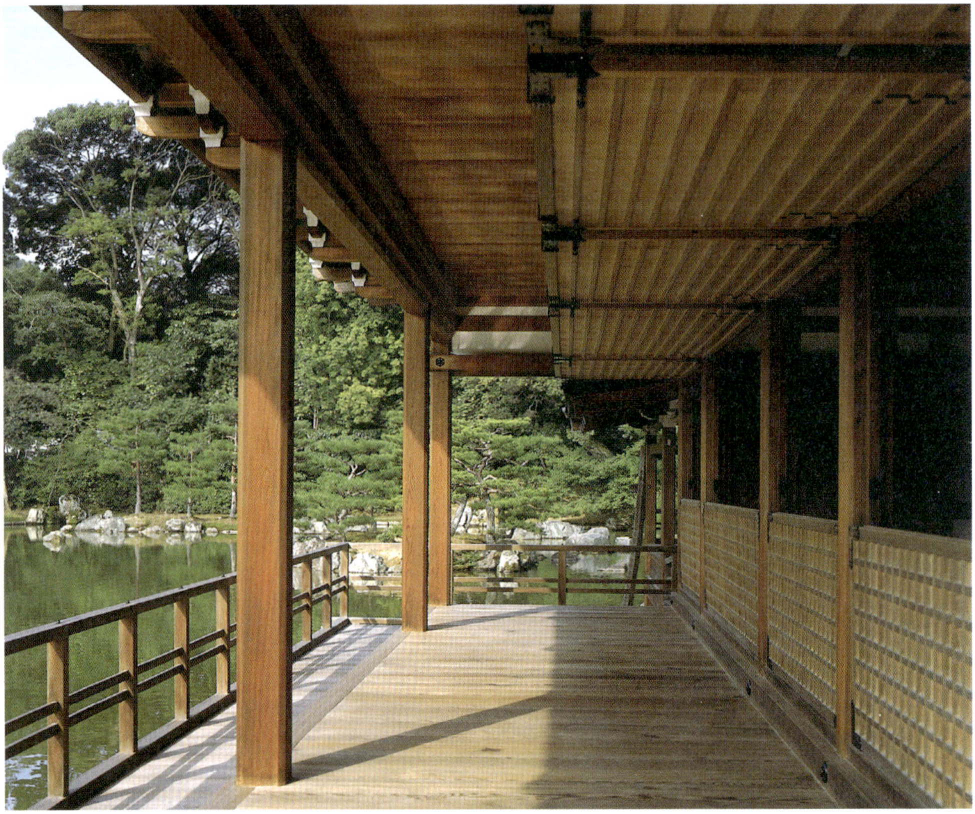

Fig. 5. Kinkakuji, first floor

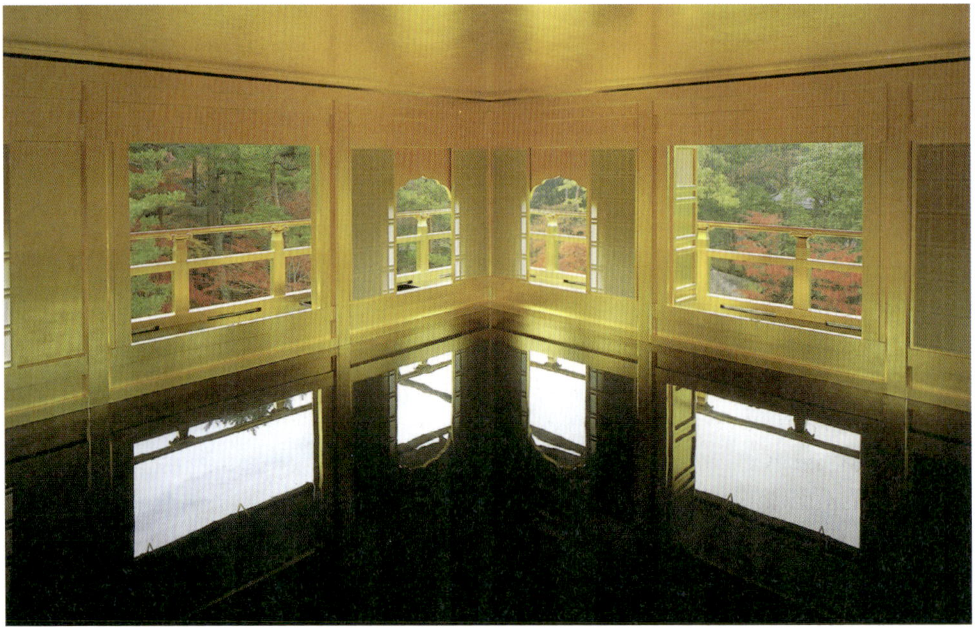

Fig. 6. Kinkakuji, third floor

Kinkakuji are notoriously unreliable. As far as it is known, during the modern era only the third floor was gilded up until the arson of 1950. While supervising the reconstruction, however, Murata referred to a timber component from a corner of the second floor that had been separately preserved after the 1904–6 reconstruction and that was being used at the time as a flower container (*hana-ire*). Because this was the only surviving timber component from the second story and bore traces of gold ornamentation, it served as a basis for covering both the second and third floors with gold foil. Miyakami Shigetaka argued that the gold foil was most likely added to the flower container at a later time, because this in situ component would have been exposed to the elements and any original gilding would have long disappeared.[26]

From approximately ten years after the reconstruction, the gold foil began to wear away and expose the black lacquer coating underneath. Because the exposed lacquer surface was being progressively eroded by ultraviolet rays, plans were made to reapply the gold foil. It took several decades to raise the money and achieve this goal. Finally, over a twenty-month span from 1986 to 1987, another major restoration enabled the reapplication of lacquer and foil, and the repainting of the ceilings. This project, known as the "Great Shōwa-Era Restoration" (Shōwa daishūfuku), was estimated to cost approximately 745 million yen (over 7.5 million US dollars) at the time. On this occasion, some 200,000 sheets of gold foil at five times the normal thickness (0.45–0.55 micrometers) were applied, totaling approximately 20 kilograms in weight. It is likely that Kinkakuji gleams more brilliantly today than it ever did in its own time, due primarily to the use of especially thick gold foil during the 1986–87 restoration.

Land of Gold

The question of why Yoshimitsu chose to ornament the building in gold, and more generally why the structure took the form that it did, has never been directly addressed. In the most general and straightforward sense, the golden profile of Kinkakuji can be understood as a marker of Yoshimitsu's kingship. As Imatani Akira has proposed, Yoshimitsu's pattern of activity demonstrates a desire to become emperor and establish the Ashikaga as the imperial clan (*uji*), an aspiration that remained unconsummated with his death in 1408.[27] Although the nature of Yoshimitsu's rule has been a subject of heated debate among historians of Japan, and Imatani's understanding of his intentionality merits revision, there is little doubt that he attempted to transcend the conventional framework of shogunal sovereignty and assume the prerogatives of an emperor or retired emperor. This plan unfolded over several decades with the assumption of a series of titles, beginning with his appointment as Acting Grand Counselor (*Gon Dainagon*) in 1378 at the age of twenty-one; conferral of the title *Junsangō*—placing him above all aristocrats, and equivalent to the ranks for empress and empress dowager—in 1383; his appointment as Grand Chancellor of State (*Dajō daijin*) in 1394; his retirement and assumption of Buddhist vows in 1395; and his attempts from 1407 onward to become a *Dajō tennō*, a title traditionally reserved for a retired emperor.

Matthew Stavros has made the important observation that architecturally, with three *shinden*-style palaces on its premises, the Kitayama Villa was designed as a site for Ritsuryō ritual and therefore can be understood as the premier locus of statecraft.[28] Esoteric Buddhist rituals for the protection of the state were also conducted within the villa's precincts; in ceremonial terms, therefore, it was the functional equivalent of the imperial palace. The Kitayama Villa can be characterized as an imperial estate, with Kinkakuji as its most spectacular structure.

Its framing as an imperial arena, however, was interregional as much as it was intramural, because Yoshimitsu's imperial sources of emulation extended overseas. His establishment in 1382 of Shōkokuji monastery, the seat of the Registry of Monks (*Sōrokushi*) and the administrative center of the Gozan system of Zen monasteries, was modeled after the Song state-sponsored temple Xiangguosi in the Northern Song capital of Kaifeng. Yoshimitsu's Chinese painting collection is understood to emulate the famous collection of Emperor Huizong (1082–1135), known in Japan through the circulation of the palace inventory, *Xuanhe Catalog of Paintings* (*Xuanhe huapu*; 1120). Indeed, Yoshimitsu is the earliest figure to impress owner's seals—"Dōyū" and "Tenzan," which were his Buddhist names—directly on the surface of paintings, a practice modeled after Chinese imperial convention. Yoshimitsu's funerary portrait even cited the same text that was inscribed on the mortuary likeness of Huizong, a eulogistic verse by the Chan monk Dahui Zonggao (1089–1163).[29]

Kinkakuji's gilding bears a direct relationship to Yoshimitsu's status as a statesman with an international purview, and the regular reception of foreign embassies at the Kitayama Villa during his final decade. He hosted a Korean emissary there in 1403, as well as three groups of delegates from the Ming between 1405 and 1407, before grandly receiving Go-Komatsu and his retinue in the third month of 1408. For these visitors, witnessing the Golden Hall would without any doubt have left one of the greatest impressions during their sojourn.

By this period, Japan was associated with gold within the interregional imagination. Intriguingly, Marco Polo's description of "a King's Palace roofed with pure gold" in Zipangu (Japan) resonates uncannily with Kinkakuji. His image of the country, however, was undoubtedly derived from descriptions circulating in China well before his time, or perhaps even among Muslim traders, who referred to the golden land of Wāqwaq, an Arabic distortion of Wakoku, another name for Japan. Gold served as the material of choice for the gilded face of Japanese diplomacy as early as the consecration of Tōdaiji's Great Buddha in 752, a ceremony attended by official delegates from the Silla Kingdom in Korea, as well as Buddhist monks from Tang China and even India. During diplomatic missions to China in the eighth and ninth centuries, Japanese delegates regularly brought large amounts of gold to fund their stays. Chinese merchants were also aware of the Golden Hall (Konjikidō) at Chūsonji in the northern Fujiwara capital of Hiraizumi. Indeed, it is possible that the Chūsonji Golden Hall, which consists of a three-bay square structure whose exterior and interior flooring is entirely sheathed in gold leaf, was conceived with a similarly interregional purview interregional purview.[30]

What is intriguing about the association of Japan with gold overseas was the relatively paltry production of gold within the archipelago, which is estimated to have been around 255 tons between the eighth and sixteenth centuries, or around 5 percent of world production before the California Gold Rush.[31] At the same time, its valuation within Japanese material culture as a means of ornamentation and expression of luxury, while significant, was arguably less so than other materials such as silk, lacquer, or mother-of-pearl. Overseas, however, it continued to serve as the signature substance reflecting the affluence of the islands. Ashikaga shoguns regularly offered gold-foil screens painted with auspicious themes to Ming emperors as tributary offerings during the fifteenth and sixteenth centuries, a practice continued on an even greater scale by the Tokugawa shoguns in relation to Korea's Joseon kings. And ten pairs of gold screens, sent by Tokugawa Ieyoshi to Netherlands' King William III, still survive in the National Museum of Ethnology in Leiden.

Thus while Kinkakuji's sumptuous exterior may have awed onlookers, it was experienced within a discursive environment in which overseas visitors were prepared and even expected to encounter aurelian manifestations of abundance. And the structure's gold-leaf surface may have born a sacral semantics that was particularly evident to those who hailed from the continent. As Yutani Yūzō has argued, Kinkakuji may even have been designed specifically to invoke the Buddhist temple Jingesi at the sacred mountain site of Wutaishan.[32]

According to a story that circulated in *Song Biographies of Eminent Monks* (*Song gaoseng zhuan*), compiled by the monk-historian Zanning (919–1001) in 988, the Tang master Daoyi, while on a pilgrimage to Wutaishan, encountered the Bodhisattva Manjusri in the guise of an old man at a three-story golden temple called Jingesi (Temple of the Golden Pavilion). Upon returning to the Tang capital of Chang'an, he informed Emperor Xuanzong of his miraculous encounter, and Xuanzong ordered the construction of a temple that evoked this visionary structure. Jingesi would become famous throughout the Buddhist world, and it was visited by the famous Japanese pilgrim-monk Ennin in the ninth century.[33]

As Yutani observes, both Kinkakuji and Jingesi are three-story golden structures written with the same set of characters, and, while Kinkakuji is believed by most to be a later appellation, Yutani proposes that in fact it may well have been the designation Yoshimitsu had in mind for his reliquary hall. Furthermore, soon after taking vows, Yoshimitsu changed his initial Buddhist name "Dōyū" to "Dōgi," adopting the same characters as Daoyi. Most significantly for the consideration of Kinkakuji's interregional context, Dōgi was the name that Yoshimitsu used to sign his letter sent to Emperor Jianwen in 1401 requesting a tributary relationship with the Ming, along with the aristocratic title "Junsangō." It is therefore possible to understand Yoshimitsu, in his capacity as a retired sovereign who had taken vows, as modeling his religious identity upon that of Daoyi, and his construction of Kinkakuji upon the example of Xuanzong. If this interpretation holds, Kinkakuji's golden surface would have resonated within a Buddhist macroculture that extends well beyond Kyoto.

Yoshimitsu's Kingship

The relationship of Kinkakuji to Yoshimitsu's sovereignty, however, is more complex and multifaceted than can be explained by its gold ornamentation alone. This relationship is intertwined with the fluid geopolitics of the East Asian region during the late fourteenth and early fifteenth centuries. Take, for example, the debate that has centered around the meaning of Yoshimitsu's embrace of the title of "King of Japan" (Nihon kokuō), bequeathed by Emperor Yongle in 1402, thereby designating Japan an official tributary of the Ming Empire. Japanese rulers had traditionally refused such a title because of the inferior status it encoded. Yoshimitsu therefore effectively reversed a diplomatic position of non-recognition that had been in place for centuries.

While there is little doubt, as Imatani and others have argued, that Yoshimitsu aspired to some form of monarchial status on a par with or even surpassing the imperial throne, his sovereignty merits more nuanced framing. His initiatives achieve greater legibility when his kingship is understood as developing multiple fronts to address differing constituencies in divergent ways. Rather than a unified construction, his lordly identity was a composite of disparate faces that evolved through dialectical engagement with the warrior, aristocratic, clerical, and international communities.

For example, there is ample reason to interpret his "King of Japan" title not as a usurpation of imperial privilege but more narrowly as the reflection of a sovereign selfhood directed primarily toward the Ming emperor and his mediators. Yoshimitsu continued to acknowledge the presence of the emperor in Japan, and the designation did not influence in any way the manner in which Yoshimitsu was referred to by others, which continued to be as either "Lord Kitayama" or "Lord Muromachi." In fact, Yoshimitsu was criticized for embracing this designation and placing himself in a position of inferiority to a neighboring sovereign, in contrast to the disposition of earlier Japanese rulers. There would have been incentive for him to downplay this title among Japan's ruling classes. Likewise, nothing about Yoshimitsu's behavior subsequent to his investiture suggests that he was the leader of a tributary state. Japan did not adopt a Ming era name, as did other states in a subordinate relationship to China. Nor did it adopt the Ming calendar. Indeed, the ritual by which Japan was designated a tributary, performed in Yoshimitsu's *shinden* palace at the Kitayama Villa, was unorthodox in that Yoshimitsu sat on a throne and received an offering from a Ming envoy, thus strongly suggesting that he viewed the relationship between Japanese and Chinese sovereigns on equal terms. As a number of scholars have proposed, economic motives loomed large in Yoshimitsu's pursuit of tributary relations with the Ming. Although he did not live long after the first tributary mission of 1404, the Ming trade was enormously lucrative, and among the many treasures on display for the 1408 visitation of Emperor Go-Komatsu at the Kitayama Villa were numerous artworks that must have been recently brought back from China.

While gold is an obvious characteristic of Kinkakuji's profile, its relationship to Yoshimitsu's political culture is more manifestly expressed in its structure. Kinkakuji is among the most eclectic examples of palatial architecture ever witnessed in Japan until that period.[34] As described earlier, its first story consists of an aristocratic *shinden*-style room, its second story is a traditional Japanese temple interior in what is known as the *wayō* style, and its third story is in the more recently imported Zen architectural style. Moreover, the origins of its syncretism resist easy analysis. The Hall of Lapis Lazuli (Ruriden) at Saihōji, the structure understood to be the most direct inspiration for Kinkakuji, was believed to have been more uniform in its architectural profile. In Kinkakuji, by contrast, all three floors are differentiated through walling and partitions, details of the architectural components, and general ambience. Every stratum of the temple hall constitutes its own distinct realm and serves different functions within the context of the villa. The first floor is appropriate to an aristocratic fishing pavilion overlooking the water, and offers lateral continuity with the *shinden* palaces and social aristocratic spaces spread out across the Kitayama campus. The second story presents a devotional space for the worship of the Bodhisattva Kannon, and possibly the Amida Buddha, both of significance to the Ashikaga family. And the upper floor was intended for the worship of the Buddha's Relic, which is why the entire structure was referred to in its time as a Relic Hall (Shariden). Until the introduction of Zen monasteries, the presence of relics in Japanese temple compounds were marked by high-rise pagodas; Zen monasteries, by contrast, often included separate temple halls for the worship of relics—a practice that was common in China. Thus, the top story at Kinkakuji introduces both a Chinese architectural program and a Chinese stylistic inflection to the structure.

Kinkakuji, while heterogeneous within the context of Japanese architecture, complements well the hybrid nature of the villa as a whole, and provides an uncannily direct analog to Yoshimitsu's own multiform stature. The multiple programs embedded within it include social spaces and private chapels, old and new architectural practices, and indigenous as well as foreign modes of enclosing space. From the exterior, it constitutes one of the premier high-rise presences at Kitayama, a beaming, golden beacon that shimmers upon the water and throughout the landscape. But this effulgence is only one component of what makes Kinkakuji worthy of attention. Its true cultural and architectural legacy lies in its vestigial manifestation of a fleeting—and for that reason all the more remarkable—moment in which Japanese kingship was reimagined as something boundlessly multifaceted, protean, and cosmopolitan.

Notes

1. Mizukami's lifelong obsession with the motives behind the arsonist's act also led to the nonfiction work *The Burning of the Golden Pavilion* (*Kinkaku enjō*, 1979), which traces Hayashi's life from his childhood in the city of Maizuru up through the Kinkakuji fire, to the young monk's death in 1956 in a mental hospital.

2. The details of this restoration are spelled out in detail in the publication *Saikon Kinkakuji* (Kyoto: Rokuonji, 1955).

3. The most thorough analysis of Murata's plan is found in Miyakami Shigetaka, "Kinkakuji," in *Nihon meikenchiku shashin senshū*, vol. 11, *Kinkakuji, Ginkakuji* (Tokyo: Shinchōsha, 1992), 92–109.

4. Matthew Stavros, *Kyoto: An Urban History of Japan's Premodern Capital* (Honolulu: University of Hawai'i Press, 2014), 68–74.

5. For a fuller discussion of Saionji and the account in *The Clear Mirror*, see P. Richard Stanley-Baker, "Mythic and Sacred Gardens in Medieval Japan: Sacral Mediation in the Rokuonji and the Saihōji Gardens," in *Sacred Gardens and Landscapes: Ritual and Agency*, ed. by Michel Conan (Washington, DC: Dumbarton Oaks, 2007), 115–52, esp. 121–35. *The Clear Mirror* is translated in George W. Perkins, trans., *The Clear Mirror: A Chronicle of the Japanese Court During the Kamakura Period (1185–1333)* (Stanford: Stanford University Press, 1998).

6. See Stavros, *Kyoto*, 96–101.

7. Zuikei Shūhō 1448. *Kanrin koroshū* (Murai 53).

8. For a detailed discussion of changes to the garden, see Hisatsune Shūji, *Kyōto Mei'enki* (Tokyo: Seibundō Shinkōsha, 1969).

9. Yoshimitsu's visit is recorded in the Zen monk Gidō Shūshin's diary *Kūge nikkō shū*. The shogun Ashikaga Takauji also visited Saihōji in the years 1350 and 1352. Later, Ashikaga Yoshimasa is known to have visited the temple on dozens of occasions. See Hisatsune, *Kyōto Mei'enki*, 160.

10. The *kōan* in question is Case18, "The Seamless Pagoda," from *The Emerald Cliff Record* (Japanese *Hekiganroku*, Chinese *Biyanlu*, 1125). It is clear from a study of this *kōan* that Musō renamed the buildings and garden sites of Saihōji to refer to Zen enlightenment.

11. For the esoteric rituals conducted there, see Stanley-Baker, "Mythic and Sacred Gardens in Medieval Japan," 138–39.

12. For more on Yoshimitsu's display, see P. Richard Stanley-Baker, "Muromachi-jidai no zashiki-kazari to bunka-teki shidōken," in *Nihon bijutsu zenshū*, vol. 11, *Zenshū ji'in to Tei'en* (Tokyo: Kōdansha, 1993), 168–73.

13. Stanley-Baker, "Mythic and Sacred Gardens in Medieval Japan," 140. For a full record of Go-Komatsu's visit, see *Record of the Imperial Visitation to Kitayama* (*Kitayama gyōkō ki*), in *Zoku gunsho ruijū* (Tokyo: Zoku Gunsho Kanseikai, 1923–33).

14. On Yoshimochi's construction of the Sanjōbōmon Palace, see Matthew Stavros, "The Sanjō bōmon Temple-Palace Complex: The First Locus of Ashikaga Authority in Medieval Kyoto," *Japan Review* 22 (2010): 3–29. Yoshimochi was believed to be full of animosity towards his father for perceived mistreatments, which conditioned his relationship to Kitayama. See Yukio Lippit, *Zen Buddhism and the Impossible Painting* (Los Angeles: Getty Research Institute, 2017).

15. *Ga'un nikken roku batsuyū*, in *Dai Nihon kokiroku*, ed. by Shiryō Hensanjo (Tokyo: Iwanami Shoten, 1961), 29.

16. *Sanetaka kōki* (Tokyo: Zoku Gunsho Ruijū Kankōkai, 1931–63), entry for December 15, 1485.

17. Yoshimasa visited the site in 1487 to study Kinkakuji. See Katsuno Ryūshin and Tamamura Takeji, eds., *Inryōken nichiroku* (*Daily Record of the Inryōken Cloister*), 5 vols. (Kyoto: Shiseki Kankōkai, 1953-1954), vol. 2, 1011. The entry concerning Ashikaga Yoshimasa's visit to Kinkakuji takes place on 1487(Chōkyō 1).6.6.

18. Miyakami, "Kinkakuji," 99.

19. Ibid., 100.

20. See Iwama Kaoru and Oka Yoshiko, eds., *Kan'ei bunka no nettowaaku—Kakumeiki no sekai* (Kyoto: Shibunkaku Shuppan, 1998).

21. As Okudaira Shunroku has noted, however, with a few exceptions these pictorial renderings mischaracterized the architecture, suggesting that painters and other urban commoners were rarely allowed on the premises. See Okudaira Shunroku, "Kinkakuji no yūraku," in Iwama and Oka, *Kan'ei bunka no nettowaaku*, 125–34.

22. According to *Inryōken nichiroku*, when Yoshimasa visited the site in 1485, Kisen Shūshō reported to him that the original Kannon statue there was destroyed during the Onin War. Kisen also told him that the third floor had a "Welcoming Descent of the Amida Buddha with Twenty-Five Bodhisattvas," but that these were also destroyed, and only painted white clouds on the walls behind remained.

23. Tamamura Takeji, "Kinkaku no karoku ni yosu," in *Nihon zenshūshi ronshū* (Tokyo: Tokyo Daigaku Shuppankai, 1975), A.661–66.

24. This argument is made by Miyakami, who studied the detailed measurements made of each of the timber components when the structure was dismantled for the 1904–6 restoration. Heavy ceiling beams only spanned the western room of the second story, suggesting that only this side of the floor would have been able to bear the load of the floor above it. Miyakami, "Kinkakuji," 105–8.

25. In appearance the top floor of such structures ends up looking like a small square hall inserted into the hip-and-gabled roof of a traditional temple structure. Another building that follows this design is the Founder's Hall (Kaisandō) at Tōfukuji Temple in Kyoto. Although the building dates to the Edo period, it is believed to resemble closely the original building dating to the Muromachi period.

26. Miyakami, "Kinkakuji," 109.

27. Imatani Akira and Kozo Yamamura, "Not for Lack of Will or Wile: Yoshimitsu's Failure to Supplant the Imperial Lineage," *Journal of Japanese Studies* 18, no. 1 (1992): 45–78.

28. Stavros, *Kyoto*, 120–23.

29. Takagishi Akira.

30. In this regard, see the discussion of northern Fujiwara culture in Mimi Hall Yiengpruksawan, *Hiraizumi: Buddhist Art and Regional Politics in Twelfth-Century Japan* (Cambridge, MA: Harvard University Asia Center, 1998), esp. 121–24.

31. These figures are cited from Miyazaki Masakatsu, "The Legend of 'Zipangu,' The Land of Gold," *Nipponia* 45 (June 2008), http://web-japan.org/nipponia/nipponia45/en/feature/feature01.html. For a recent survey that offers more detailed estimates of gold production in premodern Japan, see Katō Hiroshi, *Kin no Nihon shi* (Tokyo: Shinchōsha, 2012).

32. Yutani Yūzō, "Kinkakuji wa, Kinkakuji to shite taterareta," *Nagoya Gaikokugo Daigaku gaikokugo gakubu kiyō* 42 (2012): 304–32.

33. For a discussion of Daoyi's vision, see Yiengpruksawan, *Hiraizumi*, 152–53.

34. A case could also be made for the eleventh-century Byodo-in. See Mimi Yiengpruksawan, "A Pavilion for Amitabha," in *Buddhist Transformations and Interactions: Essays in Honor of Antonino Forte*, ed. by Victor H. Mair (New York: Cambria Press, 2017), 401–516.

Bibliography

Ga'un nikken roku batsuyū. In *Dai Nihon kokiroku*, edited by Shiryō Hensanjo. Tokyo: Iwanami Shoten, 1961.

Hisatsune Shūji, *Kyōto Mei'enki*. Tokyo: Seibundō Shinkōsha, 1969.

Imatani Akira and Kozo Yamamura. "Not for Lack of Will or Wile: Yoshimitsu's Failure to Supplant the Imperial Lineage." *Journal of Japanese Studies* 18, no. 1 (1992): 45–78.

Iwama Kaoru and Oka Yoshiko, eds. *Kan'ei bunka no nettowaaku—Kakumeiki no sekai*. Kyoto: Shibunkaku Shuppan, 1998.

Katō Hiroshi, *Kin no Nihon shi*. Tokyo: Shinchōsha, 2012.

Katsuno Ryūshin and Tamamura Takeji, eds., *Inryōken nichiroku* (*Daily Record of the Inryōken Cloister*), 5 vols. Kyoto: Shiseki Kankōkai, 1953-1954.

Lippit, Yukio. *Zen Buddhism and the Impossible Painting*. Los Angeles: Getty Research Institute, 2017.

Miyakami Shigetaka. "Kinkakuji." In *Nihon meikenchiku shashin senshū*, vol. 11, *Kinkakuji, Ginkakuji*, 92–109. Tokyo: Shinchōsha, 1992.

Miyazaki Masakatsu, "The Legend of 'Zipangu,' The Land of Gold," *Nipponia* 45 (June 2008), http://web-japan.org/nipponia/nipponia45/en/feature/feature01.html.

Okudaira Shunroku. "Kinkakuji no yūraku." in *Kan'ei bunka no nettowaaku—Kakumeiki no sekai*, edited by Iwama Kaoru and Oka Yoshiko, 125–34. Kyoto: Shibunkaku Shuppan, 1998.

Perkins, George W., trans. *The Clear Mirror: A Chronicle of the Japanese Court During the Kamakura Period (1185–1333)*. Stanford: Stanford University Press, 1998.

Record of the Imperial Visitation to Kitayama (*Kitayama gyōkō ki*). In *Zoku gunsho ruijū*. Tokyo: Zoku Gunsho Kanseikai, 1923–33.

Saikon Kinkakuji. Kyoto: Rokuonji, 1955.

Sanetaka kōki. Tokyo: Zoku Gunsho Ruijū Kankōkai, 1931–63.

Stanley-Baker, P. Richard. "Muromachi-jidai no zashiki-kazari to bunka-teki shidōken." In *Nihon bijutsu zenshū*, vol. 11, *Zenshū ji'in to Tei'en*, 168–73. Tokyo: Kōdansha, 1993.

Stanley-Baker, P. Richard. "Mythic and Sacred Gardens in Medieval Japan: Sacral Mediation in the Rokuonji and the Saihōji Gardens." In *Sacred Gardens and Landscapes: Ritual and Agency*, edited by Michel Conan, 115–52. Washington, DC: Dumbarton Oaks, 2007.

Stavros, Matthew. *Kyoto: An Urban History of Japan's Premodern Capital*. Honolulu: University of Hawai'i Press, 2014.

Stavros, Matthew. "The Sanjō bōmon Temple-Palace Complex: The First Locus of Ashikaga Authority in Medieval Kyoto." *Japan Review* 22 (2010): 3–29.

Tamamura Takeji. "Kinkaku no karoku ni yosu." In *Nihon zenshūshi ronshū*, A.661–66. Tokyo: Tokyo Daigaku Shuppankai, 1975.

Yiengpruksawan, Mimi Hall. *Hiraizumi: Buddhist Art and Regional Politics in Twelfth-Century Japan*. Cambridge, MA: Harvard University Asia Center, 1998.

Yiengpruksawan, Mimi. "A Pavilion for Amitabha." In *Buddhist Transformations and Interactions: Essays in Honor of Antonino Forte*, edited by Victor H. Mair, 401–516. New York: Cambria Press, 2017.

Yutani Yūzō. "Kinkakuji wa, Kinkakuji to shite taterareta." *Nagoya Gaikokugo Daigaku gaikokugo gakubu kiyō* 42 (2012): 304–32.

PART II

The Lure of Gold: Holy and Unholy Desires

Potable Gold: From Cordial Remedy to *Panacea* (Fourteenth-Sixteenth Centuries)

Chiara Crisciani

The development of Latin alchemy in the period between the end of the thirteenth century and the end of the fourteenth century is now well known to scholars. It was at this time that the endeavor to transmute metals (which had never really disappeared from the scene) was accompanied by a significant innovation, and a branch of alchemical research focused its full attention on the production of a medical elixir capable not only of rapidly restoring health in the case of many illnesses, but also of prolonging life itself.[1] Indeed this objective, which would become predominant in many fourteenth-century works, especially those of pseudo-Lullus, pseudo-Arnaldus, and John Dastin, was originally formulated (in terms of its doctrine, philosophy, and precepts) in various writings by Roger Bacon, as well as in short works—principally *De retardanda senectute*—which, formerly attributed to Bacon, have recently been definitively identified not to be his, and in fact were themselves the basis for Bacon's proposals.[2]

The development of Western alchemy displayed a precocious yoking of alchemy and medicine. The two disciplines shared epistemological characteristics (against their common Aristotelian background, both pursuits being in various ways subordinate to the more general field of natural philosophy). Both were divided into a theoretical and a practical part. Organic ingredients were used in alchemical processes and mineral elements could be used in the medical pharmacopoeia. Most importantly, we find alchemical texts using concepts and categories (such as radical moisture, the function of heat, blood, embryological theories) borrowed from similar medical doctrines. This intertwining becomes progressively evident, so much so that in the fifteenth century Christopher of Perugia lists in his *Elucidarius* the three proper pursuits of alchemical research as the transmutation of metals, medical alchemy for the human organism, and technical discoveries and "secrets."[3]

In the fifteenth century we also find a number of medical texts which feature aspects of medical alchemy, thereby prompting in the reader what amounts to a dual and even conflicted response. On the one hand, these texts clearly testify to a set of deep-rooted interrelationships between alchemy and medicine—indeed they deal with similar problems and deploy common basic theories (on the elements, on mixture, on the nature of blood, on radical moisture).[4] On the other hand, one is aware of fissures and inconsistencies: when alchemical texts describe alchemically produced remedies they do not explain in physiological terms the manner in which the admirable medicine works. This is the case, for example in the *Testamentum* by "Lullus" and the *Rosarium* by "Arnaldus," in which lavish praise of the therapeutic function of the elixir is not always accompanied by detailed explanations of the manner in which it acts. Indeed, the *Testamentum* goes so far as to state that the ideal physician has no need to carry out an analytical diagnosis, nor must he necessarily be familiar with the chaotic, misleading, and useless traditional collections of antidotes.[5] Conversely, in texts with a stronger medical bias, there is not always a detailed examination of the treatment from which the admirable medicine derives and the way in which it acts. There emerges therefore, in both doctors and alchemists, an apparent unwillingness to gain a deeper understanding of the practical applications of what each borrows from the other's field.

Hence, the fifteenth-century texts that display a certain eagerness to close the distance between the different sets of competences are of particular interest. These texts focused in various ways on gold, which had always been present in the traditional pharmacopoeia, but was also an ingredient or aim of alchemical doctrines and practices, which, as we have seen, in the Western world from the thirteenth century onwards had also taken on a marked medical slant and therapeutic aims.[6]

The starting point of these speculations about the golden remedy was a core of conceptions and sources, which, though composite, are quite clearly recognizable as a set. In the first place, there is Avicenna's neutral and sober pharmacological discussion of the therapeutic properties of gold mainly contained in the *Canon*: here gold is viewed as a special medicine on account of its extremely balanced nature, which makes it suitable for the purpose of "comforting" the heart.[7] However, it is listed, together with its specific properties and uses, along with other equally important "cordials," some of which are in fact ranked above it for efficacy. To this core of knowledge should be added some portions of an influential alchemical text, the *Testamentum* by Pseudo-Lullus (beginning of the fourteenth century). It is not gold that is discussed here but an elixir created from gold that has both a transmutatory and an overall therapeutic function: unlike Avicenna's gold pharmacon, this is a unique and universal remedy.[8] Preceding the *Testamentum* there was a group of booklets by pseudo-Bacon and pseudo-Arnaldus on prolongevity (the so-called texts regarding *Retardanda senectus*).[9] From these come the most intriguing contributions to the cluster we have been describing, since they discuss a gold-based medicine that not only cures but also guarantees long life and a happy comfortable old age.

To sum up, in addition to Avicenna's gold—that important but unexceptional medicine—there now appeared the admirable remedy of medical alchemy, an elixir whose twin characteristics of uniqueness and universality (it cured all illnesses) were decidedly innovative; this remedy presupposed artificially treated gold. The potability of this remedy emerges clearly, above all from the *Retardanda* texts: it was certainly this elixir that was unknowingly drunk by the old Sicilian farmer who found a pot full of liquid as he was working his fields—the results were indeed marvelous, as not only was he blessed with a long life but he also became one of the king's counsellors.[10] The same excellent effects were enjoyed by a certain man who covered his body with an unguent of equally admirable composition, but who forgot to anoint the soles of his feet, which therefore followed the normal process of aging and putrefaction, so that, throughout the rest of his long life, he was forced always to ride on horseback. Later, we find prelates and cardinals avidly drinking it.[11] And it was mixed with *cibis euchimiis*: foods, that is, that were artificially treated so as to be suitable for a diet that promoted longevity.[12] Finally, as pointed out once again by Roger Bacon, the alchemist should treat gold "by calcining and dissolving it so that it can be used in food and beverages as soon as it can be converted into human nature," thereby inaugurating what would later be the fiercely contested issue of the digestibility of gold.[13]

It is to this aggregation of progressively consolidated notions and doctrines—whose ramifications are in themselves quite complex—that various fifteenth-century texts refer: they were written by physicians, and they all focus attention on the "golden remedy." These are the *Epistola* by Thomas of Bologna;[14] an anonymous *quaestio* on the efficacy of a gold cure for the plague;[15] the *Tractatus* of an anonymous "Solemnis medicus" (connected with the Avignonese curia) on the search for potable gold;[16] the *De lapide philosophorum* by the physician and jurist Guglielmo Fabri (a functionary and member of the household of Pope Amedeus VIII);[17] the letter by Bernard of Treviso containing his answer to his friend Thomas of Bologna;[18] and the pamphlet by Giovanni "Mercurio" da Correggio (a well-informed work, albeit rhetorical rather than scientific in its aims). This group could easily be augmented, as many manuscript sources from this period have not been suitably studied, or even cataloged. For the most part these authors were connected in various ways to courtly environments. This is not surprising, as courts had always—and most clearly from the fifteenth century onwards—been the privileged context for alchemical research, which never enjoyed recognition in the universities.[19] At court its practitioners found social visibility (although this was sometimes semi-clandestine) as well as interested admirers, and forms of—albeit ambivalent and often risky—patronage. An unmistakably professional approach is taken by Thomas of Bologna, and even more so by Bernard of Treviso and by the author of the *quaestio*. The competent university style adopted by the "Solemnis medicus" is especially noteworthy;[20] while the works of Fabri and Correggio are less detailed and, above all, more rhetorical.[21]

For all these writers the alchemical preparation was "artificial" gold, in the sense that it was alchemically prepared and made potable. The purpose of the product obtained was first and foremost therapeutic: it guaranteed rapid recoveries and, in most cases, also a prolongation of life. This "treated" gold incorporated both the characteristics and the therapeutic virtues that tradition assigned to gold, and the admirable effects which the *Retardanda* attributed to the "extraordinary medicine"; in some cases, it also appropriated the advantages of other remedies (theriac, ardent water, quintessence), and it acquired astral power through its relationship with the sun, which in some of these texts was earnestly foregrounded. The actual preparation of this "medicine" was not always specifically described, and clearly it was thought that the instructions of alchemists such as "Arnaldus" and "Lullus," to whose works the reader is referred, were both sufficient and practicable. The authors were mainly concerned with the issue of administration, with the effects, and especially with what parts of the human organism the admirable remedy elected as its targets.

All these fifteenth-century texts are ideally interconnected through various points of consonance, which we are made aware of through similarities in themes and inquiry. Each author, however, privileges or accentuates a particular point of contact between alchemy and medicine, in an attempt to make sense pharmacologically and epistemologically of the new forms that medicinal gold had taken on. Space does not allow me here to discuss all these texts in detail. I will therefore limit myself to putting forward some specific points concerning the correspondence between Thomas and Bernard, and some observations on the anonymous *quaestio* on the plague.

The *Epistola* by Thomas of Bologna (Thomas de Pizan, father of Christine de Pizan, and physician and astrologer at the court of Charles V of France) was written in haste and under the pressure of growing anxiety, so it is perhaps on this account that its overexcited argumentation presents somewhat fragmentary information. Thomas had prepared and sent to the princes of France a special remedy. Now he was also sending it to his friend Bernard of Treviso, whom he describes as "secretarius nature," for an appraisal and for his scientific opinion: the medicine had been tested (*probata*) at court and "aliquid sinistre ... est reputatum" (something sinister ... is considered)—perhaps, Thomas explains, because it had been tried by fire, as if it were normal natural gold, and this misguided test might have adulterated it.[22] The princes of France were afflicted with sudden illnesses and ailments, and it was suggested at court that they had been poisoned by the new medicine. Grave suspicions had therefore been cast on the man who presented the princes with the remedy, and, though he declared himself to have been moved only by affection and deference, Thomas feared for his reputation and possibly also for his position at court (if not for his life itself).

What was this remedy? It was a "medicina facta de substantia auri processu philosophico": the gold, therefore, had been alchemically treated and strengthened.[23] Gold was chosen for its homogeneity and elemental balance, which made it the apogee of all minerals. The treatment which it underwent lead to a dynamic reinforcement of the perfect temperamental proportion of the initial gold. Such an operation entailed the (alchemical) phases and processes of *solutio*, *reductio*, *fixio*, and *inceratio*, through which the medicine was generated *ex auro*.[24] In other words, this remedy "it is nothing else than gold multiplied in its degrees being in the same proportion as it was to the initial gold."[25] Its vitality and exuberance would appear to depend upon "mercurius animatus,"[26] which therefore somehow contributed to its efficacy, and which behaved in the same way as blood does in the human organism, continuously coursing through and vivifying the body.[27]

More than once, alongside the absolute priority of the *experimentum*, Thomas points out that in this quest similitude constitutes a fundamental heuristic procedure: "Similitudinaliter in artibus philosophicis est procedendum."[28] Through what he explicitly calls an analogy (namely, that between blood and mercury), he connects the mineral nature of the preparation (which remains and must remain a metal) with the organic nature of the human body. He does not explain how the remedy, which remains solid, is absorbed by or acts in the organism. He does, however, with triumphant satisfaction, list its effects, some of which were already known, while others more newly recognized: it promotes a continual *vivificatio* (vitalizing) and the achievement of prolongevity.[29]

Certain aspects that Thomas merely hints at should here be brought more clearly to the foreground. First of all, there was the substantial interchangeability of the terms used to indicate the medicine he is discussing: in place of *medicina*, *aurum*, and *sol*, Thomas also uses *lapis philosophorum* (philosopher's stone).[30] Also noteworthy is his underscoring of the difference between this remedy and traditional ones: the *vegetales medicine de preparatione apothecali* (that is, the remedies adopted by the traditional pharmacopoeia), which were digestible (that is, they were transformed within the organism—"non mutant sed mutabuntur" Thomas observes) and whose action was therefore transitory. In the traditional pharmacopoeia, however, these were the very characteristics that lay at the basis of the variety of remedies (which was infinite and valorized precisely because of its multiplicity),[31] as well as the variety of the theories on the graduations of remedies. On the other hand, even before it became part of the alchemy of the elixir, the supremacy of the possibly unique remedy (such as that prepared by Thomas), which remained stable and therefore made those who took it incorruptible, was a typical feature of the pharmacology of the *Retardanda*.

A number of important theoretical questions remain unanswered, regarding both the way in which the remedies worked in general, and the action of the exceptional remedy (which would "traverse" the organism, modifying it but without being itself modified). Finally, the exceptionality of the medicine immediately prompts Thomas to note its miraculous operation—which, however, is only apparent and seen as such by the simpler among humans—and to draw comparisons with Christ. Thus, it is his belief that this remedy may be considered a "a miracle in nature's experiments ... not that he is a god, but that he is said to be in similitude in nature." [32] In a manner similar to this golden pharmacon, Christ, through his blood, has cured and perfected us, "by rejecting superfluities, such as sins and vices, and filling up absences, as by reforming the corruptible into the incorruptible, the mortal into the immortal."[33]

On account of its rather disconnected and concise style, Thomas's letter does not allow us to see clearly the way in which his suspected and incriminated remedy is supposed to act; indeed, the addressee of the letter himself states that he does not fully comprehend it.[34] This aspect, as well as Thomas's overall approach, is criticized in Bernard of Treviso's calmer and more structured response: he is entirely familiar with what the alchemy of the elixir might achieve, as well as with the theories put forward by "Arnaldus," but he has no qualms about voicing his very strong reservations. With implacable politeness and ruthless competence, Bernard dismantles many of the doctrinal presuppositions on which he believes that Thomas, with excessive lightness, has based his work. He starts by repeatedly pointing out that the relationship between blood and quicksilver is purely one of analogy, and that it works only *similitudinarie*;[35] it is therefore only by analogy that physiological-biological terms and concepts (body, spirit, soul, and embryological phases) may be deployed in the mineral and alchemical field. Bernard—like other contemporary physicians[36]—thus rejects any full compatibility between mineral remedies and the human organism. Quicksilver may at best be entirely purified of all *immunditia* (uncleanness), but will always "retain intact the characteristic fluidity of Mercury": this fluidity, if desiccated and turned into powder to be made potable later by combining it with water or oils, can become a remedy, but loses its nature and cannot influence a human's radical moisture.[37] Of course, through opportune treatment, various medicines with a mineral basis may be obtained, but Bernard does not believe that treated gold works as an exceptional remedy; it serves no purpose and may in fact cause damage. This is because there is too great an ontological difference between the level of inert simplicity in minerals and in gold and the complexity of the living structure of the organism.[38] He finally declares that such significant qualitative changes in quicksilver, capable of transforming it into a remedy suitable for human intake, are impossible.

The author of the *quaestio* on the *lapis* as a possible remedy against the plague, bases his work on the *Rosarium* by Pseudo-Arnaldus, which is full of praise for the marvelous alchemical medicine capable of rapidly curing all illnesses and in particular of "repelling poison from the heart," as well as restoring youth and prolonging life.[39] He too, however, is well aware of the issue highlighted by Bernard of Treviri regarding the incompatibility between mineral and living forms: indeed, he solves it with original theoretical acumen.

The anonymous *quaestio* is linked to the *Epistola* in its return to and development of the theme of blood.[40] Indeed, this foregrounding could not be otherwise in a work that aims to explore the efficacy of the alchemical *lapis* against the plague, which is here seen as a poison that causes great imbalance in the organism, specifically by corrupting the blood. The author concentrates from the very beginning on two problems: how the properties of gold become communicable and diffusive; and if and how—that is, based on what similarity between mineral and human allowing the transition—these properties exert their action on an individual who is afflicted by the plague.

What is here called *lapis* is the result of the working of the gold, which is the substance of the remedy.[41] Its elements have been treated and recomposed by means of various procedures, through which gold has become *solutum*: its various natures have become *abundantes* (strengthened) but more importantly they are now *aperte* (capable of effusion), "prompte ad comunicandum alteri de virtute sua" (quickly to communicate their virtue—that is, to restore temperamental balance).[42] The golden *lapis* that is created is none other than "aurus in gradibus suis multiplicatus stante proportione que fuit in auro primo" (the gold multiplied in its degrees, being in proportion as it was in the initial gold); it is gold *solutus*, refined and thinned down.

It is this treated gold that must be "thinned," because this is the only way in which it can interact with the organism. In the naturalistic scheme that constitutes the underlying framework of the *quaestio*, gold and human occupy a corresponding position in the stratification of the levels that form the pyramid of natural mixtures (minerals, vegetables, animals). Human and gold, both equally and perfectly balanced, occupy the vertices of the two extremes.[43] It is, however, equally true that, in this equal balance, which lies at the basis of their correspondence, the elements in the human reach the highest degree of subtility, while those of gold reach the maximum level of thickness, or coarseness (*crassities*). Such relative homogeneity—this correspondence in diversity—is the condition for a possible interaction, which can in fact only take place if gold too achieves the highest degree of elemental thinness, without, however, losing its properties or its complexional balance.

Once it has been refined and rendered diffusive, the gold preparation is able to eliminate the poison of the plague that corrupts the blood, albeit following some important precautions.[44] A material assimilation should not be attempted, as if the remedy were almost a digestible food: this would perhaps make the organism permanently incorruptible, but at the cost of an undesirable mineralization. Nor should the medicine be used when the blood is excessively or entirely poisoned: in this case, the maximum imbalance of the plagued blood and the maximum balance of the remedy would be entirely incompatible and adverse to each other. Because of the "collision" this would cause, the gold antidote would eliminate the blood entirely (it is not explained how, whether by hemorrhage or desiccation), the body would become *exhaustum* (depleted), and death would ensue immediately. To avoid the opposite but equally lethal risks of a heavy perpetuity, which would, however, be mineral, or of a lightness so evanescent as to be (literally) bloodless—both of which alternatives are clearly extreme—the golden remedy must be used at the onset of the illness, when the blood is only partly imbalanced; it is only in this phase that it is effective, progressively rectifying the blood by communicating its own balance to it. It will then function as a sort of "positive contagion," ultimately promoting the body's healing.

There are a number of interesting points here, and in particular, again, issues that remain open: among these, the most obvious difficulty concerns the manner in which the golden antidote exerts its action and is administered. Clearly it acts *ex contrario*, though not on the basis of the contraries of natural humors: it is rather on the basis of the contrast between influences—poisonous or salutiferous—which are based on material (indeed, I might say geometrical) contraries: grossness versus subtility, balance versus imbalance. It is specified that the remedy is not digestible, and, in fact, that is must not be digested: nevertheless, its functioning seems also to imply internal contact and action. Clearly the *quaestio* is located at the intersection of multiple points of view on the matter and allows them to overlap with a certain audacity.

In conclusion, these texts, and the other similar ones that have been briefly mentioned, confirm the intersection between alchemy and medicine which was pointed out at the beginning, as well as the effort to integrate the doctrines and problems presented by the two fields. Also visible, however, is a phase of strong uncertainty in scholastic pharmacology. In this situation of epistemological and practical instability, in which exchanges and loans were attempted between different disciplines (a useful, though complex and demanding endeavor), we can see a relative loss of specificity—or rather, of conceptual precision within, and a clear distinction between, the two fields. This comes to light principally in the tendency of key terms to overlap, bordering sometimes on outright interchangeability: as we have seen briefly in the preceding pages, starting from Thomas of Bologna, the terms *lapis*, gold, potable gold, elixir, and *medicina* are often rotated without any distinction. Furthermore, at least in the texts we have examined, the root issues—transferring to the remedy the traditional balance of gold, endowing it with the diffusive dynamism of the elixir, and rendering it capable of being taken in the manner in which potions were customarily taken—are not fully resolved.

Certainly, a process of pharmacological unification and simplification was taking place, exemplified by the search for a unique and universal remedy. This process would be more clearly appreciated if one considered, in addition to potable gold, the fifth essence and aqua vitae, not to mention theriac, which also entered into this circuit and whose virtues and applications, especially in medical texts on the plague, became progressively similar to those of potable gold and the fifth essence.[45] Somewhat paradoxically, however, next to this simplification one finds a process of accumulation. Often in these texts, alongside the hope of discovering a unique remedy suitable for curing all illnesses, there remain the traditional medicaments, multiple and differentiated: the golden remedy is in these cases described almost as an additive, a supplement that boosts their traditional efficacy.[46]

Such a complex and multifaceted situation was probably also the outcome of the therapeutical checkmate inflicted by the plague on scholastic medicine, which created the need to turn to other forms of research—such as alchemy—so as to attempt all possible routes to combat this terrible disease, and to rethink all those certainties that had turned out to be, in practice, so ineffectual. What is certain is that, from the fifteenth century onwards, and taking their cue from an ingredient—gold—whose more than merely mineral value prompted a wealth of symbolic connections and features, various definitions of therapeutic virtues, which were the outcome of a century-long medical tradition, started to form a coordinated whole, and combined with a new and innovative widening of the aims and prospects of alchemy, to offer unprecedented promises of rapid recovery and of long life.

Notes

1. For an overview and general interpretation, see M. Pereira, *Arcana sapienza. L'alchimia dalle origini a Jung* (Rome: new ed. Carocci, 2019); M. Pereira, ed., *Alchimia. I testi della tradizione occidentale* (Milan: Arnoldo Mondadori, 2006); C. Crisciani and M. Pereira, *L'arte del sole e della luna. Alchimia e filosofia nel med ioevo* (Spoleto: Centro italiano di studi sull'alto medioevo, 1996).

2. See n. 9 below.

3. See Christopher of Perugia, *Elucidarius artis transmutatoriae Summa maior*, in *Theatrum chemicum*, ed. by L. Zetzner, 6 vols. (Strasbourg, 1603), 4.195–266.

4. Among the many scholars who have focused on various aspects of the relationship between medicine and alchemy are D. Jacquart, "Médecine et alchimie chez Michel Savonarole," in *Alchimie et philosophie à la Renaissance*, ed. by J. C. Margolin and S. Matton (Paris: J. Vrin, 1993), 109–22; D. Jacquart, *La médecine médiévale dans le cadre parisien* (Paris: Fayard, 1998), esp. chap. 5; M. Pereira, "Medicinal and Alchemical Writings Attributed to Ramon Lull," in *Alchemy and Chemistry in the 16th and 17th Centuries*, ed. by P. Rattansi and A. Clericuzio (Dordrecht: Springer, 1994), 1–15; M. Pereira, "'Mater medicinarum': English Physicians and the Alchemical Elixir in the Fifteenth Century," in *Medicine from the Black Death to the French Disease*, ed. by R. French et al. (Aldershot: Ashgate, 1998), 26–52; M. Pereira, *L'oro dei filosofi. Saggio sulle idee di un alchimista del Trecento* (Spoleto: Centro italiano di studi sull'alto Medioevo, 1992); C. Crisciani, "Medici e alchimia nel secolo XIV: dati e problemi di una ricerca," in *Atti del congresso internazionale su medicina medievale e scuola medica salernitana* (Salerno: Centro di Studi Medicina "Civitas Hippocratica," 1994), 102–18; C. Crisciani, "Il corpo nella tradizione alchemica: teorie, similitudini, immagini," *Micrologus* 1 (1993): 189–233; C. Crisciani, "Alchemy and Medicine in the Middle Ages: Recent Studies, and Projects for Research," *Bulletin de philosophie médiévale* 38 (1996): 9–21; C. Crisciani, "Alchimia e medicina nel medioevo: complessità di un rapporto," in *Forme del sapere medico dal mondo antico al mondo modern*, ed. by C. Crisciani and P. Rossi, *L'arco di Giano. Rivista di "me-*

dical humanities" 40 (2004): 29–38; C. Crisciani, "'Experientia' e 'opus' in medicina ed alchimia: forme e problemi di esperienza nel tardo medioevo," *Quaestio* 4 (2004): 149–73; B. Obrist, "Alchemie und Medizin im 13. Jahrhundert," *Archives internationale d'histoire des sciences* 43 (1993): 210–46; A. Calvet, "Mutations de l'alchimie médicale au XVe siècle: à propos des textes authentiques et apocryphes d'Arnaud de Villeneuve," *Micrologus* 3 (1995): 184–209; finally, the essays in C. Crisciani and A. Paravicini Bagliani, eds., *Alchimia e medicina nel medioevo* (Florence: SISMEL edizioni del Galluzzo, 2003).

5. Pseudo-Lullus, *Testamentum*, ed. by M. Pereira and B. Spaggiari as *Il 'Testamentum' alchemico attribuito a Raimondo Lullo* (Florence: Sismel, 1999), 112, 412; M. Pereira, "L'alchimista come medico perfetto nel 'Testamentum' pseudolulliano," in Crisciani and Paravicini Bagliani, *Alchimia e medicina nel medioevo*, 77–108. Among the various treatises on the action of remedies written by physicians, see, for example, Arnaldus de Villanova, *Tractatus de intentione medicorum*, ed. by M. R. McVaugh (Barcelona: Universidad de Barcelona, 2000), 110–18, tr. 2, chap. 2, as well as the introduction by McVaugh, 155–62. See also the observations by the fourteenth-century physician Petrus Bonus in *Pretiosa margarita novella*, in *Bibliotheca chemica curiosa*, ed. by J. J. Manget, 2 vols. (Geneva, 1702), 2.27A.

6. E. Darmstaedter, "Per la storia dell'oro potabile," *Archeion* 5 (1925): 251–71; R. Halleux, "L'oro potabile," *Kos* 12 (1985): 49–64; J. Proust, "L''aurum potabile' au temps de la Renaissance," in *L'or au temps de la Renaissance. Du mythe* à *l'économie*, ed. by M. T. Jones-Davies (Paris: Centre de recherches sur la Renaissance, 1978), 15–26; S. Mahadissan, "The Earliest History of Gold in China as Drug of Longevity," *Hamdard* 23 (1980): 41–55, and 24 (1981): 49–55; O. Novotny, "De auro potabili," *Salzburger Beiträge zur Paracelsusforschung* 7 (1967): 13–22; C. Crisciani, "Oro potabile tra alchimia e medicina: due testi in tempo di peste," in *Atti del VII Convegno nazionale di Storia e fondamenti della chimica*, ed. by F. Calascibetta (Rome: Accademia Nazionale delle Scienze detta dei XL, 1997), 83–93; C. Crisciani and M. Pereira, "Black Death and Golden Remedies: Some Remarks on Alchemy and the Plague," in *The Regulation of Evil: Social and Cultural Attitudes to Epidemics in the Late Middle Ages*, ed. by A. Paravicini Bagliani and F. Santi (Florence: Sismel Edizioni del Galluzzo, 1998), 7–39; C. Ferragud and J. R. Bertomeu Sanchez, "Mirades sobra l'alquimia en la Valencia baixmedieval: un proces judicial sobre la producciò de l'or potable (1440–1445)," *Afers* 82 (2015): 421–66; M. Lopez Perez, *Historia del oro potable. La búsqueda alquímica de la vida eterna* (Valladolid: Glyphos, 2017).

7. *Liber Canonis Avicenne* (Venice, 1507; reprinted Hildesheim, 1964), 96ra: "De auro"; *Libellus Avicenne de viribus cordis* (published with the preceding text), 594ra.

8. Pseudo-Lullus, *Testamentum*; see also M. Pereira, "Teorie dell'elixir nell'alchimia latina medievale," *Micrologus* 3 (1995): 103–48; M. Pereira, "Un tesoro inestimabile: elixir e 'prolongatio vitae' nell'alchimia del Trecento," *Micrologus* 1 (1993): 161–87; M. Pereira, "Projecting Perfection: Remarks on the Origin of the 'Alchemy of the Elixir'," *Micrologus* 24 (2016): 73–93. Along with the *Testamentum*, this line is developed by the texts of the Pseudo-Arnaldian corpus, first by the *Rosarium*; in addition to the many studies which A. Calvet has devoted to 'Arnaldian' alchemy, see his edition of "Le 'De vita philosophorum' du pseudo-Arnaud de Villeneuve," *Chrysopoeia* 4 (1990–91): 35–79, and that of *Le Rosier alchimique de Montpellier. Lo Rosari* (Paris: Presses de l'université de Paris-Sorbonne, 1997); more recently, see A. Calvet, *Les oeuvres alchimiques attribuées à Arnaud de Villeneuve* (Paris: SEHA, 2011).

9. Pseudo-Roger Bacon, *De retardatione accidentium senectutis*, ed. by A. G. Little and E. Withington, *Opera hactenus inedita Rogeri Baconi* vol. 9 (Oxford: Oxford University Press, 1928), 1–83, 120–43; Calvet, "Le 'De vita philosophorum'"; Pseudo-Arnaldus de Villanova, *De conservanda iuventute et retardanda senectute*, in *Arnaldi Villanovani Opera Omnia* (Basel, 1585), 813–38. Of fundamental importance in clarifying the intertwining and attributions of some of these works, and especially in rejecting the attribution to Bacon of the short treatises of prolongevity (despite the undoubted and original interest Bacon took in this issue in works where his authorship is uncontested) are the essays by A. Paravicini Bagliani, "Ruggero Bacone, Bonifacio VIII e la teoria della 'prolongatio vitae'" and "Il mito della 'prolongatio vitae' e la corte pontificia del Duecento: il 'De retardatione accidentium senectutis'," in *Medicina e scienze della natura alla corte dei Papi nel Duecento* (Spoleto: Centro italiano di studi sull'alto Medioevo, 1991), 281–361; A. Paravicini Bagliani, "Bacone e l'alchimia della lunga vita," in Crisciani and Paravicini Bagliani, *Alchimia e medicina nel medioevo*, 33–54. See also Pereira, "Un tesoro inestimabile"; F. M. Getz, "To Prolong Life and Promote Health: Baconian Alchemy and Pharmacy in the English Learned Tradition," in *Health, Disease, and Healing in Medieval Culture*, ed. by S. Campbell, B. Hall, and D. Klausner (New York: St Martin's Press, 1992), 135–45; C. Crisciani, "Elixir di lunga vita (secoli XIII–XIV)," in *Elisir mercuriali e immortalità. Capitoli per una storia dell'alchimia nell'Eurasia antica*, ed. by A. Roselli, G. Orofino, and A. Sannino, *Aion* 36 (2014): 81–97; C. Crisciani, "Il 'lignum vite' e i suoi frutti," in *Le monde végétal. Médecine, botanique, symbolique*, ed. by A. Paravicini Bagliani (Florence: SISMEL, 2009), 173–203; C. Crisciani, "Prolungamento della vita: medicina e teologia (secoli XIII e XIV)," in *Médecine et religion. Collaborations, compétitions, conflits (XIIe–XXe siècles)*, ed. by M. P. Donato et al. (Rome: École française de Rome, 2013), 87–113; C. Crisciani, "Death as a Destiny and the Hope of Long Life: The Latin Middle Ages," in *Longevity and Immortality: Europe–Islam–Asia*, *Micrologus* 26 (2018): 5–25.

10. Pseudo-Roger Bacon, *De retardatione*, 45–46; Roger Bacon, *Opus majus*, 209–10; Roger Bacon, *Liber sex scientiarum*, in *Opera Hactenus inedita Rogeri Baconi* vol. 9, 182; in the *Tractatus brevis et utilis* (the prologue to his glossed redaction of the *Secretum secretorum*, ed. R. Steele and A. S. Fulton, *Opera hactenus inedita Rogeri Baconi* vol. 5 (Oxford: Clarendon, 1920)), 24, Bacon confirms that "consimilis effectus possunt fieri unguenta et pociones."

11. Calvet, "Le 'De vita philosophorum'", 72: "Et multi modernorum, specialiter de prelatis faciunt bulire pessias auri in eorum coquina. Et alii recipiunt in panniculis, cum electuariis. Et alii cum limatura, sicut in confectione que dicitur dyacameron...Et quidam utitur tenendo frusta auri in ore et salivam dicti auri deglutiunt. Et quidam alii convertuntur in aquam potabilem, et sufficit modica quantitas in auro, et est preservat<iv>um sanitatis et prolongativum generationis vite...; see also 74, on cardinal "Dominus Hugo" and the "cardinalis de Toleto," who used it with great benefit (cf. Paravicini Bagliani, "Medicina e scienze della natura alla corte di Bonifacio VIII," in *Medicina e scienze*, 263–64 and passim).

12. Pseudo-Roger Bacon, *De retardatione*, 40.

13. "Calcinando et solvendo ut possit uti eo in cibis et potibus quatinus possit converti in naturam humanam." Bacon, *Liber sex scientiarum*, 183; Bacon, *Tractatus brevis et utilis*, 23.

14. I have used the manuscript Paris, Bibliothèque nationale de France, MS lat. 11201, fols. 1r–13v (this should be compared with Cambridge, Corpus Christi College, MS 99, fols. 195–213). The title, in a later hand, is "Epistola magistri Thome de Bononia ad Bernardum Trevirensem de lapide philosophico."

15. "Quaestio an lapis philosophicus valeat contra pestem," in Zetzner, *Theatrum chemicum*, 3.186–87.

16. "Tractatus de investigatione auri potabilis editus a quodam solemni medico," Bologna, Biblioteca universitaria, MS lat. 104 (Frati, no. 138), fols. 271r–283v; see also C. Crisciani, "Solemnis medicus: suggerimenti e farmaci per una sana e lunga vita," in *Scientia, fides, theologia. Studi in onore di Gianfranco Fioravanti*, ed. by S. Perfetti (Pisa: Edizioni ETS, 2011), 402–26 (with partial edition of the text).

17. "Liber de lapide philosophorum et de auro potabili," Bologna, Biblioteca universitaria, MS lat. 104 (Frati, no. 138), fols. 245r–253v: see C. Crisciani, *Il papa e l'alchimia. Felice V, Guglielmo Fabri e l'elixir* (Rome: Viella, 2002), with an edition of the text by Fabri. The Bolognese miscellaneous codex, belonging to the Fondo Caprara, contains various texts on potable gold: in addition to the two I have mentioned here, there are a recipe for potable gold by the physician Albini di Moncalieri (fol. 310r), published by K. Sudhoff, "Eine Herstellungseinwesung für 'Aurum potabile' und 'Quinta essentia' von dem herzoglichen Leibartze Albini di Moncalieri (14. Jahrhundert)," *Archiv für die Geschichte der Naturwissenschaften und der Technik* 5 (1914): 198–201; and a "Practica de auro potabili," fols. 254r–255v. On the importance of the Fondo Caprara for scholars of alchemy, see D. Kahn, "Le fonds Caprara de manuscrits alchimiques de la Bibliothèque universitaire de Bologne," *Scriptorium* 1 (1994): 62–110.

18. Bernard of Treviso, *Responsio*, in Manget, *Bibliotheca chemica curiosa*, 2.399–408; see also D. Kahn, "Recherches sur le 'Livre' attribué au prétendu Bernard le Trévisan (fin du XV siècle)," in Crisciani and Paravicini Bagliani, *Alchimia e medicina nel medioevo*, 265–336.

19. C. Crisciani, "Alchimia, alchimisti e corti nel tardo medioevo: documenti e racconti," *Micrologus* 16 (2008): 433–57.

20. In addition to Aristotle (*Meteorologica*, *De generatione*, *De morte et vita*, *De anima*, *Ethica*, *Physica*, and *Rhetorica ad Alexandrum*), he uses a variety of medical and scientific authors: Hippocrates, Galen, Avicenna, Averroes's *Colliget*, Isaac's *De sustentatione memorie*, Constantine's *Pantegni*, Arnaldus de Villanova, Maino de' Maineri, al-Kindi, and Avenzoar.

21. C. Crisciani, "Alchimia, magia e patronage: Giovanni 'Mercurio' da Correggio," in *Società natura storia. Studi in onore di Lorenzo Calabi*, ed. by A. Civello (Pisa: ETS, 2015), 63–79 (which contains a vast bibliography of previous studies).

22. See Thomas of Bolognia, *Epistola*, fol. 6r–v: "Accidit quod regi execellentissimo Frantie illustrimisque principibus nec non duci Burgundie ac domino duci Bituric ob amoris causam aliquod munus medicinale miseram per meos legatos, quod in propriis corporibus suis ipsi mei legati examinaverunt; ... Quare vobis, ut secretario nature, refero medicinam propter reclamare scandalla mihi facta pro caritate, quoniam, ve mihi, asserunt aliter quam commisi. Medicina est probata et aliquid sinistre medicine est reputatum; et cum principes laici sint qui estimant de illo, sive bonum sive malum, ignoro ne pro caritate suscipiam odium et pro munere vituperium. Quare vobis, ut intimo amico meo, plenius de hac medicina declarabo ut ipsis et ceteris vestra reverentia pertinentius poterit respondere." Thomas hopes that his friend will conduct experiments on the preparation and that he will give him his considerations and scientific opinion; he also asks (fol. 13r) for concrete support: "Quamobrem supplico reverencie vestre quod dominum metuendum velitis accedere et ex hiis intencionem meam declarare michique rescribere quid responsi vobis fuerit allatum." Regarding the test which has been carried out on his remedy, Thomas fears precisely "de examine impertinenti, quod tamen credo sine scitu principis esse factum" (fol. 12v): his is not a preparation to transmute metals, "cum solum medicina sit ablata ad egrorum corporum reformationem et veneni expulsionem, et non ad ignis probam."

23. See ibid., fol. 6v: "Est enim medicina facta de substantia auri processu philosophico, quamvis occulte et propter malos occultando, ne indigni ad hoc speciale munus Dei et opus magnum in arte nature perveneant."

24. See ibid., fols. 8r–9r.

25. "Nihil aliud est quam aurum in gradibus suis multiplicatus stante eadem proportione que erat auri primi." Ibid., fol. 9r.

26. Ibid., fol. 8r: "sic mercurius animatus post corporis sui solutionem alias tenet qualitates"; fol. 9v: "et alius facit in operibus medicine et in corporibus humanis seu sensitivis et vegetatitivis quam crudus fecit ante."

27. Ibid., fol. 9r: "et sicut necesse est in corporibus sensitivorum esse sanguinem continue intereuntem corpus in quo vivificat, sic necesse in hac medicina mercurium animatum."

28. Ibid., fol. 7v.

29. Ibid., fols. 4v–5r: the remedy offers "sapientiam, diuturnitatem, sanitatem vite, depositionem senii, inventionem iuventutis et corpus incolume reservatum"; (fol. 5r): "hec medicina pre ceteris medicinis mundi efficacissima, nobilissima, quam non excedit quicquam" [through its] "adequata natura ideoque adeguat discoequatum, reducit ad bonam compositionem, omne superfluum inde reiciendo," since it is "excitativa bona vivificat in proportione omne mortuum, cum vita vegetabilis non sit aliud quam actio proportionalium elementorum"; fol. 11r: "hoc medicinale aurum nature generatum per artis administrationem habet vim et virtutem dupplicis medicine, scilicet expulsive et restaurative, quoniam quicquid in agentibus invenit vegetabilium et sesitivorum superflui ... reicit immediate et in presenti actum provocat proportionatum actumque renovat suspensum"; fol. 12r: "ipsa de senio habet reficere in humanis, volente deo, et per ipsam medicinaliter vita potest produci ultra actum naturaliter susceptum."

30. Ibid., fol. 12r.

31. For these differences from the *vegetales medicine de preparatione apothecali*, see ibid., fol. 11v: "Ista autem medicina non sic, quia evaporabilis non est eius commistio, sed solida...et a digestione nequit separari vel dissipari, manens sicut novus de iure excitans motum in corporibus et vivificans elementa."

32. "Miraculum in experimentis nature ... non quod sit deus, sed ut in similitudine dicatur in natura." Ibid., fol. 5r.

33. "Superflua reiciendo, ut sunt peccata et vitia, et absencia adimplendo, ut coruptibilem incoruptibilem, mortale immortale reformando." Ibid., fol. 2r.

34. Bernard of Treviso, *Responsio*, 405–6.

35. Ibid., 2.406 and passim.

36. Antonio Guainieri (a physician at the court of the Savoia) and Michele Savonarola (a physician at the court of the Estensi) are among these, although they were interested in alchemical texts and remedies and had a good knowledge of alchemical processes. See M. Savonarola, *Libellus de aqua ardenti*, in *I trattati in volgare della peste e dell'acqua ardente*, ed. by L. Belloni (Milan: Tip. di Stucchi, 1953);

D. Jacquart, "Theory, Everyday Practice and Three Fifteenth-Century Physicians," *Osiris*, 2nd ser., 6 (1990): 140–60; Jacquart, "Médecine et alchimie chez Michel Savonarole."

37. *Responsio*, 2.406, 408: "manente illaesa semper Mercurii fluxibilitate, seu humido radicali."

38. Ibid., 406a: "Lapis enim noster non habet formam formabilem, sed tantum habet formam formatam...: propterea quod homogeneus est. Corpus vero humanum et aliorum sensitivorum, est heterogeneum. Quia os, caro, sanguis, medulla, crines et ungues in ipso differenter cognoscuntur. Quod aliter est in auro, in quo quidquid inest, unicae speciei reperitur."

39. The long quotation is from Pseudo-Arnaldus, *Rosarium* (*Le Rosier alchimique*, 76A). The *Quaestio* then develops, as a sort of commentary to the text, three specific themes derived from these praises and from the special qualities of the *lapis*: its possible function as an antidote for the plague, its rejuvenating power, and its therapeutic function against "all diseases." In a number of places the *Quaestio* is conspicuously similar to Thomas' *Epistola*, though it is greatly superior in terms of cogency and argumentative clarity.

40. These reflections may usefully be compared not just with the analyses contained in medical writings on the plague, but also with the discussions on the properties of blood examined by Jacquart, *La médecine médiévale*, esp. 333–71.

41. "Quaestio an lapis philosophicus valeat contra pestem," 182: "quia aurum quod est materia lapidis philosophici"; the *lapis philosophicus* "non est compositus de sanguine humano, sed de purissima auri substantia."

42. Thus treated, gold becomes "lapis philosophicus ubi omnes naturae sunt apertae et abundantes, promptaeque ad communicandum. ... Sed nuc oritur dubium, an aurum existens in crassitie sua insolutum, cum sit in qualitatum primarum complexione omnino conforme humanae complexioni, expellat venenum, sicut facit lapis philosophicus? Et dico quod non, quia naturae non sunt in eo aperte, sed clausae: et ideo non emittit virtutem suam, sicut facit philosophicus lapis, in quo sunt naturae apertae ac abundantes ad communicandum alteri de virtute sua" (ibid., 3.183).

43. For the *impositiones,* see ibid., 182–83; for the comparisons between *complexiones*, see 183: "sciendum est, quod auri complexio, et temperati ad pondus hominis complexio in nullo differunt, quoad proportionem qualitatum primarum elementorum, sed quoad crassitiem et subtilitatem elementorum differunt permaxime"; 182: "notandum quod corpus humanum est subtilissimis elementis compositus ... et est complexio eius anatica seu aequalis, sub tamen certa latitudine"; also 186–87.

44. Ibid., 182.

45. On medical texts on the plague I refer the reader to the collection of miscellaneous texts of various geographical provenances, collected and edited by K. Sudhoff under the title "Pestschriften aus den ersten 150 Jahren nach der Epidemie des 'Schwarzen Todes, 1348," and published in *Archiv für Geschichte der Medizin* 2–17 (1909–25). New editions of these texts are ongoing, and a vast interdisciplinary debate on the plague has developed, focusing on its causes and various types of consequences: social, epistemological, doctrinal (on this issue, see the recent important work by Monica Green.

46. This is the case, for example, at the end of the treatise by the "Solemnis medicus."

Bibliography

Arnaldus de Villanova. *Tractatus de intentione medicorum*. Edited by M. R. McVaugh. Barcelona: Universidad de Barcelona, 2000.

Bacon, R. *Liber sex scientiarum*. Edited by A. G. Little and E. Withington. In *Opera hactenus inedita Rogeri Baconi* vol. 9. Oxford: Oxford University Press, 1928.

Bacon, R. *Opus majus*. Edited by Bridges J. H., 3 vols., London, 1900.

Bacon, R. *Tractatus brevis et utilis*. In *Opera hactenus inedita Rogeri Baconi* vol. 5. Edited by R. Steele and A. S. Fulton. Oxford: Clarendon, 1920.

Bernard of Treviso, *Responsio*. In *Bibliotheca chemica curiosa*, edited by J. J. Manget, 2.399–408. 2 vols. Genevae, 1702.

Calvet, A., "Le 'De vita philosophorum' du pseudo-Arnaud de Villeneuve." *Chrysopoeia* 4 (1990–91): 35–79

Calvet, A. "Mutations de l'alchimie médicale au XVe siècle: à propos des textes authentiques et apocryphes d'Arnaud de Villeneuve." *Micrologus* 3 (1995): 184–209.

Calvet, A. *Les oeuvres alchimiques attribuées à Arnaud de Villeneuve*. Paris: SEHA, 2011.

Calvet, A., ed. *Le Rosier alchimique de Montpellier. Lo Rosari*. Paris: Presses de l'université de Paris-Sorbonne, 1997.

Christopher of Perugia. *Elucidarius artis transmutatoriae Summa maior*. In *Theatrum chemicum*, edited by L. Zetzner, 4.195–266. 6 vols. Strasbourg, 1603.

Crisciani, C. "Alchemy and Medicine in the Middle Ages: Recent Studies, and Projects for Research." *Bulletin de philosophie médiévale* 38 (1996): 9–21.

Crisciani, C. "Alchimia, alchimisti e corti nel tardo medioevo: documenti e racconti." *Micrologus* 16 (2008): 433–57.

Crisciani, C. "Alchimia e medicina nel medioevo: complessità di un rapporto." In *Forme del sapere medico dal mondo antico al mondo moderno*, edited by C. Crisciani and P. Rossi, *L'arco di Giano. Rivista di "medical humanities"* 40 (2004): 29–38.

Crisciani, C. "Alchimia, magia e patronage: Giovanni 'Mercurio' da Correggio." In *Società natura storia. Studi in onore di Lorenzo Calabi*, edited by A. Civello, 63–79. Pisa: ETS, 2015.

Crisciani, C. "Il corpo nella tradizione alchemica: teorie, similitudini, immagini." *Micrologus* 1 (1993): 189–233.

Crisciani, C. "Death as a Destiny and the Hope of Long Life: The Latin Middle Ages." In *Longevity and Immortality: Europe–Islam–Asia*, *Micrologus* 26 (2018): 5–25.

Crisciani, C. "Elixir di lunga vita (secoli XIII–XIV)." In *Elisir mercuriali e immortalità. Capitoli per una storia dell'alchimia nell'Eurasia antica*, edited by A. Roselli, G. Orofino, and A. Sannino, *Aion* 36 (2014): 81–97.

Crisciani, C. "'Experientia' e 'opus' in medicina ed alchimia: forme e problemi di esperienza nel tardo medioevo." *Quaestio* 4 (2004): 149–73.

Crisciani, C. "Il 'lignum vite' e i suoi frutti." In *Le monde végétal. Médecine, botanique, symbolique*, edited by A. Paravicini Bagliani, 173–203. Florence: SISMEL, 2009.

Crisciani, C. "Medici e alchimia nel secolo XIV: dati e problemi di una ricerca." In *Atti del congresso internazionale su medicina medievale e scuola medica salernitana*, 102–18. Salerno: Centro di Studi Medicina "Civitas Hippocratica," 1994.

Crisciani, C. "Oro potabile tra alchimia e medicina: due testi in tempo di peste." In *Atti del VII Convegno nazionale di Storia e fondamenti della chimica*, edited by F. Calascibetta, 83–93. Rome: Accademia Nazionale delle Scienze detta dei XL, 1997.

Crisciani, C. *Il papa e l'alchimia. Felice V, Guglielmo Fabri e l'elixir*. Rome: Viella, 2002.

Crisciani, C. "Prolungamento della vita: medicina e teologia (secoli XIII e XIV)." In *Médecine et religion. Collaborations, compétitions, conflits (XIIe–XXe siècles)*, edited by M. P. Donato, L. Berlivet, S. Cabibbo, R. Michetti, and M. Nicoud, 87–113. Rome: École française de Rome, 2013.

Crisciani, C. "Solemnis medicus: suggerimenti e farmaci per una sana e lunga vita." In *Scientia, fides, theologia. Studi in onore di Gianfranco Fioravanti*, edited by S. Perfetti (Pisa: Edizioni ETS, 2011), 402–26 (with partial edition of the text).

Crisciani, C., and A. Paravicini Bagliani, eds. *Alchimia e medicina nel medioevo*. Florence: SISMEL edi-

zioni del Galluzzo, 2003.
Crisciani, C., and M. Pereira. *L'arte del sole e della luna. Alchimia e filosofia nel medioevo*. Spoleto: Centro italiano di studi sull'alto medioevo, 1996.
Crisciani, C., and M. Pereira. "Black Death and Golden Remedies: Some Remarks on Alchemy and the Plague." In *The Regulation of Evil: Social and Cultural Attitudes to Epidemics in the Late Middle Ages*, edited by A. Paravicini Bagliani and F. Santi, 7–39. Florence: Sismel Edizioni del Galluzzo, 1998.
Darmstaedter, E. "Per la storia dell'oro potabile." *Archeion* 5 (1925): 251–71.
Ferragud, C., and J. R. Bertomeu Sanchez. "Mirades sobra l'alquimia en la Valencia baixmedieval: un proces judicial sobre la producciò de l'or potable (1440–1445)." *Afers* 82 (2015): 421–66.
Getz, F. M. "To Prolong Life and Promote Health: Baconian Alchemy and Pharmacy in the English Learned Tradition." In *Health, Disease, and Healing in Medieval Culture*, edited by S. Campbell, B. Hall, and D. Klausner, 135–45. New York: St Martin's Press, 1992.
Halleux, R. "L'oro potabile." *Kos* 12 (1985): 49–64.
Jacquart, D. "Médecine et alchimie chez Michel Savonarole." In *Alchimie et philosophie à la Renaissance*, edited by J. C. Margolin and S. Matton, 109–22. Paris: J. Vrin, 1993.
Jacquart, D. *La médecine médiévale dans le cadre parisien*. Paris: Fayard, 1998.
Jacquart, D. "Theory, Everyday Practice and Three Fifteenth-Century Physicians." *Osiris*, 2nd ser., 6 (1990): 140–60.
Kahn, D. "Le fonds Caprara de manuscrits alchimiques de la Bibliothèque universitaire de Bologne." *Scriptorium* 1 (1994): 62–110.
Kahn, D. "Recherches sur le 'Livre' attribué au prétendu Bernard le Trévisan (fin du XV siècle)." In *Alchimia e medicina nel medioevo*, edited by C. Crisciani and A. Paravicini Bagliani, 265–336. Florence: SISMEL edizioni del Galluzzo, 2003.
Libellus Avicenne de viribus cordis. Venice, 1507; reprinted Hildesheim, 1964.
Liber Canonis Avicenne. Venice, 1507; reprinted Hildesheim, 1964.
"Liber de lapide philosophorum et de auro potabili." Bologna, Biblioteca universitaria, MS lat. 104 (Frati, no. 138), fols. 245r–253v
Lopez Perez, M. *Historia del oro potable. La búsqueda alquímica de la vida eterna*. Valladolid: Glyphos, 2017.
Mahadissan, S. "The Earliest History of Gold in China as Drug of Longevity." *Hamdard* 23 (1980): 41–55, and 24 (1981): 49–55.
Novotny, O. "De auro potabili." *Salzburger Beiträge zur Paracelsusforschung* 7 (1967): 13–22.
Obrist, B. "Alchemie und Medizin im 13. Jahrhundert." *Archives internationale d'histoire des sciences* 43 (1993): 210–46.
Paravicini Bagliani, A. "Bacone e l'alchimia della lunga vita." In *Alchimia e medicina nel medioevo*, edited by C. Crisciani and A. Paravicini Bagliani, 33–54. Florence: SISMEL edizioni del Galluzzo, 2003.
Paravicini, Bagliani, A. "Il mito della 'prolongatio vitae' e la corte pontificia del Duecento: il 'De retardatione accidentium senectutis'." In *Medicina e scienze della natura alla corte dei Papi nel Duecento*, 281–326. Spoleto: Centro italiano di studi sull'alto Medioevo, 1991.
Paravicini Bagliani, A. "Ruggero Bacone, Bonifacio VIII e la teoria della 'prolongatio vitae'." In *Medicina e scienze della natura alla corte dei Papi nel Duecento*, 327–61. Spoleto: Centro italiano di studi sull'alto Medioevo, 1991.
Pereira, M. ed. *Alchimia. I testi della tradizione occidentale* (Milan: Arnoldo Mondadori, 2006.
Pereira, M. "L'alchimista come medico perfetto nel 'Testamentum' pseudolulliano." In *Alchimia e medicina nel medioevo*, edited by C. Crisciani and A. Paravicini Bagliani, 77–108. Florence: SISMEL edizioni del Galluzzo, 2003.
Pereira, M. *Arcana sapienza. L'alchimia dalle origini a Jung*. Rome: Carocci, 2019.
Pereira, M. "'Mater medicinarum': English Physicians and the Alchemical Elixir in the Fifteenth Century." In *Medicine from the Black Death to the French Disease*, edited by R. French, J. Arrizabalaga, A. Cunningham, and L. García-Ballester, 26–52. Aldershot: Ashgate, 1998.
Pereira, M. "Medicinal and Alchemical Writings Attributed to Ramon Lull." In *Alchemy and Chemistry in the 16th and 17th Centuries*, edited by P. Rattansi and A. Clericuzio, 1–15. Dordrecht: Springer, 1994.
Pereira, M. *L'oro dei filosofi. Saggio sulle idee di un alchimista del Trecento*. Spoleto: Centro italiano di

studi sull'alto Medioevo, 1992
Pereira, M. "Projecting Perfection: Remarks on the Origin of the 'Alchemy of the Elixir'." *Micrologus* 24 (2016): 73–93.
Pereira, M. "Teorie dell'elixir nell'alchimia latina medievale." *Micrologus* 3 (1995): 103–48.
Pereira, M. "Un tesoro inestimabile: elixir e 'prolongatio vitae' nell'alchimia del Trecento." *Micrologus* 1 (1993): 161–87
Pereira, M., and B. Spaggiari, eds. *Il 'Testamentum' alchemico attribuito a Raimondo Lullo*. Florence: Sismel, 1999.
Petrus Bonus, *Pretiosa margarita novella*. In *Bibliotheca chemica curiosa*, edited by J. J. Manget. 2 vols. Genevae, 1702.
"Practica de auro potabili." Bologna, Biblioteca universitaria, MS lat. 104 (Frati, no. 138), fols. 254r–255v.
Proust, J. "L''aurum potabile' au temps de la Renaissance." In *L'or au temps de la Renaissance. Du mythe* à *l'économie*, edited by M. T. Jones-Davies, 15–26. Paris: Centre de recherches sur la Renaissance, 1978.
Pseudo-Arnaldus de Villanova. *De conservanda iuventute et retardanda senectute*. In *Arnaldi Villanovani Opera Omnia*, 813–38. Basel, 1585.
Pseudo-Roger Bacon. *De retardatione accidentium senectutis*. In *Opera hactenus inedita Rogeri Baconi* vol. 9. Edited by A. G. Little and E. Withington. Oxford: Oxford University Press, 1928.
"Quaestio an lapis philosophicus valeat contra pestem." In *Theatrum chemicum*, edited by L. Zetzner, 3.181–87. 6 vols. Strasbourg, 1603.
Savonarola, M. *Libellus de aqua ardenti*. In *I trattati in volgare della peste e dell'acqua ardente*, edited by L. Belloni. Milan: Tip. di Stucchi, 1953.
Sudhoff, K. "Eine Herstellungseinwesung für 'Aurum potabile' und 'Quinta essentia' von dem herzoglichen Leibartze Albini di Moncalieri (14. Jahrhundert)." *Archiv für die Geschichte der Naturwissenschaften und der Technik* 5 (1914): 198–201.
Sudhoff, K. "Pestschriften aus den ersten 150 Jahren nach der Epidemie des 'Schwarzen Todes, 1348." *Archiv für Geschichte der Medizin* 2–17 (1909–25).
Thomas of Bologna. "Epistola magistri Thome de Bononia ad Bernardum Trevirensem de lapide philosophico." Paris, Bibliothèque nationale de France, MS lat. 11201, fols. 1r–13v.
"Tractatus de investigatione auri potabilis editus a quodam solemni medico." Bologna, Biblioteca universitaria, MS lat. 104 (Frati, no. 138), fols. 271r–283v.

El Dorado: God's Accursed Gift to America

Thomas B.F. Cummins

> They [the Tainos] beat the gold into thin sheets ... because for them it has no value (*riqueza*) except for its beautiful appearance.
> (*Carta de Diego Álvarez Chanca*, 1495[1])

> It is his [Philip II's] Indian Golde that indaungereth and disturbeth all the nations of Europe.
> (Walter Raleigh, *The Discoverie of ... Guiana*[2])

"El Dorado" is a phrase born in America that needs no translation into almost any language, yet it stands for so many different things both then and now, including a Cadillac and an airport. The phrase originates in the imagining of America as a gilded paradise.[3] In Christopher Columbus's Fourth Letter of 1503, he wrote:

> Genoese, Venetians and all who have pearls, precious stones and other things of value, all carry them to the end of the world in order to exchange them, to turn them into gold. Gold is most excellent. Gold constitutes treasure, and he who has it may do what he will in the world, and may so attain as to bring souls to Paradise.[4]

Karl Marx would later cite this passage in *Capital*, writing: "Gold is a wonderful thing. Whoever possesses it is lord of all he wants. By means of gold one can even get into Paradise." He goes on to say that "Since gold does not disclose what has been transformed into it, everything, commodity or not, is convertible into gold. Everything becomes saleable and buyable. ... Not even are the bones of saints, and still less are more delicate res sacrosante, extra commercium hominum able to withstand this alchemy."[5]

In a footnote Marx cites, in an adulterated form, from Shakespeare's *Timon of Athens*, in which gold rather than vegetable roots is discovered by Timon,

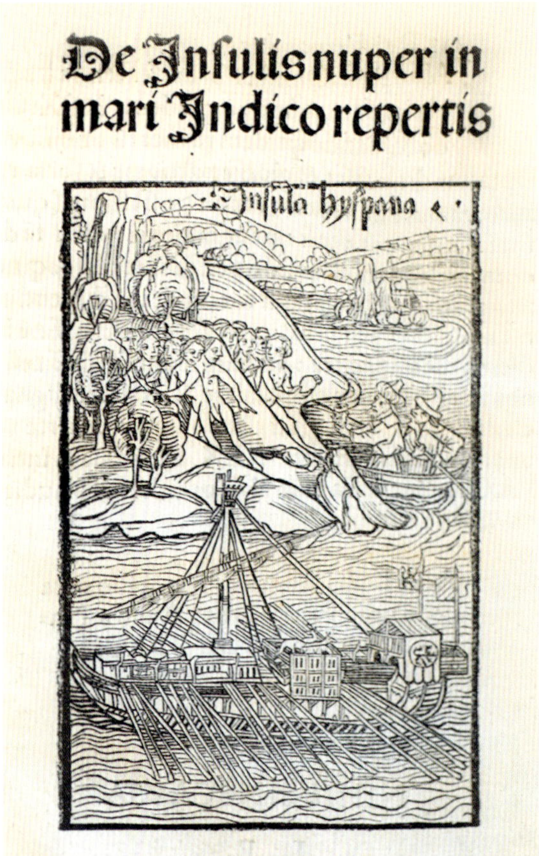

Fig. 1. Haintz Narr Master, frontispiece to Christopher Columbus, *Epistola de insulis nuper inventis* (Basel, 1493). Cambridge, MA, Harvard University, Houghton Library

who declares how gold can make "black white, foul fair, Wrong right; base noble; old young; coward valiant. He then turns to the dark side of gold, calling it "This yellow slave" and "common whore of mankind" that "Will knit and break religions, bless the accursed, / Make the hoar leprosy adored, place thieves / And give them title, knee and approbation / With senators on the bench.[6]" In citing Shakespeare, Marx again takes us back to the sixteenth-century and a "Golden Age" as it was called in Spain and England in terms of their literature and the arts.[7] But, more importantly, the alchemy of gold to which Marx refers is palpable in these sixteenth-century texts and images as the metal became abundant, leading to a new reality in terms of the discovery of the "New World" and its place in the world's economy and imagination. This is because the gold and silver coming from America poured into the world economy, fueling not only trade, art, and imagination but also horrific acts of inhumanity, and thereby "blessed the accursed" whether they desired such blessings or not. Or, to cite Raleigh, "Indian Golde ... indaungereth and disturbeth all the nations of Europe."

Gold was the protagonist in the very first images of America. It appears as the catalyst of exchange in the frontispieces of the different editions of Christopher Columbus's 1493 letter, which are the only woodcut images that illustrate the text (except for one edition).[8] The frontispieces are all essentially the same and depict the narrative moment when the admiral and his men first come ashore (fig. 1). The Basel 1493 edition is the most direct illustration of the first meeting. Here one sees immediately the first instant of interaction: it is an image of engagement and dread, a frozen historical moment of initial suspense. Some of the natives flee from the Spaniards while others approach Columbus and his men, who offer glass beads, mirrors, and other things in exchange for gold, which is presumably represented in the orb that that the leading Taino holds. It is an exchange in which the "true" value of gold is something that the natives do not understand, as Diego Chanca's letter cited above, directly states.[9]

Theodor de Bry, in the fourth part of his series of great voyages (*Americae pars quarta*), depicts in the frontispiece of the volume the three ships of Columbus sailing into the idolatrous paradise of the New World, represented by a mountain populated with naked or near-naked Tainos who climb up the mountainsides toward a demonic figure seated within an alcove at the summit (fig. 2a). We see only the stern of the closest ship as it passes through the mountain, such that the reader/viewer is also drawn into the scene and therefore into the content of the book itself as they take the imaginary text/image journey. This, of course, is the intent of sixteenth-century frontispieces (termed *portada* or "doorway" in Spanish), which metaphorically lead the viewer/reader into the substance of the book, but here they also share in the discovery of America and the entrance into this wholly unknown world of riches.[10]

In plate IX of the same work, based on Girolamo Benzoni's text, one sees Columbus's arrival on the shore of America. De Bry basically repeats the theme of the first images of Columbus's letter, but he narrativizes these frontispieces by conflating several passages from the letter (fig. 2b). The Taino are depicted in the foreground as they come to greet Columbus, carrying objects of gold to offer to the explorer and his crew. A cross is being raised in the middle ground. In the background, naked natives flee the encroachment of other Spaniards, just as shown in the foreground of *Epistola de insulis* (see fig. 1). De Bry's image economically captures Columbus's text and the intertwining of gold, religion, and paradise. The objects that the Tainos offer to Columbus are European-style necklaces and vessels, thus ingrepresent the idea of golden luxury as cast by European goldsmiths. These forms are an index of wealth that will be used again, as we shall see, to convey the great ransom paid by the Inca leader Atahualpa, after being taken prisoner in Cajamarca by Pizarro and his men.

As Columbus and Chanca wrote, the Taino did not appreciate the "true" value of gold, and they traded it for "trinkets" of little "true" value, especially glass beads, which the Spaniards carried in anticipation of such an exchange. Such images as those of de Bry fired the European imagination of the wealth to be had for the asking in America. For the Taino, however, the value of scarcity was not in the gold but in beads and in how these beads and glass could be used or better transformed into valued material to create and enhance the beauty and

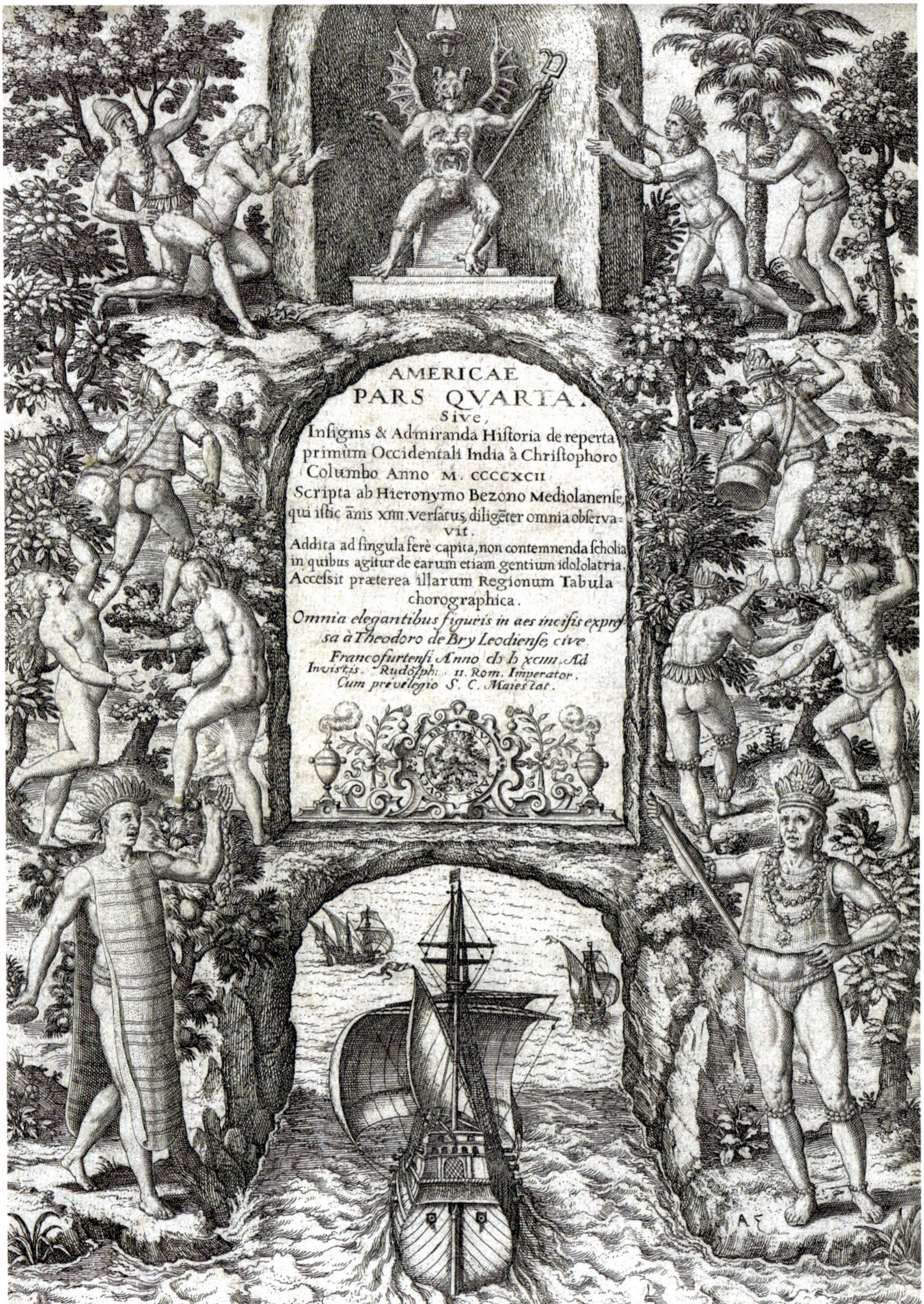
AMERICAE
PARS QVARTA.
Sive,
Inſignis & Admiranda Hiſtoria de reperta
primùm Occidentali India à Chriſtophoro
Columbo Anno M. CCCCXCII
Scripta ab Hieronymo Bezono Mediolanenſe,
qui iſtic ānis XIIII. verſatus, diligēter omnia obſerva-
vit.
Addita ad ſingula ferè capita, non contemnenda ſcholia
in quibus agitur de earum etiam gentium idololatria.
Acceſsit præterea illarum Regionum Tabula
chorographica.
Omnia elegantibus figuris in aes inciſis expreſ-
sa à Theodoro de Bry Leodienſe, cive
Francofurtenſi Anno clↄ lↄ XCIII. Ad
Invictis. Rudolph: II. Rom. Imperator.
Cum previlegio S. C. Maiestat.

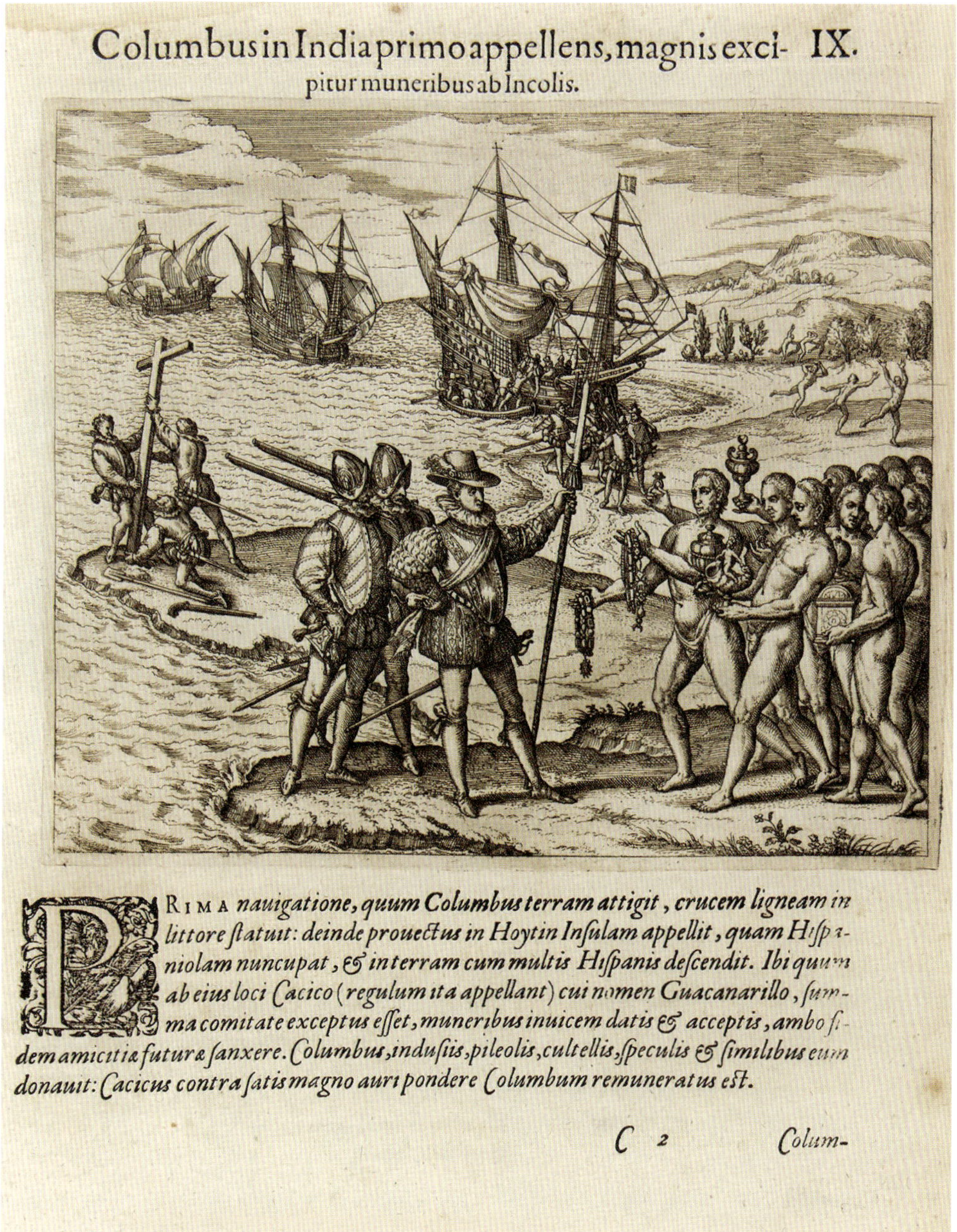

Columbus in India primo appellens, magnis exci- IX.
pitur muneribus ab Incolis.

PRIMA *nauigatione, quum Columbus terram attigit, crucem ligneam in littore statuit: deinde prouectus in Hoytin Insulam appellit, quam Hispaniolam nuncupat, & in terram cum multis Hispanis descendit. Ibi quum ab eius loci Cacico (regulum ita appellant) cui nomen Guacanarillo, summa comitate exceptus esset, muneribus inuicem datis & acceptis, ambo fidem amicitiæ futuræ sanxere. Columbus, indusiis, pileolis, cultellis, speculis & similibus eum donauit: Cacicus contra satis magno auri pondere Columbum remuneratus est.*

C 2 *Colum-*

Fig. 2a–b. Theodor de Bry, frontispiece and engraving of Columbus, in *Americae pars quarta. Sive, insignis & admiranda historia de reperta primùm occidentali India à Christophoro Columbo anno M CCCCXCII scripta ab Hieronymo Bezono Mediolanense*, 34.5 × 24.2 cm (Frankfurt am Main: Typis Ioannis Feyrabend, impensis Theodori de Bry, 1594)

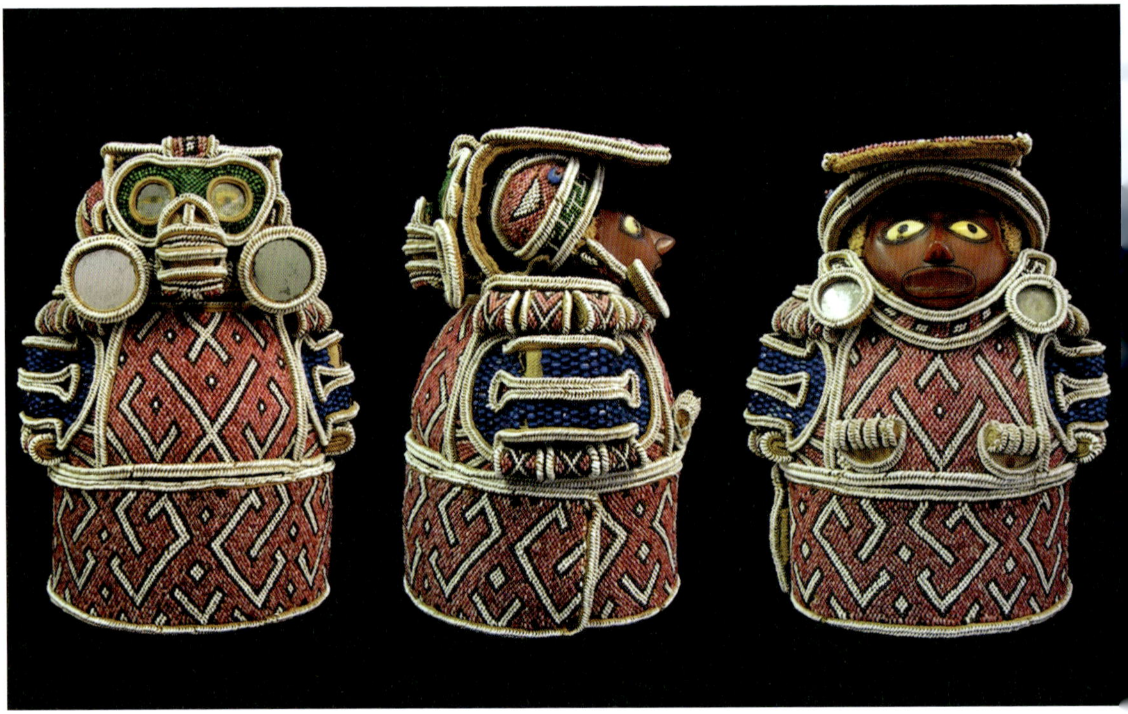

Fig. 3. Zemi, Caribbean, early sixteenth century, rhinoceros horn and glass beads, 315 × 245 mm. Rome, Museo delle Civiltá—Museo Nazionale Preistorico Etnografico Luigi Pigorini. Three views, featuring a human mask of rhinoceros horn (right), and a bat face of green glass beads (left)

sacredness of their world. Normally, in the West, glass beads are understood as a substitute for more precious gems, and they are mostly used as personal adornment, strung as a necklace or bracelet. But clearly this was not the case for the Taino, and we can appreciate the value they had by how they appear on a Taino zemi (a Caribbean religious sculpture) from the very early part of the sixteenth century (fig. 3).[11] It is a Janus-faced work that may have been worn as a headdress, lathe-formed and covered with a fiber netting, to which some 1200 small, drawn, emerald-green beads and 450 deep-blue, four-sided, cornerless beads are attached. The glass beads are combined with shell beads and mirrors to form a beautiful synthesis of rich fields of solid color and patterned design that convey the vitality of the zemi in new material and visual terms.[12]

This is a spectacular object that encompasses the material dimensions of early world trade (the face is made from rhinoceros horn).[13] What is significant is that the desire for gold and the trade for it using glass beads may seem unequal in exchange value, but that assumption presupposes one set of values,

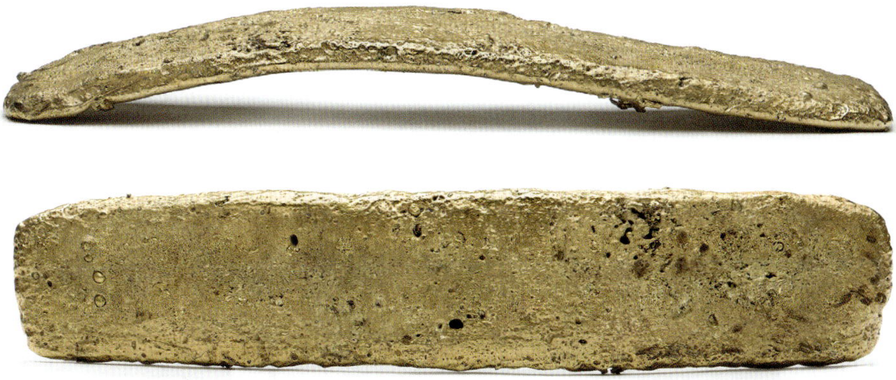

Fig. 4. Gold ingot, Tenochtitlan, cast 1519, 1.930 kg, 93.98% gold, 5.24% copper, 0.78% iron, 26.5 × 5.5 cm, 1.5 cm thick. Mexico City, Museo Nacional de Antropología. The ingot was lost in 1520 and found in 1981 in Mexico City, northeast of the Alemada Central, where Tenochititlan's canal was located

predicated on European notions of gold, as both Columbus and later Marx articulated. The desire for glass beads among the Taino, Mexica, and others was parallel to the desire for gold on the part of the Europeans. The items and the desire for them were inextricably bound together, such that they created an expanding glass-bead industry in Italy, Spain, and Mexico in the sixteenth century and Peru in the seventeenth century, as gold and silver mines were opened throughout America.[14]

Here one might recognize the relationship between gold and Christianity: for Europeans, both are true, as opposed to America's false religion and false values. I therefore turn to some very early objects and images in America and Europe that manifest this intersection in differing ways and contexts. The examples and their discussion and analysis are intended to demonstrate the centrality of gold in the very formation of the early modern global world created by European expansion, and the European values attributed to the intrinsic properties of gold.

Two of the very first golden objects are well known and come from the same historical crucible. They mark in different ways and forms the early horrific events of the Spanish invasion and sacking of Tenochtitlan, the city of the Mexica (Aztec). The first is a four-pound gold bar unearthed in Mexico City some thirty-two years ago (fig. 4).[15] It is forged from what once was the "treasure" of the Aztec in Tenochtitlan when it was seized by Cortés and his troops in 1519. In Book 12 of the *Florentine Codex*, a 1578 Franciscan-commissioned and -organized manuscript that terminates with the history of the conquest, we see and

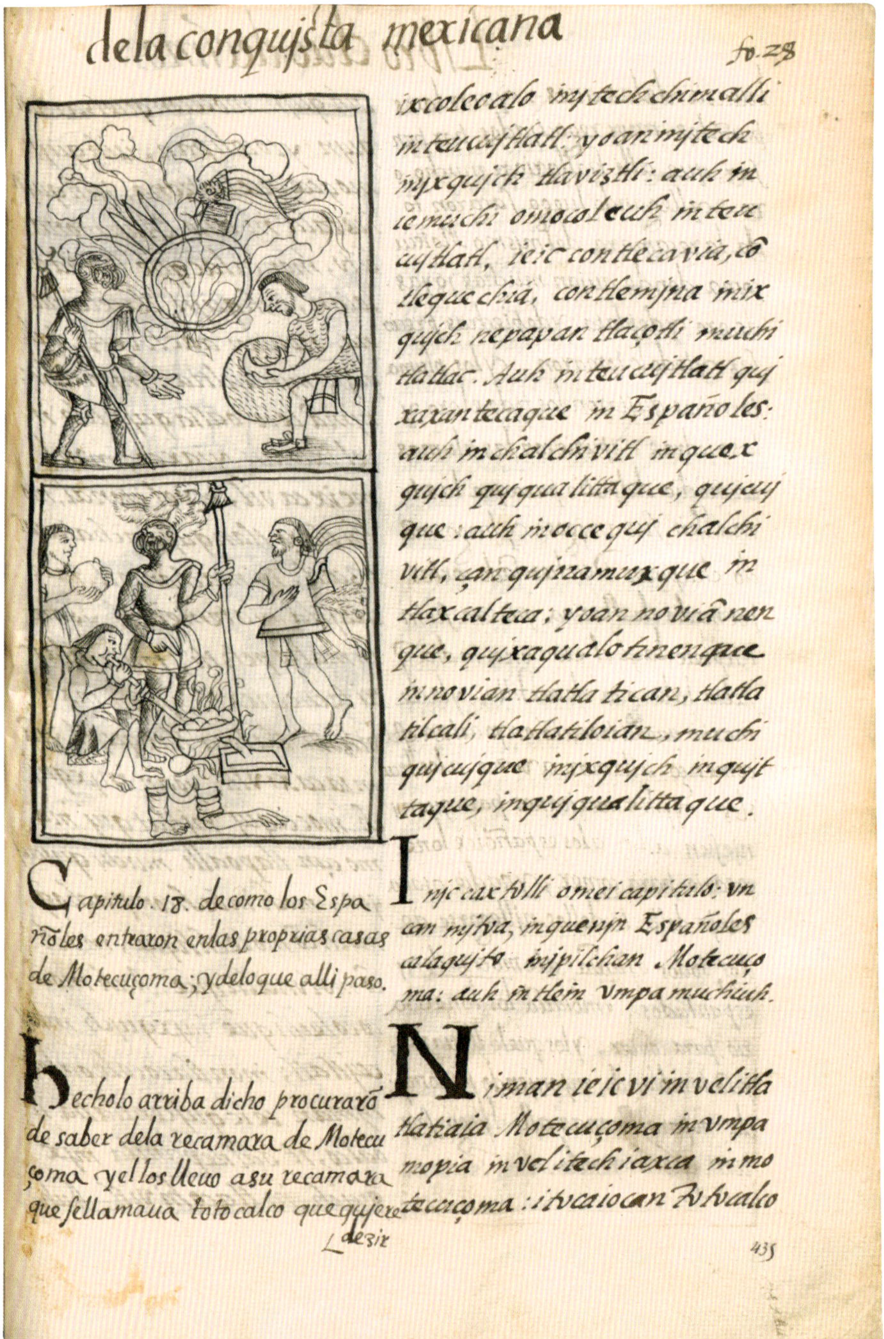

Fig. 5. Sacking of Montezuma's treasury and casting of gold ingots, ink and color on paper, in Bernardino de Sahagún, *Historia general de las cosas de Nueva España* (*Florentine Codex*), 1577, Book 12, fol. 28r. Florence, Biblioteca Medicea-Laurenziana, Palat. 218–20

read how Moctezuma was forced to reveal where his precious items were stored in a room called "teucalco" (treasure room) (fig. 5).[16] There the Aztec kept "all the things of rich feathers [their most valued commodity] and other precious things of feathers and of gold and precious stones ... which the Spaniards pulled out" and "the Spaniards began to remove the gold from the featherwork and shields ... and by removing the gold they destroyed all of the featherwork and rich jewels and they melted it down and cast it into ingots" (comenzaron los españoles a quitar el oro de los plumajes, y de las rodelas, ... y por quitar el oro destruyeron todos los plumajes y joyas ricas y fundieronlo y hizeron barretas).[17]

The following illustration, on folio 28r, depicts the two stages of the looting as described. The pen and ink drawing in the upper panel shows the removal of the gold from the featherwork and the bottom one shows the crucible into which the melted gold flows from a native forge.[18] Whereas some images of artisans in the *Florentine Codex* draw upon the those in Jost Amman's 1568 *Das Ständebuch* as a source,[19] this image seems to record directly, if not in a schematic conflation, the protagonists: the Spanish conquistador, who oversees the disassembly of the Mexica things for the gold, and his ally (a Tlaxcalan), who desires the residue of their destruction, the feathers. The narrative elements are a bit visually unclear in the drawing in the top panel, and it is only by reading the text that one understands what has been depicted. The actions of the figures in the foreground in the lower panel, who are interacting in the forging of the precious metal in three stages, are dramatically rendered and much more decipherable in terms of the event. First, the plundered gold is brought to the crucible, where an Aztec heats the coals by blowing air into it. The Aztec gold then pours into a mold to create the bars. This sequence gives definitive identity to the pictorial narrative of the two images.

The crudely cast gold ingot is the materialization of this pictorial event, and it was serendipitously found nearly 500 years after it was cast. Its state of conservation speaks to the incorruptibility of gold, as well as to its capacity to be transformed into whatever is desired. In this case it is gold's transformation from a glittering adornment on the prized Mexica featherwork to an object of Spanish desire as nearly pure gold—of no aesthetic value and intended solely for its portability and exchange value.[20] Almost immediately after the Spanish desecration of the Aztec treasury and the casting of the gold bar, they and their Tlaxcalan allies were driven out of Tenochtitlan. The need to flee, fighting their way out of the city, meant that whoever was carrying this newly cast gold bar was either killed and fell into one of the canals, where the gold bar sunk with his body, or he threw it down in an attempt to escape as quickly as

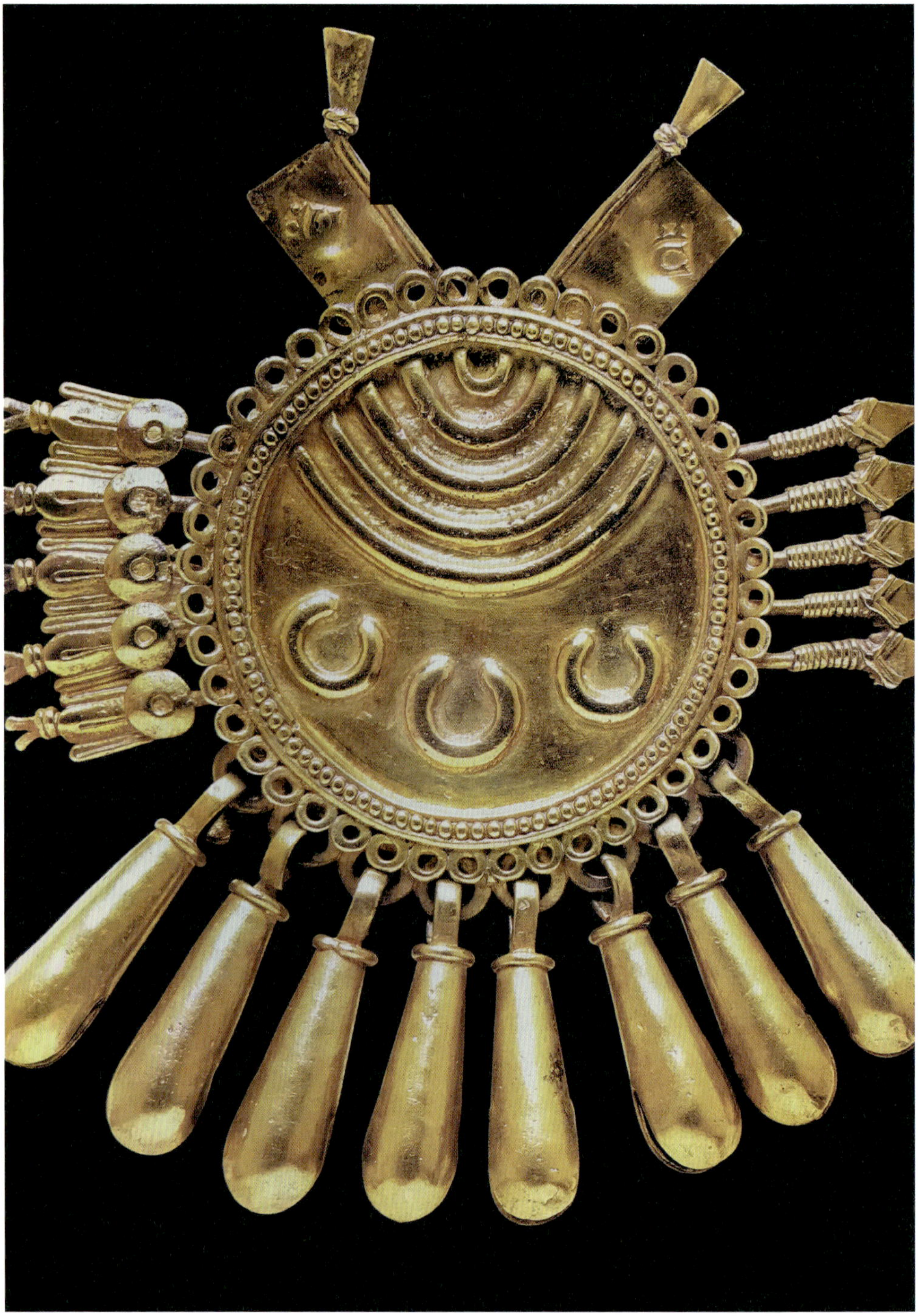

Fig. 6. Shield pendant with darts, Mixtec (Ñudzavui), ca. 1500, gold, 10.5 × 8.5 cm. Veracruz, Museo Baluarte de Santiago

possible. That we will never know, but today it no longer represents its sixteenth-century value but has become an incorruptible glittering witness to brutal conquest, concomitant greed, and its global consequences.[21]

Another gold object from almost exactly the same historical moment is an Aztec/Mixtec gold pendant formed into the shape of a shield (*chimalli*) with darts (fig. 6). It has survived unlike most other Aztec and Mixtec gold pieces because it was lost at sea in a shipwreck off the coast of Veracruz, the port of entry to Mexico. Found by a fisherman in 1975, it represents the transition of gold from a Mexican context to a Spanish one. That is, it is at the stage before the forging of the gold bar found in Mexico City, but it is no longer an object belonging to the Mexica (Aztec). It is in the interstitial stage of the history of gold: it is Mexica in form and substance (it is not pure gold, as is the bar) but it has become a possession of the crown, an object belonging to the treasury of the Holy Roman Emperor, Charles V. This transformation is marked in its form and iconography, by its failed transportation to Spain, by its discovery in a near-perfect state at the bottom of the ocean off Veracruz, and finally by the marks embossed on the two banners that rise behind the shield at the top. Each one is stamped by a seal that marks the royal fifth, or the portion that belonged to Charles V as Holy Roman Emperor and Charles II as King of Spain.[22] One sees impressed into the gold the letter "C" with a crown above it, signifying the portion that belongs to the political person of the king.[23] Gold and people, as Francesco Carletti described in 1606, were transformed into the property of others, by their possession and their marking with a seal/brand, and began circulating in a world of international commerce, looting, and enslavement.[24]

Some of the very first images that survive from Mexico are also about gold as being both things made of gold and the precious metal as a transactional medium in the marketplace. The earliest image of gold as a new medium of exchange used for both new things brought by the Spaniards and new things made by the Mexicans for the Spanish is a painting made some thirty-seven years after Columbus wrote his letter and some sixty-five years before Shakespeare penned *Timon of Athens* (and three and a half centuries before Marx wrote *Capital*). It was created in the town of Huejotzingo by *tlacuilos* (Mexican painters/scribes), as a record of expenses and was subsequently called as witness in a lawsuit between Hernán Cortés and the members of the first Audiencia (viceregal court of judges) of Mexico, especially Nuño de Guzmán (fig. 7).[25]

In this image and transcribed testimony by the *tlacuilos*, who were members of the *atepetl* (community) of Huejotzingo, we can see and hear the kinds of alchemy to which Marx and Shakespeare allude, as they play out in the New

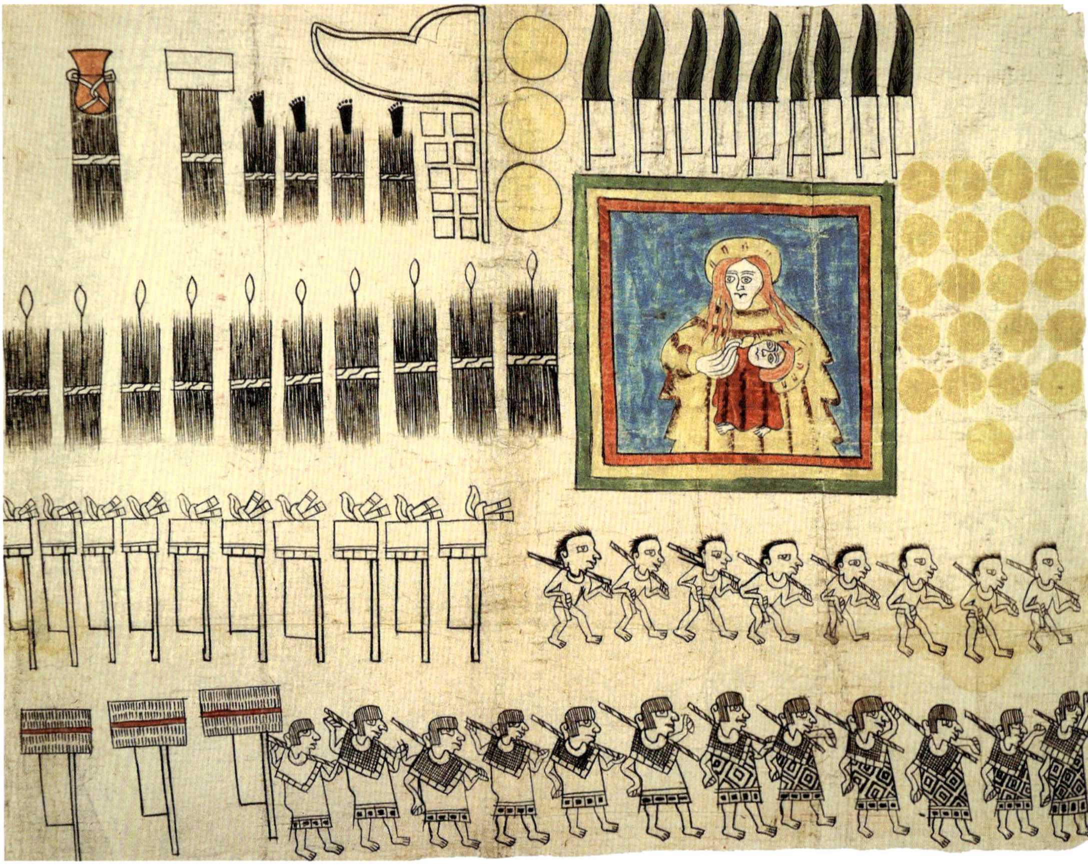

Fig. 7. Painting no. 5 of the "Tribute Account," pigment on *amate* paper, 41.1 × 52.7 cm, from the *Codex Huejotzingo*, Puebla, Mexico, 1529. Washington, DC, Library of Congress, Manuscript Division, Harkness Collection

World, where gold was not really a currency of consequence before the arrival of the Spaniards. One painter, named Lucas, begins by describing the content of the painting from the right, where there are twenty-one solid gold disks arranged in four vertical rows of five with the odd disk at the bottom. These disks represent the twenty-one portions of gold that were spent to equip Don Tomé, Señor de Huejotzingo, with a horse so that he could accompany Nuño de Guzmán to war. No glyph nor Aztec number is used to represent either the amount or the gold itself. Rather, the color yellow indicates the gold and the twenty-one yellow circles represent the precise quantity. This is very different from the quantity of things that were demanded as tribute represented on the viewer's left.

It is the next section of the painting to which Lucas refers in his testimony, where one sees the striking image of the Virgin and Child implanted in the composition. Handled unlike any of the other images, the three-quarter-length frontal view of the haloed Virgin holding Christ is startling. The figures have the same hard dark outline as the others but the interiors are filled with color, with various tonal gradations to indicate the volume and folds of their garments. The frame, the solid colored background, and the frontal figures isolate this image from the rest. But its distinctive formal qualities are based on the uniqueness of the object that this image is meant to represent.

Only here in relation to the Virgin is the order of discrete objects patterned on the page broken. One's eye is thus drawn to the Virgin. But Lucas first mentions the two rows of human figures below, and by this ordering one begins to find the transformative narrative of the production of the referent: the standard with the depiction of the Virgin. The images in this part of the document are not simply isolated ciphers which only refer externally to the oral narrative; they also refer to each other in a temporal sequence of action. They pictorially present the sequence of causal action that Lucas gives in his testimony when he notes that Nuño de Guzmán requested an image of the Virgin Mary made of gold and feathers to take to war with him. Because the village did not have either the gold or the feathers to make the image, they were forced to sell twenty slaves to Indian merchants. These are the twenty figures shown, eight men in one row and twelve women in the other.

At this point, one is still in the realm of expenditure, to which all the other figures as objects refer. The slaves—except for gender differentiation and clothing—are stereotypical and have no identity other than as ciphers for objects of commerce. But, unlike the other objects of value, such as the twenty-one disks of gold, their purchase value and purpose is not left to an oral narrative that, in this instance, because it is legal testimony, takes on a written form. Rather the value of the slaves is represented by what they purchased. Their value of exchange with the merchants is represented above the image of Virgin by nine glyphs of feather bundles, each of which contains twenty feathers, and to the left of the Virgin by three disks, representing the amount of gold required.

Value here is still represented by Mexican glyphs and pictographs of objects but the action of market exchange is now implied by that value being represented twice, by different objects of equal exchange value. The value is represented a third time by the image of the Madonna, which is the transformation of that exchange value into representation. Lucas narrates the transformation:

> And from the said ingots of gold the said image of Santa Maria was made and it was made as broad and as long as more than half an arm. And the said nine

> bundles of plumage were of the long and rich kind which the said Indians value very highly, and they placed the said feathers all around the said image after the manner of an enclosure. And when it had been made after this fashion, the said lord and leading men of the said town, and this witness with them, brought it to the said Nuño de Guzmán with said overseer who is named Gibaja. And they gave it to the said Nuño de Guzmán in the presence of this witness, and he received it.

The image in the painting refers to the Christian religious icon that the leaders of Huejotzingo had produced and given to Nuño de Guzmán to be carried to war by him. Although it is represented through an analog image and thus appears unique, its uniqueness is not based on the supernatural power of the image within a Christian context; rather it is unique as an image in the painting because it refers to a specific object produced in Huejotzingo at a cost. Its presentation appears awkward because what is recorded is new, outside the standards of Mexican representation. It is a representation of an alien image that by its likeness and certainly its reproduction and its size in relation to the other figures on the page indicates a sense of wonder and display of artistic virtuosity. Nevertheless, the first purpose of the likeness reproduced here is to signify material value within the mode of Mexican production and exchange value. Thus, the dependent sequential order of Lucas's testimony regarding the Virgin and the images related to it voices the pictorial representation of a temporal transformational narrative of economics: the real contestation of power that the word of God brought and that brought the word of God. This, then, is not a Christian image but an image of an object that is a Christian image. The Madonna has been transformed, metamorphized through the careful surrounding of it by other figures to having the semiotic status of a cipher, a glyph. It therefore achieves the value of a trope within the Mexican system.

Gold, then, became a medium of exchange that through its alchemy could transform slaves into feathers and then into an image of their exchange. Mexican gold, although in reality rather scarce as circulating currency, quickly became an index of European economic values impressed upon America. Mexico was not the great source of gold and Leonardo López Luján writes: "that means that the Aztec obtained relatively little gold, compared with the ancient societies of Colombia, Ecuador and Peru. Mexico's archaeological collection amounts to a mere 500 or so pieces of gold, all pretty tiny. And that's in three decades of excavations." Warwick Bray, another scholar of pre-Columbian gold, writes that " if you gathered together all the ceremonial gold artifacts from the Aztec capital that have survived today, you could quite easily fit them

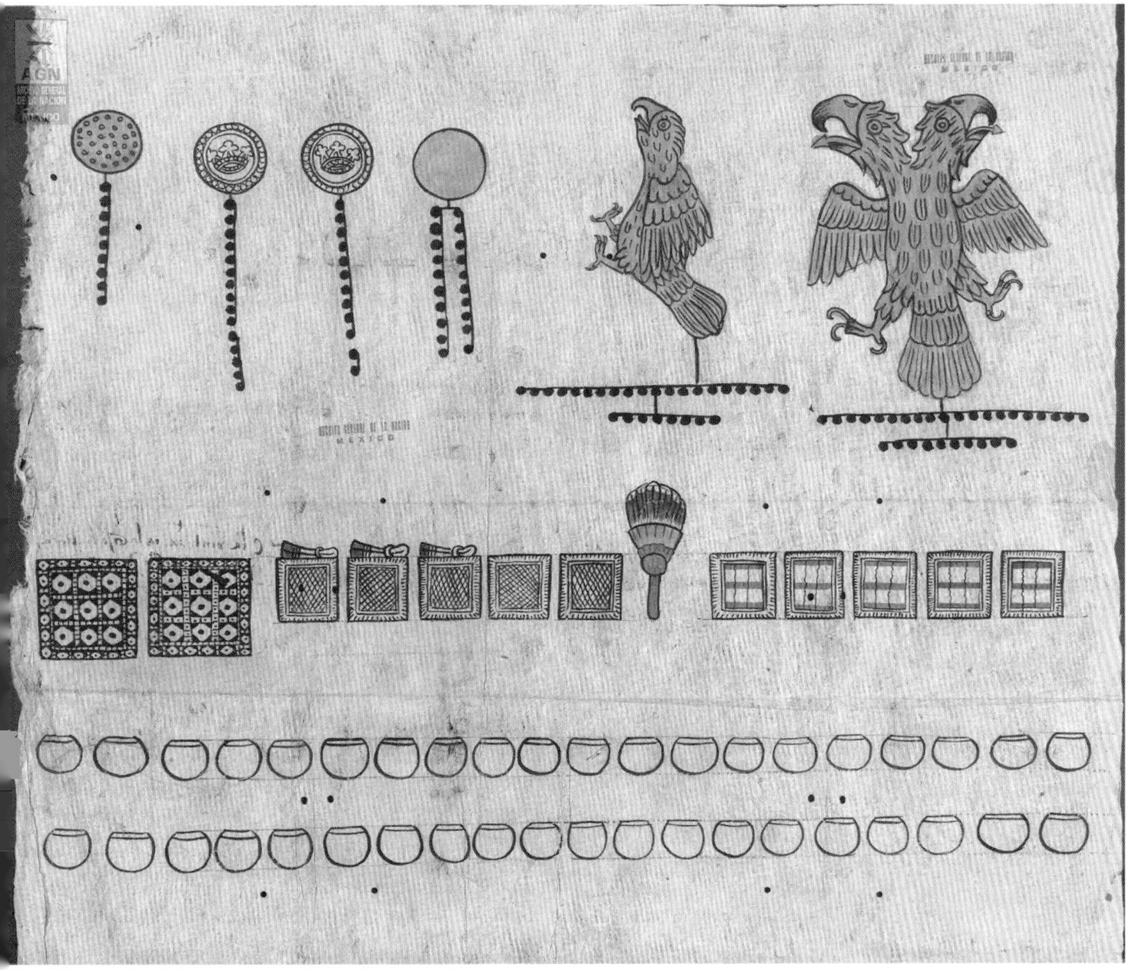

Fig. 8. The possessions of Martín Ocelotl, 1540, European paper, 43 × 47 cm. Mexico City, Archivo General de la Nación de México, Inquisición, vol. 37, expediente 4, fols. 132–47

into your cupped hands." Indeed, gold working has a much longer history of production and development in South America and only arrived in Mexico around 900 AD.[26]

Nonetheless, the second image of gold from America comes from Mexico and again appears in a painting that was introduced as evidence in a court case (fig. 8). This time it was a case presented before the Inquisition against Ocelotl, who was born before the conquest but converted to the Roman Catholic faith, when he was baptized and given the Christian name Martín. This was a key conversion for the newly arrived invaders as Martín Ocelotl was an Aztec priest in Tenochtitlan who in 1519 was imprisoned by Moctezuma II for

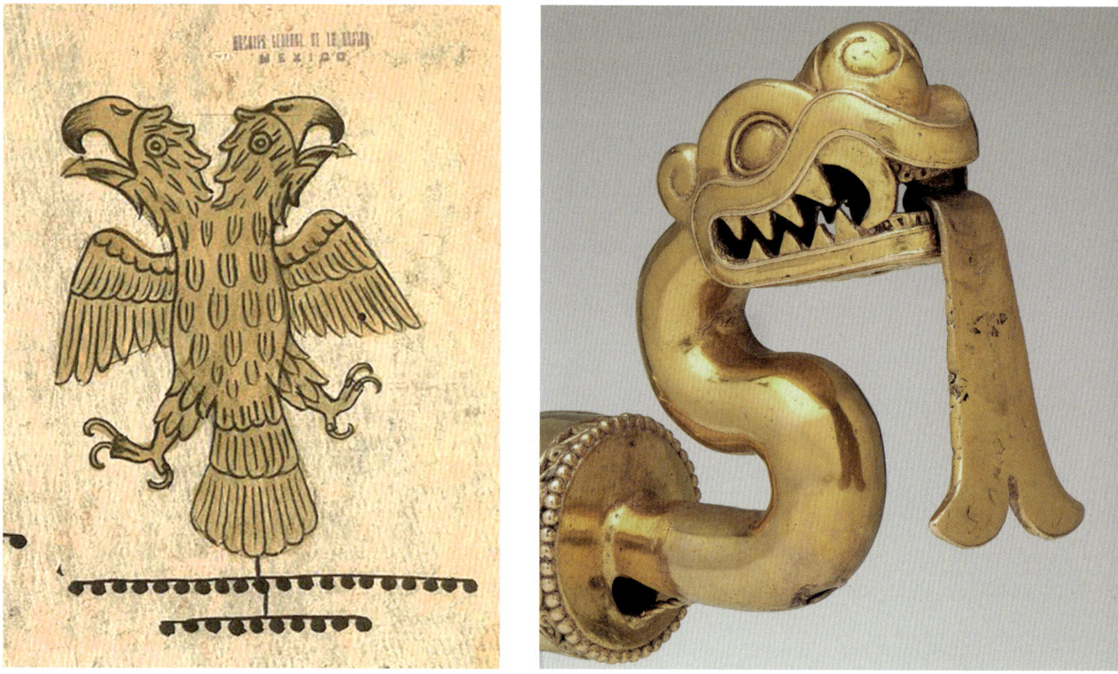

Fig. 9a: The possessions of Martín Ocelotl, detail; 9b: Serpent labret with articulated tongue, Aztec, 1300–1521, gold, 6.67 × 4.45 × 6.67 cm, 51.35 g. New York, The Metropolitan Museum of Art, accession no. 2016.64

reading omens unfavorable to the emperor.[27] After the conquest of Tenochtitlan, Martín Ocelotl appeared to be a model new Christian but in fact he led a dual existence, performing native religious rites and prognostications. He was finally swept into the maw of the Inquisition in 1536 for being an apostate and idolator.[28] His case was given to Bishop Juan de Zumarraga, who before coming to New Spain had been an inquisitor rooting out witches in the Basque area of northern Spain. The bishop presided over Martín Ocelotl's trial in 1540 and Ocelotl was exiled and sent to Seville. The painting was introduced into the trial as evidence of his possessions.[29] In March 1540 these possessions were seized and the Office of the Inquisition auctioned them off. One sees from left to right different coin values in silver and gold, the gold to the farthest right having the highest value and looking very much like what is represented in the Huejotzingo manuscript discussed above. Further to the right are two golden objects of considerable value, as indicated below them. The furthest object to the right is an odd golden amalgamation of Aztec and Holy Roman imperial images: the bicephalic eagle is clearly based on the Hapsburg royal insignia that was now on display throughout New Spain (Mexico).

However, this is also clearly an Aztec cast piece as can be seen in the detail (fig. 9a). The painter has taken great care to depict the tongues of the two eagle heads as they extend from their mouths. An Aztec labret seems to show us what the artist is referencing here (fig. 9b). When the labret was worn, a serpent head would sinuously curl from the lower lip to end above the wearer's upper lip, where the mouth opens and a golden tongue extends outward. The tongue is an independent piece and is loosely attached so that as it was worn it would move as a snake's tongue does in reality. In the painting for the trial evidence, the depicted tongues of the bicephalic eagle appear to be equally independent and it would seem that an Aztec goldsmith had cast it so as to unite two distinct but compatible elements of power. One body of power, however, triumphed over the other and the golden bicephalic eagle was seized, never to be seen again, just as Martín Ocelotl was never to be seen again, being lost at sea as he journeyed to his exile in Seville.

It was in the same year that the Huejotzingo painting was created that the conquest of Peru began, which, as Gustave Flaubert defined in his *Dictionary of Received Ideas*, is a "Country in which everything is made of Gold." Or, as the great Andean chronicler Guaman Poma de Ayala would write in his 1615 *Nueva coronica i buen gobierno* about what happened when the news of Peru reached Spain, "there was an enormous uproar in all of Spain, day and night among their dreams, everyone crying 'the Indies, the Indies, gold silver, gold silver of Peru.' Even the musicians sang the romances 'Indies, gold and silver'.'[30] His first image of the exchange between an Inca lord and a Spaniard has the Inca ask in Quechua "Do you eat this gold?" (cay coritacho micunqui); the Spaniard answers in the plural, and therefore presumably for all Spaniards, "We eat this gold" (este oro comemos).

This excitement was generated in reality, as Peru became the place where one of the world's great ransoms was raised.[31] Atahualpa, the Sapa Inca, lord of the Inca Empire, was pulled from his litter by Pizarro and held captive at Cajamarca in the Andes. He offered to fill a room as high as he could reach with gold, which he did. This is the subject of Theodor de Bry's *Americae pars sexta*, which translates and illustrates Benzoni's text concerning the conquest of Peru. In the foreground of the historiated frontispiece Atahualpa is carried in a litter. He and his retinue are posed in profile before a mountain that is being worked for its gold (fig. 10).[32] This image is a harbinger of the wealth that would come first from Atahualpa's ransom and then from the gold and silver mines of Peru, and which generated the Spanish expression "vale un Peru," meaning more or less "you've hit the jackpot." A later image in the same

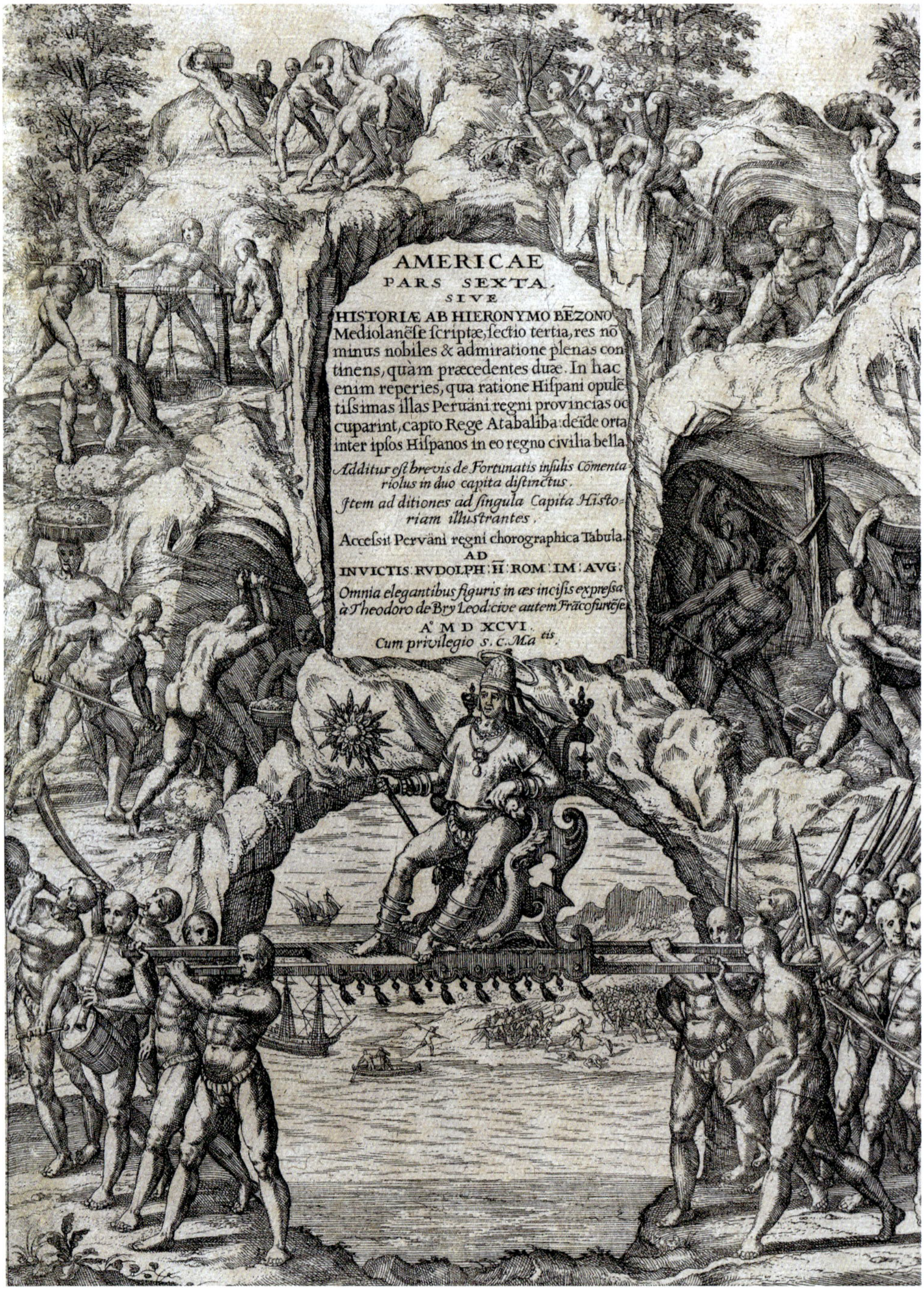

Fig. 10. Theodor de Bry, frontispiece, engraving, 34.5 × 24.2 cm, in *Americae pars sexta sive Historiae ab Hieronymo Benzono* (Frankfurt am Main, 1596). It depicts the mining of one of the Peruvian mountains and the Inca king, Atahualpa, at its base, borne on a litter

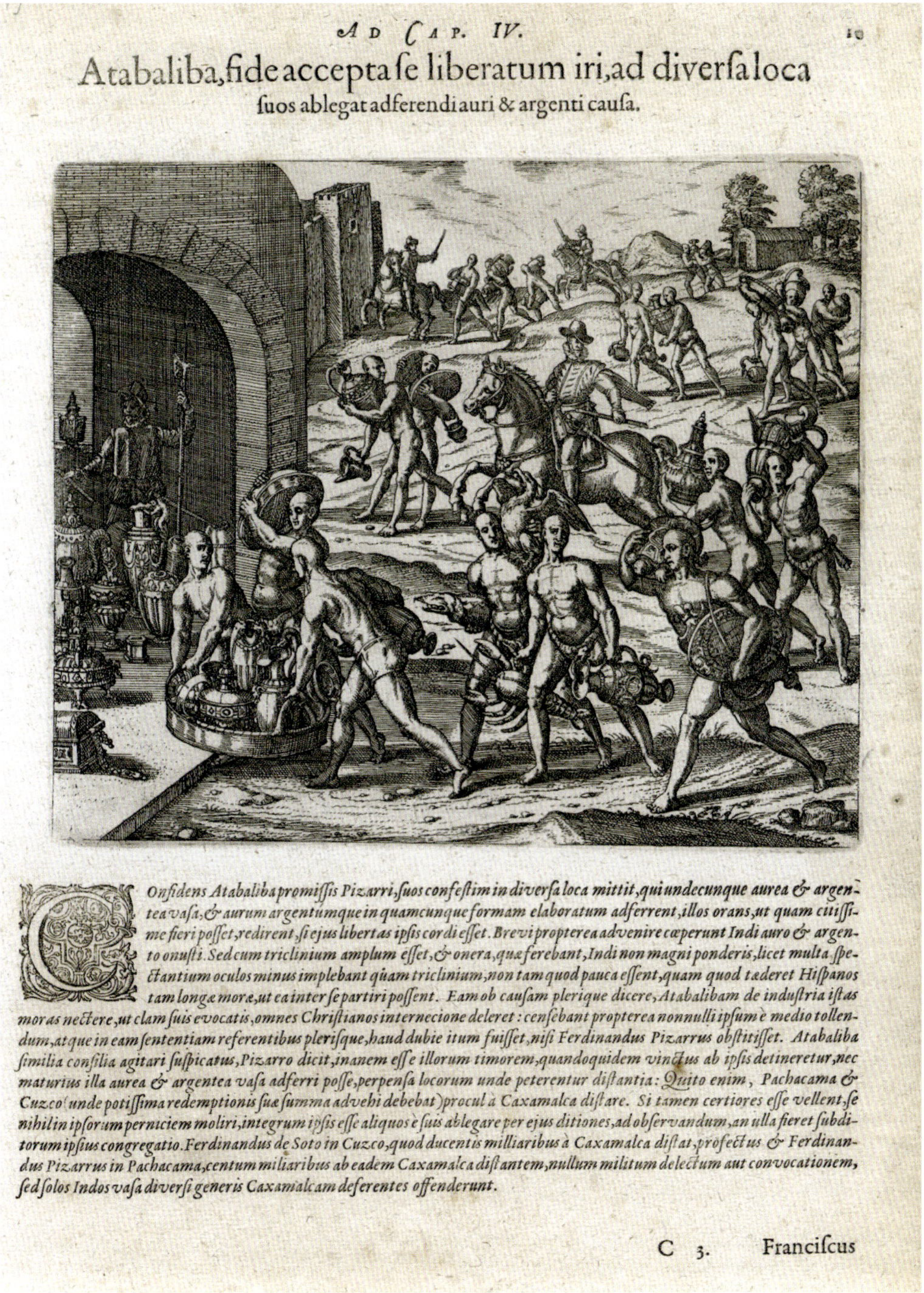

AD CAP. IV. 10

Atabaliba, fide accepta ſe liberatum iri, ad diverſa loca ſuos ablegat adferendi auri & argenti cauſa.

Confidens Atabaliba promiſſis Pizarri, ſuos confeſtim in diverſa loca mittit, qui undecunque aurea & argentea vaſa, & aurum argentumque in quamcunque formam elaboratum adferrent, illos orans, ut quam citiſſime fieri poſſet, redirent, ſi ejus libertas ipſis cordi eſſet. Brevi propterea advenire cœperunt Indi auro & argento onuſti. Sed cum triclinium amplum eſſet, & onera, quæ ferebant, Indi non magni ponderis, licet multa ſpectantium oculos minus implebant quam triclinium, non tam quod pauca eſſent, quam quod tæderet Hiſpanos tam longæ moræ, ut ea inter ſe partiri poſſent. Eam ob cauſam plerique dicere, Atabalibam de induſtria iſtas moras nectere, ut clam ſuis evocatis, omnes Chriſtianos internecione deleret: cenſebant propterea nonnulli ipſum è medio tollendum, atque in eam ſententiam referentibus pleriſque, haud dubie itum fuiſſet, niſi Ferdinandus Pizarrus obſtitiſſet. Atabaliba ſimilia conſilia agitari ſuſpicatus, Pizarro dicit, inanem eſſe illorum timorem, quandoquidem vinctus ab ipſis detineretur, nec maturius illa aurea & argentea vaſa adferri poſſe, perpenſa locorum unde peterentur diſtantia: Quito enim, Pachacama & Cuzco (unde potiſſima redemptionis ſuæ ſumma advehi debebat) procul à Caxamalca diſtare. Si tamen certiores eſſe vellent, ſe nihil in ipſorum perniciem moliri, integrum ipſis eſſe aliquos è ſuis ablegare per ejus ditiones, ad obſervandum, an ulla fieret ſubditorum ipſius congregatio. Ferdinandus de Soto in Cuzco, quod ducentis milliaribus à Caxamalca diſtat, profectus & Ferdinandus Pizarrus in Pachacama, centum miliaribus ab eadem Caxamalca diſtantem, nullum militum delectum aut convocationem, ſed ſolos Indos vaſa diverſi generis Caxamalcam deferentes offenderunt.

C 3. Franciſcus

Fig. 11. Theodor de Bry, engraving, 34.5 × 24.2 cm, in *Americae pars sexta sive Historiae ab Hieronymo Benzono*, chap. 4, p. 10, showing the ransom payment of Atahualpa brought to Pizarro at Cajamarca

volume depicts the Inca leader being pulled from his litter and taken captive by Pizarro at Cajamarca in 1532. There he supposedly pledged to fill the room where he was imprisoned with the gold of Tahuantinsuyu.

De Bry also then depicts (fig. 11) the Incas who arrive from all over the empire bringing golden objects, which are described by the anonymous chronicler of *La Conquista del Peru llamado la nueva Castilla* (1534) and listed in the inventory of all that reached Seville intended as the king's fifth for the emperor, Charles V.[33] These are sculptures of men, women, and children, an ear of corn, drums, and many vessels. What the Incas carry to Cajamarca in this engraving reflects what the Taino brought to Columbus some forty years earlier, as imagined by de Bry. There is in fact no need to differentiate between the goldwork of the Taino and the Inca. Rather, late Renaissance vessels, coffers, and necklaces suffice to represent Inca objects of gold. This is a very different depiction of native gold work and what the Spaniards did with it from how Mexica gold is depicted as being pulled from the more precious Mexica featherwork as it is described and depicted in the *Florentine Codex* (see fig. 5). More importantly, there is no correspondence between Inca forms and those depicted by de Bry. But in truth, whereas Dürer saw Aztec gold work and marveled at its art, there was no opportunity for de Bry to have seen anything of Inca goldwork.[34]

Sir Walter Raleigh, whose own *Briefe and True Report of the New Found Land of Virginia* launched what would later become known as de Bry's Grand Voyages, wrote in his 1596 *Discoverie of the Large, Rich, and Bewtiful Empyre of Guiana* that

> we are now daily threatened. But if we now consider of the actions both of Charles the fifte, who had the Maydenhead of *Peru*, & the aboundant treasures of *Atabalipa*, together with the affaires of the Spanish king now living. … It is his [Philip II's] Indian Golde that indaungereth and disturbeth all the nations of Europe.[35]

Pizarro's own persona became emblematically connected to his acquired golden ransom in his coat of arms, which was wrapped around the corner of his family's newly built home on the plaza in Trujillo, Extremadura (fig. 12). In the lower part of the coat of arms, we can see the bust portrait of a chained Atahualpa with his arms thrust into baskets of gold, as described in the patent gifted by Charles V.[36]

A similar allegorization of the Inca and Mexica leaders and the wealth of their communities appears in a Mexican manuscript illustration, in which their portraits are to be seen as the personification of the conquest of Peru and Mexico respectively. Brought to Spain in 1585 by the ambassadors from Tlaxcala, the manuscript, entitled *Descripción de la ciudad y provincia de Tlaxcala de las Indias y del mar océano para el buen gobierno y ennoblecimiento dellas*, was presented to Philip II. The text details the history of Tlaxcala and the rights and privileges granted to it by his father, Charles V. The emperor bestowed these for the Tlaxcalans' alliance with and vital support of Hernán Cortés in the conquest of Mexica.

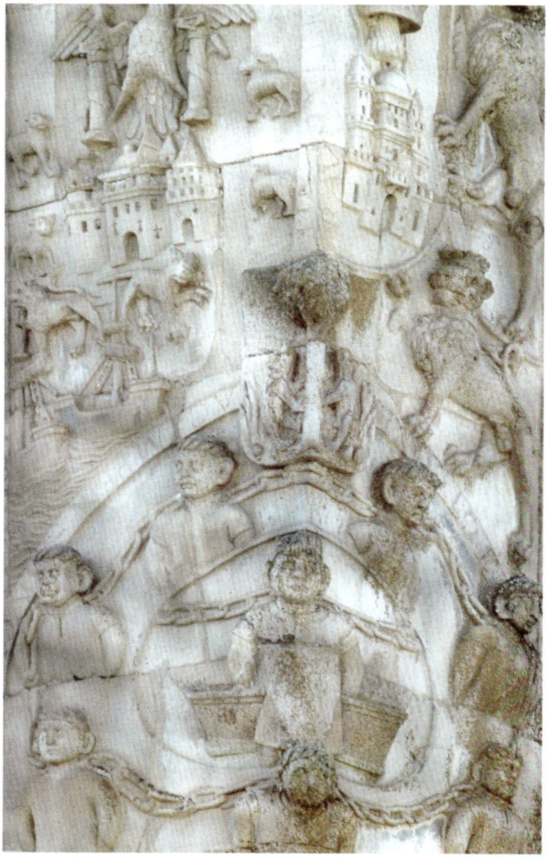

Fig. 12. Detail of the coat of arms of Francisco Pizarro, ca. 1570. Trujillo, Plaza Mayor, Palacio de la Conquista, commissioned by Hernando Pizarro

On folio 248v, the author, Diego Muñoz Camargo, represents the wealth of the New World as it is offered up to Spain by its conquering heroes (fig. 13a).[37] We first see Pizarro who stands looking down and with his right arm over the shoulder of a kneeling figure, personifying Peru. The figure is identifiable as the crownless Atahualpa, whose named portrait appears on the recto of the same folio. Pizarro's gesture is not protective but is made in supplication as he offers not only Atahualpa but also the golden wealth of Peru, represented by an open coffer filled with coins; and behind him are the golden vessels and gold bars of Atahualpa's ransom (see fig. 11). Before this pair of conquered and conqueror, we see Cortés, who similarly stands, his arm over the shoulder of a kneeling Mexican woman, presumably La Malinche, his translator, consort, and mother of his child Martín, while he holds a crucifix in his left hand. Before their feet is another allegorical coffer of New Spain's riches. They all face toward the next folio, which depicts Columbus kneeling before the equestrian portrait of Charles V as both religious and political leader of the Spanish Empire, who receives the globe (Nuevo Mundo) from the explorer's outstretched hand. The crown is composed of two defining elements: the

13a

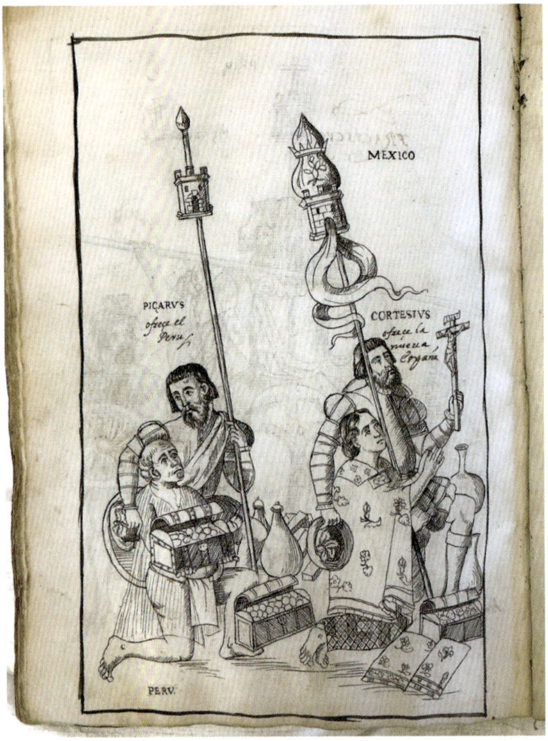

13b

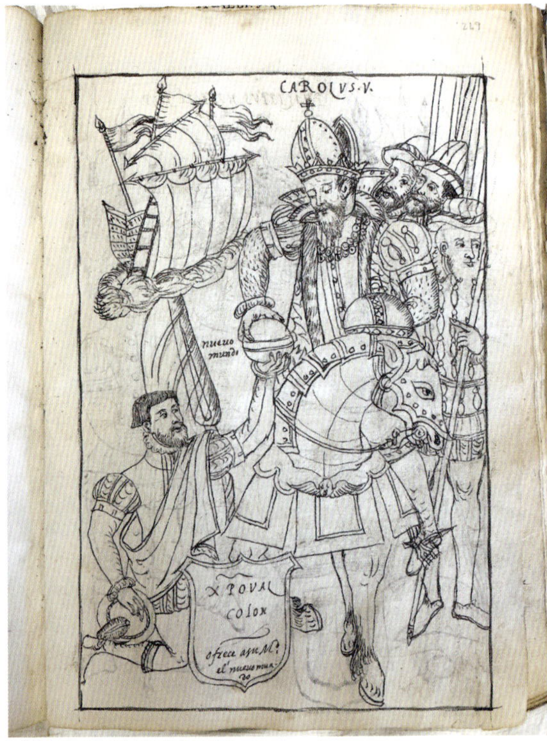

Fig. 13a–b. Diego Muñoz Camargo, *Pizarro offers Peru, Cortés offers New Spain* and *Columbus offers the New World to Charles V*, in *Historia de Tlaxcala*, 1585, fols. 248v and 249r. Glasgow University Library, Special Collections, MS Hunter 242 (U.3.15)

circlet or diadem in the shape of a royal crown (Charles was Charles II, King of Spain); and the miter, symbolizing the divine right of the emperor to rule (as Charles V, Holy Roman Emperor) (fig. 13b).[38]

This representation is rather accurate, as the golden ransom of Atahualpa that reached Charles V arrived partly in the original Andean form but much more in a new form, as solid gold bars, called *lingotes*. Moreover, those Inca objects that did reach Spain did not last long. They were quickly melted down in order to help finance other imperial interests. In fact, of the thousands of golden objects given in ransom, not one has survived, as far as is known.[39] Someone wearing gold jewelry today is probably wearing some fragment of the Incas' gold, but that is the extent of its presence in the contemporary world, aside from Renaissance gilding of churches, palaces, and other things.

One ship alone, *Nuestra Señora de Atocha*, bound for Spain but which sank during a hurricane in 1622, carried more than forty tons of gold and silver. Like the golden Aztec pendant, these gold bars lay at the ocean's bottom until

14a

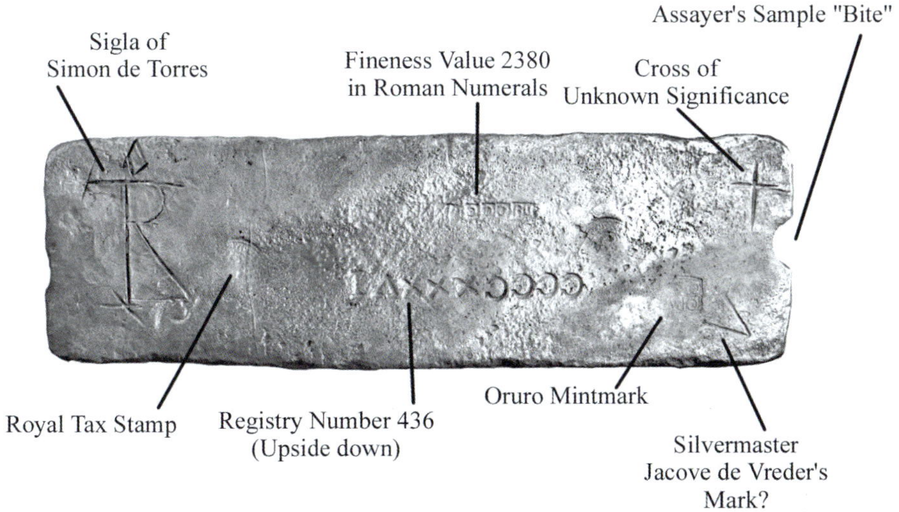

14b

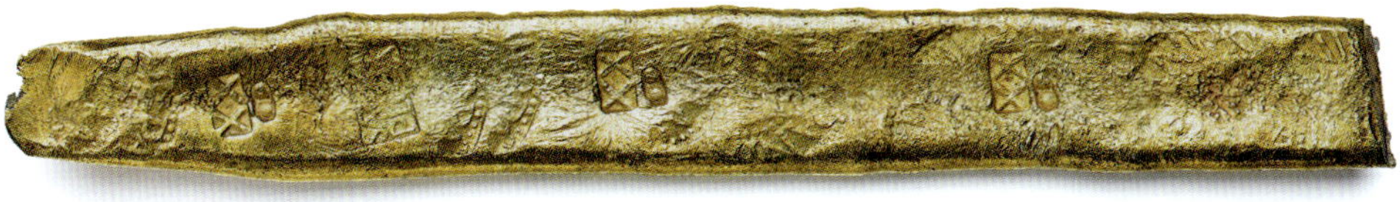

Fig. 14a–b. Silver (12.2 × 38.5 cm, 8.6 cm thick., 2.44 kg) and gold (2.6 × 21 cm, 0.8 cm thick., 426 g) ingots from the *Nuestra Señora de La Atocha*, before 1622. Key West, Florida, Mel Fisher Museum

they began to be recovered in 1973, when the sunken ship and its cargo were found.[40] In addition to the gold and silver ingots, which were the bulk of the *Atocha*'s cargo, there were gold and silver objects of colonial Inca form and design that are unique. Their recovery, like that of the gold Aztec pendant, demonstrates how much has been lost in the crucible of time and fire. All the bars recovered from the *Atocha*, both gold and silver, are more or less alike in form; however, each ingot is marked with a variety of different signatures, as can be seen in two examples (fig. 14a–b). Aside from the date of foundry and the silver maker's and assayer's marks, common to all the bars, the distinguishing mark is the owner's mark (*sigla*) pressed into the precious metal.[41] This last mark is not unlike the owner's mark burned into the flesh of men and women as they became treated as property, as described of the slave market by Francesco Carletti only sixteen years earlier.[42]

In economic reality, silver was the universal equivalent that truly spurred world trade, as Kris Lane's essay in this volume discusses. But gold continued to be the symbolic standard of wealth and power of Spain as well as Italy. How else can we understand Sir Walter Raleigh's comments, who himself sought gold in America and promised it to his queen. Yet he was not wrong in his assessment. The fabulous ransom paid by the Inca sovereign, Atahualpa, which stripped the golden cladding of the walls of Cuzco's most sacred temple, the Coricancha (Golden Enclosure), arrived in Spain to be melted into coin, so as to allow Charles V to finance fully his successful campaign against Barbarossa and his Turkish stronghold in Tunis.[43]

The desire for gold leads us to questions about the other transcendent values that gold held in the early modern world. One value that is critical is the metaphorical use of gold as God's gift to America, as first expressed by Columbus. Such evangelical sentiment was continuously voiced in the sixteenth and seventeenth centuries. Pablo Joseph de Arriaga, for example, wrote in his tract on the extirpation of idolatry in Peru that "there are few who [would] wish to visit the heathens if not by the door of gold and silver."[44] In fact, the gold and silver mines of Peru depicted by de Bry in his frontispieces were already understood as God's gift to the Christian Spaniards, as laid out in a 1571 defense of the conquest:

> these mountains are filled with gold ... and the earth is mixed with gold dust. What does this mean except that what God did with us and these miserable gentiles is what a father would do who has two daughters: the one very beautiful and fair, very discreet and full of grace and charm, and the other very ugly, bleary-eyed, stupid and brutish. If the first is to marry, she needs no dowry, rather just place her in the castle and there gentlemen will come running in competition to see who can marry her. For the ugly, slow, stupid unfortunate one, this is not sufficient rather [it is necessary] to give her a great dowry, many jewels, rich clothes, sumptuous houses ...
>
> God did the same with them and us. We were once all infidels: Europe, Asia; but in their nature [resided] great beauty, many sciences, discretion. Little was required by which the Apostles and apostolic men wed these souls with Christ by the faith of baptism. ... But these [other] nations were ugly, rustic, stupid, unskilled, dreary-eyed and were in need of a great dowry. And so, [God] gave them mountains full of gold and silver, and fertile valleys because [drawn] by their scent men came, as God wished, to preach the Gospel and baptize them and make these souls the bride of Christ. ...
>
> Thus I say of these Indians [of Peru] that one of the means of their predestination and salvation were their mines, treasures, and riches because we see clear-

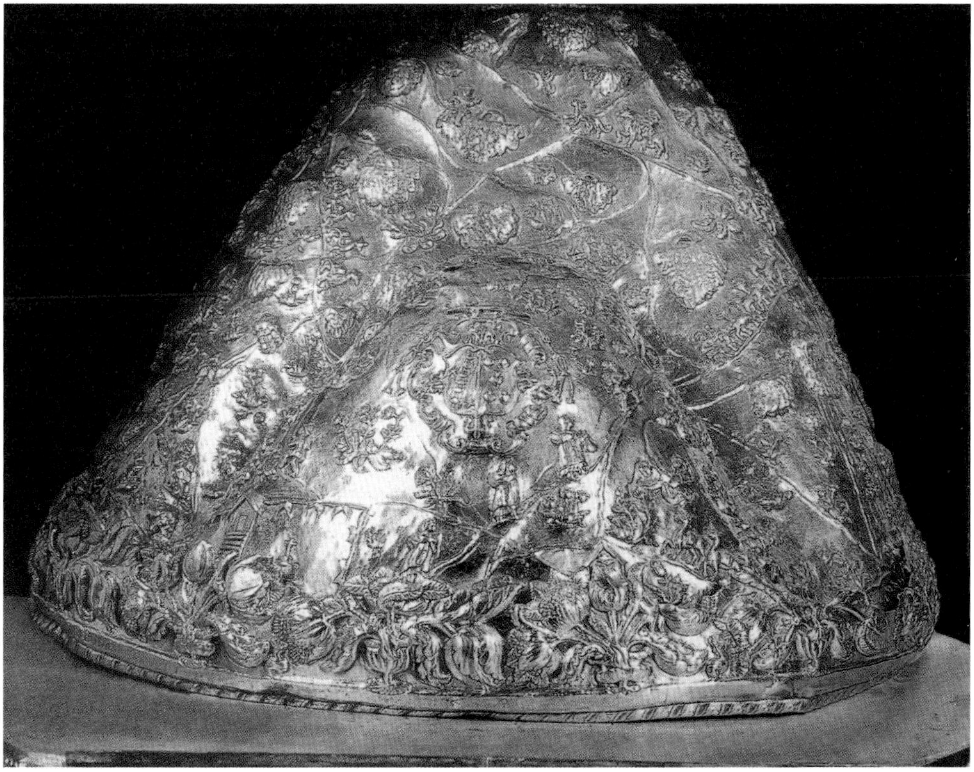

Fig. 15. Luis Niño, pedestal in the form of the Mountain of Potosí for the sculpture of the *Virgin of Charity* in Villarobledo, Spain, 1519, 33 × 46 cm

> ly that where they are the Gospel goes flying and in competition and where there is none [of these riches] it is a means of disapproval because the Gospel will never reach there, as it is seen by long experience that the land where there is not this dowry of gold and silver neither the captain nor soldier would wish to go nor even the minister of the gospel! Then good are the mines of the barbarians since God gave them to them so that they might carry the faith and Christianity to them for ... their salvation.[45]

This is truly a remarkable passage, as not only is Peru gendered as a woman, as all America was,[46] but the country is presented as the ugly daughter for whom God has had to provide a great dowry: her precious metals lie in her ground, her maidenhead, anticipating the natural desire of the Spanish suitor, just as Raleigh writes. Peru's intrinsic allure sets into circulation God's gift of wealth bestowed on these otherwise miserable lands. In exchange, God's gift returns transformed as divine grace and salvation. The mines of Peru thus become a

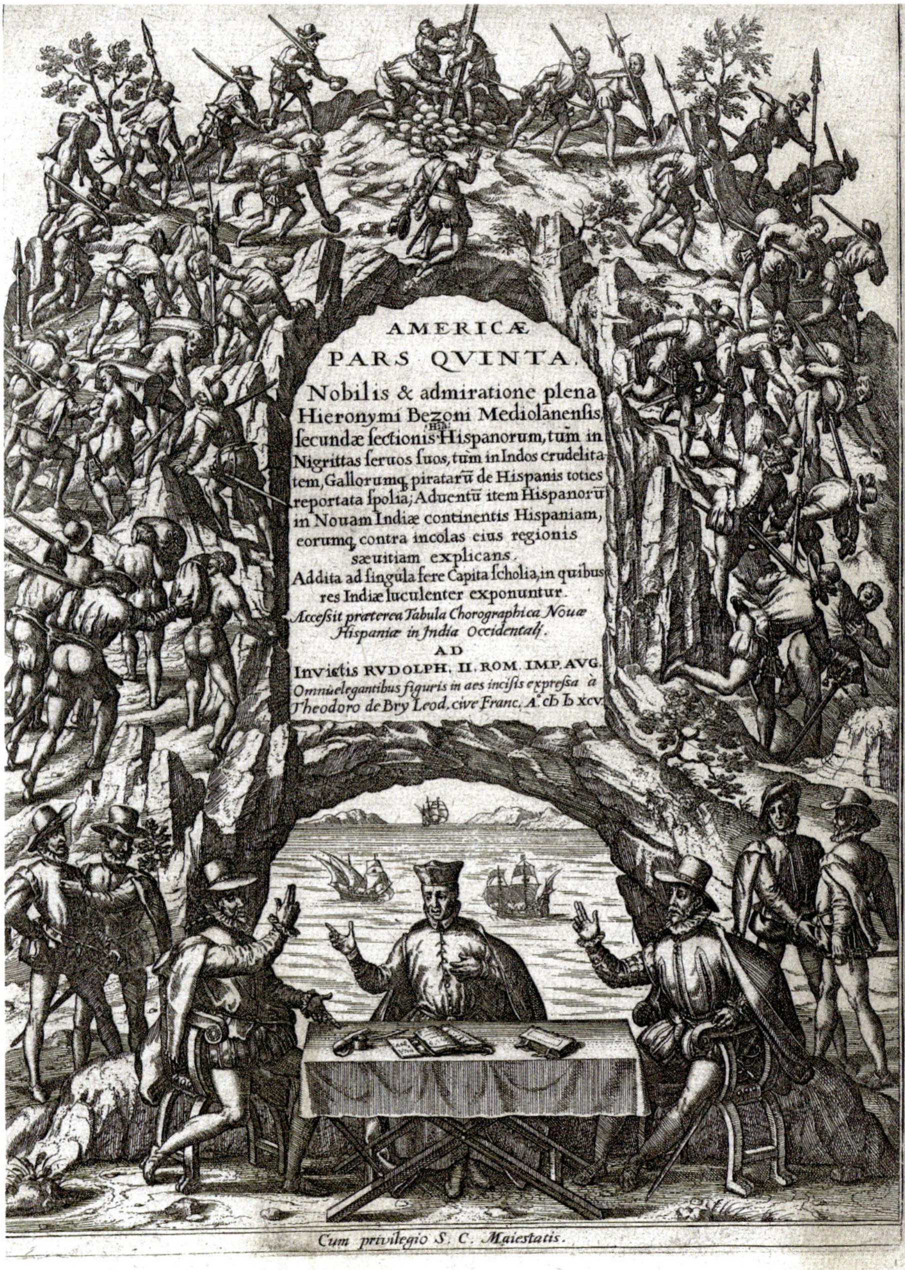

Fig. 16. Theodor de Bry, frontispiece, engraving, 34.5 × 24.2 cm, in *America pars quinta nobilis & admiratione plena Hieronymi Benzoni* (Frankfurt am Main, 1595). This is the second volume dedicated to Benzoni's text. A desiccated rocky mountain replaces the luxuriant landscape of the Caribbean, and heavily burdened Indians, forced by armed Spaniards, ascend on the left toward the summit, where Spaniards are depicted raising the cross, from which they then descend on the left

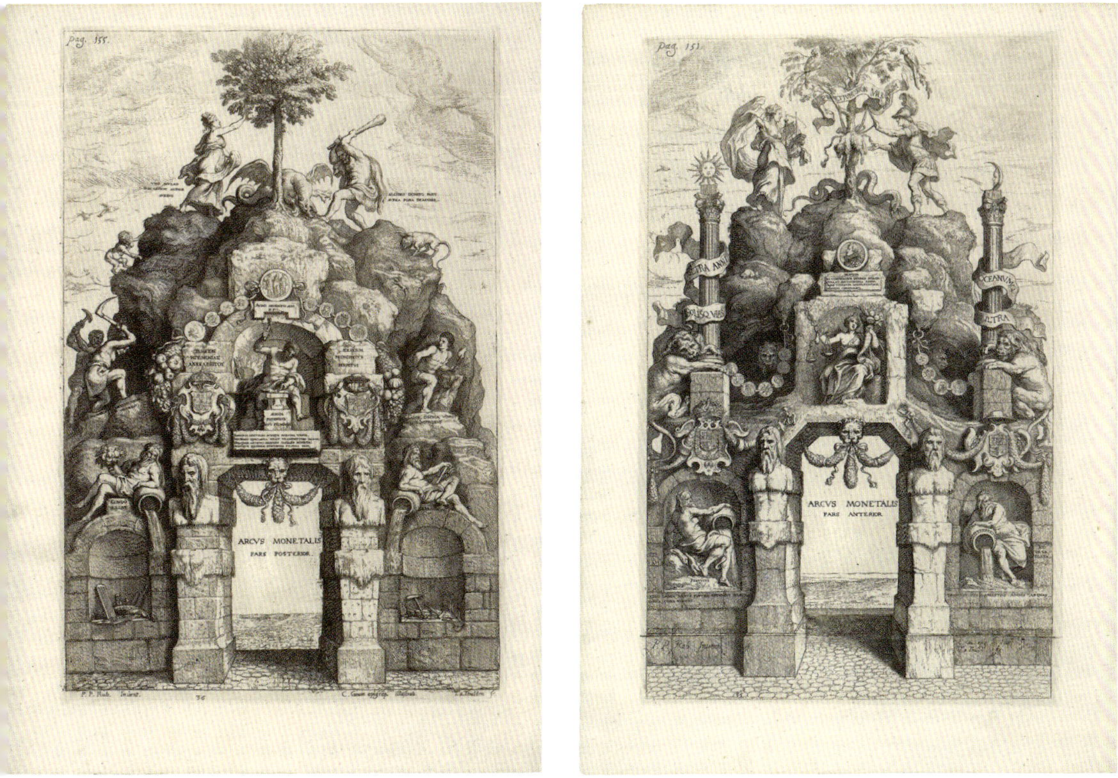

Fig. 17a–b. Theodoor van Thulden, *The Arch of the Mint* (front and back), engraving after Peter Paul Rubens, in Jan Caspar Gevaerts, *Pompa Introitus ... Ferdinandi Austriaci* (Antwerp, 1642)

metaphor as well as a reality. The inextricable connection between the material treasures of America's ore to be extracted and the pagan souls to be saved is articulated in the great seventeenth-century book written by the Peruvian friar Juan Meléndez, *Tesoros verdaderos de las Yndias*.[47]

In the exchange between America and Europe one might ask how this becomes translated. In part, the mines maintained the role of the image of salvation in the guise of a 1719 sculpture by Luis Niño of the most famous mine of all America, the silver mine of Potosí, commissioned by the Archbishop and Viceroy of Peru, Diego Morcillo Rubio de Auñón, as a pedestal for a sculpture of the *Virgin of Charity* in his hometown church of Villarobledo, Spain (fig. 15). His coat of arms is embossed on the surface, as are figures of men, women, and pack animals (llamas) as they ascend to work the veins of silver ore or descend with their loads of silver. This silver model is simultaneously simple and complex. It is a sculpture of a worked mine materialized by the very ore extracted from what it represents, a natural treasure, that is also a fully material articulation of the metaphor of God's dowry in order to bring the Gospel to Peru, and simultaneously the literal support of a Christian sculpture in Spain, where it can still be seen and venerated.

More importantly, the idea of the mines of the mountains of America became emblematic of its new history, for good and bad, throughout Europe as a common trope. Theordore de Bry used the mountains as the motif for the frontispieces of several volumes of his voyages.[48] For the fifth part, we see Spaniards ascending into the rugged Andes and planting the cross (fig. 16), just as the figures ascend the silver sculpture of Potosí that serves as the pedestal for a devotional sculpture. In the sixth part, we see the mountain now being mined, as Atahualpa appears below on his golden litter (fig. 10).

De Bry's frontispieces were the inspiration for one of the temporary arches designed by Peter Paul Rubens for the entrance of Ferdinand II of Austria into Antwerp in 1635, which we know from the engravings by Theodoor van Thulden in *Pompa Introitus ... Ferdinandi Austriaci*, which Jan Caspar Gevaerts published with his explanatory text in 1642 (Figs. 17a–b).[49] The imagery on what is called "The Arch of the Mint" alludes to or directly depicts the wealth that came from the conquest of America. Hercules is one of the classical figures whose heroic deeds were understood to also express allegorically the expansion of the Spanish Empire and the acquisition of the treasures of New Spain and Peru.

This classical mythological and modern allegorical relationship can be seen on the front of the arch, the summit of which depicts Hercules slaying the dragon that guards the golden apples of the Hesperides, while the figure of Hispania gathers them from the tree. On the back side of the arch Jason and the Golden Fleece appear at the summit of the mountain, just as the raising of the cross and the demonic figure feature at the top of the de Bry frontispieces (see figs. 2a and 16). The legend reads *pretivm non vile laborvm* (the reward of his labors is not worthless). According to a contemporary account of the entry, this was thought to mean not only that the Golden Fleece was well worth the trouble that Jason took to obtain it, but also that "the great usefulness of money sweetens the labor of the minters." Here, in the text, we can read of the figures that appear in de Bry's image of the mountainscape as it is being worked (fig. 10) but are absent in Ruben's design. The figure of the Golden Fleece is also, of course, a direct reference to the modern Order of the Golden Fleece, founded by Philip the Good, Duke of Burgundy (through whom Charles V took possession of the lowlands); Charles V and his son and grandson were grand masters in the order, and their portraits often depict them wearing the gold chain-link necklace of the order. At the sides are the pillars of Hercules that were a part of Charles V's new personal device, which expresses the Hapsburg expansion into what was for them was a new world.[50] Classical mythology was the screen through which the once unknown could be imagined. Thus, while the riches of Mexico and Peru flowed into Seville, the now legendary conquistadores Pizarro and Cortés were understood as "the new Jasons and Argonauts", as Gevaerts calls them.

Rubens abandons allegory to give a more realistic glimpse of the mines of Potosí on the other side of the arch. On the left, two workmen strike at the rock with their picks as they search for veins of ore. On the right, two men, one of whom holds a candle, are seen as they emerge from the mouth of a mine carrying loads of ore upon their backs. (Similar episodes are illustrated in the engraved title of the 1596 sixth part of Theodor de Bry's *America*.) In the great niche over the portal sits Vulcan, who with hammer and tongs is forging a golden thunderbolt on an anvil; on the block beneath the anvil is the legend *avrvm potentivs ictv fvlmineo* (gold is more powerful than the thunderbolt). The river gods have found a place above the niches, and from their urns "the streams of gold-producing Peru" spill over the stones below. The other river is Maranon, a branch of the Amazon that comes out of the Peruvian Andes.[51] Thus, by the seventeenth century, America was both a real source and a metaphor for wealth unlike any other part of the world. These images have a recursive effect in the imagination, through mixing contemporary wealth with ancient mythology, and they entered both the repertoire of artists and the dreams of Europeans, as Guaman Poma had written.[52]

Gold, of course, already had pride of place in the artistic production of the Islamic and Christian worlds before global expansion, as the essays of Dunlop and Balbale in this volume discuss. However, the sheer quantity of gold increased exponentially through first looting and then mining in the Americas, as Lane's essay details in terms of what took place in Nueva Granada (present-day Colombia). These new sources and quantities of gold led the historian John Elliot to write: "How far, indeed, would Renaissance and Baroque art, as an art heavily dependent on gold and silver ornamentation, have been possible without the riches of the Indies?"[53] They would certainly have been possible, but perhaps would not have taken quite the same appearance. No one, to my knowledge, has ever traced where the gold came from that was used in late Renaissance, Mannerist, and Baroque art and architecture. We do know, however, that the gilded interiors of Mexico and Peru and later Brazil were made possible by the immense amount of gold and silver available locally. Not only

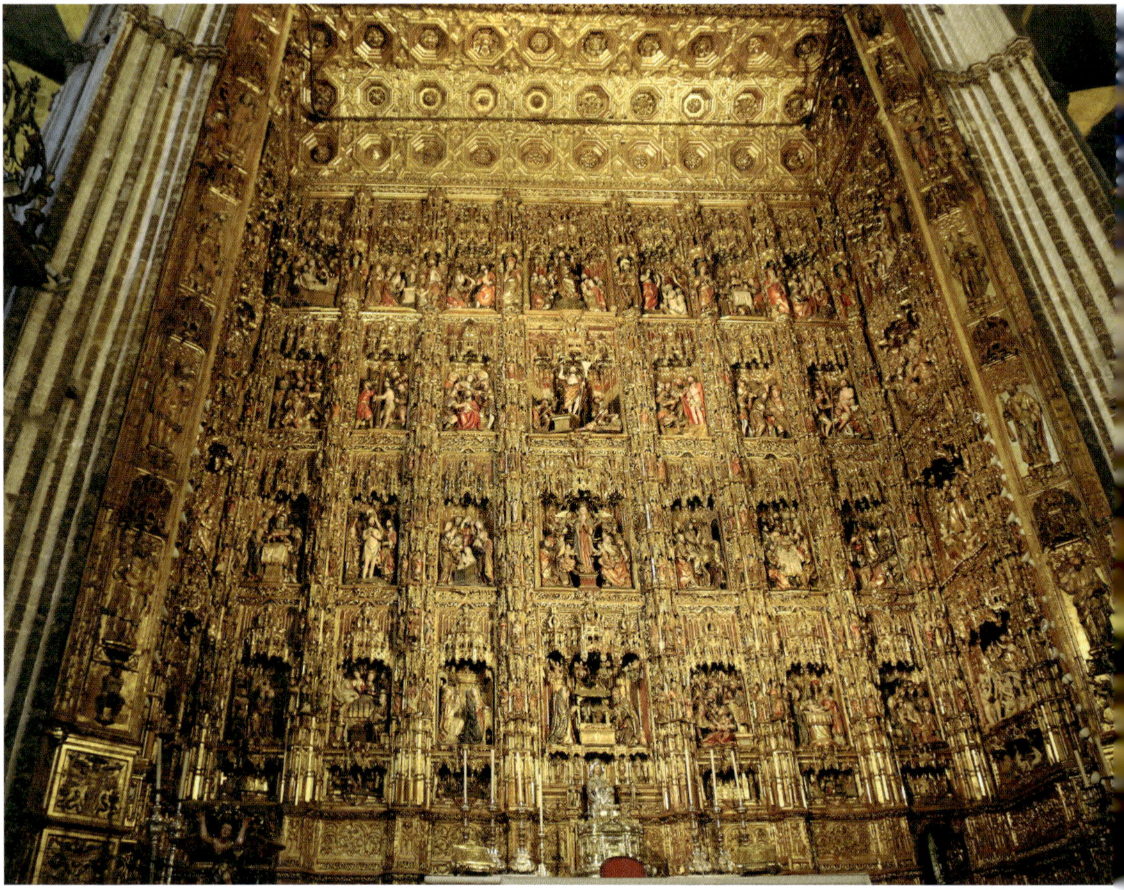

Fig. 18. Pierre Dancart, high altar, 1564, gilded wood. Seville, Cathedral

were streets in Peru literally paved with silver bars that were laid down for the entries of viceroys and the like, but altars, paintings, frames, clothes, and vessels were covered in gold.

Finally, we may ask how this might have translated literally and figuratively to Europe. If we look at the high altar in Seville Cathedral, designed by the Flemish artist Pierre Dancart, we can imagine the possibilities (fig. 18). It was begun in 1482, before Columbus discovered America, but gold began to pour into Seville as it was being built. The altar would have been nearly impossible to gild it as it now appears if it were not for that gold, and so the gilding took place as it neared completion in 1564. This soaring retable is, in some ways, not only a place of veneration and salvation writ through the gilded life of Christ, but its architecture conjures up the natural geography of the mountains from

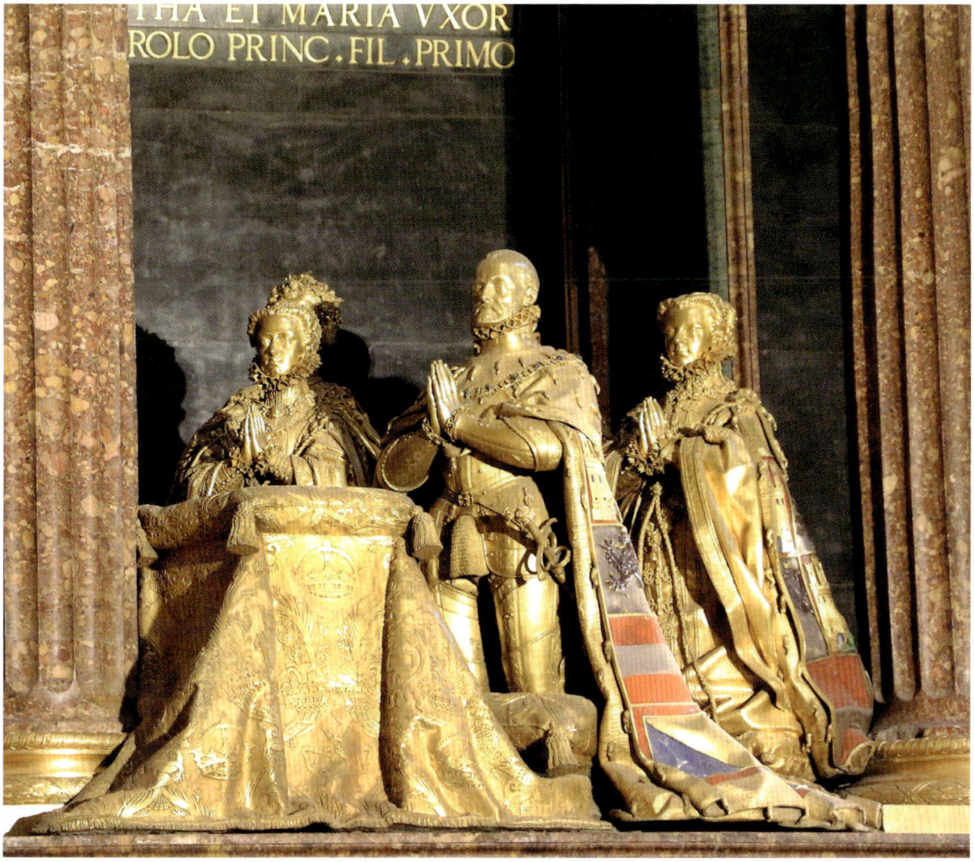

Fig. 19. Pompeo Leoni, tomb sculpture of Philip II, Anne of Austria, Isabella de Valois, Mary of Portugal, and Don Carlos, 1598, gilded bronze, 1,70 × 1. 80 m. El Escorial, Monasterio de San Lorenzo, Capilla mayor

which the gilding came. We might ask also how much of the enormous surface that depicts Christ's life is also the sacrifice of the Indies first gathered by Columbus and his sons and then by Cortés and Pizarro and so many others.

For certain, some of the gold of America rendered such service in Spain and Italy. Tradition has it that some of the very first gold brought back by Columbus and presented to Queen Isabella was then given to Pope Alexander VI, and used to gild the magnificent coffered ceiling of Santa Maria Maggiore in Rome.[54] Whether or not tradition is fact is not important here, as it is clearly in line, at least imaginatively, with how the gold from America was turned to aesthetic production in Europe by various painters, architects, and sculptors. Among those artists who had privileged access to this newfound wealth were Leone Leoni and Pompeo Leoni. They created numerous sculptures for Philip II, including the magnificent, gilded statues by Pompeo of the royal Spanish family kneeling in perpetual prayer before the altar in the chapel of the Monastery of San Lorenzo in the Escorial (fig. 19).[55]

The letters between the monarch and the sculptors demonstrate that there was a collaboration between a very devout patron and the artists at many levels. But, in terms of gold and where it came from and how it came to Spain, we can read (in a similar vein to that in Carletti's account discussed in the introduction) in a register of May 14, 1581 that the gold that Philip II was sending to Milan (19 baras del oro) to be used for the gilding of the effigies of the royal family at the Escorial had come from America. It had just arrived as the royal fifth from America, brought by the Capitan General of the Fleet, Martín Perez Olazábal, from New Spain.[56] Truly, this was a Christian "el dorado."[57]

One final set of images from a legal record of how gold was demanded as tribute paid to the Marqués del Valle occurs in the *Codex Tepetlaoztoc* (*Codex Kingsborough*) (fig. 20a and b). Again, these were painted by native artists (*tlacuilos*), as was the Huejotzingo painting (see Figure 9), and it too was entered in a legal case as the community's petition to the Audiencia in Mexico City. The images, painted on European paper, were created in 1554, specifically to be used as evidence by the community of the excessive demands made by Cortés but brought against the encomendero Juan Velázquez de Salazar, who continued the excess.[58] We first see the three years of tribute demanded by Cortés and overseen by his minions, and the consequences that led to the lawsuit that details tribute from 1527 to 1551. After the foundational history of the community and the genealogy of the ruling families in order to establish their legal rights, the images of tribute appear.

In the very first image (fig. 20a) one can see the type of gold that was shipped to Madrid some thirty years after the painting was made, and then forwarded to Pompeo Leoni's studio. The tribute demanded by Cortés is represented by three groupings of forty rectangular bars/ingots of gold, which are glossed by the phrase "estos son los tejuelos de oro." Their rectangular shape recalls the cruder *bara/tejuela* forged in Mexico City and lost in the hasty retreat of Spanish. The text relates that each *tejuelo* ought to be equivalent to thirty pesos of "oro de minas." Placed before the repetitive images of the gold bars is a magnificent painting of a "rudela de pluma y oro" (a shield of feathers and gold). In the center is an anthropomorphic butterfly with human hands and head.

Fig. 20a–b. *Codex Tepetlaoztoc* (*Codex Kingsborough*), Nahua, Mexico, 1554, paper and pigment, closed 29.8 × 21.4 cm, fols. 8r and 9r. London, British Museum, AM2006, DRG. 13964

20a

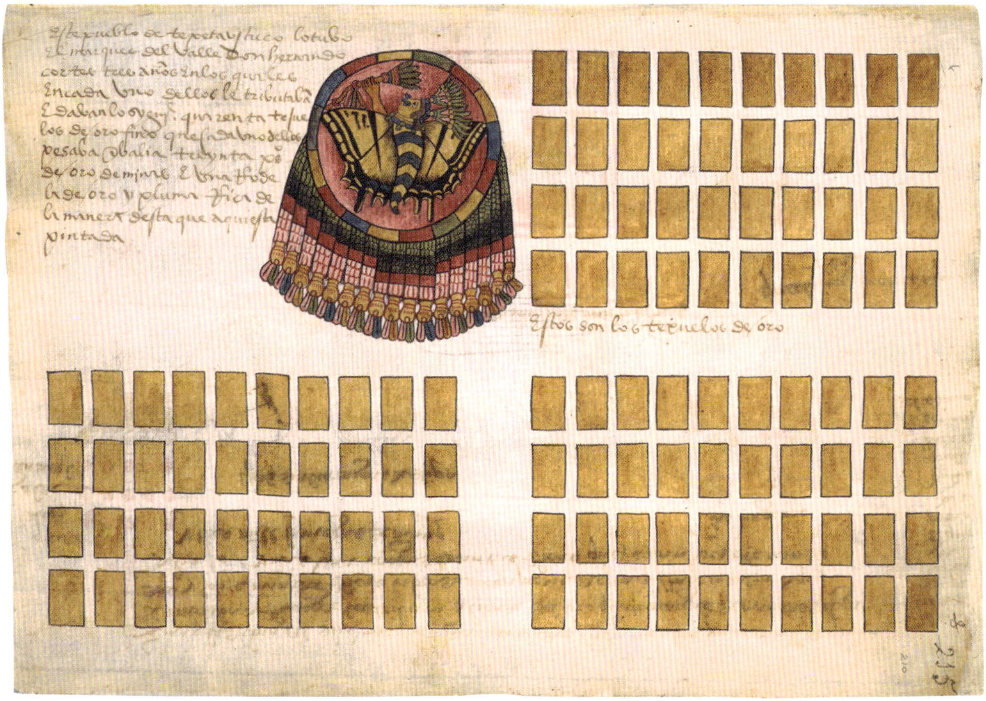

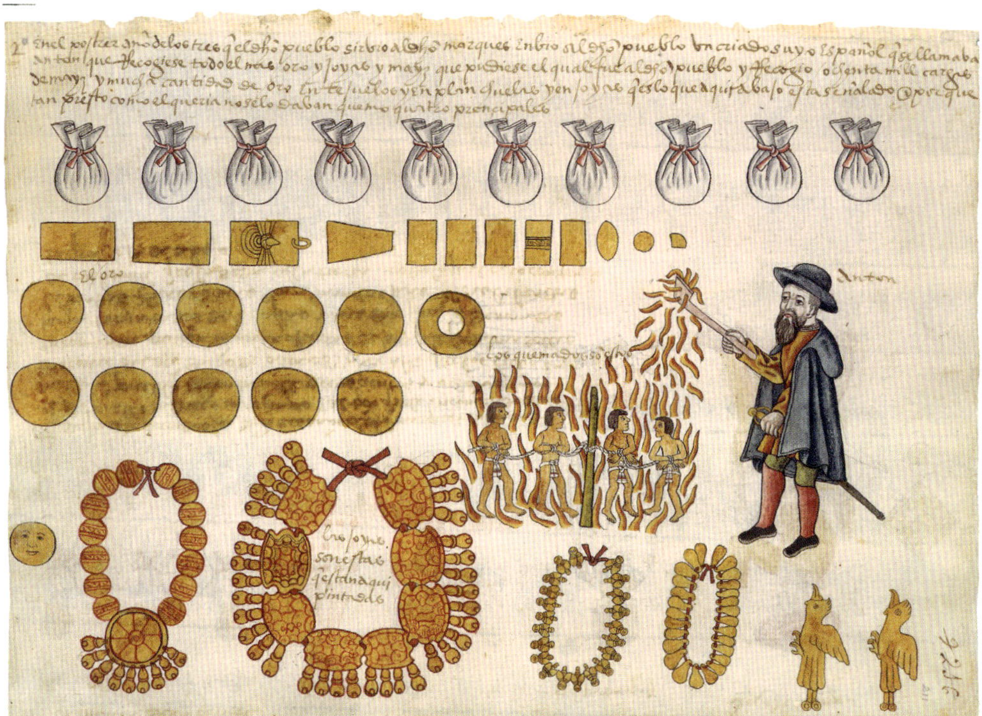

20b

The bottom is flecked with gold bells. This is the type of feathered object that was despoiled by Cortés and his band in Tenochtitlan, and which is depicted in Book 12 of Bernardino de Sahagún's *Florentine Codex* (fig. 5). There we see the gold that was stripped from the feather objects and melted in the crucible to form gold bars. Rendered here, the carefully and beautifully crafted image of the feathered butterfly is identified as possibly representing the goddess Xochiquetzal, who was the goddess of beauty and love and patroness of the duties of the household, the happy lives of women, and single soldiers. Diego Durán, a Dominican friar, wrote in the last third of the sixteenth century that she was "the protectoress of painters and weavers, of gold and silver smiths as ... all those who practiced the imitative arts."[59]

One can see the extreme irony here of the image of beauty and then terror that is the consequence of noncompliance as depicted on folio 9 (fig. 20b). Here, one sees Cortés's majordomo, Antón, who with a torch ignites the fire around four bound leaders of the community. They are punished because they were not forthcoming with the tribute as demanded: the gold, 80,000 loads of corn (shown above the gold), and six pieces of golden jewelry (depicted below). The first gold necklace that we see has a round, central shield-like form similar to the gold shield found off the coast of Veracruz (fig. 6), which may suggest that it too once belonged to a larger necklace. The ocher-painted disks are also familiar pictorial forms as they occur in the Huejotzingo manuscript (fig. 7). Even the small golden pendants of eagles, the last items on the page, conjure up the possessions depicted in the possessions of Martín Ocelotl (fig. 8). There is, in the end, a recursivity to the rendering of the New World's gold as depicted by artists in New Spain, as golden objects that become monetarily valued and then depicted as abstractions (yellow disks) as the substance of pure economic value.

The Escorial sculptures and Tepetlaoztoc paintings are radically different images of and about gold, from radically different places, cultures, and contexts. How, then, are we to understand gold in a global context without seeing its antithetical expressions of piety, economics, and extreme inhumanity at its cruelest, whether in the form of slavery or of torture? They are the two sides of the same coin. One presents the golden royal family of Spain in pious everlasting prayer. The other is yet another financial account from New Spain of the gold extracted through force. In this pictorial manuscript, the visceral pain and suffering is placed alongside economic value and greed, just as Carletti recounts the economics of trade as Dutch threw enslaved people into the ocean to drown in order to have room for the objects that could be sold in the

Dutch marketplace, as mentioned in the introduction to this volume.[60] And so, finally, we see the gold of the Indies shining in the Monastery of San Lorenzo, where it gilds the eternal prayers of a different "el dorado" now entered into the kingdom of heaven, while the gold of the Indies is forced from the lords of Tepetlaoztoc, who are not consumed by the imaginary fire of eternal damnation but by the very real fires of a hell on earth.

Notes

1. This assessment of value was made in Chanca's description of the gold jewelry that the Taino lord Guacamarí gave as a gift to the Spaniards: "Este oro facian en fojas muy delgadas, porque lo quieren para facer carátulas é para poderse asentar en betún que ellos facen, si ansí no fuese no se asentaria. Otro facen paratraer en la cabeza é para colgar en las orejas é narices, ansi que todavia es menester quesea delgado, pues que ellos nada de esto hacen por riqueza salvo por buen parescer." "Carta de Diego Álvarez de Chanca," *Historia del Nuevo Mundo*, 14 March 2008, http://www.historiadelnuevomundo.com/docs/Carta-Relacion-Doctor-Chanca.pdf, accessed June 29, 2022.

2. Walter Raleigh, *The Discoverie of the Large, Rich, and Bewtiful Empyre of Guiana: With a Relation of the Great and Golden Citie of Manoa (which the Spanyards Call El Dorado) and the Prouinces of Emeria, Arromaia, Amapaia, and Other Countries, with Their Riuers, Adioyning: Performed in the Yeare 1595*, ed. by Neil L. Whitehead (Norman: University of Oklahoma Press, 1997), 127.

3. For a modern study, see John Hemming, *The Search for El Dorado* (London: E. P. Dutton, 1978). The first mention of "el indio dorado" (the gilded Indian) occurs in 1534, when the Spanish moved from the coast of present-day Ecuador to the highlands and received news of a golden kingdom to the north (ibid., 52–53). What that probably referred to was the Muisca polity in the high plains of Bogotá. The term "el dorado" is in fact best known from the early seventeenth century, in the description of the Muisca in the inauguration ritual of their new leader: "They used to make a large raft from reeds on that lake, adorned and decorated as splendidly as they could. ... They stripped the heir to his bare flesh, anointed him with sticky soil, and covered him in ground and pulverized gold, so that everything on the raft was covered in this metal. They placed him standing on the balsa with mounds of gold and emeralds at his feet to offer to the gods. He was joined by four highest-ranking chieftains sumptuously dressed with feathers and crowns, bracelets, leggings, earrings all made of gold ... and they went to the middle of the lake. There, the golden Indian made his offerings by throwing into the middle of the lake all the gold and emeralds he carried. And the four chieftains who went with him did the same and once the raft started towards the land those on shore began to dance in a circle to the sound of flutes and rattles. And by this ritual they received their new chief and recognized him as their lord and master. ... It is this ceremony that originated the celebrated name of 'El Dorado.'" (Juan Rodríguez Freyle, *Conquista y descubrimiento del Nuevo Reino de Granada de las Indias Occidentales del Mar Océano* (Bogotá, 1890; written 1636), fols. 4v–5r, 5v.)

4. "... genoveses, venecianos y toda gente que tenga perlas, piedras preciosas y otras cosas de valor, todas las llevan hasta el cabo del mundo para las trocar, convertir en oro: el oro es excelentísimo, del oro se hace tesoro, y con él, quien lo tiene hace cuanto quiere en el mundo, y llega a que echa las ánimas al Paraíso." As Hemming writes (*In Search of El Dorado*, 5), Columbus was deeply influenced by Paolo Toscanelli's letter to sail westward to China and Japan, where "temples were, and palaces were covered with gold."

5. Karl Marx, *Capital: A Critique of Political Economy. Vol. I, Part 1, The Process of Capitalist Production*, trans. Ernest Untermann (New York: Cosimo Inc., 2007; first published in German 1867), 148.

6. "Earth, yield me roots!
[Digging]
Who seeks for better of thee, sauce his palate
With thy most operant poison! What is here?
Gold? yellow, glittering, precious gold? No, gods,
I am no idle votarist: roots, you clear heavens!
Thus much of this will make black white, foul fair,
Wrong right, base noble, old young, coward valiant.
Ha, you gods! why this? what this, you gods? Why, this
Will lug your priests and servants from your sides,
Pluck stout men's pillows from below their heads:
This yellow slave
Will knit and break religions, bless the accursed,
Make the hoar leprosy adored, place thieves
And give them title, knee and approbation
With senators on the bench: this is it
That makes the wappen'd widow wed again;
She, whom the spital-house and ulcerous sores
Would cast the gorge at, this embalms and spices
To the April day again. Come, damned earth,
Thou common whore of mankind, that put'st odds
Among the route of nations, I will make thee
Do thy right nature." (William Shakespeare, *Timon of Athens*, (ca. 1606): 4.3.23–44.)
Marx's citation places the emphasis slightly differently so as to make his point about gold and money.

7. The concept of a golden age exists within Shakespeare's work, as enunciated in *The Tempest*, when he has Gonzalo say: "I would with such perfection govern, sir, T' excel the Golden Age" (ca. 1610, 2.1.161–62).

8. The Basel Latin edition of 1493 has four illustrations: Christopher Columbus, *Epistola de insulis nuper inventis* (Basel: Michael Furter für Johann Bergmann, de Olpe, 1493).

9. For a discussion of the first images of America, as they appear in the frontispiece of Columbus's letter, see Thomas B.F. Cummins, "The Indulgent Image: Prints, Natives and the New World," in *Contested Visions in the Spanish Colonial World*, ed. by Ilona Katzew (Los Angeles: LACMA and Yale University Press, 2011), 203–5, 289–92.

10. De Bry's composition is derived from two prints. The older is from the frontispiece of Columbus's *La lettera dell'isole che ha trovato nuovamente il Re di Spagna*, by Giuliano Dati, printed in Florence in 1493; the second is the print of a broadsheet for Amerigo Vespucci's *Mundus Novus* (Nuremberg, 1505–6). For a hand-colored example, see Herzog August Bibliothek, Wolfenbüttel.

11. For the earliest account of the zemi, see Ramón Pané, *An Account of the Antiquities of the Indies*, trans S. Griswald (Durham, NC: Duke University Press, 1999; from the Spanish, ca. 1498).

12. Joanna Ostapkowicz et al. "Integrating the Old World into the New: An 'Idol from the West Indies'," *Antiquity* 91, no. 359 (2017): 1314–29.

13. While it is presumed that the presence of the rhino indicates an African connection, the Asian rhinoceros became a subject of great interest as a gift in the first decade of the sixteenth century and was the subject of one of Albrecht Dürer's most famous prints, of 1515, based only on a textual description: see ibid.

14. Alexander Menaker, "Beads," in *Magdalena de Cao: An Early Colonial Town of the North Coast of Peru*, ed. by Jeffery Quilter (Cambridge: Peabody Museum Press, 2020), 189–207. Beads continued to be used for barter in the Caribbean well into the seventeenth century. For example, 258 beads (ca. 34% glass, 17% cut crystal, 14% ceramic, 35% organic), manufactured in Venice, Paris, and Spain, and one agate bead from central India, all used to barter along the coasts of Colombia and Venezuela, were recovered from the 1622 shipwreck of *Buen Jesús y Nuestra Señora del Rosario*: see Sean A. Kingsley, "Tortugas Shipwreck (*Buen Jesús Nuestra Señora del Rosario*), 1622," https://shiplib.org/index.php/shipwrecks/iberian-shipwrecks/spanish-and-the-new-world/dry-tortugas-shipwreck-1622/, accessed June 29, 2022.

15. My discussion and analysis here is taken from the wonderful analytic and interpretive work of Leonardo López Luján, *José Luis Ruvalcaba Sil* "El tejo de oro y la noche triste" *Arqueología Mexicana* 27, no. 161 (2020): 14–21. I thank him for generously sharing it with me.

16. For a description of the *Florentine Codex*, see Jeanette Peterson and Kevin Terraciano, eds., *The Florentine Codex: An Encyclopedia of the Nahua World in Sixteenth-Century Mexico* (Austin: University of Texas Press, 2019).

17. Bernardino de Sahagún, *Historia general de las cosas de Nueva España (Florentine Codex)*, 1577, Biblioteca Medicea Laurenziana, Florence, Palat. 218–20, Book 12, fols. 27v–28r. See www.wdl.org/en/item/10096/view/1/47/, accessed June 29, 2022.

18. This link between the gold ingot and the image in Book 12 of the *Florentine Codex* is made in López Luján, "El teje de oro y la noche triste."

19. Jeanette Peterson, "The Florentine Codex Imagery and the Colonial Tlacuilo," in *The Work of Bernardino de Sahagún: Pioneer Ethnographer of Sixteenth-Century Aztec Mexico*, ed. by J. Klor de Alva, H. B. Nicholson, and E. Quiñones Keber (Albany: Institute for Mesoamerican Studies, SUNY, 1988), 273–93.

20. Only sixty years earlier, gold-adorned Christian liturgical objects and images in Constantinople were destroyed and melted down for their gold. For a stunning and brilliant comparison of the images and texts of the Turkish sacking of Constantinople and the Spanish sacking of Tenochtitlan and destruction of golden objects, see Eleni Kefala, *The Conquered: Byzantium and America on the Cusp of Modernity* (Washington, DC: Dumbarton Oaks, 2020).

21. In 1622, another gold bar was on its way to Spain aboard the ship *Santa Margarita*, when it sank off the coast of Florida in a hurricane, with some 9,000 ounces of gold. Recovered in the late twentieth century, along with many other things of value, the bar was placed in the Mel Fisher Museum within a plexiglass box, such that visitors could reach in and pick it up, feeling the weight of gold and history melded into one, without being able to pull it out (a kind of monkey box/trap). In 2010, the bar was brazenly stolen when two men, later apprehended, simply cut into the plexiglass and removed it.

22. Allison Caplan, "Shield Pendant with Darts," in *Golden Kingdoms: Luxury Arts in the Ancient Americas*, ed. by Joanne Pillsbury, Timothy Potts, and Kim N. Richter (Los Angeles: J. Paul Getty Museum and Getty Research Institute, 2017), 267, cat. no. 222. I am also indebted to Ji Mary Seo's excellent unpublished study "All That Glitters: Aztec Gold before and after the Spanish Conquest of Mexico."

23. Charles V would take certain portions for himself and family, which were different from the royal fifth owed to the Spanish king.

24. Francesco Carletti, *Ragionamenti del mio viaggio intorno al mondo*, ed. by Adele Dei (Milan: Mursia, 1987; from a manuscript of 1606), 38.

25. For a more detailed analysis of the painting, see Thomas B.F. Cummins, "The Madonna and the Horse: Alternative Readings of Colonial Images," in *Native Artists and Patrons in Colonial Latin America*, ed. by Emily Umberger and Thomas B.F. Cummins, *Phoebus* 7 (1995) 52–83; Thomas B.F. Cummins, "From Lies to Truth: Colonial Ekphrasis and the Act of Crosscultural Translation," in *Reframing the Renaissance: Visual Culture in Europe and Latin America, 1450–1650*, ed. by Claire Farago (New Haven: Yale University Press, 1995), 152–74, 326–29.

26. Dorothy Hosler, *Sounds, Colors, and Meanings in the Metallurgy of Ancient West Mexico* (Cambridge MA: MIT Press, 1995).

27. His religious or priestly status or position in Tenochtitlan and then Mexico City is at best ambiguous: see, for example, J. Jorge Klor de Alva, "Martín Oceotl: Clandestine Cult Leader," in *Struggle and Survival in Colonial America*, ed. by David G. Sweet and Gary B. Nash (Berkeley: University of California Press, 1981), 128–41; Munehiro Kobayashi, "Modalidades de la vida de los indígenas texcocanos de la década de 1530: un análisis de los tres procesos inquisitoriales de los indios," *Annals of Latin American Studies* 15 (1995): 19–52.

28. The literature on Martín Oceotl is vast. See Patricia Lopes Don, "Franciscans, Indian Sorcerers, and the Inquisition in New Spain, 1536–1543," *Journal of World History* 17, no. 1 (2006): 27–48.

29. Robert H. Barlow, "Las joyas de Martín Ocelotl," *Yan: ciencias antropológicas* 3 (1954): 56–59; Xavier Noguez, "Las joyas de Martín Océlotl," *Arqueología Mexicana* 142 (2019): 12–13.

30. Felipe Guaman Poma de Ayala, *Nueva crónica i buen gobierno* (ca. 1615), ed. by J. Murra and R. Adorno, trans. by J. Urioste (Mexico: Siglo XXI, 1980), 371–72.

31. Thomas B.F. Cummins, "The Golden Calf in America," in *The Idol in the Age of Art: Objects, De-*

votions and the Early Modern World, ed. by Michael Cole and Rebecca Zorach (Farnham: Ashgate, 2009), 99–104.

32. This set of figures derives from the frontispiece of the first book detailing the conquest of Peru, published in Seville. It ultimately derives from a large print by Burgkmair: see Thomas B.F. Cummins, "Indulgent Image," 201–23; 289–92.

33. *La conquista del Peru llamado nueva Castilla* (Seville: Bartolome Perez, 1534). For the gold and silver from the ransom of Atahualpa sent from Peru to Charles V, see the various inventories, beginning with Hernando Alvarez, "Relación del oro que recibimos de Herando Pizarro por el mes de Hebrero del año pasado mil é quientos é trienta é cuatro años," in José Toribio Medina, *La imprenta en Lima (1584–1824)*, vol. 1, facsimile ed. (Santiago de Chile: Fondo Histórico y Bibliográfico José Toribio Medina, 1966), 163–74. For an abbreviated English version, see Samuel K. Lothrop, *Inca Treasure as Depicted by Spanish Historians* (Los Angeles: Southwest Museum, 1939), 48–51.

34. Dürer famously wrote of his reaction on seeing Aztec items exhibited by Charles V in Brussels in 1520: "I saw the things which have been brought to the King from the new land of gold, a sun all of gold a whole fathom broad, and a moon all of silver of the same size, also two rooms full of armor of the people there, and all manner of wondrous weapons of theirs, harness and darts, very strange clothing, beds, and all kinds of wonderful objects of human use, much better worth seeing than prodigies [myths, fairy tales]. These things were all so precious that they are valued at 100,000 florins [guilders]. All the days of my life I have seen nothing that rejoiced my heart so much as these things, for I saw amongst them wonderful works of art, and I marveled at the subtle Ingenia of men in foreign lands. Indeed, I cannot express all that I thought there." Albrecht Dürer, *Diary of His Journey to the Netherlands, 1520–1521*, ed. by J.-A. Goris and G. Marlier (Greenwich, CT: New York Graphic Society Ltd., 1971), 53–54.

35. Raleigh, *Discoverie of the Large, Rich, and Bewtiful Empyre of Guiana*, 127.

36. "On a silver field, a king in carnation, bound by two golden chains, flanked by two trunks, on which the king lays his hands. The image bordered in azure [blue] and loaded with seven monarchs in carnation bound by a golden chain. It is divided into three parts. In the first section, on a silver background, a sable [black] eagle crowned with gold, embracing two silver columns, joined by a silver banner that reads PLUS ULTRA in sable lettering. In azure, a city [Túmbez, where Pizarro came ashore in Peru]; in silver, a lion and a tiger standing on their hind legs; and on waves of azure and silver, two ships with drawn sails. A double border contains a vert [green] background with eight silver sheep, and around that, a silver banner with sable lettering which reads *Carol Caesaris auspitio et labore ingenio ac impensa ducis Pizarro inventa et pacata*. In the second section, a silver lion with a golden crown held by a golden chain holds a golden F between its front paws, and around it a silver banner with the lettering *Indefesso labore meo. Fidem pro oculis habens tot comparavi divitas*. The third section has an azure border with seven golden griffins bound with a gold chain. Each griffin holds an azure banner. The coat of arms is crested with a helmet in gold and azure. Parting from the helmet is a demi-lion in gold wielding an unsheathed sword dripping in blood. Above the lion is a crown, which marks the emblem as that of a marquis. Over everything is a smaller coat of arms bearing the emblem of the Pizarro family [a vert pine tree on silver, with golden fruits, and two sable bears on their hind legs]." Real provision de Don Carlos y Juana al Marques Francisco Pizarro, gobernador del Perú, por al que le conceden el uso de nuevas armas en su escudo, además de sus antecesores y de las concedidas anteriormente en otras dos ocasiones. Todas las cuales están descritas detalladamente con sus respectivas leyendas, la última de las cuales está en lengua india (22-12-1537). Archivo General de las Indias, Seville, Lima 565 L. 2, fols. 327r–329r.

37. The narrative pen and ink images appear at the end of the text and are based upon a set of murals and other pictorial documents produced in Tlaxcala.

38. The royal crown of Rudolph II, commissioned in 1602, is the best example of this form of the imperial crown of the Hapsburgs. It is made of pure gold, which perhaps came from America, as well as being topped by an emerald cross, the emeralds of which came from Nueva Granada (present-day Colombia). Rudolph's interest in objects and materials from America is well known, including his collection of feather paintings from New Spain. However, this double royal authority over Church and State as held by Charles V was even more important in the imaginary of the Tlaxcalan ambassadors because, as King of Spain, Charles V and Philip II also embodied the Spanish accord with the papacy known as the Patronato Real. This accord granted the King of Spain the authority to appoint Church officials as well as oversee Church finances. The Patranato Real developed late in the Catholic retaking of Spain from Islamic control and the victory at Granada, but it was developed further as Spain and Portugal expanded to the New World. In origin it "had feudal and contractual overtones. ... [However,] Ferdinand foresaw the possible enlargement of the role of the patron into that of ruler of an empire. ... The end result gave the monarchy an opportunity to push patronal rule beyond the original powers into a quasi-pontifical rule of the clergy [in America]." W. E. Shiels, *King and Church: The Rise and Fall of the Patronato Real* (Chicago: University of Chicago Press, 1961), 8.

39. It is possible that many of the golden objects in the inventory of Charles V's possessions made at his death at Yuste (1558–59) were from these objects. They are enumerated under the category entitled "Joyas de las Yndias." The first items listed most certainly came from Peru, and they were perhaps a part of Atahualpa's ransom that reached Seville intact. The first object is "una caxa de plata y oro en que están un yndio y una yndia con una alabarda y en lo angosto que todo pesa como se esta diez y siete marcos quatro oncas y siete octavas." The next object is described as a golden ear of corn: "Una caña de oro de la muestra del trigo de las Yndias que esta en dos pedazos y es de oro de catorze quilates que peso diez marcos y seys oncas y una ochava." The third object is directly related to Peru: "Un par de zapatos de las Yndias del Peru." See "Inventario postmórtem 1558–1559, Archivo General de Simancas, Valladolid, Contaduría Mayor de Cuentas, 1ª época, leg.1145," in *Los inventarios de Carlos V y la familia imperial*, vol. 1 (Madrid: Fernando Villaverde Ediciones, 2010), 320. In fact, we can be fairly sure that the first two items listed in Charles's collection clearly came from the ship bearing Atahualpa's ransom. In an inventory made in Seville of the things received as part of the king's fifth, we find "a stalk of maize, of gold with three leaves and two ears," followed by "A panel of gold and silver which enclosed the figures of an Indian and woman of medium size" (as translated in Lothrop, *Inca Treasure as Depicted by Spanish Historians*, 50). What happened to them after 1559 we will probably never know. Ironically, in the same inventory of Charles, several Mexican feather shields embellished with gold were despoiled of the gold, just as they had been in Tenochtitlan by Cortés, as depicted and described in the *Florentine Codex* (Fig. 5) ("Inventario postmórtem," 323).

40. Thomas B.F. Cummins, "'Let me see! Reading is for them': Colonial Andean Images and Objects 'como es costumbre tener los caciques señores'," in *Native Traditions in the Postconquest World*, ed. by Elizabeth Boone and Thomas B.F. Cummins (Washington, DC: Dumbarton Oaks Research Library and Collections, 1998), 118–30.

41. For the passenger lists of the *Atocha* and *Margarita* and the relationships of those lists and the ingots recovered from the shipwrecks, see Corey Malcom, "The 1622 Tierra Firme Fleet: An Account of the Disaster and the People" (Mel Fisher Maritime Museum Series of Occasional Papers in Maritime Heritage Research No. 1, 2019).

42. "Poi ciascun padrone li fa segnare o, per dire piú propriamente, marcare della sua marca che si fa fare d'argento e poi infocata al lume della candela di sego, con il quale se unge la scottatura e segno che si fa loro sopra il petto overo sopra un braccio o dietro la spalle per reconoscerli." Carletti, *Ragionamenti del mio viaggio*, 38.

43. As Charles wrote, "I would love to see it all but given the time it would take to bring it here, I think it would be enough to send me some of the most unusual gold and silver work. You can coin all the rest ... [given] our need for money" to attack Tunis; as cited in Geoffrey Parker, *Emperor: A New Life of Charles V* (New Haven: Yale University Press, 2019), 357.

44. Pablo Joseph de Arriaga, *La extirpación de la idolotría en el Perú* (1621) (Cuzco: Centro de Estudios Regionales Andinos "Bartolomé de las Casas," 1991), 156.

45. "todas estas montañas están llenas dello, y tierras hay (que) en las casas y en los campos y adonde quiera, está la tierra mesclada con polvo de oro. ¿Que significa esto sino que se hubo Dios, con estos gentiles miserables y con nostoros como sea un padre que tiene dos hijas: la una muy blanca, muy discreta y llena de gracias y donaires, la otra muy fea, lagañosa, tonta y bestial? Si ha de casar la primera, no ha menester (darle) dote sino ponerla en palaçio, que allí andarán en competencia los señores sobre quién se casará con ella. A la fea, trope, neçia, degraçiada, no basta esto sino darle gran dote: muchas joyas, ropas ricas, sumptuosas casas, y con todo eso Dios y ayuda.

Lo mismo hiço Dios con éstos y con nosotros. Todo eramos infieles: esa Europa esa Asia; mas, en lo natural, gran hermosura, muchas ciençias, discreción. Poco fue menester para que los apóstoles y varones apostólicos desposasen estas almas con Jesucristo por la fee del bautismo. Mas estas naçiones, criaturas eran de Dios; y para la bien aventurança, capaçes deste matrimonio con Jesucristo; mas eran feos, rústicos, tontos, inhábiles, lagañosos, y era menester gran dote. Y así, les dio hasta las montañas de oro y plata, tierras fértiles y deleitosas, porque a este olor hubiese gentes que por Dios quisiesen ir a esta predicación evangélica y los baustisaen y quedasen estas alamas esposas de Jesucristo ...

Así, digo destos indios que uno de los medios de su presestinaçión y salvaçión fueron estas minas, tesoros y riquesas, porque vemos claramente que donde hay va el Evangelio volando y en competençia; y adonde no la hay sino pobres, es medio de reprobaçción porque jamás llega allí el Evangelio, como por gran experiençia se ve que, a las tierras donde no hay este dote de oro y plata, ni hay soldado ni capitán que quiera is, ni aun ministro del Evangelio. Luego, buenas son las minas entre estos bárbaros, pues Dios se las dio para que llevasen la fee." *El Anonimo de Yucay frente a Bartolomé de Las Casas* (1571), ed. by Isacio Pérez Fernández (Cuzco: Centro de Estudios Regionales Andinos "Bartolomé de las Casas," 1995), 158–60.

46. The most famous allegorical image of America, as a recumbent female, is found in Jan van der Straet's (Stradanus's) image of Columbus's discovery of the New World in *Nova Reperta* (translated as *New Inventions of Modern Times*), ca. 1590.

47. After detailing the riches taken from Potosí and elsewhere in America, Meléndez writes: "como nos llevan el Tesoro material valiéndose delo mismo, que han trabajado, fatiga sacaron de las entrañas de las peñas nuestros manos, para hacernos después guerra conello, se aprovecharan mejor destos Tesoros espirituales, y verferafderas, paraque todos unidos en una Fe, y en una paz, que es Cristo Nuestro Señor, que solo puede unir los corazones mas opuestos" (Juan Meléndez, *Tesoros verdaderos de las Yndias*, 3 vols. (Rome: Nicolas Angel Tinassio, 1681), 1.48), and "Lee mis libros (vuelvo á decir) con piedad, y hallarás mucho oro, y purissimo, entre sus desaliños, y mucha plata, y finissima, entre sus escorias; y hace rico de una vez de lo que truxo un indio, si para poderlo ser en tantos años, no te han vastado las Yndias" (ibid., 3.37).

48. See Cummins, "Golden Calf in America."

49. My discussion of the arch is taken directly from Elizabeth McGrath, "Rubens's Arch of the Mint," *Journal of the Warburg and Courtauld Institutes* 37 (1974): 191–217.

50. Earl E. Rosenthal, "Plus Ultra, Non plus Ultra, and the Columnar Device of Emperor Charles V," *Journal of the Warburg and Courtauld Institutes* 34 (1971): 204–28; and Earl E. Rosenthal, "The Invention of the Columnar Device of Emperor Charles V at the Court of Burgundy in Flanders in 1516," *Journal of the Warburg and Courtauld Institutes* 36 (1973): 199–211.

51. Aneta Georgievska-Shine and Larry Silver, *Rubens, Velázquez, and the King of Spain* (Farnham: Ashgate, 2014), 92–95, 103–6.

52. The riverine elements of Ruben's design for an ephemeral arch make their way into permanent sculptural form in Bernini's 1651 Fountain of Four Rivers in the Piazza Navona in Rome: see Joseph Connors, "Borromini's House of Books," *Annali di architettura* 31 (2019): 135–44.

53. John Elliot, *The Old World and the New 1492–1650* (Cambridge: Cambridge University Press, 1970), 65.

54. According to the official Vatican site describing Santa Maria Maggiore, "The coffered ceiling was designed by Giuliano Sangallo and later completed by his brother Antonio. Tradition has it that the first gold brought from the New World, which Isabella and Ferdinand of Spain offered to Alexander VI, was utilized for the ceiling's gilding." See http://www.vatican.va/various/basiliche/sm_maggiore/en/storia/interno.htm, accessed May 14, 2021. I thank Thomas Gruber for bringing this tradition to my attention. Such a donation by Isabella and the use of the gold by Alexander for the basilica's coffered ceiling is fully understandable, given Alexander's pronouncement of his *Inter caetera* of 1493, which recognized by papal donation to the Spanish kings all the lands more than 100 leagues west of the Cape Verde Islands. The basilica soon became the focus of Alexander's architectural ambitions; for a full analysis of his project, see Philip J. Jacks, "Alexander VI's Ceiling for S. Maria Maggiore in Rome," *Römisches Jahrbuch für Kunstgeschichte* 22 (1985): 63–82.

55. For a discussion of the history of the production of these sculptures, see Almudena Pérez de Tudela Gabaldón, "El cenotafio de Carlos V en la Basílica del Escorial," and Augustín Bustamante García, "El grupo sepulcra de Felipe II," in *Leone & Pompeo Leoni. Actas del Congreso Internacional*, ed. by Stephan Schroder (Madrid: Museo Nacional del Prado, 2012), 132–48 and 149–59.

56. Eugene Plon, *Les maîtres italiens au service de la maison d'Autriche. Leone Leoni, sculpteur de*

Charles-quint, et Pompeo Leoni, sculpteur de Philippe II (Paris: E. Plon, Nourrit et Cie, 1887), 416. Eight years later, in 1589, he was again commander of the fleet, when it was partially destroyed by a hurricane off the coast of Florida.

57. I have earlier written of this image of Philip as a "Christian el dorado," as the term "el dorado" designating a gilded king comes from an early seventeenth-century text by Juan Rodríguez Freyle, who describes the coronation of a new leader of the Muisca (the people who lived in the high plains of Bogotá) involving him being covered in gold: see note 4 above; also Thomas B.F. Cummins, "The Gilded Body and Brilliant Wall: Ornament in America before and after the European Contact," in *Ornament Between Globalism and Localism*, ed. by Gulru Necipoglu and Alina Payne (Princeton: Princeton University Press, 2016), 238–47.

58. See Perla Valle, "Estudio," in *Códice de Tepetlaóztoc (Códice Kingsborough), Estado de México*, 2 vols. (Mexico: Espejo de Obsidiana Ediciones, S.A de C.V., El Colegio Mexiquense a. C., 1994), 2.11 n.3.

59. Diego Durán, *Historia de las Indias* (1581), as cited in Valle, "Estudio," 2.57.

60. There were enslaved people in Holland, many of whom were brought to Holland by those returning from America. However, there was no major slave market in Holland. Rather, the Dutch slave trade was focused on the colonies. Because the *Zeelandia* and the *Langebarke* intended to return directly to Holland, where enslaved people held no mercantile value for them, and because those people took the space of the seized valued commodities in the Dutch markets, they were expendable.

Bibliography

Álvarez, Hernando. "Relación del oro que recibimos de Herando Pizarro por el mes de Hebrero del año pasado mil é quientos é trienta é cuatro años." In José Toribio Medina, *La imprenta en Lima (1584–1824)*, vol. 1, 163–74. Facsimile ed. Santiago de Chile: Fondo Histórico y Bibliográfico José Toribio Medina, 1966.

Anonymous. *La conquista del Peru llamado nueva Castilla*. Seville: Bartolome Perez, 1534.

El Anonimo de Yucay frente a Bartolomé de Las Casas (1571). Edited by Isacio Pérez Fernández. Cuzco: Centro de Estudios Regionales Andinos "Bartolomé de las Casas," 1995.

Archivo General de las Indias, Seville, Lima 565 L. 2.

Arriaga, Pablo Joseph de. *La extirpación de la idolotría en el Perú* (1621). Cuzco: Centro de Estudios Regionales Andinos "Bartolomé de las Casas," 1991.

Barlow, Robert H. "Las joyas de Martín Ocelotl." Yan: ciencias antropológicas 3 (1954): 56–59.

Bustamante García, Augustín. "El grupo sepulcra de Felipe II." In *Leone & Pompeo Leoni. Actas del Congreso Internacional*, edited by Stephan Schroder, 149–59. Madrid: Museo Nacional del Prado, 2012.

Caplan, Allison. "Shield Pendant with Darts." In *Golden Kingdoms: Luxury Arts in the Ancient Americas*, edited by Joanne Pillsbury, Timothy Potts, and Kim N. Richter, 267, cat. no. 222. Los Angeles: J. Paul Getty Museum and Getty Research Institute, 2017.

Carletti, Francesco. *Ragionamenti del mio viaggio intorno al mondo* (1606). Edited by Adele Dei. Milan: Mursia, 1987.

"Carta de Diego Álvarez de Chanca." *Historia del Nuevo Mundo*, 14 March 2008, http://www.historiadelnuevomundo.com/docs/Carta-Relacion-Doctor-Chanca.pdf.

Columbus, Christopher. *Epistola de insulis nuper inventis*. Basel: Michael Furter für Johann Bergmann, de Olpe, 1493.

Connors, Joseph. "Borromini's House of Books." *Annali di architettura* 31 (2019): 135–44.

Cummins, Thomas B.F. "From Lies to Truth: Colonial Ekphrasis and the Act of Crosscultural Translation." In *Reframing the Renaissance: Visual Culture in Europe and Latin America, 1450–1650*, edited by Claire Farago, 152–74, 326–29. New Haven: Yale University Press, 1995.

Cummins, Thomas B.F. "The Gilded Body and Brilliant Wall: Ornament in America before and after the European Contact." In *Ornament Between Globalism and Localism*, edited by Gulru Necipoglu and Alina Payne, 238–47. Princeton: Princeton University Press, 2016.

Cummins, Thomas B.F. "The Golden Calf in America." In *The Idol in the Age of Art: Objects, Devotions and the Early Modern World*, edited by Michael Cole and Rebecca Zorach, 77–104. Farnham: Ashgate, 2009.

Cummins, Thomas B.F. "The Indulgent Image: Prints, Natives and the New World." In *Contested Visions in the Spanish Colonial World*, edited by Ilona Katzew, 201–23, 289–92. Los Angeles: LACMA and Yale University Press, 2011.

Cummins, Thomas B.F. "'Let me see! Reading is for them': Colonial Andean Images and Objects 'como es costumbre tener los caciques señores'." In *Native Traditions in the Postconquest World*, edited by Elizabeth Boone and Thomas B.F. Cummins, 118–30. Washington, DC: Dumbarton Oaks Research Library and Collections, 1998.

Cummins, Thomas B.F. "The Madonna and the Horse: Alternative Readings of Colonial Images." In *Native Artists and Patrons in Colonial Latin America*, edited by Emily Umberger and Thomas B.F. Cummins. *Phoebus* 7 (1995): 52–83.

Don, Patricia Lopes. "Franciscans, Indian Sorcerers, and the Inquisition in New Spain, 1536–1543." *Journal of World History* 17, no. 1 (2006): 27–48.

Dürer, Albrecht. *Diary of His Journey to the Netherlands, 1520–1521.* Edited by J.-A. Goris and G. Marlier. Greenwich, CT: New York Graphic Society Ltd., 1971.

Elliot, John. *The Old World and the New 1492–1650.* Cambridge: Cambridge University Press, 1970.

Freyle, Juan Rodríguez. *Conquista y descubrimiento del Nuevo Reino de Granada de las Indias Occidentales del Mar Océano* (1636). Bogotá, 1890.

Georgievska-Shine, Aneta, and Larry Silver. *Rubens, Velázquez, and the King of Spain.* Farnham: Ashgate, 2014.

Guaman Poma de Ayala, Felipe. *Nueva crónica i buen gobierno* (ca. 1615). Edited by J. Murra and R. Adorno; translated by J. Urioste. Mexico: Siglo XXI, 1980.

Hemming, John. *The Search for El Dorado.* London: E. P. Dutton, 1978.

Hosler, Dorothy. *Sounds, Colors, and Meanings in the Metallurgy of Ancient West Mexico.* Cambridge MA: MIT Press, 1995.

"Inventario postmórtem 1558–1559, Archivo General de Simancas, Valladolid, Contaduría Mayor de Cuentas, 1ª época, leg.1145." In *Los inventarios de Carlos V y la familia imperial*, vol. 1. Madrid: Fernando Villaverde Ediciones, 2010.

Jacks, Philip J. "Alexander VI's Ceiling for S. Maria Maggiore in Rome." *Römisches Jahrbuch für Kunstgeschichte* 22 (1985): 63–82.

Kefala, Eleni. *The Conquered: Byzantium and America on the Cusp of Modernity.* Washington, DC: Dumbarton Oaks, 2020.

Kingsley, Sean A. "Tortugas Shipwreck (*Buen Jesús Nuestra Señora del Rosario*), 1622." Accessed June 29, 2022. https://shiplib.org/index.php/shipwrecks/iberian-shipwrecks/spanish-and-the-new-world/dry-tortugas-shipwreck-1622/.

Klor de Alva, J. Jorge. "Martín Oceotl: Clandestine Cult Leader." In *Struggle and Survival in Colonial America*, edited by David G. Sweet and Gary B. Nash, 128–41. Berkeley: University of California Press, 1981.

Kobayashi, Munehiro. "Modalidades de la vida de los indígenas texcocanos de la década de 1530: un análisis de los tres procesos inquisitoriales de los indios." *Annals of Latin American Studies* 15 (1995): 19–52.

López Luján, Leonardo José Luis Ruvalcaba Sil, "El tejo de oro y lanoche triste." *Arqueología Mexicana* 27, no. 161 (2020): 14–21.

Lothrop, Samuel K. *Inca Treasure as Depicted by Spanish Historians.* Los Angeles: Southwest Museum, 1939.

Malcom, Corey. "The 1622 Tierra Firme Fleet: An Account of the Disaster and the People." Mel Fisher Maritime Museum Series of Occasional Papers in Maritime Heritage Research No. 1. 2019.

Marx, Karl. *Capital: A Critique of Political Economy. Vol. I, Part 1, The Process of Capitalist Production.* Translated by Ernest Untermann. New York: Cosimo Inc., 2007. First published in German 1867.

McGrath, Elizabeth. "Rubens's Arch of the Mint." *Journal of the Warburg and Courtauld Institutes* 37 (1974): 191–217.

Meléndez, Juan. *Tesoros verdaderos de las Yndias.* 3 vols. Rome: Nicolas Angel Tinassio, 1681.

Menaker, Alexander. "Beads." In *Magdalena de Cao: An Early Colonial Town of the North Coast of Peru*, edited by Jeffery Quilter, 189–207. Cambridge: Peabody Museum Press, 2020.

Noguez, Xavier. "Las joyas de Martín Océlotl." *Arqueología Mexicana* 142 (2019): 12–13.

Ostapkowicz, Joanna, Fiona Brock, Alex C. Wiedenhoeft, Rick Schulting, and Donatella Saviola. "Integrating the Old World into the New: An 'Idol from the West Indies'." *Antiquity* 91, no. 359 (2017): 1314–29.

Pané, Ramón. *An Account of the Antiquities of the Indies* (ca. 1498). Translated by S. Griswald. Durham, NC: Duke University Press, 1999.

Parker, Geoffrey. *Emperor: A New Life of Charles V.* New Haven: Yale University Press, 2019.

Pérez de Tudela Gabaldón, Almudena. "El cenotafio de Carlos V en la Basílica del Escorial." In *Leone & Pompeo Leoni. Actas del Congreso Internacional*, edited by Stephan Schroder, 132–48. Madrid: Museo Nacional del Prado, 2012.

Peterson, Jeanette. "The Florentine Codex Imagery and the Colonial Tlacuilo." In *The Work of Bernardino de Sahagún: Pioneer Ethnographer of Sixteenth-Century Aztec Mexico*, edited by J. Klor de Alva, H. B. Nicholson, and E. Quiñones Keber, 273–93. Albany: Institute for Mesoamerican Studies, SUNY, 1988.

Peterson, Jeanette, and Kevin Terraciano, eds. *The Florentine Codex: An Encyclopedia of the Nahua World in Sixteenth-Century Mexico*. Austin: University of Texas Press, 2019.

Plon, Eugene. *Les maîtres italiens au service de la maison d'Autriche. Leone Leoni, sculpteur de Charles-quint, et Pompeo Leoni, sculpteur de Philippe II.* Paris: E. Plon, Nourrit et Cie, 1887.

Raleigh, Walter. *The Discoverie of the Large, Rich, and Bewtiful Empyre of Guiana: With a Relation of the Great and Golden Citie of Manoa (which the Spanyards Call El Dorado) and the Prouinces of Emeria, Arromaia, Amapaia, and Other Countries, with Their Riuers, Adioyning: Performed in the Yeare 1595.* Edited by Neil L. Whitehead. Norman: University of Oklahoma Press, 1997.

Rosenthal, Earl E. "The Invention of the Columnar Device of Emperor Charles V at the Court of Burgundy in Flanders in 1516." *Journal of the Warburg and Courtauld Institutes* 36 (1973): 199–211.

Rosenthal, Earl E. "Plus Ultra, Non plus Ultra, and the Columnar Device of Emperor Charles V." *Journal of the Warburg and Courtauld Institutes* 34 (1971), 204–28.

Sahagún, Bernardino de. *Historia general de las cosas de Nueva España* (*Florentine Codex*). 1577. Biblioteca Medicea Laurenziana, Florence, Palat. 218–20.

Shiels, W. E. *King and Church: The Rise and Fall of the Patronato Real.* Chicago: University of Chicago Press, 1961.

Valle, Perla. *Códice de Tepetlaóztoc (Códice Kingsborough), Estado de México.* 2 vols. Mexico: Espejo de Obsidiana Ediciones, S.A de C.V., El Colegio Mexiquense a. C., 1994.

Blood Money: Asante Gold, Art, Power, and Identity in Historic Ghana

Suzanne Preston Blier

Ye de sika na epe sika (Money is used to earn money)
(Twi proverb: Earning money is hard if you start with nothing)

There is nothing as important as wealth (*Sika sene, biribiara nsen bio*)
(Ivor Wilks, *Asante in the Ninteenth Century*, 673)

Blood Money is the subject of a popular 2009 film from Ghana, whose title and subject, *Sika Mu Sakawa* (literally to penetrate in gold), speaks to the potent corrupting influences of gold.[1] The film is set in the present in the former Gold Coast, long a vital West African source for this shiny yellow, highly valued staple of global economics. In this film, we witness a pregnant zombie-like woman, her body bathed in deep red lighting, in the throes of birthing. She soon delivers not a human baby but instead, and doubly perversely, a pile of paper money. She has become through evil acts a money-making machine, a human ATM. In the local Twi language, the *sika* of the film's title means both gold and money. *Sakawa* (to put or to penetrate) is a borrowed word from Hausa, the language of the group of Muslim traders from northern Nigeria who for centuries have been involved in long-distance commercial engagements here, including money exchange; today it also means "internet fraud." This film and related productions address the sometimes dire situations in which young people with little hope of employment turn to immoral or criminal activities.[2]

Blood Money (literally *sika mogya*) also references the larger genre of films from Ghana and Nigeria that has developed since 1997: films that draw on Hollywood horror tropes to convey both the corrupting influence of financial greed and the misuse of traditional ritual practices for personal gain, sometimes with bloody ends.[3] The film might have been titled *Gold Medicine* (*sika aduro*; *mogya*[4] *sika aduro*—literally blood money medicine), a frame that generates reference to the idea that money can be gained from evil sources through magic or supernatural means. Put another way, since money frequently appears and disappears in ways not readily understood, this reflects the likely presence (or lack) of supernatural action.[5] In Ghana, since "magic" is seen to require sacrifice, and the scale of one's offering is believed to impact the size of financial benefit, it is believed that blood enhances the power of magic: "If someone loses money quickly or crashes a newly acquired car then these are seen as signs that the gods have taken their payback."[6]

Ill-gotten gain takes on new meaning. Today when one sees a large palatial residence in southern Ghana, particularly where one has little knowledge of the occupants, much less the sources of their income, one may say, only partially in jest, that "blood money" is behind it. This is not an unusual phenomenon in Africa, where increasingly we see deep economic imbalances and vast disparities between the very wealthy and the very impoverished individuals who define the new global capital arena.[7] While scholars largely consider the underlying issues at play within colonial and post-colonial framing, earlier eras are also relevant.

In 1857, the Basel missionary David Baum wrote of the Akan that "Gold is their god."[8] These ideas also point to strong local Akan beliefs that money (wealth) derives not only from inheritance, gifts, work, and even criminal acts, but also, and equally importantly, from potent ritual offerings, chief among these being blood sacrifices. In this sense blood evokes not only ancestry (blood relationships, kinship ties) but also violence. In many African contexts, including Ghana, medicine refers to a broad array of potions and powders, as well as ritual actions that are believed to improve one's condition, heal a person, or even protect one, alongside an array of sorcery-linked materials—so-called bad medicine, including magical objects (*suman*) and those ritual actions and related materials that help advance one's personal interests, often to the detriment of others.[9] The local proverb, "money/gold is blood" (*sika fit mogya*) speaks to this as well, and more specifically to the fact that money calls/attracts supporters (one's own and self-appointed) to one's side. Gold could also be used to attract the spirit world—*abosom* (deity, power, divinity; pl. *obosum*)—or Nyame, the Supreme Deity, to earth through a ceremony in which gold and medicinal forms positioned in a brass pan featured prominently. Expanding from these associations, it is not surprising that gold figured prominently in various local rites of transition. It was used not only as marriage payment (fees to the bride's father (determined by that individual's merit) but also at funerals (a small amount was tied into the deceased's cloth and sprinkled on the body for the journey to the other world).[10] Finally, gold, as we will see, featured prominently in the array of religious rites and festivals.

Gold remained at the core of Akan history and politics.[11] But there were important class and gender considerations regarding its use. Local coastal women were observed by Pieter de Marees in 1602 to be "eager traders"; yet reports beginning in the nineteenth century indicate that Akan women were forbidden from holding scales—as also was the king (Asantehene, "parent of all parents").[12] At the same time, it was the royal matrilineage who held not only the largest lands, but also the greatest gold-dust hoards, and the largest quantities of enslaved persons.[13] "There is nothing as important as wealth" (*Sika sene, biribiara nsen bio*) admonishes a local aphorism. While on the surface, this would seem obvious, as noted by Ivor Wilks, what this really references is the view that, for the Asante, each individual is a "trustee of the legacy of the ancestors on behalf of the generations yet unborn, [and this] carried the implication that the good citizen was the one who worked to bequeath more to his successors than he had acquired from his predecessors."[14] Gold dust (*sika-futuro*) served as both local and foreign trade currency.[15] It was employed to buy not only produce and locally manufactured goods but also foreign items.[16] Key among the latter were armaments (assuring a ready supply of war prisoners), along with salt, liquor, brass vessels, and luxury import textiles such as silk.

Local practices helped check the acquisition of gold for private wealth accumulation.[17] More important was the unique mutability of gold as a "transferential agent."[18] Once accumulated, wealth could not be discarded, and as such generated sizable complexities, based in part on the means through which it had been acquired—specifically, whether it was based on inheritance or personal earnings, in the latter case most often through war or trade. Nor could gold easily be borrowed for less dire reasons since, in the early nineteenth century, according to the traveler William Hutton, "Interest of money is 33⅓ per cent for every forty days."[19] Hutton also recorded that, in the same way that royal blood was sacred and could not be shed, so too a "considerable quantity of gold" would be buried with the body of royalty and other rich individuals. Due to its very sacredness, gold could not be used except in a very few circumstances: for key ceremonies, in "extreme national distress," and to "redeem capital" from enemy hands. So sacrosanct was the substance, indeed, that death was the punishment for anyone in the market or elsewhere who found a piece of gold and kept it.[20]

Gold has been mined in the broader Akan area for centuries. Prior to the Arabian conquest of North Africa, gold from the Bambuk and Bure areas furnished local and foreign markets, extending northward to Ancient Ghana (in modern Mauritania), Jenne-Jeno (in Mali), and later sites involved in the trans-Saharan trade to Islamic centers in North Africa, and through these sites to Europe and the Middle East. Indeed, it was in large measure to gain control of this gold trade that Europeans—initially the Portuguese in the mid-fifteenth century, followed by Spanish, Danish, Swedish, Dutch, German, and British—established large coastal forts in the area. The early development of these forts speaks as much to the importance of gold for key European goods (among these liquor, fine textiles and home furnishings, and large and smaller firearms), as to the concomitant transatlantic slave trade.

Gold was, of course, also the principal local currency and so ample was its availability that the early nineteenth-century traveler T. E. Bowdich learned that when the two marketplaces of the Asante capital of Kumasi were washed by the local citizens under the eyes of the market supervisor or chief toll-collector, some 800 ounces of gold were recovered.[21] Gold working was generally done in a secluded place, in artisan communities near the capital that specialized in this art. Local goldsmiths, who were familiar with the distinctive properties of the different metals, also cast works of brass.[22] In this work, in addition to the requisite earthen cylindrical-form furnace and bellows, these smiths made use of special anvils, hammers, tongs, spatulas, and iron needles (used in part to fashion the wax for casting).

The Materiality of Gold

The red-yellow color of gold carries symbolic weight. It evokes both the reddish-yellow color and the heat of the life-giving motion and vibrancy of the sun, activating the circulation of key elements in it. As in the film *Blood Money*, red also recalls bloodlines (the ancestors), through whom birth and well-being are nurtured. Finally, red points to the bloodshed associated with the violence that features in both war and some acts of self-interest. Red, in short, is linked at once to life and ancestry and to political power and violence (including sorcery). The technology of gold reflects this too. The earliest form of weights comprised bright red seeds with black "eyes." These seeds derive from the *Abrus pecatorius* bush (known locally as *damma*). This use of *damma* seeds suggests a kind of vegetal complement to the idioms of power with which gold plays a key part.

Gold as a material form carries properties suggestive of the kind of transformative engagement that is important in religious healing, political action, and sorcery. At once rough and smooth, hard and soft, shiny and dull, plastic and stable, gold has properties similar to an amulet (*asuman*; pl. *suman*). The search for gold nuggets is similarly linked. Often success in turning up the rare nugget is simply a question of chance (or, as framed by some locally, sorcery).

The processes of transforming gold-rich soil into gold dust cleanses this highly desirable material (through washing) and adds coolness (*dwa*) to the notably hot substance. Most of the gold that was found went to the king, but there was still enough to change the life of a lucky individual.[23] Even if the riverbeds had dried, certain plants were believed to reveal the good fortune that might lie within; but in this context, too, "blood medicine" is in play.

Gold shares deep philosophical and religious complements with the soul (*kra*), in particular that part of the soul considered the life force or spiritual essence of each individual (*sunsum*), acquired from one's father, yet vulnerable to attack by witches or other spirit forces. The large amounts of gold maintained within the family and clan are termed *kra sika* (soul's gold). The annual Odwira New Yam Festival also becomes the annual soul-washing rite. There is a key philosophical and moral link, too. Gold weights often reference local proverbs or aphorisms (*abebusem*; pl. *mmebusem*) that convey similar themes. To strengthen the soul, special gold jewelry forms were worn. In weighing gold, related ideas of maintaining balance and well-being are simultaneously engaged. In principle, gold could only be used for rituals (such as ceremonies of thanksgiving to the ancestors—including Odwira) and in cases of unforeseen emergencies. In either instance, the gold was considered a loan that had to be repaid. This took inherited gold largely outside the dynamics of regular economic engagement and meant that large ceremonies such as Odwira historically had a vital financial role as well.

Unsurprisingly, gold had political weight. In many ways, all gold was linked to the king. As Bowdich noted in the early nineteenth century: "the King is heir to the gold of every subject, from the highest to the lowest." At death, all gold in principle returned to the king, although there were exceptions:

> In practice it would seem that a small estate, of the ordinary farmer for example, was left intact, to be apportioned by the family of the deceased. Conversely, the estates of ... functionaries of the bureaucracy, were wholly at the disposal of the government. In other cases, the estate was carefully appraised by the agents of the Treasury, after which its distribution was decided upon.[24]

Gold also came to the crown through other means: tributes by dependent kingdoms, taxes on enslaved individuals sold or purchased on the coast, import duties on goods from the coast, payment following the deaths of each royal subject, and the direct confiscation of wealth of disgraced individuals or those found guilty of misdeeds. Elephant hunters and miners, among others, were the subject of special annual taxes by the king and local chiefs.[25] There were yet further funding sources too. Traders sometimes were stopped along key highways by royal wardens, and required to pay a fee in gold dust before continuing on their way.[26] Perhaps the most surprising practice is one that relates directly to art works. During the annual Odwira ceremony, people were asked to melt down and recast their gold. The new items were taxed (20 percent for every 100 ounces); in this way, not only was new art making encouraged but taxes were regularly drawn from the population.[27]

Gold powder and other precious goods were stored in special metal boxes or chests (*adaka*). These included not only the principal state gold-dust container, the Adaka Kese or Great Chest, but also smaller family-held forms, in the shape of cast brass vessels (*kuduo*) (fig. 1). *Kuduo* and these other containers held not only gold dust and nuggets as well other valuable forms associated with the ancestors and other spiritual powers for safe keeping. Each family kept this in a special room; for royals, gold was often stored in its own house—the Sikadan (the gold house: *sika dan*) as well as at the royal cemetery of Bantama.

The *kuduo* of past rulers were positioned before their coffins and blackened stools. In other contexts, gold-filled *kuduo* were buried with local elites.[28] The securing of these gold-filled vessels at Bantama underscores the inherent link between gold, the state, and the royal ancestors as capital assets of the Asante nation as a whole. Consistent with this, *kuduo* were also associated with purification of the *kra*.[29] In their form they address the long history of gold commerce in the area. The system itself owes much to the early gold trade and early import objects such as fourteenth-century elite brass Mamluk vessels, poised on the shrines of river gods linked to the gold trade. These Islamic forms underscored the use of local gold in the trans-Saharan trade economy many centuries earlier. Incised geometric surface decorations on the *kuduo* reference this source, alongside other motifs, including the curving elements of *sunsum* discs and geometric gold-weight decorations. Figural scenes on top of these vessels evoke both important ceremonial scenes, where gold features prominently, and proverbs and aphorisms involving humans and animals—many linked to ideas of social engagement and collaboration.

Gold was thus the very glue uniting politics, religion, and art. This potent glue served as a vital complement to the sun, the source of one's life force, vitality, or *kra*, as well as that of the state itself. The soul was considered in vital ways to be immortal;[30] at birth, a child's matrilineal ancestor's soul—also representing the supreme being, Nyame—was sent from heaven to the child as their own *kra*. Nyame is believed to have created and now control the universe

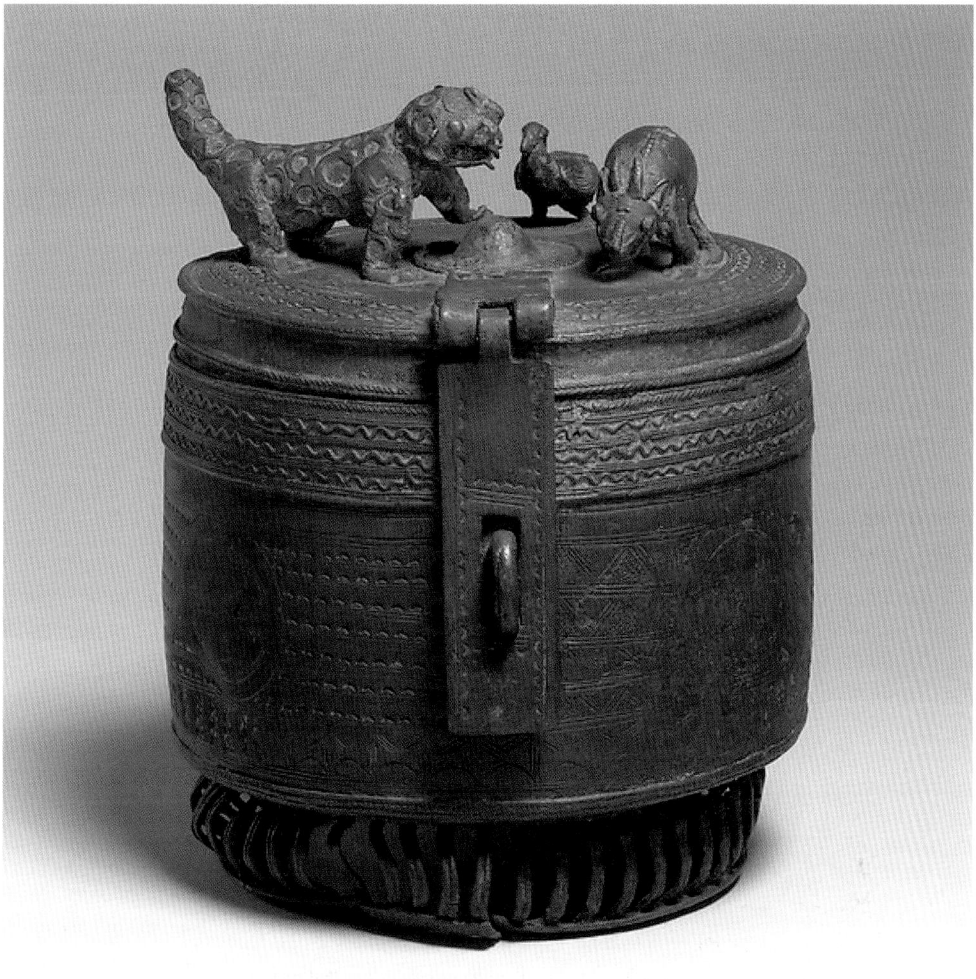

Fig. 1. Asante *kuduo* gold-dust container, Ghana, nineteenth or twentieth century, brass, 17 × 14 × 16.5 cm. New York, The Metropolitan Museum of Art, accession no. 1978.412.384ab

and its natural phenomena (water bodies, mountains, and forests), which are identified not only as his offspring but also to hold special powers in their own right. Within this schema are a variety of spirit entities—*abosom* (generally inhabiting local temples, shrines and altars, and trees, where they are propitiated)—who function as vital intermediaries between humans and Nyame.[31]

Ancestors played an important role as intermediaries, as also referenced in the form of the stools—now blackened by smoke and heaped with offerings—which served as altars and access sites for the spirits of the deceased. In key ways, the ancestral belief system was both very local (family by family, lineage by lineage) and also led by the Asante king, whose ritual and political authority underscored this role, particularly as played out in large state ceremonies, in the course of which the Asantehene would borrow the necessary gold from the ancestors at the royal cemetery (Bantama) where it was stored.[32] These events are occasions when "blood medicine" is a feature of mass public engagement. The king might likewise loan gold accoutrements to a key ambassador or officer for large ceremonies such as Odwira to enhance the splendor of his suite.[33] This enhanced both the circulation of gold and related ideas of power engagement.

Elephant Tails Versus Golden Seats

Gold and the question of blood money become especially trenchant in the ongoing balance and competition between inherited wealth and self-made wealth. As we will see, this competition is framed by two key art forms linked to power: the monarch's gold-covered throne (*Sika Dwa Kofi,* "the Friday-born Golden Stool"; fig. 2); and a gold-decorated elephant-tail fly whisk (*sika mmera*), which is a key emblem of self-made wealth and power. The display of gold-rich jewelry forms by the king and court (fig. 3) also comes into play, as does the array of gold ornaments (*abosodee*) secured to the gold-handled state swords (*keteanofena*) that reference not only the role of inherited wealth but also the key dangers involved in acquiring it. These state swords were used in oath-swearing rites and were sometimes given as important gifts (fig. 4).

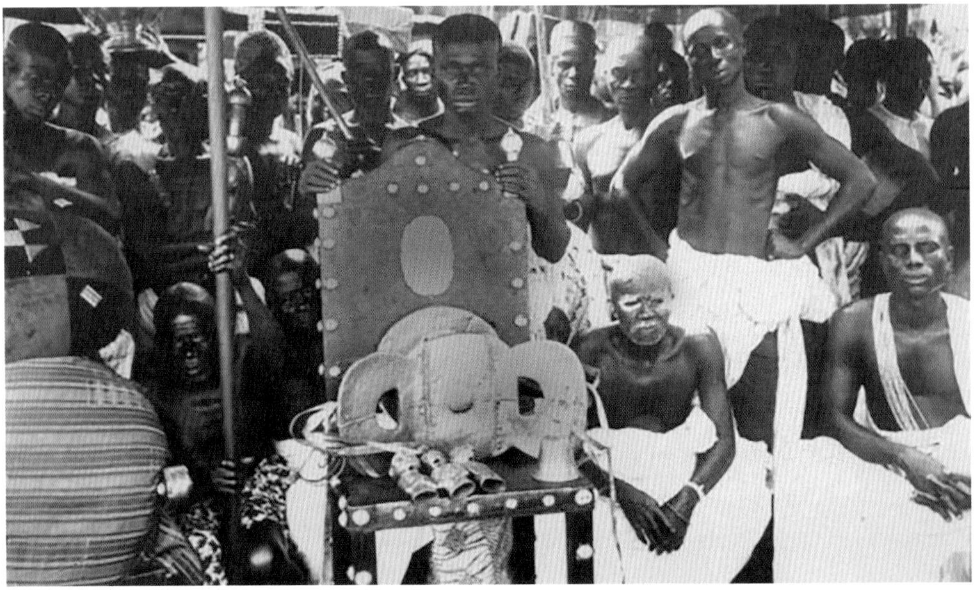

Fig. 2. Asante Golden Stool, Ghana, reputedly 1701, wood with gold leaf

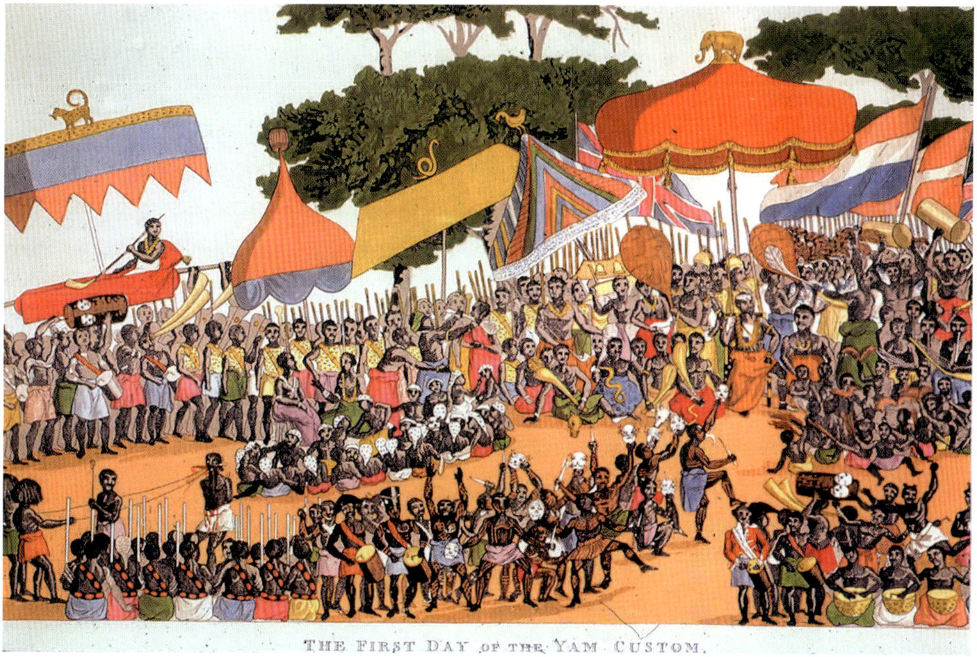

Fig. 3. R. Havell & Son, "The First Day of the Ashanti Yam Ceremony," engraving, in T. E. Bowdich, *Mission from Cape Coast Castle to Ashantee* (London: John Murray, 1819)

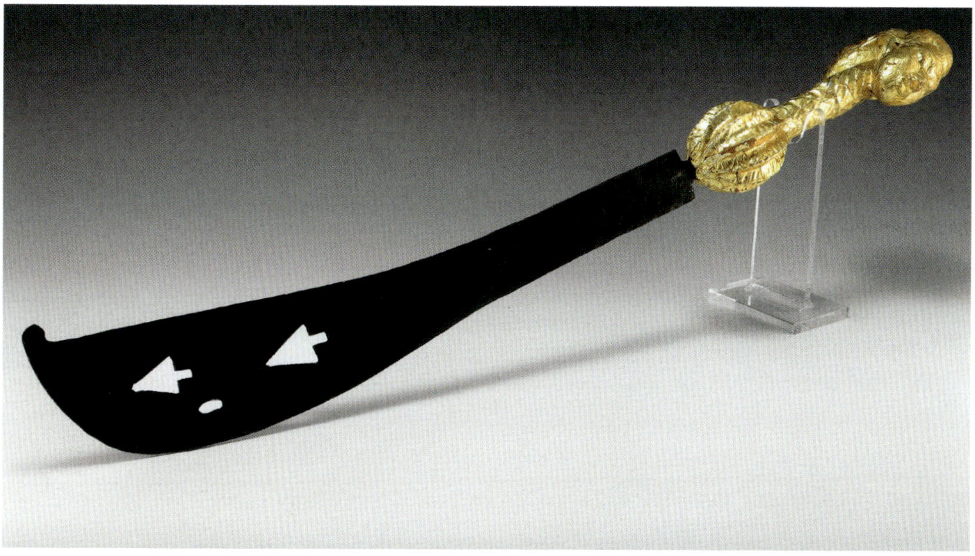

Fig. 4. Asante ceremonial sword, Ghana, 1975, gold, iron and wood, 69.9 × 7.6 cm. Grand Rapids, Michigan, Gerald R. Ford Presidential Museum, gift of S. E. Quarm, Ambassador of Ghana

The ongoing oppositional dynamic of inherited wealth versus earned or appropriated wealth represented in the primacy of the Golden Stool conveyed in large measure through the Asantehene, on the one hand, and the "Golden Elephant Tail," on the other, can be seen in various contexts.[34] As noted by Ivor Wilks, the king in some ways embraced both dynamics: "He became responsible for the custody of the *Sika Mmra* or Golden Elephant's Tail which was the formal symbol of the nation's wealth just as the *Sia Dwa* or golden stool was that of its political sovereignty."[35] While each king created his own *sikamena* (holder of the elephant's tail), this elephant tail had to be acquired individually.

To be a person of wealth—someone who earned the wealth themself—was a huge honor. As one Akan maxim puts it, "One becomes famous not by being noble born but by being wealthy" (*odehye nhyehye, na sika na ehyehye*).[36] How was self-made wealth defined? *Asikafo* (person of wealth, sing. *sikani*) referred to "rich men who own large estates, and are capable of granting large loans; in ancient times, they owned many slaves."[37] Central among the related investment rationales were vital social concerns: having persons as affiliates (whether free or unfree) was key because social prestige was fundamental to one's identity as someone of wealth.[38] Blood medicine in this context assumed identities with real and fictitious kinship ties.

The person accorded the title of holder of the elephant tail was distinguished in public by a symbolically potent elephant tail being carried in front of him in procession. A dance miming the elephant hunt, in the course of which its tail was cut, carried related significance, recalling not only the importance of the hunt in early Akan history, and how difficult it was to fell an elephant (known as "the big one," *esono*), but also the identity of this animal as unpredictable and both physically and spiritually dangerous.[39]

If the Golden Elephant Tail was the symbol of self-made wealth, the Golden Stool was the most salient icon of inherited wealth. The story of its appearance is now well known. In 1701, following a decisive military victory over the Denkyira, as Osei Tutu, founder of the state, sat beneath a tree, a wooden stool wrapped in gold sheathing floated down from the sky and came to land on his lap, thereby providing a sacred symbol of his right to rule.[40] As such the Golden Stool became the paradigmatic symbol of the new Asante nation or state, replacing as it did all older stools as referents of political power.[41] Its name, "Friday's Golden Stool," refers to the fact that the assembled chiefs had been invited on a specific Friday (*Fiada-fofie*) to witness a divine act. When the stool floated down from heaven, those in attendance cheered the event and were told by Osei Tutu that this very stool enshrined the *kra* or life force of the entire Asante nation.[42]

Despite ongoing references to the king as "the one who sat on gold,"[43] the Golden Stool was too sacred to ever sit on; in public rituals it was accorded its own special European-style chair, positioned atop an elephant-hide mat. There were specific rules accorded to it as well. The Golden Stool could never be duplicated elsewhere in the realm (a factor that led to several wars), and its theft was assumed to portend the nation's demise.[44] Defending this sacred stool in turn assumed the larger significance of defending the collective *sunsum* of the Asante against attack, illness, or other harm.[45] Accordingly, the one who was enstooled as proprietor of this Golden Stool was believed to hold core spiritual power to mediate between material and spiritual worlds. The new Asante king who came to the throne was ideally a descendant in Osei Tutu's paternal line, even if he gained power through his matrilineal descendance (carrying key elements of historic ancestry), even if, in some ways, Asante royal thrones (passed down from each incumbent to the next) were also of great importance. In the same way that blood (war, death, slavery, sacrifice) featured in the founding of the Asante state (the victory over the Denkyira), so too it was involved in maintaining this stool as an ongoing royal symbol and force—both by defeating those who might try to claim this right with their own golden stools, and in sacrifices and gold displays in key festivals involving the stool, Odwira among them.

Gold, Souls, and Sculptural Arts

Given the identity of gold with the soul (*kra*) and beliefs, it should not surprise us that gold plays a key role in the regular cleansing of the soul to help safeguard it from serious harm— specifically through the *sunsum* disk or *akrafokonmu* ("soul-washer's disk"—literally "soul people's pendant") (fig. 5). These are worn in such a way that the disk rests on the center of the chest, directly on top of the solar plexus. Worn occasionally by the king, by young girls during puberty ceremonies, and by funeral ceremony mourners, these pendants are most closely identified with royal attendants (*akrafo*) believed to represent the king's soul. Some of these attendants are prisoners of war, but all generally are selected because they are born on the same day of the week as the king; together they are tasked with renewing and maintaining the vitality of the king (and the nation) in their roles as "soul-washers"—those who cleanse the soul of the state. The disks are among the best-known royal regalia forms; they also constitute a sizable portion of the king's (and hence the state's) wealth.

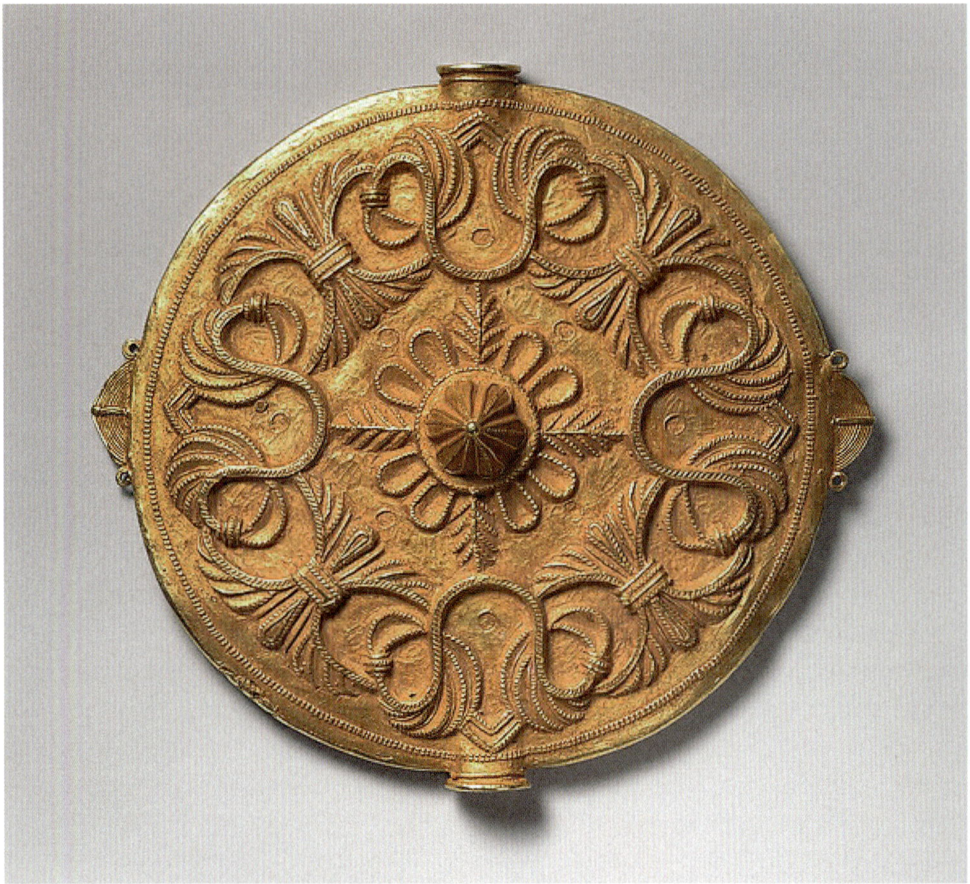

Fig. 5. Akan soul-washer's disk, Ghana, eighteenth or nineteenth century, gold, diameter 14 cm. New York, The Metropolitan Museum of Art, accession no. L.1982.92

The *akrafokonmu* surfaces are decorated with forms suggestive of both radiating solar beams (the source of *kra*) and a multi-pedal flower said to grow near where gold is found. As described by T. E. Bowdich, the King Osei Tutu Kwame Asiba wore a form resembling "a full-blown rose, one leaf rising above the other until it covered his whole breast."[46]

This circular form of the *sunsum* pendant evokes key ideas of Asante governance, which finds expression in an Asante saying, *wonsa ka bi*, referencing the circular meeting of authorities and subjects in a village where people come together in a public discussion:

> The Asante symbol that goes with this axiom has the form of a wheel with big spokes. In *akom* performances the outer ring of the wheel symbolizes the audi-

ence and the inner circle symbolizes the position of the deities that possess the traditional priestesses or priests. The spokes represent the channels through which the audience can come in to dance.[47]

There is also interesting performative resonance between the dance forms and the functions of the soul-washer's disk. The spiraling, encircling radial or petal motif accordingly complements the open circular dance movements of *abosom* priestesses, who are seen to evoke the binding and releasing of powerful evil spiritual forces (often seen as deriving from witchcraft) to prevent them having a bad impact.[48]

There are a number of other Asante gold decorative forms; these include various jewelry items—rings, bracelets, armlets, anklets, toe and finger rings, necklaces, pectorals—and tobacco pipes, hair ornaments, sandal, and hats, as well as chair decorations, musical instruments (horns, drums), sword motifs, and umbrella finials. The array of motifs ranged from traditional forms like star clusters, crescents, and shells to import goods such as bells, watches, keys, padlocks, and manacles. While most of these were specifically made by goldsmiths (*sikadwumfoo*), in some cases gold nuggets themselves were introduced.[49] Hutton's 1821 description of young ten- to twelve-year-old girls is particularly striking: "Each of them had a large piece of solid rock-gold suspended round the neck, at least ten or twelve ounces, value forty or fifty pounds."[50]

Whether one was the Asante king, a minister, a lesser chief, or one of their attendants, it was not only the subject portrayed that was significant but also the sheer massing of gold regalia—here a key sign of social position.[51] One's office could also be indicated through gold motifs, as, for example, the captain of the messengers (a gold horn), the executioner (a massive gold hatchet on the breast), or the keeper of the treasury (symbols of his service—boxes, scales and weights of solid gold).[52]

Some of the most interesting gold sculptures comprise shimmering gold leaf sheets superimposed on a carved wooden core. These often elaborate scenes (*kyeame poma*) were poised atop tall wooden staffs that were carried by the king's linguists (who served as royal advisers, spokesmen, interpreters) and were also distinguished by their rich gold surface. Akan proverbs and an array of political symbols serve as the basis of these motifs, forming a strong "visual–verbal nexus" similar to that found in other Akan arts, here made all the more interesting because of their association with royal spokesmen and interpreters.[53] The gold ornaments on state swords are also often quite elaborate. Such swords (*afenakwa*), which date back to the mid-eighteenth century, had an important role in oath-swearing rituals.[54] The gold sculptures on these elite swords include powerful animals (rams, leopards), trophy heads, military equipment (canons, rifles, powder barrels), and import punch bowls, sugar bowls and teapots. All serve as symbols of power and authority.

A key part of the symbolic import of gold involves the pageantry of the gold display itself (see fig. 2). Nowhere is this more strikingly conveyed than in the early nineteenth-century reports of the British visitors T. E. Bowdich and William Hutton. Bowdich writes of one display:

> manillas and rude lumps of rock gold, hung from their left wrists, which were so heavily laden as to be supported on the head of one of their handsomest boys. Gold and silver pipes and canes dazzled the eye in every direction. Wolves and rams heads as large as life, cast in gold, were suspended from their gold handled swords, the blades shaped like round bills and rusted in blood.[55]

Regarding the king himself, Bowdich adds:

> He was seated in a low chair, richly ornamented with gold; he wore a pair of gold castanets on his finger and thumb, which he clapped to enforce silence. The belts of the guards behind his chair, were cased in gold and covered with small jaw bones of the same metal; the elephants tails, waving like a small cloud before him, were spangled with gold, and large plumes of feathers were flourished amid them. ... the royal stool, entirely cased in gold, was displayed under a splendid umbrella.[56]

Hutton writes similarly of the king that:

> His majesty was seated in a low chair, the back of which was profusely studded with gold nails, and ornamented with small pieces of gold. ... he wore a necklace of aggry beads and small pieces of gold. Saphies, cased in gold, were suspended over his shoulder, and he had a number of gold rings upon his fingers, and gold castanets on his finger and thumb. His wrists, knees, and ancles were richly adorned with bracelets and knee-bands of the finest gold and aggry beads ...[57]

The glistening glare of gold, its massing and differentiation, left a lasting impression both on foreign visitors like Hutton and Bowdich and more importantly on the tens of thousands of local pageant onlookers and participants.

It was meant to! For this was a political display of extraordinary import—one that legal strictures and religious rites were intended in part to reinforce. As Hutton wrote: "The majestic appearance of the cabboceers and captains, the richness of their dresses, the glittering and costly gold ornaments which were seen everywhere, as far as the eye could reach, had a most imposing effect."[58]

Gold Mining

Historically, the largest quantity of gold from southern Ghana came from surface mining in riverbed valleys and the sides and crests of hills, collected in shallow openings or pits (*mmoaboa*) often no more than one to three meters deep.[59] Shallow surface digging was so much a part of the local landscape that, over the years, the land became "honey-combed [and] ... dangerous to walk on."[60] Sometimes a hundred or so such pits were documented within a single acre.[61] Coastal gravel and sands were also rich in gold, and occasionally nuggets washed out in the heavy rains. Such was the case when Portuguese travelers visited in the mid-fifteenth century and were stunned to discover locals panning gold.[62] Jean Barbot would note in 1732 the remarkable sight of young men bearing calabash gourd bowls or shallow brass vessels and diving into rapidly flowing streams to scoop up gold-rich nuggets from the stream bottoms.[63] More generally, however, the major gold source locations, processes of opening, and contexts of use were closely guarded secrets to be shielded from foreigners.[64] The color of the local earth (blue-black or grayish in hue) was believed to offer clues; so too did the presence of certain plant forms that might indicate gold-rich soils. In the late seventeenth century, during a war between the Asante and the gold-rich Adanse power, the military advance of the latter temporarily stopped when gold was found; the troops were put to work to "wash the soil" for gold.[65]

While much of the gold mining was often undertaken historically in small family groups, slavery was a key factor in more centralized Akan states, including the Asante. Gold was so important to the state that it has been estimated that between 1482 and 1632 some 12,000 enslaved individuals were imported to participate in both the deep mine excavation and agricultural work.[66] Locally enslaved individuals (generally prisoners of war), pawns (family members sold into slavery for debts), and hired labor (migrants, among others) were a vital factor in this process.[67] Deep-shaft mining was largely done by these same populations. Such work was highly dangerous and identified not only with frequent injury and filth but also with the broader impact of an array of "unfriendly" spirits.[68] Over the centuries, many of these workers took up residence in agricultural plantations around Kumasi, assimilating into Asante society. While this slavery factor was important in the local gold economy, from the eighteenth century onward enslaved persons also became a component of Asante foreign trade.[69]

The sacredness of gold factored into the mining process, with local gods playing a key role. These deities, including the Earth Goddess (Bona) and various local river gods (Tano and others), were important not only in finding gold but also in assuring the safety of miners.[70] Local rivers like the Tano came to be known both for their rich ores and for the gods who could be relied on to supply and refurbish this shiny yellow substance. Care had to be taken by the workers to follow certain rules, especially those linked to pollution. Not only were royals and women not allowed to do this work (nor could they touch the goldsmithing equipment) but, if a man were to commit adultery with a goldsmith's wife, he had to pay a fine that included a fee for the necessary purification rituals to be performed on the goldsmith's tools and anvil.[71] Following the death of a chief, or the desecration of land through violence or other actions, special additional ceremonies and offerings were undertaken to bring about purification and pacification (*asubo*), to assure a bountiful return of gold.[72] Prior to the digging of a new mine shaft, for example, a chicken would be offered by a local priest to the ancestors, who were considered the ultimate owners of the land.[73] After a specific gold find, a libation of eggs, plantains, or pounded yam was presented to the local spirits of the Earth, who, without such signs of respect, might hide their gold sources from those seeking to find them.[74] Should a miner die inside a shaft, the mine would generally be abandoned and "fetish" would be applied to the site, in part to protect others from harming themselves there.[75] This practice conveys much about enduring ideas of blood medicine.

Miners would not only seek the blessings of deities prior to beginning work. They might also employ special plant-rich medicinal solutions to wash their faces in order to "open their eyes" to the golden "glow" marking the surface of the earth beneath which the gods had secured the gold.[76] And the presence of gold could be found through other means—including the dreams of ancestors.[77]

Miners would avoid evil thoughts while mining. Pollution was also a concern: miners avoided sex the night prior to mining in order to be in a state of greatest purity; and menstruating women would keep their distance from the gold fields. If a mine went dry, this was viewed as being due to improper acts. A priest would be called to make additional offerings to the local Earth spirits to bring back the gold, which was thought to have moved to another site; these offerings were paid for by the miners themselves. The mining or panning of gold was also not allowed on sacred days to the local gods or ancestors, including the days beginning and ending the Adae rites in honor of the ancestors (see more on these rites below).[78] This practice also allowed the various family members who mined to celebrate with the rest of their families key annual festivals such as Adae or Odwira. To continue gold mining during religious rites was viewed as potentially leading to death by living burial within the mine itself at a future date.[79]

Although surface or shallow-pit mining could take place all year round, gold mining was generally seasonal work. River panning was normally undertaken in the early rainy season months (March–May); deep-shaft mining was largely dry season work (December—April). In the intervening periods, farmwork was undertaken. Gender also factored in gold-mining activities: the deep mine shafts were dug largely by men, while women took a lead in the labor-intensive work of washing the auriferous materials to extract the ore. With the first heavy rains of April, when shimmering gold-rich grains washed out of the soil, children and others began the search in roadways, ditches, and streambeds.[80]

Not all Akan areas were as auriferous as others and not all gold was the same; purity might range from 85 to 95 percent.[81] Whereas in the Gyman area a 9-foot shaft might bring viable gold resources, and would furnish sizable numbers of gold nuggets (*sika pokowa*), in other areas, including the Asanti, Denkyera, and Wassa areas, the shaft would often have to reach 22 feet. Sometimes these deeper gold shafts (*amenapeaa nkron*—which are normally 3–4 feet in diameter) could even extend to 50 or 100 feet.[82] The deeper shafts had cut steps running along the sides to the bottom or bamboo ladders. The base of the deep-shaft mines expanded outward, creating a bell-shaped space. The interior roof was supported by bamboo lashed together by cords, with cross-timber reinforcement to prevent cave-ins. Often horizontal tunnels were used to connect to nearby shafts. A series of small openings were used for ventilation; fires might also be lit at the base of the shaft to help draw in oxygen to the depths. Fire was used elsewhere to heat the ore-rich stone. This was followed by cold water, causing the rock to crack and allowing the auriferous ore to be extracted. Small clay palm-oil lamps with cotton wicks helped miners see within this difficult setting.[83] In deep mining shafts the ore-rich material was placed in cane baskets secured to long fiber cords so that they could be dragged to the surface.[84]

Regardless of how the gold was acquired, it had to be washed. A set of wide differentially sized wooden "gold panning bowls" (*sika koro, akoro*) were used to separate the gold from sand or pebbles. The separation through panning of the valuable gold from sand, gravel, and other detritus was difficult and laborious, necessitating multiple washing stages where the rough debris was placed in the wooden bowl and slowly shaken and rotated multiple times to find just a few grains of gold. The process was repeated five or six times, the last (smallest) of these vessels often being painted black so that the gold was readily visible.[85] The gold discovered through this arduous process was carefully placed in *etwa* leaves.

In royal mines, chiefs stationed near the area supervised activities and sometimes participated in the gold extraction themselves; these individuals served both as the king's gold keepers and as treasury officials.[86] No gold shaft or pit for mining could be dug without the chief responsible for the land being informed.[87] Land ownership factors also affected distribution. The gold was classified based on size, which ranged from gold dust (*sika future*), to smaller nuggets (*mpokowa* and *nsanma*), to large nuggets (*sika po*)—the latter two classes both being destined for the king. The king for his part might redistribute this new gold to any "rising captains" (individuals who had performed their professional roles well) without the requisite loan fees, with the understanding that it be returned after two to three years; this loan was intended to help launch the individual's career.[88] These various gold categories served in turn as the basis for taxation. All gold nuggets other than those owed to the local ruler of the land went to the king; one-third of gold dust went to the chief from whose land the gold was recovered, another third went to the specific local family owners of the land, and the final third went to the miners themselves. If the work was done by pawns or enslaved persons, the owning king or chief received the full gold quantity, a factor that likely encouraged this class of gold workers.[89] Local rulers would receive one-third of the smaller nuggets destined for the Asantehene, in part as reimbursement for the costs of any related sacrifices.[90]

Gold Weights and Their Artistic Parallels

Gold had to be weighed. The system of gold weights and weighing was closely linked to the development of the Akan political order and Asante empire.[91] De Marees, in 1602, was the first to describe the weighing and use of gold, noting the employment of copper weights and "small copper scales, with circular pans which they make hollow like an orange-peel, suspended by very long strings" (fig. 6).[92] The beam-form scales (*nsania*) were balanced on the thumb, with a cast-brass gold weight (*abrammuo*; pl. *mrammuo*) positioned in

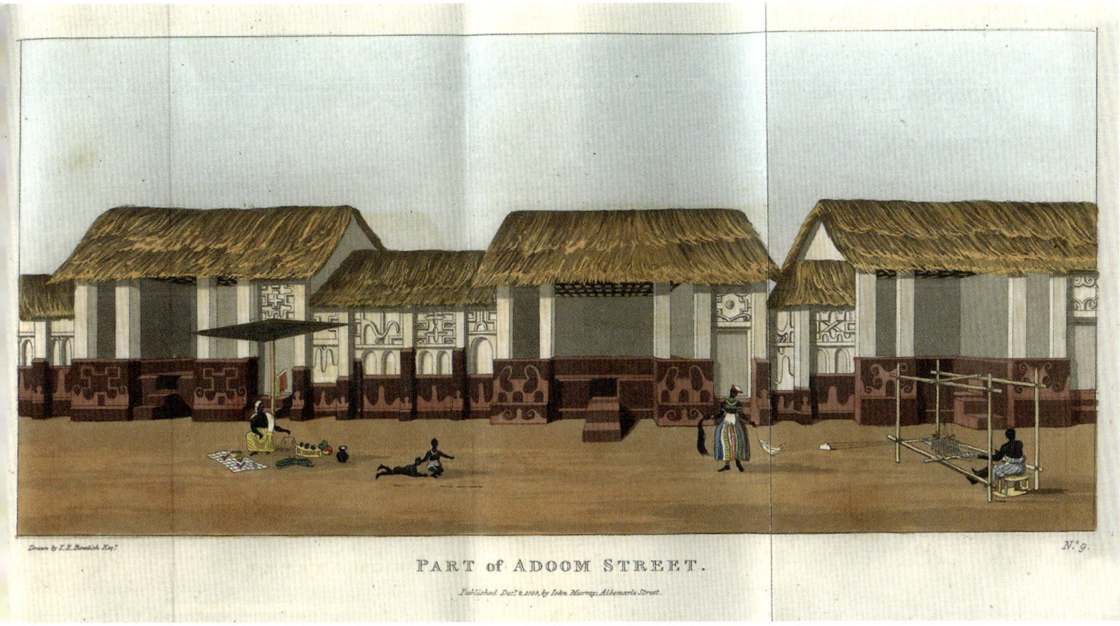

Fig. 6. R. Havell & Son, "Part of Adoom Street," engraving, showing gold weighing in front of residences on Adoom Street in the Asante Capital of Kumasi (Ghana), in Bowdich, *Mission from Cape Coast Castle to Ashantee*, p. 90, fig. 2.3

one pan, as gold dust was added to the other with a special sheet-hammered brass spoon (*saawa*).[93] Each merchant had a separate *nsania* and *mrammuo* to measure gold currency; so too did every Akan male of any merit.[94] Most individuals had a series of weights. The base unit (the *peredwan*)—linked to both the Islamic mithqal and the European ounce—carried a value of approximately 2 ounces of gold dust; in turn it was the basis for fractional or multiple weights (*asuanu*: ½; *osua*: ¼; *nsoansa*: ⅛) which were employed for external trading, with smaller units (*damba*, *taku*, *domafo*, and *doma*) for internal trading or to pay fines or fees.[95] Court-affiliated gold-weighers (*fotosanfo*) measured the gold dust for fines; they also sometimes used weights as royal messages, their meanings conveying ideas based on the core symbolic motifs of their decorative elements.[96]

Because of their symbolic importance, gold weights were items that royals would give to officials and others as rewards. Significantly, not all transactions were equal. While all payments to and from the state treasury were in gold, the king's weights were about one-third heavier than other weights, making each transaction with a royal a "source of emolument to the household."[97] At the same time, in order to safeguard against cheating, gold dust was often weighed on both the buyer's and the seller's scales, and most merchants (and families) owned large numbers of weights.[98]

We should not be surprised to learn that gold weights, like gold, were deemed to have sacred import. Sick children were sometimes given gold weights to wear as protective amulets or objects of healing.[99] Leather-encased amulets intended to ward off danger and illness would also occasionally include similar gold-weight motifs, underscoring their important links to the soul and related apotropaic associations. Key gold-weighing paraphernalia, including the bag in which the weights were stored, was identified with the souls and well-being of the owners; this paraphernalia (*afutuo*) was passed on within the family as core inheritance, although some weights were also bequeathed as gifts. Safeguarded as key icons of the state and its treasury (*sannaa*) in the palace shrine room, the weights were only taken outside for public display in key ceremonies such as the annual soul-washing (Odwira).[100] As such the larger gold-weighing system was fundamentally linked to ideas of royal religion and power.

Like the weight measures, the decorative elements on these weights were diverse and changed considerably over time. Early on it was the *aya* seed that was used to measure gold dust, drawing in part on the importance of the *aya* fern (whose distinctive chevron-leafed pattern also appears in gold weights) as a symbol of strength (hardiness) and resourcefulness because it grows in many different conditions. Simple pieces of metal or stone (*karibo*) were also used early on as weights. And brass beads, watch mechanisms, and bits of scrap metal could serve in this role.

Most later Asante gold weights, however, were cast of copper alloy (zinc-rich brass) in the well-known lost-wax process. Early Akan brass weights shared much in common with Islamic weights: both in the weight values themselves and in their key decorative elements. This is not surprising since the early gold trade involved Muslim partners on both sides of the Sahara, who facilitated and controlled this vital remunerative trade. The earliest brass weights (dating to ca. 1400–1700 CE) are geometric in form (fig. 7), drawing inspiration from Islamic weighing traditions used in the trans-Saharan trade; in the second phase of weights (1700–1900 CE) representational (often figurative forms) prevailed. These weights are discussed in great detail by Timothy Garrard.[101]

The early Islamic-based geometric weights are distinguished by their diverse base shapes and inclusion of bar-like elements that may have helped in handling. Disks, ovals, semicircles, and stepped squares are among the most common shapes; some are smooth, others are notched at the edge or defined by circular cavities or raised plugs or dots. Sometimes their surfaces are decorated with straight or curving lines, dots, spirals, star forms, crosses, triangles, or chevrons. Similar decorations were also included in locally made leather-encased Islamic amulets (*safi*, *sebe*), fashioned according to a possible source in the early Kufic script of Arabic. Related forms can sometimes be dated: triangles and rectangles are mostly fifteenth century; trefoils, quatrefoils, cinquefoils, and stepped or pyramidal forms appeared in the sixteenth century.

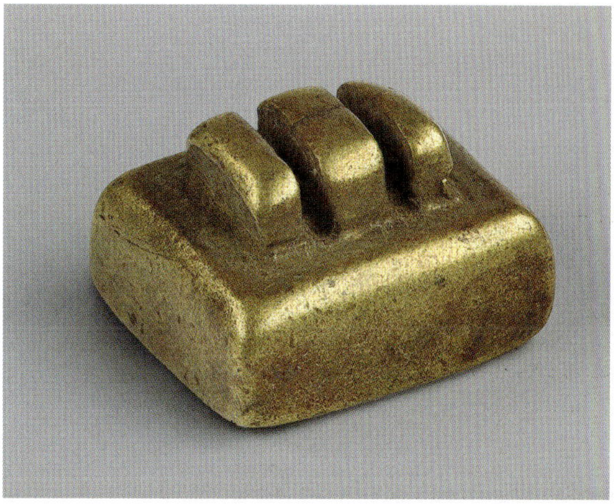

Fig. 7. Akan gold weight, Ghana, date unknown, brass, 1.1 × 1.8 × 1.5 cm, 16.2 g. Muséum de Toulouse, ancient collection of French botanist Jean Baur, inv. no. MHNTETH.2010.25.054

Some weights had clear-cut local symbolism, as for example the stepped pyramidal shapes that evoke the importance of raised stepped platforms (*sumpene)* used as seats for chiefs in public rites—in this context suggesting both political hierarchy and sacral authority. The evening star and crescent- moon shapes similarly evoke both religious ideas and political relationships. Abstract forms of animals (from lizards and crocodiles to birds) also appeared. And everyday items were represented: lozenge shapes are seen to complement mirrors; simple combs are suggested by joined parallel bars. Other forms include European-form keys (Y-shaped weights decorated with two or three raised bars).[102]

When Portuguese sailors arrived on the coast of Ghana in 1482—soon to be joined by the Danish, English, Dutch, Germans, and others—the forts they established sought to control the gold trade and related commercial engagement. The trans-Saharan trade continued, only somewhat diminished after the fall of Muslim Granada in 1492, and the discovery of new gold sources soon after in the Americas. But the forms of the gold weights changed. A new (European) weighing system came into play involving, not only a new weight calibration system but also new styles of weights. As noted above, early brass weights tended to be mold-made and solid brick-like forms, cast in an array of geometric shapes; later weights were more often hand-crafted forms, and included an array of human and animal figurative motifs. Sometimes actual objects from nature—such as insects or seed pods—were cast in brass, which is very easy to do in the lost-wax method. Even with these changes, however, earlier geometric brass weights continued to be made and used.

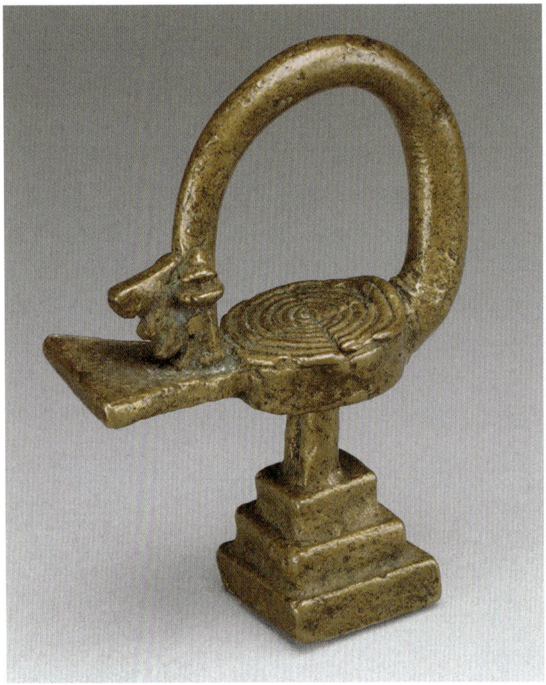

Fig. 8. Akan gold weight in the form of the *sankofa* bird, Ghana, post-seventeenth century, brass, 2.5 × 7 × 3.2 cm. New York, Brooklyn Museum, Carll H. de Silver Fund, 45.11.5

The later figural works are notably diverse, and goldsmiths often had large stocks of weights they could turn to as samples and models to compare their work to.[103] These motifs included humans (shown in various activities such as talking, making offerings, oath-taking, or hunting) and human activities, particularly warfare (weapons, decapitated heads, jaws, femurs). Males appear more frequently than females or children. Though somewhat abstract in form, the human shapes are easy to read through their gestural details, distinctive coiffures, and clothing forms. Animals are common, particularly wild animals (leopards, snakes, antelopes, porcupines, monkeys, fish, shell fish, frogs, wild birds, beetles, and insects), rather than domestic beasts, with the exception of chickens (fig. 8). This is believed to be in part because of their importance in proverbs or their identities as family referents. A sizable number of direct castings of insects, plant forms, or seeds are also found. All these weights date to the sixteenth century and later.

Manufactured objects are common too. Local forms included not only gold weighing spoons and *kuduo* gold-dust vessels, but also other key utility and cultural items such as agricultural tools (hoes, adzes, axes), specialty items (bellows, prongs, horse harness parts), everyday vessels (pots, pans), elite items such as badges, and even musical instruments—lute harps (*sankuo*), gongs, and side-blown ivory horns (*akoben*) that frequently accompanied chiefs in ceremonies (voicing actions and names in cadences complementing tonal Twi language). Portrayals of local shields (*ekyem*) and swords (*akrafena*, "swords of the soul") carried both political and spiritual import, the latter featuring in private ceremonies linked to the *kra* of the king or chief and featuring prominently in the annual ceremony of Odwira as part of the soul-cleansing rites.

Gold weights in the form of elephant-tail fly whisks were particularly important because they referenced power, self-made stature, and wealth accumulation. Leather sandals (*mpaboa*)—a tradition originating in the north—were seen to suggest not only movement but also protection, due to their status associations and local and Qur'anic amulet-like functions. Fly whisks (*bodua*) and round or rectilinear fans (*papa*) were identified with coolness and warding off danger. Sometimes weights were cast in the form of local amulets (*asuman*), including both items created by humans (beads) and those drawn from nature (leopard's teeth, claws, shells, feathers). Islamic protection was sometimes referenced: for example the Qur'anic texts enfolded in a leather, cloth, or metal surround—the *safi* or *sebe* mentioned above). In other contexts, these amulet forms were worn on the body or affixed to swords or stools.

Import-linked motifs detailed in these gold weights range from weapons (cannons, muskets, pistols, powder barrels, swords) and flags to money chests (*adaka*, complete with iron bands and studs), furniture (chairs, clocks, desks, cabinets), crotal bells, and spoons. Locks and keys (*safoa*), referencing wealth and status, along with tobacco pipes and belt buckles, were also common. Interestingly, some of these import forms also had local ritual significance: for example, cannons were sounded during important ceremonies to frighten away evil; and crotal bells were affixed to shields, clothing, and jewelry because of their apotropaic associations.

Despite the striking variety, certain motifs appear with greater frequency, among these a crocodile eating a mudfish (*kuwamu*), rams' horns (*dwanimen*), and stepped platforms (the clay platforms called *sumpene* used in local rituals). Swastika shapes (*futuo-bo* or *futuro-bo),* sometimes called "monkey feet," are similar to those that marked the surfaces of iron tools in Mali and Bourkina Faso to the north. These swastika forms were seen to have apotropaic and fertility associations in the Akan area; they were sanctified with chicken offerings to bring more gold dust; and one such weight was to be found in every collection.[104]

Whether referencing local or import forms, many of these brass weights were identified with social maxims and proverbs, hence the reference to them as proverb weights (*mmebusem*).[105] These proverbs also add to the signification of the forms; their meanings are complex and interpreted in sometimes quite personal ways.[106] Weights bearing salient proverbs were sent by the court to convey royal interests, for example a weight portraying a gong to suggest that something was widely known, or an elephant tail to underscore the fact that all power came from the king.[107] Gold weights more generally were seen to have an important didactic and pedagogical role for people of all ages and status, and were sometimes quoted as such in court hearings (verbalizing social norms in key kinds of relationships).[108] For example, a gold weight bearing the common crossed crocodile motif referenced the call for unity provided by the saying "a family has many throats but only one stomach."[109]

References to Gold Weights in Other Arts

These gold-weight symbols were often associated with specific factors of history, family identity, or circumstances linked to the deceased, although popular proverbs were also represented—including references to individual attitudes and behavior. As such they carry related meanings into the broader community and public arena. The association of gold and associated weights with the spiritual world and one's soul was important and the other contexts in which gold-weight motifs appeared are consistent with this. They range from the central columns of chiefs' and other stools, to architectural reliefs on shrines and the residences of chiefs and other local elites (particularly on the front porches or verandas (*adampan*) where business was carried out), to the stamped cloth known as *adinkra* widely worn at funerals as a sign of protection and unity in these events that brought so many members of the family back together.

Among the most striking of these public gold-weight motifs found in other art contexts is the tradition of architectural bas reliefs (see fig. 6) found on the facades of local temples and the compounds of local elites arrayed along the four main avenues and the smaller streets of the capital, Kumasi. These motifs derive from the same sources as local gold weights—a virtual encyclopedia of local proverbs, aphorisms, objects, and experiences. In rare cases, gold was applied to buildings: for example, the window frames of the king's bedroom in the palace were reportedly encased in gold and silver.[110]

The architectural examples of bas reliefs on both elite and religious edifices included an array of animal forms, among others: a bird with its head turned backward (the importance of drawing insight from the past); two birds facing each other and eating (peaceful living and mutual engagement); rams' horns (two pairs of spiral forms—referencing deity, sacrifice, power, and protection, as well as the desire to avoid trouble); a crocodile (trusting those in the know; spiritual knowledge from the deep); a crocodile with a mudfish in its mouth (that the powerful should not harm weaker members); a feline (precision and quietude; the slow swift power of the deities). Other motifs include the ladder of death (a web of diagonal lines suggesting the inevitability of death, hence shared values); the path of a dancing priest (a field of swirling motifs—referencing the priest's undulating dance path; the use of spirits for protection); a stool (chieftaincy; the union of spirits and humans); and four kola nuts (a quatrefoil—offerings to the gods to avoid misfortune). Hunters also appear (strength and bravery, as well as readiness to search out evil).[111] That these same forms are found in Akan gold weights reaffirms the conjoined factors of politics, religion, and social well-being in them. Gold, well-being, family, and religion were all closely linked. Interestingly, in light of these connections, red pigment is applied to the lower surfaces of temples and homes. This color—a key referent to gold—is linked to ideas of spiritual and political engagement: to life (the sun), kinship (blood), and sacrifice (offerings).

Asante Ceremony: Gold, Renewal, and Purification

Gold figured prominently in local ceremonies. One such rite, called Adae (resting place) served as the key venue for honoring the ancestors. As part of this rite, the chief, along with key elders, visited the shrine where the blackened seats of the ancestors and the gold powder-filled *kuduo* containers (see fig. 1) were kept. The ancestral seats are cleansed and anointed with propitiations for the ancestors, each of whom is invoked and commemorated with blessings and appeals for well-being. In addition to the regular Adae rites, which in some areas take place every six weeks, the Asante hold an annual ceremony called Odwira ("purify" in Twi; see fig. 3). This new year and new yam harvesting festival generally takes place in October–November as a kind of Adae rite writ large, a time when the ancestors are honored through offerings of food and drink. Odwira dates back to 1697–99 when the Asante celebrated the victory over the Denkira that provided their independence. As noted earlier, closely associated with this victory was the 1701 establishment of the sacred Golden Stool, the potent Asante symbol of nationhood.

The most sacred Odwira rites take place at the royal burial ground (mausoleum) of Bantama, on what was once the outskirts of Kumani, where sheep (evoking peace) are among the sacrifices offered to the bones of past kings and their ancestral stools (encapsulating the spirits of these dead) to help assure a safe Odwira and both prosperity and well-being through the subsequent year.[112] Here too gold was prominent:

> Bantama was the second and last burial place of the ancient Kings of Asante—The Mausoleum. It was a long building approached by a gallery and partitioned into small cells; the entrance of each cell was covered with a silk curtain; in each cell was the sacred skeleton of a King in preservation. The different seg-

> ments of each skeleton had been carefully and artfully joined together with gold wires, and placed in a coffin adorned with slabs of gold. For each skeleton there were a table, a chair, a dish, and a water jug; and around each coffin had been placed ... a sword, a musket, sandals, and some other personal articles that had been the favourites of each particular King during his life time.[113]

It is here at Bantama, in the course of the Odwira libations, that the Asantehene prays for everyone's well-being and for help from the ancestors to prevent "any evil at all to come upon us" in the new year.[114]

It is at Bantama too, prior to the announcement of the opening date of Odwira, that the Asantehene borrows the necessary *sika future* (gold dust), jointly belonging to the ancestral chiefs and comprising a key part of the royal property, that is reserved exclusively for rituals such as Odwira or emergencies such as war. This gold dust is secured within the state brass *kuduo* containers, which themselves are key symbols of ritual purification (*esubo*), closely linked to the *kra* of the state, and which are, on this occasion, carefully positioned in front of the coffins of the Asante ancestral rulers.[115]

Part of Odwira is a profoundly public rite including an elaborate royal procession, in which the king, queens, ministers, chiefs, and other elites appear in their richest regalia and perform an array of dances to the accompaniment of vibrant drum rhythms. During this dazzling state march, described in its own right as a "gold mine," the king is carried above the crowd in a gold-studded palanquin (see fig. 3). The Golden Stool is carried in this procession too, eventually being displayed on its own special seat (*hwedom*). The populace, in turn, pledge loyalty to the king, providing food, water, firewood, and other necessities to the court. During the festival, especially deserving individuals are recognized by the king for their valor and other accomplishments. An individual being elevated to captain would kneel in front of the king and receive three soft strikes on his head from the state gold-handled sword, following which an oath of allegiance was sworn. Finally, Odwira is an occasion for grand feasting. The king offers liquor to the population, "poured into several brass pans and placed in various parts of the capital for the populace to drink." During this potentially "licentious" time, "law was temporarily suspended that day."[116] Also participating in the larger Odwira rite are the group of *akrafo* ("souls of the king")—distinguished by their gold disk-shaped *sunsum* chest pendants (see fig. 5). This group historically included both war captives and free individuals whose lives were in service to the king and state, and who would accompany him in death. The king would meet with various of his chiefs during Odwira, sharing drinks (both palm wine and European liquor), while also hearing cases and settling disputes. Both local calabash gourds and expensive imported silver punchbowls were used on such occasions.

Eating newly harvested yams (the consumption of which prior to Odwira was forbidden) is naturally a central part of the rite; and yams are presented at the shrines of key gods (*abosom*) and the various mortuary houses, including Bantama.[117] These events are important as part of the new yam harvest rite and New Year celebration because Odwira symbolizes the king's and the Asante state's rebirth, and the vital support of his subjects. As suggested in the well-known Akan proverb, it is "people that make a chief's stool great" (*nnipa na ema Ahennwa ye kesee*).[118] The king and the state are only as successful as their followers; Odwira is the occasion that defines this most strongly.[119]

A broader cleansing of the capital, the palace, the king, the court, and the population at large was a vital part of the Odwira festival. Protection was crucial, and the king would carefully tour the capital, inspecting it and pouring libations at key boundaries (particularly where important roads began).[120] Cleaning the capital (its people, places, and artworks), washing the king's soul, and purifying the nation more generally, to remove accumulated defilement, would eventually follow as key parts of Odwira rite. The cleansing of local architecture and artworks is of special interest. As Anti observes, "the King performed the ceremony of ablution, when he washed the various ancestral royal Stools, and purified the palace and the city."[121] He and other chiefs would cleanse the palace walls, windows, door, rooms, and furnishings such as bedposts with water—here assuming the role of priest.[122] "The purification rite was performed to keep away evil spirits from the King's bedrooms, and to ward off danger that might befall the King's household as well as the whole capital."[123]

Cleansing also included the recasting of historic sculptures of gold. As Anti explains, "it was the time for melting down any of the royal gold ornaments considered outmoded, to be fashioned into new patterns. This was determined by the state policy rather than by fashion."[124] These new works were a prominent focus since, during this well-attended festival, "all the gold ornaments that had been recast in preparation for the Odwira were publicly displayed."[125] It is hard to imagine an event anywhere more closely identified with the promotion of artistic creativity.

There was more cleansing to come and, indeed, "once these ablutions were concluded, the principal rite of purification was set in motion."[126] The court and others would process to the local stream. Brass basins containing the king's shrines and *asuman* (magical charms; sing. *suman*), which were covered with a white cloth on top of which were gold ornaments, were carried here as well. Hutton provides an overview of this remarkable "day of ablution" to cleanse the soul *(akradware)* of the king and the state:

> Before sunrise the King, accompanied by his Chiefs, captains, Nobles and a crowd of people connected with the washing of the Stools, would set out to a marshy place called Sareso and a stream, Dra, where the ablution ceremony would take place. There were Chiefs who had been raised to special status responsible for washing the royal articles of furniture and the various Stools in this ceremony. They would wash the royal chairs, different Stools, the gold and silver plates, and the brass pans in which were kept the royal gods and the magic medicines. After this function, the King would move a little farther from the spot to the stream, Dra, where he would wash his own body himself. Among the articles of toilet such as sponge, towel, comb and soap, was the King's dressing mirror which required two people to carry because of its size. To complete the operation, about 20 sheep were immersed in the stream so as to wash them for sacrificing.[127]

The soul-washers (*nkradwarefo*), wearing white cloths and distinguished by their prominent *sunsum* pendants, were a key part of this procession as well.[128] The Asantehene, his family, the large numbers of office holders and their retinues were all dressed in white as they moved in state to the river for purification—a rite intended to distance dangerous spirits. At the river, the king would take up an *adwera* branch (from a semi-woody member of the medicinal mint family that helps reduce inflammation) and submerge it in a vessel of the pure sacral water.[129] This plant-embued water was then sprinkled on the Golden Stool.[130] The use of this water-steeped *adwera* plant in rites to sanctify one's soul in *esubo* purification ceremonies is consistent with its use in decreasing the inflammation of illness. The rubbing of white clay on one's body on this occasion was also consistent with the larger theme of cooling and healing.

As we have seen, the royal bath did not just involve the king and his followers who processed to the river, but also the Golden Stool, the ancestral stools, and key deity shrines. Some of the items that were brought to the stream for cleansing were unusual, including: "much regalia and all the Asantehene's household effects." Some were clearly high-status imported goods, among them "pictures, mirrors, dressing cases and other fancy boxes." These same furnishings were then displayed before the population, a rich array of items "including several magnificent silver teapots, 'crew stands' and a variety of champagne goblets."[131] A key purpose of this display was to impress onlookers with the wealth and power of the state.

Basins and bottles of sacred river water were brought back to the capital for further purification rites, as

> people started for the palace in a procession, led by the King's chief priests and fetishmen. These priests were followed by servants who held in their arms brass basins full of water into which from time to time the priests dipped some leaves to sprinkle the water on the public by way of purification.[132]

The whole process was notably interactive: "The King's fetish men walk first, with attendants holding basins of sacred water, which they sprinkle plentifully over the chiefs with branches, the more superstitious running to have a little poured on their heads, or even on their tongues."[133] In addition to the cleansing river water and offerings, medicinal plants were employed, because they were "believed to be magic medicine, having power to scare away the ghosts."[134]

Conclusion

By way of conclusion, let me quote here part of the Asantehene's Odwira prayer during the associated rites of purification—prayers intended to enhance the prosperity, security, and well-being of the larger population and the state:

> Friday born Golden Stool I sprinkle water upon you, may your power return sharp and fierce.
> The edges of the years have met.
> May the nation prosper;
> May the women bear children;
> May the hunters kill meat;
> We who dig for gold, let us get gold to dig, and grant that I get some for the upkeep of my kingship.[135]

What is clear in this prayer, as in the various examples cited in this essay, is the importance of gold—and art—in the larger functioning of the Asante state, as well as the striking way in which different contexts of wealth identity play a part. The wealthiest group (the royal family) is not allowed to spend the multi-generational accumulated wealth except during key ceremonies (such as Odwira) or severe emergencies. Art features prominently both in the related display of status and power, and in the accumulation of more wealth, through the melting and recasting of arts of gold and the special "rigged" weighing system that benefitted the royal family in related transactions. At the same time, whether one achieved one's wealth through inheritance or individual accomplishment—whether through success in the hunt, in war, through farming, or by mining gold—all such gold accumulation was associated with ideas of potential pollution concerning either ill-gotten gains or personal acts that were identified as harmful.

Notes

1. Evans Kumi Wademor, dir., *Sika Mu Sakawa*, 2009, Ghana: Miracle Films. In English and Akan. DVD. Carmela Garritano, "Blood Money, Big Big Men and Zombies: Understanding Africa's Occult Narratives in the Context of Neoliberal Capitalism," *manycinemas* 3 (2012), n.6.

2. Garritano, "Blood Money."

3. See also ibid., on the relationship between occult films such as this within the context of Neoliberal capitalism.

4. From *mogyagu* (bloodshed).

5. G. Knight, "Ghana's Sakawa Superstition: Magic in the Digital Age," April 6, 2011, https://grahamghana.wordpress.com/2011/04/06/ghana%E2%80%99s-sakawa-superstition-magic-in-the-digital-age/.

6. Ibid.

7. A number of scholars have written about this phenomenon linked to the cult of winners and issues of sorcery, the occult, and the underbelly of popular culture, both in Ghana and elsewhere in Africa: see Misty L. Bastian, "'Bloodhounds Who Have No Friends': Witchcraft and Locality in the Nigerian Popular Press ," in *Modernity and Its Malcontents: Ritual and Power in Postcolonial Africa*, ed. by Jean Comaroff and John Comaroff (Chicago: University of Chicago Press, 1993), 129–66; Peter Geschiere, *The Modernity of Witchcraft: Politics and the Occult in Postcolonial Africa*, trans. by Janet L. Roitman (Charlottesville: University Press of Virginia, 1997); Birgit Meyer, "The Power of Money: Politics, Occult Force, and Pentecostalism in Ghana," *African Studies Review* 41, no. 3 (1998): 15–37; Jane Parish, "The Dynamics of Witchcraft and Indigenous Shrines among the Akan," *Africa: Journal of the International African Institute* 69, no. 3 (1999): 426–47; J. Comaroff and J. Comaroff, "Alien-Nation: Zombies, Immigrants, and Millennial Capitalism," *South Atlantic Quarterly* 101, no. 4 (2002): 782; Achille Mbembe, *On the Postcolony* (Oakland: University of California Press, 2002); Tobias Wendl, "Wicked Villagers and the Mysteries of Reproduction: An Exploration of Horror Movies from Ghana and Nigeria," *Postcolonial Text* 3, no. 2 (2007), https://www.postcolonial.org/index.php/pct/article/view/529; T. C. McCaskie, "The United States, Ghana and Oil: Global and Local Perspectives," *African Affairs* 107, no. 428 (2008): 313–32; and Alice Armstrong, "'Sakawa Rumours': Occult Internet Fraud and Ghanaian Identity," in *Cosmos, Gods and Madmen: Frameworks in the Anthropologies of Medicine*, ed. by Roland Littlewood and Rebecca Lynch (Oxford: Berghahn Books, 2016), 67–92.

8. R. Addo-Fening, *Akyem Abuakwa 1700–1943: From Ofori Panin to Sir Ofori Atta* (Trondheim: Norwegian University of Science and Technology, 1997), cited in Emmanuel Ababio Ofosu-Mensah, "Historical Overview of Traditional and Modern Gold Mining in Ghana," *International Research Journal of Library, Information and Archival Studies* 1, no. 1 (2011): 6–22.

9. Ursula M. Read, "Madness and Miracles: Hoping for Healing in Rural Ghana," in Littlewood and Lynch, *Cosmos, Gods and Madmen*, 62 n.8. See also McCaskie, "United States, Ghana and Oil."

10. Timothy F. Garrard, *Akan Weights and the Gold Trade* (York: Longman Group Ltd., 1980), 106; Janet Hess, "Embedded Objects: The Asante Goldweight, Subjectivity Formation, and Social Control," *Semiotica* 118 (1998): 295–305.

11. T. C. McCaskie, "Accumulation, Wealth, and Belief in Asante History I: To the Close of the Nineteenth Century," *Africa* 53, no. 1 (1983): 26. See also Garrard, *Akan Weights*; M. D. McLeod, *The Asante* (London: British Museum Publications, 1981).

12. Garrard, *Akan Weights*, 170–71, 174–75.

13. Kwame Arhin, "Gold-Mining and Trading among the Ashanti of Ghana," *Journal des Africanistes* 48, no. 1 (1978): 97.

14. Ivor Wilks, *Asante in the Nineteenth Century: The Structure and Evolution of a Political Order* (Cambridge: Cambridge University Press, 1975), 673.

15. Ibid., 418.

16. There were other currencies in place historically as well: among these early on were forged pieces of iron, and cowrie shells (originally from the Indian Ocean) came to this area from the north. See Emmanuel Ababio Ofosu-Mensah, "Traditional Gold Mining in Adanse," *Nordic Journal of African Studies* 19, no. 2 (2010): 140.

17. Wilks, *Asante in the Nineteenth Century*; Arhin, "Gold-Mining and Trading," 97.

18. McCaskie, "Accumulation, Wealth, and Belief in Asante History I," 27.

19. William Hutton, *A Voyage to Africa: Including a Narrative of an Embassy to one of the Interior Kingdoms, in the Year 1820* (London: Longman, Hurst, Rees, Orme and Brown, 1821), 317.

20. Ibid.

21. Thomas Edward Bowdich, *Mission from Cape Coast Castle to Ashantee with a Statistical Account of That Kingdom and Geographical Notices of Other Parts of the Interior of Africa* (London: John Murray, 1819), 319–20.

22. Garrard, *Akan Weights*, 104–5 and passim.

23. A larger set of local forms and terms are associated with the production and use of gold, including the balance scales (*akontuma*) to weigh the gold dust, gold dust seives (*huhuamoah*), and scoops (*famfa*; pl. *mfamfa*) to remove impurities from the gold dust. The equipment includes special paired leather satchels or bags (*kotokuo*; pl. *nkotokwaa*) that hold a chief's gold treasure, gold weights, and balance, as well as the single larger leather bag (*futuo*) of cloth or animal skin with which this equipment is wrapped. A number of people held special gold-linked offices: these ranged from the state head treasurer (*gyasehene*) and state exchequer (*gyasewa fekuo*), to the guardian of the royal gold-weight bag (*fotosanfohene*, "keeper of the leather bag"), the official treasury gold-weigher (*fotosanfo*), and the master goldsmith (*sikananfo;* pl. *sikadwumfo*).

24. Cited in Wilks, *Asante in the Nineteenth Century*, 697.

25. Arhin, "Gold-Mining and Trading," 93.

26. J. K. Fynn, *Asante and Its Neighbours, 1700–1807* (London: Longman, 1971), 120.

27. Arhin, "Gold-Mining and Trading," 93.

28. Frank Kwesi Adams, *Odwira and the Gospel: A Study of the Asante Odwira Festival and Its Significance for Christianity in Ghana* (Eugene, OR: Wipf & Stock, 2011), 231.

29. Ibid., 102; T. C. McCaskie, *State and Society in Pre-Colonial Asante* (Cambridge: Cambridge University Press, 1995), 160.

30. Adams, *Odwira and the Gospel*, 134.

31. Ibid.

32. Ibid., 132.

33. Hutton, *Voyage to Africa*, 325.

34. McCaskie, *State and Society in Pre-Colonial Asante*, 47–48.

35. Wilks, *Asante in the Nineteenth Century*, 415.

36. Ibid., 697.

37. Ibid., 693.

38. Wilks 1993: 135.

39. McCaskie, *State and Society in Pre-Colonial Asante*, 43.

40. R. S. Rattray, *Ashanti Law and Constitution* (Oxford: Clarendon Press, 1929), 277; Osei Agyeman Kyerematen, *Kingship and Ceremony in Ashanti* (Kumasi: UST Press, 1969), 1–5.

41. Wilks, *Asante in the Nineteenth Century*, 112.
42. McCaskie, *State and Society in Pre-Colonial Asante*, 128.
43. Arhin, "Gold-Mining and Trading," 89.
44. Ibid.; R. S. Rattray, *Ashanti* (Oxford: Clarendon Press, 1923), 289–90.
45. McCaskie, *State and Society in Pre-Colonial Asante*, 168.
46. Bowdich, *Mission from Cape Coast Castle to Ashantee*, 38.
47. Louise Françoise Müller, "Dancing Golden Stools: Indigenous Religion as a Strategy for Identity Construction in Ghana," *Fieldwork in Religion* 5, no. 1 (2010): section 1.3, https://scholarlypublications.universiteitleiden.nl/access/item%3A2910787/view.
48. Ibid.
49. Ofosu-Mensah, "Traditional Gold Mining in Adanse," 142.
50. Hutton, *Voyage to Africa*, 241.
51. McLeod, *Asante*, 75.
52. Bowdich, *Mission from Cape Coast Castle to Ashantee*, 37–38.
53. Herbert M. Cole and Doran H. Ross, *The Arts of Ghana* (Los Angeles: UCLA Museum of Cultural History, 1977), 9–12.
54. Hutton, *Voyage to Africa*, 365.
55. Bowdich, *Mission from Cape Coast Castle to Ashantee*, 35.
56. Ibid., 39.
57. Hutton, *Voyage to Africa*, 216–17.
58. Ibid, 212–13.
59. Ofosu-Mensah, "Historical Overview of Traditional and Modern Gold Mining," 10.
60. Arhin, "Gold-Mining and Trading," 90.
61. Ofosu-Mensah, "Traditional Gold Mining in Adanse," 136.
62. Ofosu-Mensah, "Historical Overview of Traditional and Modern Gold Mining," 12.
63. Ibid.
64. Ofosu-Mensah, "Traditional Gold Mining in Adanse," 132 nn.41–42. See also Garrard, *Akan Weights*, 17.
65. Ofosu-Mensah, "Traditional Gold Mining in Adanse," 129–30.
66. Nana S. Achampong, *Adinkra (ī'kŏn')-cepts: [Concept Ikons of the Asante Akan of West Africa]* (2011), 20, https://docplayer.net/47338068-Adinkra-i-kon-cepts.html. Joseph Dupuis (*Journal of a Residence in Ashanti* (London: H. Colburn, 1824), lviii) was informed that eight to ten thousand "slaves" were employed in washing the beds of streams, presumably for the rulers. In this context, "slaves" could mean simply subjects, or include free men.
67. Arhin, "Gold-Mining and Trading," 93.
68. Ofosu-Mensah, "Historical Overview of Traditional and Modern Gold Mining," 12.
69. A. Norman Klein, "The Two Asantes: Competing Interpretations of 'Slavery' in Akan-Asante Culture and Society," in *The Ideology of Slavery in Africa*, ed. by Paul E. Lovejoy (Beverly Hills: Sage, 1981), 149–52.
70. Ofosu-Mensah, "Traditional Gold Mining in Adanse," 143.
71. Rattray, *Ashanti*, 301; Garrard, *Akan Weights*, 117–19.
72. Ofosu-Mensah, "Traditional Gold Mining in Adanse," 143.
73. Ibid., 130.
74. Ibid., 131.
75. Ibid., 134, 136; Arhin, "Gold-Mining and Trading," 94.
76. Garrard, *Akan Weights*, 48; Ofosu-Mensah, "Traditional Gold Mining in Adanse," 130–32.
77. Ofosu-Mensah, "Traditional Gold Mining in Adanse," 129–30.
78. Arhin, "Gold-Mining and Trading," 94.
79. Ofosu-Mensah, "Traditional Gold Mining in Adanse," 131–32.
80. Arhin, "Gold-Mining and Trading," 90.
81. Wilks, *Asante in the Nineteenth Century*, n.102.
82. Arhin, "Gold-Mining and Trading," 90.
83. Ofosu-Mensah, "Traditional Gold Mining in Adanse," 133.
84. Each mining form had its own tool box: chisels (*soso* or *tofa*) for deep shafts; small iron shovels (*soso toa*) and a special digging adze, a form of hoe with a six-inch-long iron head (*aso*), for shallow digging;

another iron shovel (*soso tupre*) and wooden pole-form digging stick with an iron tip (*tabono*) for turning over the sand and stones when searching riverbeds.

85. Garrard, *Akan Weights*, cited in Ofosu-Mensah, "Historical Overview of Traditional and Modern Gold Mining."

86. Ofosu-Mensah, "Traditional Gold Mining in Adanse," 129, 134.

87. Ibid., 129.

88. Hutton, *Voyage to Africa*, 325.

89. Ofosu-Mensah, "Traditional Gold Mining in Adanse," 137.

90. Arhin, "Gold-Mining and Trading," 93; Ofosu-Mensah, "Traditional Gold Mining in Adanse," 131.

91. Cole and Ross, *Arts of Ghana*, 72.

92. Cited in Garrard, *Akan Weights*, 172–73.

93. Garrard, *Akan Weights*, 173.

94. Arhin, "Gold-Mining and Trading," 93; Timothy F. Garrard, "Studies in Akan Goldweights," *Transactions of the Historial Society of Ghana* 13 (1972): 1–20, 149–62, and 14 (1973): 1–16, 149–68.

95. Rattray, *Ashanti Law and Constitution*, 114–15; Garrard, "Studies in Akan Goldweights"; Arhin, "Gold-Mining and Trading," 93.

96. Garrard, *Akan Weights*, 202.

97. Hutton, *Voyage to Africa*, 325.

98. Garrard, *Akan Weights*, 174, 176–77.

99. Ofosu-Mensah, "Traditional Gold Mining in Adanse," 139.

100. Garrard, *Akan Weights*, 179, 192.

101. Garrard, *Akan Weights*, is my key source for this section.

102. McLeod, *Asante*, 48.

103. Ofosu-Mensah, "Traditional Gold Mining in Adanse," 138.

104. Rattray, *Ashanti*, 308; Garrard, *Akan Weights*, 196.

105. McLeod, *Asante*, 124, 128.

106. Hess, "Embedded Objects."

107. Garrard, *Akan Weights*, 202.

108. Cole and Ross, *Arts of Ghana*, 81; Garrard, *Akan Weights*, 193.

109. McLeod, *Asante*, 128.

110. Hutton, *Voyage to Africa*, 242.

111. Eric Appau Asante, Steve Kquofi, and Stephen Larbi, "The Symbolic Significance of Motifs on Selected Asante Religious Temples," *Journal of Aesthetics and Culture* 7, no. 1 (2014): 1–11.

112. A. A. Anti, *The Ancient Asante King* (Ghana: Volta Bridge, 1974) 26, 31–32, 40, 43; Kwame Arhin, *The City of Kumasi Handbook: Past, Present, and Future* (Legon. The Institute of African Studies, University of Ghana, 1992).

113. Anti, *Ancient Asante King*, 40. This description continues: "The Bantama ritual was a process of exhuming the bones of a late King from his temporary royal burial place near the palace and removing them to Bantama, the last resting place. It was also the time of giving drink to the old ones. It was only at midnight that the ritual was performed. The funeral cortege started from the palace cemetery. ... Before the King and the cortege arrived at Bantama, the skeleton of each King had already been removed from its coffin and displayed on its bed near its table, ready to receive the King's food and drink. Without sandals on, and without any gold ornaments on his body, the King would enter the first cell with his cloth adjusted about his loins. ... [After the key sacrifice] His blood was collected in the bowl and used in smearing the chair, table, musket and the skeleton. In this way all the different cells were visited and rituals performed in the same way as in the first."

114. Adams, *Odwira and the Gospel*, 43.

115. Ibid., 43.

116. Hutton, *Voyage to Africa*, 48; Adams, *Odwira and the Gospel*, 102.

117. Anti, *Ancient Asante King*, 26, 29, 31–32, 40, 43; Arhin 1992; Adams, *Odwira and the Gospel*, 11, 43, 47, 134.

118. P. Appiah, K. A. Appiah, et al. "Bu me bE 'Akan proverbs'," Accra, Centre for Intellectual Renewal, 2000, cited in Müller, "Dancing Golden Stools," section 1.4; McCaskie, *State and Society in Pre-Colonial Asante*, 231.

119. Müller, "Dancing Golden Stools," section 1.4.
120. Ibid.
121. Anti, *Ancient Asante King*, 49.
122. McCaskie, *State and Society in Pre-Colonial Asante*, 233; Adams, *Odwira and the Gospel*, 47.
123. Anti, *Ancient Asante King*, 50.
124. Ibid, 49.
125. McCaskie, *State and Society in Pre-Colonial Asante*, 232.
126. Ibid., 231.
127. Anti, *Ancient Asante King*, 49–50.
128. Adams, *Odwira and the Gospel*, 102.
129. Complementary rites on other occasions include a special pre-dawn river bath for widows to mark the end of the mourning period: see Joseph Oduro-Frimpong, "Sakawa: On Occultic Rituals and Cyber-fraud in Ghanaian Popular Cinema," Southern Illinois University Carbondale Working Paper presented to the Media Anthropology Network e-seminar, European Association of Social Anthropologists, January 18–February 1, 2011, https://www.easaonline.org/downloads/networks/media/35p.pdf.
130. Adams, *Odwira and the Gospel*, 102.
131. McCaskie, *State and Society in Pre-Colonial Asante*, 232.
132. Anti, *Ancient Asante King*, 50.
133. Bowdich, *Mission from Cape Coast Castle to Ashantee*, 280.
134. Anti, *Ancient Asante King*, 50.
135. Adams, *Odwira and the Gospel*, 47; see also McCaskie, *State and Society in Pre-Colonial Asante*, 233.

Bibliography

Achampong, Nana S. *Adinkra (ɒkŏn')-cepts: [Concept Ikons of the Asante Akan of West Africa]*. 2011. https://docplayer.net/47338068-Adinkra-i-kon-cepts.html.

Adams, Frank Kwesi. *Odwira and the Gospel: A Study of the Asante Odwira Festival and Its Significance for Christianity in Ghana*. Eugene, OR: Wipf & Stock, 2011.

Akyeampong, Emmanuel. *Drink, Power and Cultural Change: A Social History of Alcohol in Ghana, c. 1800 to Recent Times*. Portsmouth, NH: James Currey, 1996.

Anti, A. A. *The Ancient Asante King*. Ghana: Volta Bridge, 1974.

Arhin, Kwame. "Gold-Mining and Trading among the Ashanti of Ghana." *Journal des Africanistes* 48, no. 1 (1978): 89–100.

Arhin, Kwame. *The City of Kumasi Handbook: Past, Present, and Future*. Legon. The Institute of African Studies, University of Ghana, 1992.

Armstrong, Alice. "'Sakawa Rumours': Occult Internet Fraud and Ghanaian Identity." In *Cosmos, Gods and Madmen: Frameworks in the Anthropologies of Medicine*, edited by Roland Littlewood and Rebecca Lynch, 67–92. Oxford: Berghahn Books, 2016.

Asante, Eric Appau, Steve Kquofi, and Stephen Larbi. "The Symbolic Significance of Motifs on Selected Asante Religious Temples." *Journal of Aesthetics and Culture* 7, no. 1 (2014): 1–11.

Ayesu, Solomon Marfo. 2015 "Empirical Study of Akuapem Odwira Festival and Traditional State Symbols: A Means for Design and Production of Textile Regalia for Akuapem Paramount Chief." MFA thesis, Industrial Art and Textile Design Department, Kwame Nkrumah University Science and Technology, Ghana, 2015.

Bastian, Misty L. "'Bloodhounds Who Have No Friends': Witchcraft and Locality in the Nigerian Popular Press." In *Modernity and Its Malcontents: Ritual and Power in Postcolonial Africa*, edited by Jean Comaroff and John Comaroff, 129–66. Chicago: University of Chicago Press, 1993.

Bowdich, Thomas Edward. *Mission from Cape Coast Castle to Ashantee with a Statistical Account of That Kingdom and Geographical Notices of Other Parts of the Interior of Africa*. London: John Murray, 1819.

Cole, Herbert M., and Doran H. Ross. *The Arts of Ghana*. Los Angeles: UCLA Museum of Cultural History, 1977.

Comaroff, J., and J. Comaroff. "Alien-Nation: Zombies, Immigrants, and Millennial Capitalism." *South Atlantic Quarterly* 101, no. 4 (2002), 779–805.
Dupuis, Joseph. *Journal of a Residence in Ashanti*. London: H. Colburn, 1824.
Fynn, J. K. *Asante and Its Neighbours, 1700–1807*. London: Longman, 1971.
Garrard, Timothy F. *African Gold*. New York: Prestel, 2011.
Garrard, Timothy F. *Akan Weights and the Gold Trade*. York: Longman Group Ltd., 1980.
Garrard, Timothy F. "Studies in Akan Goldweights." *Transactions of the Historial Society of Ghana* 13 (1972): 1–20, 149–62, and 14 (1973): 1–16, 149–68.
Garritano, Carmela. "Blood Money, Big Big Men and Zombies: Understanding Africa's Occult Narratives in the Context of Neoliberal Capitalism." *manycinemas* 3 (2012): 50–65.
Geschiere, Peter. *The Modernity of Witchcraft: Politics and the Occult in Postcolonial Africa*. Translated by Janet L. Roitman. Charlottesville: University Press of Virginia, 1997.
Hess, Janet. "Embedded Objects: The Asante Goldweight, Subjectivity Formation, and Social Control." *Semiotica* 118 (1998): 295–305.
Hutton, William. *A Voyage to Africa: Including a Narrative of an Embassy to one of the Interior Kingdoms, in the Year 1820*. London: Longman, Hurst, Rees, Orme and Brown, 1821.
Klein, A. Norman. "The Two Asantes: Competing Interpretations of 'Slavery' in Akan-Asante Culture and Society." In *The Ideology of Slavery in Africa*, edited by Paul E. Lovejoy, 149–67. Beverly Hills: Sage, 1981.
Knight, G. "Ghana's Sakawa Superstition: Magic in the Digital Age." April 6, 2011. https://grahamghana.wordpress.com/2011/04/06/ghana%E2%80%99s-sakawa-superstition-magic-in-the-digital-age/.
Kyerematen, Osei Agyeman. *Kingship and Ceremony in Ashanti*. Kumasi: UST Press, 1969.
Mbembe, Achille *On the Postcolony*. Oakland: University of California Press, 2002.
McCaskie, T. C. "Accumulation, Wealth, and Belief in Asante History I: To the Close of the Nineteenth Century." *Africa* 53, no. 1 (1983): 23–43.
McCaskie, T. C. "Accumulation, Wealth, and Belief in Asante History II: The Twentieth Century." *Africa* 56, no. 1 (1986): 3–23.
McCaskie, T. C. *Asante, Kingdom of Gold: Essays in the History of an African Culture*. Durham, NC: Carolina Academic Press, 2015.
McCaskie, T. C. "The United States, Ghana and Oil: Global and Local Perspectives." *African Affairs* 107, no. 428 (2008): 313–32.
McCaskie, T. C. *State and Society in Pre-Colonial Asante*. Cambridge: Cambridge University Press, 1995.
McLeod, M. D. *The Asante*. London: British Museum Publications, 1981.
Meyer, Birgit. "The Power of Money: Politics, Occult Force, and Pentecostalism in Ghana." *African Studies Review* 41, no. 3 (1998): 15–37.
Müller, Louise Françoise. "Dancing Golden Stools: Indigenous Religion as a Strategy for Identity Construction in Ghana," *Fieldwork in Religion* 5, no. 1 (2010): 32–57, https://scholarlypublications.universiteitleiden.nl/access/item%3A2910787/view.
Oduro-Frimpong, Joseph. "Sakawa: On Occultic Rituals and Cyberfraud in Ghanaian Popular Cinema." Southern Illinois University Carbondale Working Paper presented to the Media Anthropology Network e-seminar, European Association of Social Anthropologists, January 18–February 1, 2011. https://www.easaonline.org/downloads/networks/media/35p.pdf.
Ofosu-Mensah, Emmanuel Ababio. "Historical Overview of Traditional and Modern Gold Mining in Ghana." *International Research Journal of Library, Information and Archival Studies* 1, no. 1 (2011): 6–22.
Ofosu-Mensah, Emmanuel Ababio. "Traditional Gold Mining in Adanse." *Nordic Journal of African Studies* 19, no. 2 (2010): 124–47.
Parish, Jane. "The Dynamics of Witchcraft and Indigenous Shrines among the Akan." *Africa: Journal of the International African Institute* 69, no. 3 (1999): 426–47.
Pescheux, Gérard. *Le royaume asante (Ghana). Parenté, pouvoir, histoire, XVIIe–XXe siècles*. Paris: Karthala, 2003.
Rattray, R. S. *Ashanti Law and Constitution*. Oxford: Clarendon Press, 1929.
Rattray, R. S. *Ashanti*. Oxford: Clarendon Press, 1923.
Read, Ursula M. "Madness and Miracles: Hoping for Healing in Rural Ghana." In *Cosmos, Gods and Madmen: Frameworks in the Anthropologies of Medicine*, edited by Roland Littlewood and Rebecca Lynch, 45–66. Oxford: Berghahn Books, 2016.

Ross, D. H. "The Iconography of Asante Sword Ornaments." *African Arts* 11, no. 1 (1977): 16–25.
Schildkrout, Enid. "The Kingdom of Gold." *Natural History* 105, no. 2 (1996): 36–47.
Wademor, Evans Kumi, dir. *Sika Mu Sakawa*. 2009. Ghana: Miracle Films. In English and Akan. DVD.
Wendl, Tobias. "Wicked Villagers and the Mysteries of Reproduction: An Exploration of Horror Movies from Ghana and Nigeria." *Postcolonial Text* 3, no. 2 (2007). https://www.postcolonial.org/index.php/pct/article/view/529.
Wilks, Ivor. *Asante in the Nineteenth Century: The Structure and Evolution of a Political Order*. Cambridge: Cambridge University Press, 1975.
Wilks, Ivor, *Forests of Gold: Essays on the Akan and the Kingdom of Asante*. Athens: Ohio University Press, 1993.

PART III

The Economies of Gold

The Genoese Merchant Network and Gold (ca. 1450–1530)

Carlo Taviani

The Genoese Diasporic Network in the Atlantic

The purpose of this essay is to shed new light on the network of Genoese merchants who traded into the southern Iberian Peninsula, the Atlantic islands, and West Africa between the fifteenth and early sixteenth centuries. In Africa they collected and traded in gold, as well as other goods and enslaved people. As the merchants involved in the gold trade are the main subject, those who dealt in other goods and in enslaved people will only be partly considered.

Genoese traders were scattered throughout the many different places where they resided and traded. For a long period of time, spanning the fourteenth to seventeenth centuries, their presence stretched all the way from Asia (the Indian Ocean) to Africa and the New World. They lived and did business in far-flung lands, in the areas bordering the Tatars on the Black Sea, in Syria, Egypt, and the Low Countries, and extended their influence toward the Iberian Peninsula, a trading hub for commerce with the Atlantic islands—Madeira, the Canaries, and Cape Verde—and West Africa. At the beginning of the sixteenth century this Atlantic trade was beginning to flow toward the New World.

For these merchants, their hometown of Genoa remained a tiny patch of ground in comparison with the vast trading areas over which they formed a diasporic merchant network.[1] It has been claimed that, at least for the entire fifteenth century, gold flowed out of central Africa—one of the world's leading suppliers of the metal—to Genoa, which was one of the cities in Europe that was hungriest for gold.[2] Later Genoese traders invested in the New World, dominating the silver market of the Spanish Empire. The studies of Enrique Otte, Ruth Pike, David Igual Luis, and others have proved how extensive and interconnected these Genoese trading networks were, both in Europe and on the African side of the Atlantic.[3] Once the merchants had settled abroad—even if they kept up contact with their native Genoa—it made little sense for them to bring goods back to their hometown. As we shall see, Genoa remained the capital and the notarial hub for their activities, but their actual trade at that point had shifted westward. Perhaps it was the simple fact of the geographical location of the Genoese diasporic network—and not merely the balance of trade, as maintained by Jacques Heers—which discouraged the flow of goods back toward Genoa. Capital flowed out of Genoa, notarial records were stored in Genoa, but many Genoese merchants did not live and trade there. They continued to be based in the Iberian Peninsula and traded across the Atlantic.

During the early modern age some of the most mathematically transferable equivalents of gold were financial practices and institutions. Items such as shares of public debt or shares of joint stock companies, financial institutions such as the public debt system or the huge banks, and financial practices like double-entry bookkeeping and accounting techniques all typically arose out of a desire and need for gold. Whenever there was a shortage of gold, financial institutions kept the market alive. Many financial transactions were gold *in effigy*, fictional instruments that represented an exchange of the precious metal. Until the early sixteenth century, groups of merchant bankers who traded in gold from West Africa were also actively involved in the financial institutions of the city-states of Renaissance Italy. Florentines, Venetians, and Genoese were the most active, between the twelfth and early seventeenth centuries. Genoa was a center for financial innovation and, even more than Venice and Florence, it projected itself into North and West Africa. At the beginning of the fifteenth century the Genoese consolidated their public debt and founded a huge bank, the Casa di San Giorgio (1407–1805), which lasted for centuries.[4] Economic historians maintain that the Casa di San Giorgio was created because there was a scarcity of gold in Genoa.[5] In 1444 its bank failed: it had pledged to exchange fictional coins for gold and real coins and it could not honour this promise. It reopened in 1530.[6]

The following pages, exploring this period, will also briefly show how some of the financial institutions that developed in Genoa were directly correlated to the quest for, the presence of, or the scarcity of gold; they and the social networks of the Genoese merchants were tightly interwoven.

The search for gold

In Genoa gold was an invisible commodity. It is difficult to find references to it and hard to know where it will turn up in the sources. In the fifteenth century the Genoese were looking for gold mainly in Africa but not only there. They also went to great lengths to find it closer to home, mining it in small quantities in Liguria, the area around Genoa. The right to prospect for precious metals and gold was granted by the commune of Genoa to anyone willing to

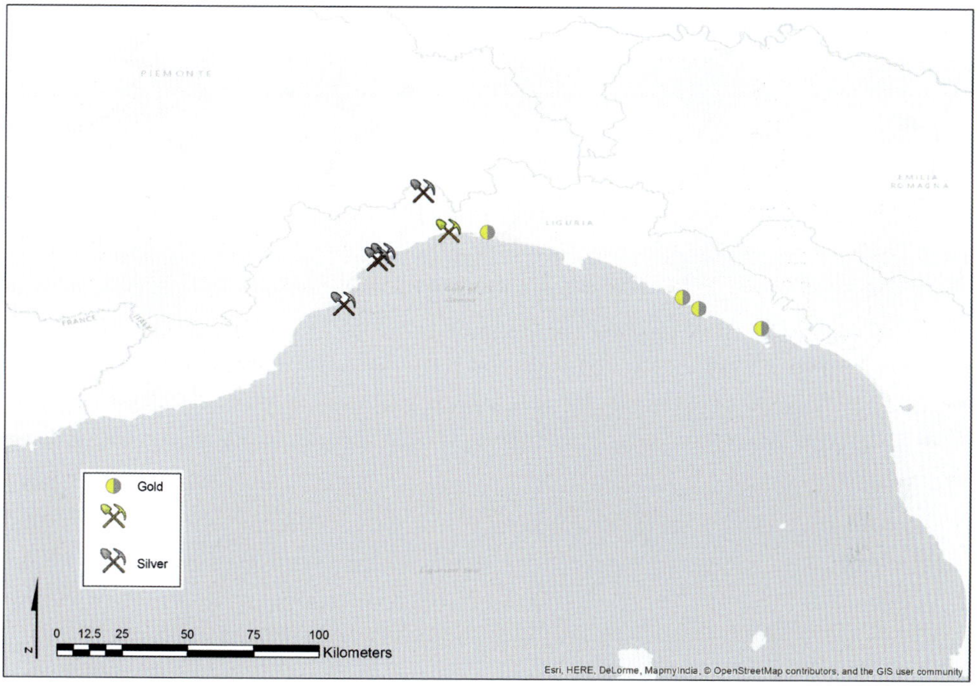

Map 1. Gold and Gold Search in Liguria (1465-1481)
In 1465 Boniforte Rotulo declares he has found various veins of precious metals. Gold in the small river of Albunega, in Voltri, silver in the mountains of Arenele, gold again in Faiallo in the Mountains of Arenzano, silver in Celle and Albisola, in Stella, and Rossiglione. In 1473 Francesco Pammaleo—doctor in utroque—obtained the permission from the commune of Genoa to search for gold until up to the following 22 years in the areas of Levanto and Framura. The concession says every vein, stone, rock "auri or argenti". Again in 1474 magister Iacobus de Presbiteri received the task to search for gold, silver or copper in the land close to La Spezia. In 1481 Pietro Orabono obtained another permission to search for gold, silver and other metals in the river Polcevera

Sources: Archivio di Stato di Genova, Archivio Segreto, 733 C and Giuseppe Pipino, *Liguria mineraria. Miscellanea di giacimentologia, mineralogia e storia estrattiva* (Ovada: Tipografia Pesce, 2005)

make the effort. Once this privilege had been issued, the right to dig anywhere in the area granted prevailed over any other jurisdictional claim (institutions or persons). Gold prospectors crossed fences and trespassed into private lands and gardens in order to dig them up and overturn the soil. The Genoese commune strongly encouraged the privatization of rights and lands, and many lands were granted to powerful Genoese families, such as the Fieschi, Doria, Spinola, and Fregoso, and to the commune's creditors, the Casa di San Giorgio, which possessed and governed with full territorial authority Corsica, Crimea, and the Lunigiana. However, the right to excavate under the ground remained in the hands of the commune. The concessions also gave permission to look for other metals such as silver and iron. Map. 1 shows where gold and silver had been found and the attempts made to find them for the period 1465–81. There are only a few studies on this subject, but it appears that results of this gold search in Liguria bore little fruit.

Most of the gold came from overseas. A customs register of 1377 which was discovered by John Day shows the flow of gold into Genoa: from Palermo (1000 Genoese lire), from Valencia (6000 Genoese lire), from Malaga (6000 Genoese lire), and from Seville (9500 Genoese lire).[7] The main source of gold was Africa, from where it was next taken to the Iberian Peninsula. From Spain the Genoese traded it in Flanders and England and also brought it back to Genoa. Until around 1250 gold came to Genoa in the form of a powder known as "de paiola". In later documents we sometimes see mentions of *aurum tiberi*, which derives from *Al-tibr* (from the word for gold in Arabic or perhaps from the Insula Tiberi, a mythological island in Africa where Europeans believed sub-Saharan gold originated). References to *aurum tiberi* are rare and there are few studies about it. After 1250 the metal was often transported in the form of *doblas* of *aurum tiberi* that were probably minted in the cities of North Africa.

Apart from the information contained in the 1377 register studied by Day, it is difficult to obtain any quantitative data for Genoa in other periods.[8] According to Enrique Otte, who studied the Genoese in Spain, the reason for the scarcity of gold was that it was forbidden to take the metal out of the Iberian Peninsula.[9] Jacques Heers maintained that once the gold got to Spain from Africa it tended to stay there, arguing the balance of trade was not in favor of the Genoese.[10] In addition to silk and other merchandise from Spain, various goods from northern Europe (London, Bruges, etc.) kept the balance in favor of Spain. Thus, at the end of the fifteenth century, Spain, and the Nasrid Sultanate of Granada in particular, functioned as distribution hubs for different types of goods, and the Genoese ruled the market and the trade in that area. Perhaps Heers's explanation will be partially reframed with future studies on Genoese merchant networks and their diasporical structure. The Genoese were among the most important traders in Spain and they later reinvested in finance the profits they made from trading in the fifteenth and early sixteenth centuries, eventually becoming merchant bankers, during what Felipe Ruiz Martín referred to as the "golden century," and even bankers to King Philip II.

Eurocentric Approaches

The story of the African gold trade and the American gold and silver trade to major European financial centers like Genoa—but also to Portugal and Spain—is an oft-heard tale. It is a very Eurocentric narrative, peppered with words like "expansion", "discovery", "adventure" (the European "expansion" toward Africa, the "discovery" of the New World, etc.). From the late nineteenth century until only a few decades ago erudite scholars (such as Charles de la Roncière) scoured the archives for details about early modern explorers, and they found precious documents. These scholars tended to focus on the biographical details of important explorers. Obvious instances are the extensive literature on Christopher Columbus's origins or debates over whether Antonio da Noli was the discoverer of Cape Verde.[11] However, there is also an extensive literature on the lesser-known Genoese Antonio Malfante, the first European to bring back information about Timbuktu after his journey to southern Algeria (1447), or the Genoese Antoniotto Usodimare, who together with Alvise Cadamosto traveled to Guinea (1455), or Niccoloso da Recco, who rediscovered the Canaries (1341). Most of the so-called explorations of the Genoese were devoted to the search for gold: to give just one example, gold was the reason why Antonio Malfante gathered information about Timbuktu.

Updating our understanding of late fifteenth-century Genoese trade can provide us with an opportunity to view the relationships between Africa and European traders from a different perspective. The so-called Genoese explorers need to be contextualized as part of the story of the Genoese trading networks. As geographically vast as these trading networks were, and however much we may revise our view of their so-called explorations, they represent what were essentially commercial contacts between Europeans and Africa. The so-called explorers were only the tips of the icebergs of wider trading networks. This perspective may help us to gain a better view of relations between Africa and Europe—at least in precolonial times—a view that is less Eurocentric, since it considers "exploration" to be a component of commercial exchange and exploitation.

New Old Sources: The Notaries

Scholars such as Enrique Otte, Ruth Pike, Antonia Fabregas, and others studied the fifteenth- and sixteenth-century Genoese diaspora by focusing on documents in Seville and to a lesser extent from other Spanish cities, and even the scarce documentation of the Portuguese archives, all of which have proved extremely useful.[12] Surprisingly, the documentation from Genoa itself has not been studied systematically.[13] The classic sources for trade are merchant ledgers. As Richard Goldthwaite has proved after carefully sifting through the vast Florentine archives, Florence represents the best place to find merchants ledgers in Renaissance Italy—and probably the best in the world. In Genoa, though some ledgers remain and others have not yet been properly located or studied, the same kind of treasure trove does not exist and we have to fall back on notarial deeds.[14] These are of various types and contain many different kinds of information. There are proxies, wills, arbitrations, and a few other deeds (such as the *naulizatio*, which was an itinerary of ships) or various forms of insurance. While there is no scholarly consensus, it is likely that most notarial deeds related to trade were written in order to prevent potential conflicts arising among the parties. Even certain wills may be considered as documents drafted to prevent conflicts among heirs.

Because of their great variety, any systematic study of Genoese notarial documents would be quite a daunting task. That, together with the lack of a complete index, is probably the reason why Fernand Braudel, Carlo Cipolla, and Robert Sabatino's project to use notarial archives in Genoa never came to fruition and remained a dead letter.[15] The present essay provides information on various case studies related to the gold trade. So far, my project has investigated a sample of around 300,000 notarial deeds and I have selected a few thousand of them that contain references to the Genoese network in the Iberian Peninsula. In this essay I refer to the deeds of the notary Simone Canella. Two of his folders contain the majority of documents used in the following survey.[16] The Genoese documentation could accompany—and the resulting analysis be enriched by—a study of the documentation housed in Seville (notarial archives and Casa da India archives), Lisbon (Archivo do Torre do Tombo), and the Canaries (notarial archives). As I mentioned in the introductory paragraph, the Genoese merchant network during the period considered here (ca. 1450–1530) mainly operated in the Atlantic islands and the Iberian Peninsula and its commercial ties with Genoa were weak (even black enslaved people are mentioned only very rarely in the Genoese documentation). The notarial connection was, however, stronger and more important, though the reason why these notarial sources were produced or ended up in Genoa has not been investigated until now.

Often the investment for trading came from Genoa, from members of older generations of the same family, people who had accumulated money from businesses in other places, such as the Levant (the Black Sea, which was a Genoese territorial domain before the Ottoman conquest, or in the eastern

Mediterranean Sea, such as Chios, and Cyprus, as in the case of the Centurione family). More often, however, notarial deeds contain information about commercial conflicts between two families or groups of merchants which were then resolved in front of a Genoese notary and—more importantly—using Genoese witnesses and mediators (as in the case studies presented here below: those of the Centurione against the Marihoni and a case involving the sale of writing paper). Genoese mediators played an important role in resolving these kinds of disputes, since they were often socially or economically linked to the parties involved in the conflict. This may be why the merchants of the Genoese diaspora employed Genoese notaries even when they themselves were living far away. Genoese notarial deeds and the social, economic, and kinship ties within Genoese society performed a regulatory function whenever conflicts arose.

Case Studies

The North African Route

Gold was more than just a commodity. It had a financial value and that is why, even though we do not see much information about it in Genoa, it has left more of a trace in the documents than African enslaved people or merchandise usually traded in the Atlantic islands, the Iberian Peninsula, Flanders, and England, goods like melegueta pepper, *oricello*, or exotic animals. Scholars have already explored the itineraries of the gold trade, and the archival research in Genoa, after looking at various notarial deeds, confirms the results of current research, as well the tales of old sources such as Antonio Malfante. Gold flowed mainly out of central Africa to Tunis and Oran. Genoese had been settled in North Africa since at least the thirteenth century and there were many Genoese trading posts, such as Ceuta. Some of these places were even under Genoese jurisdiction.

Information about this trade emerged only occasionally and mostly when conflicts arose. For example, a group of nine merchants who were trading in gold in 1474 appealed to the commune of Genoa because it had not respected their fiscal rights. A law from the mid-fifteenth century stated that gold and silver from Tunis could not be taxed by the commune. That was what the merchants wished to prove and for that purpose they signed a petition in front of a notary. The petitioners included members of the most important families of the Genoese nobility, including the Cattaneo, Spinola, Lercari, Imperiale, and Di Negro: Francesco Cattaneo, Ambrogio di Negro, Andalò Imperiale, Ambrogio Lercari, and Napoleone and Teodoro Spinola.[17] Among them were also Gabriele Marihoni and Tommaso and Gerolamo Pallavicino. The Pallavicino were a large merchant family, closely interrelated with other families; the Marihoni were small but they played an important role in the so-called exploration of fifteenth-century Africa by financing the famous Antonio Malfante.

Timbuktu, Antonio Malfante, and the Marihoni

In 1446, on a ship owned by Gerolamo Savigonone, the Genoese Antonio Malfante arrived in the port of Honein, in the company of Percivalle Marihoni. Marihoni subsequently left Africa, while Malfante moved southward into the Sahara, joining a caravan of local traders which reached the oasis of Tuat in what is today southern Algeria. From Tuat Malfante wrote a letter to Marihoni which later became one of the most famous accounts of Timbuktu and the sub-Saharan trade during precolonial times. The letter contains various details about trade, food, customs, and geography. It describes how Jewish merchants dominated trade in the vicinity of Tuat and enjoyed the protection of the Maghrebi lords of the district. It also describes how the rich Maghrebi merchant who protected Malfante there had a family network which extended from Tlemcen toward Timbuktu, a distance of around 2000 miles. Some of these details still provide interesting information which has been confirmed by modern studies. For example, the report of a widespread merchant network in the Sahara corresponds to recent archaeological finds. Archaeological studies conducted by Anne Haour looked at the trading territory of a certain family group in ancient Mali, where one family alone, as Malfante relates, covered a vast region, sometimes as large as the entire Iberian Peninsula.[18] It is also interesting that Malfante mentions copper, saying that copper from Romania (the Genoese word for the maritime area of the Byzantine Empire) was "always in great demand throughout the land of the Blacks."[19] As the work of Hilmar Krueger has proven, the Genoese brought copper into Africa at least until the thirteenth century.[20] However, Malfante makes no mention of a copper trade from Genoa, which probably means that at the time he was writing Genoese merchants were no longer taking the metal to Africa, as they had once done.

Gold was the most important commodity for Malfante, and information about the gold trade was what really interested him. He inquired of the lord he was living with about the sources of gold and was told that where the metal came from and how it got there were shrouded in secrecy. His host informed him that he had lived fourteen years in the "land of the Blacks" and nobody knew anything about this trade, perhaps because it came from even more distant lands. The secrecy surrounding sub-Saharan gold and the reports of an inaccessible chain of merchants operating in a very far land, in the deepest heart of Africa, are mentioned in many sources. A rare Genoese ledger from 1431—partially broken up and lost during the Second World War and only recently recovered—records the activities of a Genoese merchant in Oran, Urbano Leoni, and it contains the names of various Maghrebi traders.[21] Data like this is not easy to come by, since western European commercial contracts and sources usually do not list the names of Islamic traders during this early period.[22] From this ledger we can see that the Marihoni family was involved in the gold trade.[23] This information reinforces the possibility that Malfante was looking for another path to trade not only in various goods but also in gold.

Another Genoese family of traders, who lived and traded in Spain, was probably interested in the gold trade. At the death of Malfante, two Genoese merchants who lived and traded in Majorca, Giovanni and Nicola Centurione, collected his money, goods, and all the wealth he had accumulated during his journeys in Africa and brought them to Genoa.[24] It is even possible that they—and not only the Marihoni—were behind Malfante's travels.[25] This probable hypothesis could be reinforced by looking at the activities of the Centurione in the southern Iberian Peninsula.

The Centurione Family and the Quest for Gold

From the middle of fifteenth century to the beginning of the sixteenth, various members of the Centurione family traded in gold and they were among the richest merchants and bankers in Genoa. In 1447, only three years after the huge bank of the Casa di San Giorgio closed, and the same year that Antonio Malfante made his expedition to southern Algeria, a law was passed in Genoa that fixed the exchange rate in gold. The law stated that all *cambiali* had to be paid in gold and that at least one-third of all payments had to be made in gold or in gold florins. This was done in order to stabilize transactions and it also served to stabilize the exchange rate between gold and silver coins. While other cities had pegged payments at fixed rates to gold (Florence in 1464, and Bruges in 1434), it may be that in the case of Genoa the measure had something to do with the financial turmoil besetting the bank of the Casa di San Giorgio just then. It was the Centurione family who proposed this law, so it is possible that this family was lobbying for new legislation while at the same time investing in Malfante's expedition for gold.

A preliminary examination of the portion of the notarial deeds mentioned above and an analysis of the secondary literature led to the results in Table 1 which shows a small dataset of the Centurione family's involvement in the quest for gold, covering at least fifty years, from 1465 to 1513. In 1465 Nicholas

NAME	PARTNERSHIP	LOCATION	DATE	GOLD	PURPOSE
Federico Centurione	Unknown	Mina de Oro (El Mina Castle in West Africa)	1486	attempt	
Federico Centurione	Stefano Centurione and Giuliano Calvo	New World	1507	attempt	
Federico Centurione	Unknown	Portugal	1513		Received gold "de la Tyba" (aurum tiberi)

Table 1. The Centurione Family and the Gold Trade

and Jacobo Marihoni were engaged in a dispute with Francesco Centurione and Thomas Piccamiglio. The disagreement turned on a quantity of wheat and Valencian drapes which were exchanged in the Kingdom of Tlemcen for sub-Saharan gold (*aurum tiberi*).[26] The Marihoni gave to Centurione and Piccamiglio 628 doblas and 2 tominas of gold (*aurum tiberi*). A group of mediators, people known to both the parties, resolved the conflict. The mediators were Taddeo Spinola, Luca Pinelli, and Johannis and Franciscus Spinola. This notarial deed involved the families of both the Centurione and the Marihoni. From a selection of documents it is evident that the same names of merchants appear over and over again. When the Genoese had to trade with sub-Saharan Africa via North Africa, the network able to reach these places and traders was tiny. That is why it may be useful to look at other goods and not just gold in order to identify who was investing in the quest for that metal.

Expanding the Network

In the 1465 document signed by the Marihoni and Centurione families, mention is made of a certain Taddeo Spinola acting as intermediary. His name evokes a crossroads in the heart of the Sahara. From another document related to another commercial dispute we learn that in 1451 Spinola brought writing paper from Genoa to Africa. At the time Genoa was important for writing paper, since artisans from Fabriano, an Italian town traditionally known for manufacturing paper, moved to Genoa and the Genoese hinterland—most of them to Voltri—and began producing paper there from the middle of the fifteenth century.[27] The 1452 document contains a rare reference to trade with sub-Saharan Africa.[28] In September 1451, in Malaga, Rafael Barixonus sold twelve bales of writing paper (*papirrum pro scribendo*) to Domenicus Buroni at the price of 6.5 doblas. Some of the bales were not in good condition. Domenicus, in a ship owned by Taddeo Spinola and with the help of the sailor, Gabriel Pardus from Saona (near Genoa), sailed to Oran in North Africa, where he tried to sell the paper to a Muslim merchant. He received only 3.5 doblas for each of five bales and 7 doblas for each of the other seven.[29] Gabriel Pardus acted as intermediary with the Muslim merchant. What is interesting here is that the notarial deed mentions that the Muslim merchant was someone who had many contacts with black merchants (a "mauro speciario qui multum frquentat in terra nigrorum mercatorio modo"). This short phrase used in the context of a sale suggests that the paper was ultimately destined for the merchants of sub-Saharan Africa. Upon his return to Genoa, Domenicus Buroni sued Rafael Barixonus. Since the latter was himself Genoese and because Genoese paper was an important commodity, it is highly probable that the cargo originated in Genoa. We know the facts of the case from a *testificatio*, a notarial deed reporting the information provided by various witnesses. The notary recorded in Genoa the information provided by Domenicus Buroni, Gabriel Pardus, and Taddeo Spinola.

In recent years many efforts have been made to preserve the libraries of Timbuktu, which have been threatened by the political instability of the region and by jihadists, and various attempts have been set up to transport thousands of manuscripts to Bamako, the capital of Mali.[30] This process has also encouraged the study of old manuscripts in Timbuktu's libraries. According to the most recent research, there is no evidence of writing paper in Timbuktu or Djenné-Djenno before the seventeenth century.[31] Thanks to the works of Paolo de Moraes Farias, we know that stone epigraphs were quite common in ancient Mali, where the oldest epigraphs have been dated to the twelfth century, but no paper documents of the same age have yet been found.[32] While the Genoese document does not directly mention either Timbuktu or Djenné-Djenno, it is likely that "the land of the Blacks" refers to regions south of the Sahara and possibly to the cities in present-day Mali. The document which names Taddeo Spinola may be one of the oldest reports of the presence of writing paper in sub-Saharan Africa. While the document does not refer to the gold trade as such, it is important here because it helps to identify a group of people who were trading between Genoa, the southern Iberian Peninsula, and Africa. Taddeo Spinola is connected to the Centurione who traded in gold, and Gabriel Pardus was acquainted with the Maghrebi merchants. These could prove to be interesting individuals to focus on in any future studies on the gold trade.

A preliminary screening of the sources shows that, together with the families mentioned above, members of other families, either in Genoa or in other Italian cities, traded with the Marihoni and the Centurione. Francesco Pinelli, a relative of Luca Pinelli (who acted as mediator in the notarial deed mentioned above, which was signed by the Centurione and the Marihoni in 1465), was among the main backers of Christopher Columbus. The Centurione also collaborated with the Florentine Medici family from at least 1465 to 1486. Piero and Lorenzo de' Medici did business with the Centurione in various commercial centers: London, Florence, and Bruges.[33] The Medici family had many connections in Europe with different merchants, but the Centurione connection is worth exploring in order to obtain new information about Medici artistic and scientific patronage and their collecting practices of African objects (such as ivory).[34]

Conclusion

This essay has focused on the gold trade and the Genoese merchant networks associated with it in the period ca. 1450–1530. The case studies have looked especially at the Marihoni and the Centurione families. The former actively financed Malfante's search for gold in Africa. There are pieces of evidence indicating that the Marihoni were trading in gold in various instances: Malfante's attempt to find gold (1447), in Tunis (1474), in Oran (1431), and in cooperation with—or in competition with—the Centurione (1465). From at least the 1460s until the 1510s the Centurione family were similarly active in seeking gold from Africa. It may be possible to explore the wider extension of this network by looking at the families of the Spinola, Pinelli, and Medici. Since not many Genoese families traded with West and sub-Saharan Africa, and since the routes toward sub-Saharan Africa were only explored by a handful of Genoese, if we wish to trace the gold routes for the end of the fifteenth century we need to consider other goods as well, such as paper. The later period was marked by different commercial trends.

In 2002, a fresco by the seventeenth-century painter Bernardo Strozzi was discovered in the Palazzo Lomellini in Genoa, which once belonged to the Centurione family. It depicts an allegory of the New World and was dedicated to the Centurione, who had funded Columbus while he was trading sugar in Madeira during the 1470s and later his enterprise in the New World. The reality and the myths surrounding Columbus's voyages are paradigmatic in this regard. After his services at Madeira, postils in a manuscript mention that he went to the Castle of El Mina on the Guinea coast.[35] Later he moved on toward the Americas. A similar "swerve" away from Africa and out across the Atlantic characterized the Genoese gold-trading networks. While during the fifteenth century the Genoese were mainly interested in gold, in the sixteenth they were dealing in other goods, such as enslaved people whom they brought from Africa via the Atlantic islands to the New World. This becomes clear if we look closely at key players like the Centurione family, who invested first in the African trade and later in the Americas. The legal and administrative hub of these social networks was based in Genoa and archival documents remained in Genoa. As the sixteenth century opened, the Genoese merchants became increasingly Spanish-based and when they moved to the Americas they probably disappeared from the Genoese records, but that part of the story still needs to be tracked down systematically.

Appendix: Notarial Deeds

Transcriptions are by Davide Gambino.

ASG, *Notai antichi*, 874/I, notary Giacomo Rondanina, doc. no. 118
October 18/23, 1452, Genoa.

Testificatio.

In nomine Domini, amen. Noverint universi presens publicum instrumentum testimoniale inspecturi quod in mei notarii publici et testium infrascriptorum ad hoc vocatorum specialiter et rogatorum presentia personaliter constitutus Gabriel Pardus de Saona navigator, testis summarie productus et receptus ad instantiam Raffarelis Buroni civis Ianue tanquam patris et coniuncte persone Dominici Buroni eius filii sic summarie probare volentis ad eternam rei memoriam et ne fides veri pereat per dictum <testem> et testificationem ipsius testis, videlicet <quod> Raffael Barixonus civis Ianue anno proxime preterito de mense septembris vendidit in Marica dicto Dominico ballas undecim papirri pro bono et mercantile, videlicet pro scribendo, pro pretio dublarum sex cum dimidia, et sic ipse Dominicus dictum papirrum in modum predictum emit a dicto Dominico; in quibusquidem ballis undecim papirri deinde reperte fuerunt per dictum Domenicum balle quinque papirri non boni nec mercantilis pro scribendo dum ipsas vendere velet in loco Orani, in quo loco ipsas duci fecerat ipse Dominicus, quod cessit in maximum damnum et preiuditium ipsius Dominici, <qui> dictas ballas quinque vendidit in loco loco Orani ad racionem dublarum trium cum dimidia et reliquas ballas, que erant bone et mercantiles prout esse debebant, vendidit in eodem loco ad racionem dublarum septem pro singula balla.

Interrogatus dictus Gabriel sub eius iuramento eidem delato per me notarium infrascriptum de veritate dicenda super premissis, sub dicto eius iuramento corporaliter tactis scripturis testificando dixit vera essa omnia et singula suprascripta, salvo quod non proprie recodatur si dicte balle papirri essent decem vel undecim.

Interrogatus de causa scientie, respondit quia ipse testis dicto tempore erat in Marica et dictus Dominicus sibi testi dixit quod emerat dictum papirrum a dicto Raffaele pro scribendo et sic publice dicebatur in dicto loco Mariche et <in> navi domini Thadei Spinule, super qua oneratus fuit dictus papirrus et conductus in loco Orani, inter iuvenes et marinarios dicte navis et de hoc inter prenominatos erit publica vox et fama, et quia ipse testis deinde vidit dictum papirrum in dicto loco Orani, in quo loco eum vendidit dictus Dominicus cuidam mauro speciario qui multum frequentat in terra nigrorum mercatorio modo; quam venditionem fecit dictus Dominicus mediante ipso teste, ex quo causam habuit videndi dictum papirru, ex quo etiam scit que testificatur.

Interrogatus quotennis est, respondit etatis annorum triginta quinque vel circa.

Interrogatus si est de proximo recessurus et ad quasvis Mondi partes iturus, respondit quod est recessurus de proximo de presenti civitate Ianue et iturus Saone ubi habitat.

Interrogatus quantum habet in bonis, respondit florenorum ducentorum et ultra.

Interrogatus si attinet producenti, respondit non. Interrogatus si ad eum spectat commodum vel incommodum, respondit non.

Interrogatus si fuit doctus vel rogatus ferre presens testimonium, respondit non.

Super alis generalibus diligenter interrogatus recte respondit.

De quibus omnibus etc.

Actum Ianue in platea Palatii ducalis, videlicet ad bancum curie dominorum viceducum, anno a Nativitate Domini MCCCCLsecundo, indictione XV[a] secundum Ianue cursum, die Iovis XVIII octobris in tertiis; presentibus testibus Bartholomeo de Viacava, lanerio et Quilico de Serravale quondam Antonii, civibus Ianue vocatis et rogatis.

In nomine Domini, amen.

Thadeus Spinula <etc.>

Interrogatus ipse Thadeus sub eius iuramento eidem delato per me notarium infrascriptum de veritate dicenda super premissis, sub dicto eius iuramento, corporaliter tactis scripturis, testificando dixit se hec scire de preditctis, videlicet quod verum est quod dictus Dominicus dicto anno et mense emit dictas ballas undecim papirri a dicto Raffaele in dicto loco prout sibi dixit dictus Dominicus; nescit tamen quo pretio, quia non recordatur, sed communiter papirrus pro scribendo venditur in dicto loco pro duplis sex pro singula balla, et quas ballas undecim dictus Dominicus oneravit in dicto loco super navi ipsius testis et illas exoneravit in dicto loco Orani, in quo loco illas vendidit cuidam mauro, nescit tamen quanto pretio, et dixit idem Dominicus ipsi testi quod in dictis ballis undecim reperierat ballas quinque papirri pro lacerando, et hoc est quod scit de predictis.

Interrogatus de causa scientie, respondit per ea, que super dixit et fuit testificatus et quia vidit dictum Dominicum onerare in dicta eius navi dictum papirrum, et quia dictus Dominicus ante emptionem ipsius papirri dixit ipsi testi quod illum emere volebat.

Interrogatus si interfuit dicte emptioni dicti papirri, respondit non.

Interrogatus quotennis est, respondit etatis annorum triginta quatuor et ultra.

Interrogatus si ad eum spectat commodum vel incommodum, respondit non.

Interrogatus quantum habet in bonis, respondit florenorum ducentorum et ultra.

Interrogatus si attinet producenti respondit non.

Super aliis etc.,

De quibus omnibus etc.

Actum Ianue in platea Palatii ducalis videlicet ad bancum curie dominorum viceducum, anno a Nativitate Domini MCCCLsecundo, indictione XV, secundum Ianue cursum, die lune XXIII octobris in vesperis, presentibus testibus Benedicto de Franchis de Pagano et Quilico de Serravale, civibus Ianue vocatis et rogatis.

ASG, *Notai antichi*, 869/I, notary Simone Canella, doc. no. 150
March 31, 1466, Genoa.

(SC) Yesus
Sententia arbitralis

In nomine Domini, amen. Nos Tadeus Spinula, Lucas Pinelus quondam Luce et Iohannes Franciscus Spinula, arbitri, arbitratores, amicabiles compositores et comunes amici ellecti et asumpti per et inter Nicolaum Marihonum, civem

Ianue quondam Quilici suo proprio nomine et nomine et vice Iacobi Marihoni quondam Antonioti, pro quo suo proprio nomine de solemni rati habicione promixit etc., sub etc., ex una parte, et Tomam Picamilium quondam Cosme ac Franciscum Centurionum domini Filippi, ex parte altera, vigore et ex forma publici instrumenti compromissi rogati manu tui notarii infrascripti die quinta presentis mensis martii; visis igitur dicto compromisso et contentis in eo, potestate et balia nobis vigore ipsius attributa et concessa per dictas partes, peticionibus et requisicionibus coram nobis oretenus factis per dictas partes, responsionibus, confessionibus et contradicionibus factis per dictas partes dictis peticionibus et requisicionibus, et auditis dictis partibus semel et pluries et quicquid dicte partes dicere et allegare voluerunt, omnia potius arbitrorum et arbitratorum eligentes quam strictum iuris rigorem, Christi, beatissimeque Virginis Marie nominibus invocatis, eosque semper habentes pre oculis et in mente, dicimus, pronunciamus, condemnanus, declaramus, arbitramur et arbitramentamur ut infra.

Videlicet quia omnes tres concordes condemnamus et condemnatos esse pronunciamus et declaramus dictos Tomam Picamilium et Franciscum Centurionum ad acceptandum dictis Iacobo et Nicolao Marihonis dublas sexcentas vigintiocto et tominos duos cum dimidio auri tiberis, videlicet dublas quadringentas decem novem et tominum medium pro tercia parte monete misse in Tenes, loci Barbarie, per dictos Iacobum e Nicolaum occaxione emendi furmenta cum Iacobo Perozino et dublas centum nonaginta novem et tominos duos pro tercia parte diversorum frumentorum emptorum in Orano per dictos Iacobum et Nicolaum ac uno equo et onustorum in duobus pasagiis, ac dublas decem pro tercia parte naulorum granorum onustorum in galeis Venetorum, in summa ascendentes ad dictas dublas sexcentas viginti octo et tominos duos cum dimidio.

Ex adverso condemnamus et condemnatos esse pronunciamus et declaramus dictos Iacobum et Nicholaum Marihonos ad dandum et solvendum dictis Thome Picamilium et Francisco Centuriono dublas trecentas viginti auri tiberis et sunt pro libris trecentis viginti monete Valentie, que dicti Tomas et Franciscus solverunt in Valentia pro dictis Iacobo et Nicolao Bartolameo Centuriono.

Item condemnamus et condemnatos esse pronunciamus et declaramus dictum Iacobum et Nicolaum ad dandum et solvendum dictis Tome et Francisco dublas sexaginta novem auri tiberis et sunt pro tercia parte processus certorum furmentorum venditorum in Ermeria, quorum processus pervenit in dictos Iacobum et Nicolaum.

Item condemnamus et condemnatos esse pronunciamus et declaramus dictos Iacobum et Nicolaum ad dandum et solvendum dictis Tome et Francisco dublas ducentas septuaginta septem et tominum medium auri tiberis pro processu tercie partis de peciis centum pannorum Valentie venditorum per dictos Iacobum et Nicolaum in regni Trimiceni.

Item condemnamus et condemnatos esse pronunciamus et declaramus dictos Iacobum et Nicolaum ad retinendum penes eos omne id et totum quicquid et quantum habebant et seu dare debebant quovis modo quondam Iacobo Perozino a tempore mortis dicti quondam Iacobi citra, donec et quousque cognitum fuerit si spectent dictis Tome et Francisco.

Et in casu quod dictis Tome et Francisco adiudicatio esset, tunc et eo casu ex nunc condemnamus dictos Iacobum et Nicolum ad eis debitum faciendum de dicta tali adiudicatione fienda, quantum pro bonis dicti quondam Iacobi Perozini existentibus penes dictos Iacobum et Nicolaum.

Mandantes presentem nostram sententiam per dictas partes et quamlibet earum observari debere sub pena contenta in dicto compromisso.

Lata, datta, sentenciata et pronunciata est ut supra hec presens nostra sententia et lecta, testata et publicata est per me Simonem Canellam notarium subscriptum Ianue in Bancis sub porticu illorum de Nigro, ad bancum residentie mei notarii subscripti, anno dominice Nativitatis millesimo quadrigentesimo sexagesimo sexto, indicione terciadecima secundum cursum Ianue, die lune trigesima prima marcii, hora vigesima tercia in circa; presentibus testibus Petro Iohanne de Saulo quondam Manuelis et Lodixio de Ingibertis Antonii civibus Ianue, ad hec vocatis et rogatis.

Notes

1. The term "diaspora" is used to refer to landless people, like Jewish merchants or Armenians. While it is true that the Genoese state did officially control Liguria (in Italy) and possessed territories abroad, the size of these areas shrank. For the use of diaspora as related to the Genoese merchants in a different period, see Catia Brilli, *Genoese Trade and Migration in the Spanish Atlantic, 1700–1830* (Cambridge: Cambridge University Press, 2016).

2. Jacques Heers, *Gênes au XVe siècle. Activité èconomique et problèmes sociaux* (Paris: SEVPEN, 1961).

3. Ruth Pike, *Enterprise and Adventure: The Genoese in Seville and the Opening of the New World* (Ithaca: Cornell University Press, 1966); David Igual Luis and Germán Navarro Espinach, "Los genoveses en España en el tránsito del siglo XV al XVI," *Historia. Instituciones. Documentos* 24 (1997): 261–332; David Igual Luis, "Valencia y Sevilla en el sistema económico genovés de finales del siglo XV," *Revista d'historia medieval* 3 (1992): 79–116; Toby Green, *The Rise of the Trans-Atlantic Slave Trade in Western Africa, 1300–1589* (Cambridge: Cambridge University Press, 2011).

4. Heinrich Fick, "Über Begriff und Geschichte der Aktiengesellschaften," *Zeitschrift für das gesamte Handelsrecht* 5 (1861): 1–63.

5. Erik Aerts, "The Casa di San Giorgio and the 'Monetary Famine' of the Late Middle Ages," in *La casa di San Giorgio. Il potere del credito*, ed. by Giuseppe Felloni (Genoa: Società Ligure di Storia Patria, 2006), 27–62.

6. Alfonso Assini, "L'importanza della contabilità nell'inventariazione di registri bancari medioevali," in *Il Banco di San Giorgio nel '400. Gli archivi degli istituti e delle aziende di credito e le fonti d'archivio per la storia delle banche tutela, gestione, valorizzazione* (Rome: Ministero per i beni culturali e ambientali. Ufficio centrale per i beni archivistici, 1995), 269–70; Giuseppe Felloni, "I primi banchi pubblici della Casa di San Giorgio (1408–45)," in *Banchi pubblici, banchi privati e monti di pietà nell'Europa pre-industriale. Amministrazione, tecniche operative e ruoli economici. Atti del convegno, Genova, 1–6 ottobre 1990, Atti della Società Ligure di Storia Patria*, n.s. 31, no. 2 (1991): 225–46.

7. Heers, *Gênes au XVe siècle*, 69.

8. John Day, *Les douanes de Gênes, 1376–1377*, 2 vols. (Paris: SEVPEN, 1963).

9. Enrique Otte, *Sevilla y sus mercaderes a fines de la Edad Media* (Seville: Universidad de Sevilla, 1996).

10. Heers, *Gênes au XVe siècle*, 163.

11. For the "tedious literature" on Cape Verde's "discovery," see Green, *Rise of the Trans-Atlantic Slave Trade*, 97 n.4.

12. Nunziatella Alessandrini, "Carlo Antonio Paggi a Lisbona (1656–1666): un approccio allo studio delle relazioni diplomatiche fra Genova e il Portogallo," in *Con gran mare e fortuna. Circulação de mercadorias, pessoas e ideias entre Portugal e Itália na época moderna*, ed. by Nunziatella Alessandrini et al. (Lisbon: Faculdade de Letras da Universidade de Lisboa, 2015), 115–34; Nunziatella Alessandrini, "Os italianos na Lisboa de 1500 a 1680: das hegemonias florentinas às genovesas" (PhD diss., Universidade Aberta, Lisbon, 2009); Luisa D'Arienzo, ed., "La presenza degli italiani in Portogallo al tempo di Colombo," special issue, *Nuova raccolta colombiana* 14 (2003); Luisa D'Arienzo, "Banchieri e mercanti genovesi in contatto con Cristoforo Colombo in Portogallo," in *Case commerciali, banchieri e mercanti italiani in Portogallo. Convegno* (Lisbon: Istituto italiano di cultura in Portogallo, 1998), 51–66; Domenico Gioffrè, "Documenti sulle relazioni fra Genova ed il Portogallo dal 1493 al 1539," *Bulletin de l'Institut historique Belge de Rome* 33 (1961): 179–316; João Silva de Jesus, "A Casa de Viseu, o comércio da Guiné e os genoveses," in *A herança do Infante*, ed. by Artur Teodoro de Matos and João Paulo Oliveira Costa (Lisbon: CEPCEP CHAM, Câmara Municipal, 2011), 305–22.

13. Adela Fábregas García has investigated some Genoese archival documents, such as the Spinola ledgers. See Adela Fábregas García, *Un mercader genovés en el Reino de Granada. El libro de cuentas de Agostino Spinola (1441–1447)* (Granada: Grupo de Investigación Toponimia, Historia y Arqueología del Reino de Granada, 2002); Adela Fábregas García, *La familia Spinola en el reino nazarí de Granada. Contabilidad privada de Francesco Spinola (1451–1457)* (Granada: Grupo de Investigación Toponimia, Historia y Arqueología del Reino de Granada, 2004). D'Arienzo, "La presenza degli italiani in Portogallo," quotes only a few Genoese notarial deeds.

14. Not many merchant ledgers survive in Genoa. See the Sauli ledgers in the Archivio Sauli Pallavicino and in the Archivio Spinola di Tassarolo. The Fondo Famiglie in the Archivio di Stato di Genova contains some interesting ledgers (see Archivio di Stato di Genova, Pandetta del Fondo Famiglie). Some unstudied and unpublished ledgers (completely unknown)—probably of the Spinola families—remain in the Archivio Spinola di Tassarolo. For the account book of Giovanni Piccamiglio, see Jacques Heers, *Le livre de comptes de Giovanni Piccamiglio, homme d'affaires génois, 1456–1459* (Paris: SEVPEN, 1959). For the ledgers of the Alberti family, see Richard A. Goldthwaite, Enzo Settesoldi, and Marco Spallanzani, *Due libri mastri degli Alberti. Una grande compagnia di Calimala (1348–1358)* (Florence: Cassa di Risparmio di Firenze 1995).

15. Yale University Library, Manuscripts and Archives, Robert Sabatino Lopez Papers, MS 1459.

16. Archivio di Stato di Genova, Notai Antichi, 869 and 870.

17. Archivio di Stato di Genova, Notai Antichi, 904, notaio Tommaso Duracino, documento 153 (March 24, 1474), quoted in Laura Balletto, "Famiglie genovesi nel Nord-Africa," in *Dibattito su grandi famiglie del mondo Genovese fra Mediterraneo ed Atlantico. Atti del Convegno, Montoggio, 28 ottobre 1995*, ed. by Geo Pistarino (Genoa: Accademia ligure di scienze e lettere, 1997), 58. See also Rossana Urbani, "Genova e il Maghrib tra il '400 e '500," in *Genova, la Liguria e l'oltremare tra Medioevo e età moderna* (Genoa: Università di Genova, Istituto di Scienze Storiche, 1976), 201.

18. Anne Haour, *Outsiders and Strangers: An Archaeology of Liminality in West Africa* (Oxford: Oxford University Press, 2013).

19. Antoine Malfante, "The Letter of Antoine Malfante," in *The Voyages of Cadamosto and Other Documents on West Africa in the Second Half of the Fifteenth Century*, trans. and ed. by Gerald Roe Crone (London: Hakluyt, 1937), 89.

20. Hilmar C. Krueger, "The Wares of Exchange in the Genoese-African Traffic of the Twelfth Century," *Speculum* 12, no. 1 (1937): 66.

21. The ledger was divided into two parts: Archivio di Stato di Genova, Fondo Famiglie 7 and Fondo Famiglie, Ignoti 229. It is now in Fondo Famiglie 7. I was able to locate the two parts with the help of Davide Gambino.

22. In Genoese sources it is sometimes possible to find the names of North African merchants. See the Spinola ledgers (above n.14).

23. Archivio di Stato di Genova, Fondo Famiglie 7, fol. 14v.

24. Raffaele Di Tucci, *Nuovi documenti e notizie sul genovese Antonio Malfante, il primo viaggiatore europeo nell'Africa occidentale (1477)* (Rome: R. Societa geografica italiana, 1934), 118.

25. Charles de la Roncière, "Découverte d'une relation de voyage datée du Touat et décrivant en 1447 le bassin du Niger," *Bulletin de géographie historique et descriptive* 32 (1917): 1–28.

26. Heers, *Gênes au XVe siècle*, 493, citing Archivio di Stato di Genova, Notai Antichi, 869, 150. See appendix for the transcription of this document.

27. Enrico Pedemonte, *La carta. Storia, produzione, degrado, restauro* (Venice: Marsilio, 2008).

28. The notarial deed was quoted in Heers, *Gênes au XVe siècle*, 226. The original documenti is in Archivio di Stato di Genova, Notai Antichi, 874, Giacomo Rondanina, I, 118 (January 15, 1452). See the appendix for a transcription.

29. We should remember that to ransom a Genoese prisoner in 1462 cost around 190 doblas and that 1 dobla (*aurum tiberi*) was equivalent to 1 Valentian lira.

30. Charlie English, *The Quest for Timbuktu and the Fantastic Mission to Save Its Past* (New York: Riverhead Books 2017).

31. No manuscripts from before the seventeenth century have been located in sub-Saharan Africa. See Jonathan M. Bloom, "Paper in Sudanic Africa," in *The Meanings of Timbuktu*, ed. by Shamil Jeppie and S. Bachir Diagne (Cape Town: HSRC Press, 2008), 53–54; Michaelle Biddle, "New Strategies in Using Watermarks to Date Sub-Saharan Islamic Manuscripts," in *The Arts and Crafts of Literacy: Islamic Manuscript Cultures in Sub-Saharan Africa*, ed. by Andrea Brigaglia and Mauro Nobili (Berlin: De Gruyter, 2017), 31 (this survey on Nigerian manuscripts mentions no older manuscript than those of the 1650s).

32. Paolo F. de Moraes Farias, *Arabic Medieval Inscriptions from the Republic of Mali: Epigraphy, Chronicles, and Songhay-Tuareg History* (Oxford: Oxford University Press for the British Academy, 2003).

33. See various documents in Archivio di Stato di Genova, Notai Antichi, 870.

34. Ezio Bassani and William Buller Fagg, *Africa and the Renaissance: Art in Ivory* (New York: Center for African Art, 1988).

35. Paul Hair, "Was Columbus' First Very Long Voyage a Voyage from Guinea?," *History in Africa* 22 (1995): n.3.

Bibliography

Aerts, Erik. "The Casa di San Giorgio and the 'Monetary Famine' of the Late Middle Ages." In *La casa di San Giorgio. Il potere del credito*, edited by Giuseppe Felloni, 27–62. Genoa: Società Ligure di Storia Patria, 2006.

Alessandrini, Nunziatella. "Carlo Antonio Paggi a Lisbona (1656–1666): un approccio allo studio delle relazioni diplomatiche fra Genova e il Portogallo." In *Con gran mare e fortuna. Circulação de mercadorias, pessoas e ideias entre Portugal e Itália na época moderna*, edited by Nunziatella Alessandrini, Susana Bastos Mateus, Mariagrazia Russo, and Gaetano Sabatini, 115–34. Lisbon: Faculdade de Letras da Universidade de Lisboa, 2015.

Alessandrini, Nunziatella. "Os italianos na Lisboa de 1500 a 1680: das hegemonias florentinas às genovesas." PhD diss., Universidade Aberta, Lisbon, 2009.

Assini, Alfonso. "L'importanza della contabilità nell'inventariazione di registri bancari medioevali." In *Il Banco di San Giorgio nel '400. Gli archivi degli istituti e delle aziende di credito e le fonti d'archivio per la storia delle banche tutela, gestione, valorizzazione*, 263–83. Rome: Ministero per i beni culturali e ambientali. Ufficio centrale per i beni archivistici, 1995.

Balletto, Laura. "Famiglie genovesi nel Nord-Africa." In *Dibattito su grandi famiglie del mondo Genovese fra Mediterraneo ed Atlantico. Atti del Convegno, Montoggio, 28 ottobre 1995*, edited by Geo Pistarino, 49–71. Genoa: Accademia ligure di scienze e lettere, 1997.

Bassani, Ezio, and William Buller Fagg. *Africa and the Renaissance: Art in Ivory*. New York: Center for African Art, 1988.

Biddle, Michaelle. "New Strategies in Using Watermarks to Date Sub-Saharan Islamic Manuscripts." In *The Arts and Crafts of Literacy: Islamic Manuscript Cultures in Sub-Saharan Africa*, edited by Andrea Brigaglia and Mauro Nobili, 27–68. Berlin: De Gruyter, 2017.

Bloom, Jonathan M. "Paper in Sudanic Africa." In *The Meanings of Timbuktu*, edited by Shamil Jeppie and S. Bachir Diagne, 45–59. Cape Town: HSRC Press, 2008.

Brilli, Catia. *Genoese Trade and Migration in the Spanish Atlantic, 1700–1830*. Cambridge: Cambridge University Press, 2016.

D'Arienzo, Luisa, ed. "La presenza degli italiani in Portogallo al tempo di Colombo." Special issue, *Nuova raccolta colombiana* 14 (2003).

D'Arienzo, Luisa. "Banchieri e mercanti genovesi in contatto con Cristoforo Colombo in Portogallo." In *Case commerciali, banchieri e mercanti italiani in Portogallo. Convegno*, 51–66. Lisbon: Istituto italiano di cultura in Portogallo, 1998.

Day, John. *Les douanes de Gênes, 1376–1377*. 2 vols. Paris: SEVPEN, 1963.

Di Tucci, Raffaele. *Nuovi documenti e notizie sul genovese Antonio Malfante, il primo viaggiatore europeo nell'Africa occidentale (1477)*. Rome: R. Societa geografica italiana, 1934.

English, Charlie. *The Quest for Timbuktu and the Fantastic Mission to Save Its Past*. New York: Riverhead Books 2017.

Fábregas García, Adela. *La familia Spinola en el reino nazarí de Granada. Contabilidad privada de Francesco Spinola (1451–1457)*. Granada: Grupo de Investigación Toponimia, Historia y Arqueología del Reino de Granada, 2004.

Fábregas García, Adela. *Un mercader genovés en el Reino de Granada. El libro de cuentas de Agostino Spinola (1441–1447*. Granada: Grupo de Investigación Toponimia, Historia y Arqueología del Reino de Granada, 2002.

Farias, Paolo F. de Moraes. *Arabic Medieval Inscriptions from the Republic of Mali: Epigraphy, Chronicles, and Songhay-Tuareg History*. Oxford: Oxford University Press for the British Academy, 2003.

Felloni, Giuseppe. "I primi banchi pubblici della Casa di San Giorgio (1408–45)." In *Banchi pubblici, banchi privati e monti di pietà nell'Europa pre-industriale. Amministrazione, tecniche operative e ruoli economici. Atti del convegno, Genova, 1–6 ottobre 1990. Atti della Società Ligure di Storia Patria*, n.s. 31, no. 2 (1991): 225–46.

Fick, Heinrich. "Über Begriff und Geschichte der Aktiengesellschaften." *Zeitschrift für das gesamte Handelsrecht* 5 (1861): 1–63.

Gioffrè, Domenico. "Documenti sulle relazioni fra Genova ed il Portogallo dal 1493 al 1539." *Bulletin de l'Institut historique Belge de Rome* 33 (1961): 179–316.

Goldthwaite, Richard A., Enzo Settesoldi, and Marco Spallanzani, *Due libri mastri degli Alberti. Una grande compagnia di Calimala (1348–1358)*. Florence: Cassa di Risparmio di Firenze 1995.

Green, Toby. *The Rise of the Trans-Atlantic Slave Trade in Western Africa, 1300–1589*. Cambridge: Cambridge University Press, 2011.

Hair, Paul. "Was Columbus' First Very Long Voyage a Voyage from Guinea?" *History in Africa* 22 (1995): 223–37.

Haour, Anne. *Outsiders and Strangers: An Archaeology of Liminality in West Africa*. Oxford: Oxford University Press, 2013.

Heers, Jacques. *Gênes au XVe siècle. Activité èconomique et problèmes sociaux*. Paris: SEVPEN, 1961.

Heers, Jacques. *Le livre de comptes de Giovanni Piccamiglio, homme d'affaires génois, 1456–1459*. Paris: SEVPEN, 1959.

Igual Luis, David. "Valencia y Sevilla en el sistema económico genovés de finales del siglo XV." *Revista d'historia medieval* 3 (1992): 79–116.

Igual Luis, David, and Germán Navarro Espinach. "Los genoveses en España en el tránsito del siglo XV al XVI." *Historia. Instituciones. Documentos* 24 (1997): 261–332.

Krueger, Hilmar C. "The Wares of Exchange in the Genoese-African Traffic of the Twelfth Century." *Speculum* 12, no. 1 (1937): 57–71.

La Roncière, Charles de. "Découverte d'une relation de voyage datée du Touat et décrivant en 1447 le bassin du Niger." *Bulletin de géographie historique et descriptive* 32 (1917): 1–28.

Malfante, Antoine. "The Letter of Antoine Malfante." In *The Voyages of Cadamosto and Other Documents on West Africa in the Second Half of the Fifteenth Century*, translated and edited by Gerald Roe Crone, 85–90. London: Hakluyt, 1937.

Otte, Enrique. *Sevilla y sus mercaderes a fines de la Edad Media*. Seville: Universidad de Sevilla, 1996.

Pedemonte, Enrico. *La carta. Storia, produzione, degrado, restauro*. Venice: Marsilio, 2008.

Pike, Ruth. *Enterprise and Adventure: The Genoese in Seville and the Opening of the New World*. Ithaca: Cornell University Press, 1966.

Pipino, Giuseppe. *Liguria mineraria. Miscellanea di giacimentologia, mineralogia e storia estrattiva*. Ovada: Tipografia Pesce, 2005.

Silva de Jesus, João. "A Casa de Viseu, o comércio da Guiné e os genoveses." In *A herança do Infante*, edited by Artur Teodoro de Matos and João Paulo Oliveira Costa, 305–22. Lisbon: CEPCEP CHAM, Câmara Municipal, 2011.

Urbani, Rossana. "Genova e il Maghrib tra il '400 e '500." In *Genova, la Liguria e l'oltremare tra Medioevo e età moderna*, 185–206. Genoa: Università di Genova, Istituto di Scienze Storiche, 1976.

Gold, Islam and the Spanish "Reconquista"

Abigail Krasner Balbale

Introduction

Among Don Quixote's many fantastical adventures is one focused on the magical golden helmet of the Moor Mambrino.[1] This helmet, already well known by Cervantes's time from chivalric romances in Spanish, French and Italian, was said to have belonged to a giant Moorish king. Made of pure gold, it was said to be capable of protecting its wearer against injury. One day, riding with his loyal squire Sancho, Don Quixote sees a rider approaching with a shiny golden object on his head, and is convinced it is a knight wearing the magical gold helmet. Although Sancho tries to dissuade him, Don Quixote charges at the man, who is a barber protecting himself from rain by carrying his brass basin on his head. Chasing off the barber and taking the bowl, Don Quixote notices that a piece of the helmet (which he calls it a sallet or *celada*) is missing, since the basin was designed with a cut-out for the neck of the man receiving a haircut.[2] He exclaims,

> This famous piece of the enchanted helmet, by some strange accident, must have fallen into the hands of one who could not recognize or estimate its value, and not knowing what he was doing, and seeing that it was made of purest gold, he must have melted down one half to take advantage of its high price, and from the other half he made this, which resembles a barber's basin, as you say. Be that as it may, I recognize it, and its transmutation does not matter to me...[3]

The helmet Don Quixote imagines is powerful because it is gold and associated with Islam; it is incomplete because that gold is malleable, and can be melted by someone choosing greed over preserving a magical object. Of course, the basin he captures is not gold, not a helmet and not "Moorish" at all. Yet, Don Quixote's fantasies reveal a world populated by people and objects that are not always what they seem, and that refuse to obey attempts to craft a pure, Christian Spain.

Like much in the novel, this fragmentary basin evokes a past that, by 1615, when the second volume of *Don Quixote* was published, was simultaneous banished and omnipresent. Like the brass bowl that glinted in the sun like a mythical golden helmet, the world of Spain in the seventeenth century shimmered with contradictions: a nation that sought to present itself as Christian and European but that introduced itself with ceremonies and objects that, to its northern neighbors, evoked Moorishness; a nation in which the styles, forms, and materials of a shared past still circulated even as the craftsmen who created them were forced into exile.[4]

Attitudes toward gold reflect some of these contradictions. For medieval European Christians who depended upon gold mined south of the Sahara, the material carried associations with Islam, Muslim traders and Africa; and in the Iberian peninsula, fine goldwork was linked to al-Andalus. By the later Middle Ages, when the Christian kingdoms of Spain and Portugal found new trade routes, trans-Saharan traders were not the only source of pure gold, and yet Granada, the last remaining Muslim kingdom on the Iberian peninsula, became inextricably linked with the finest gold jewelry, horse trappings and portable objects. After the city's conquest, and especially after the forced conversions of its Muslim inhabitants, lay and ecclesiastical authorities tried to limit the production and consumption of "morisco"-style jewelry.[5] Yet, even as the Moriscos were tried and sentenced by the Inquisition for crypto-Islam, even as they were expelled from the peninsula, and even as the New World mines offered up vast new treasures, gold maintained its association with Islam. Apologists for the expulsion argued Moriscos hoarded gold, or contaminated it, and that expelling them would restore wealth and purity to Spain.

This chapter interrogates some of the many meanings of gold on the Iberian peninsula between the twelfth and seventeenth centuries, as the growing Christian kingdoms sought to assert a new Catholic identity, and as the Muslim presence on the peninsula shrank, first through a protracted series of conquests and then with forced conversion and, eventually, expulsion. Gold objects, often manufactured by Muslim or Morisco craftsmen, traveled throughout the peninsula and became symbols of royal luxury, martial bravery and chivalry. These objects and the courtly ceremonies that used them became hallmarks of Spanishness, deployed in imperial and royal celebrations north of the Pyrenees.[6] At the same time, "morisco" gold could stand in metonymically for the danger of Islam, and its use was regulated, banned, and criticized by lay and ecclesiastical authorities. Policing this gold represented an attempt to distance Christian Spain from its long-standing intimacy with Islam. As Mary

Douglas has written, "ideas about separating, purifying, demarcating and punishing transgressions have as their main function to impose system on an inherently untidy experience. It is only by exaggerating the difference between within and without, about and below, male and female, with and against, that a semblance of order is created."[7] Spanish attitudes toward gold in the years of the so-called "Reconquista" reflect an attempt to demarcate the boundaries between Christianity and Islam, Spanishness and Moorishness, and to create a "semblance of order."[8] But, as we will see, the untidiness born of hundreds of years of intimacy among people and objects that resist classification was difficult to banish.

Three Objects in Motion

In this section, I will discuss three gold iconic, imbricated objects, from a coin minted by a Castilian king to a helmet and a necklace traditionally attributed to the Nasrid kingdom. Each object challenges classification into the systems that organize museum galleries and fields of research; each is a product of a period and a place when the movement of objects and people made such boundaries illusory. Each object also highlights how material, form and technique honed in al-Andalus became the elite aesthetic of much of the Iberian peninsula. The later process of Christianizing the Iberian peninsula consisted of the gradual imposition of regulations attempting to enforce boundaries, including on the production and consumption of objects like these.

The objects are arranged more or less chronologically, from the first gold coin minted by a Christian on the Iberian peninsula, the twelfth-century dinar of Alfonso VIII, to a gold necklace likely produced in the sixteenth century. These objects serve as entrées into discussions of religion and culture in the mixed societies of the Iberian peninsula.

The Gold Dinar of Alfonso VIII

For much of Europe in the medieval period, gold was closely connected to the Islamic world. Many of the earliest gold coins minted by European rulers, including the *taris* of Roger II, were based on Islamic models. But Roger's *taris* were crude imitations with illegible inscriptions. On the Iberian peninsula, the first gold coins minted by a Christian reflected a different level of familiarity with Arabic and with Islamic practices (fig. 1). Alfonso VIII of Castile was the Christian monarch in question, and the coins follow the model of Arabic language gold dinars closely.[9] They were based on the dinars given to Alfonso in tribute by his vassal, Muḥammad ibn Sa'd ibn Mardanīsh (known in Latin as *Rex Lupus*,

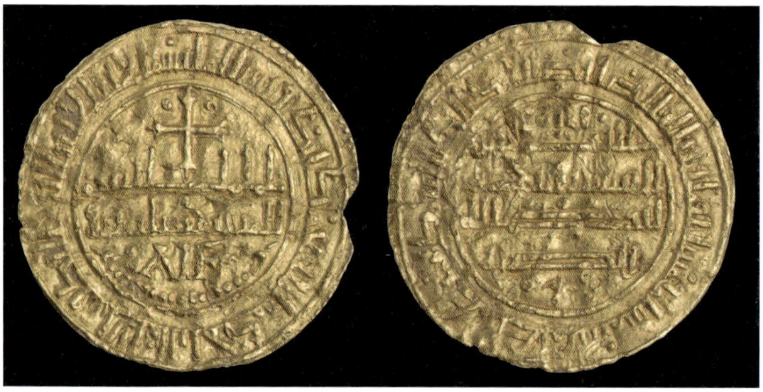

Fig. 1. Gold dinar or maravedi of Alfonso VIII, minted Toledo 1226 Safar (1188-89 AD), 3.72 g, diameter 26 mm. New York, American Numismatic Society, 2014.9.2.

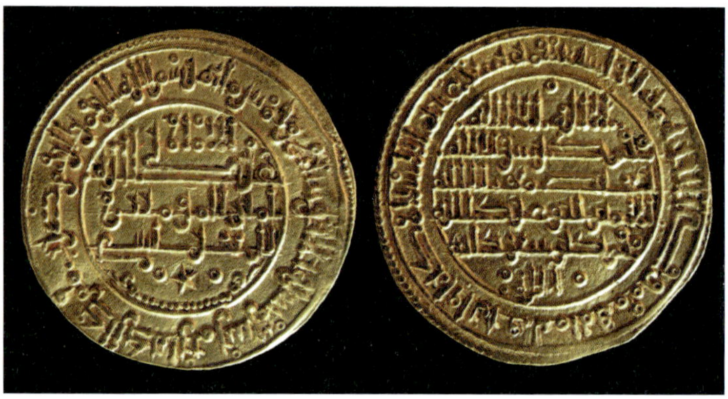

Fig. 2. Dinar of Muḥammad ibn Saʿd Ibn Mardanīsh, Murcia, 563 AH/1167-68 AD, obverse and reverse. 3.86 g, diameter 25 mm. Madrid, Tonegawa Collection

the wolf king), who ruled from Murcia from 1147 to 1172 CE. Ibn Mardanīsh's gold dinars, known in Christian sources as *morabetinos lupinos* (fig. 2), and given in the tens of thousands annually to his Christian allies, had become a currency of record in the western Mediterranean.[10] Alfonso VIII's armies fought alongside those of Ibn Mardanīsh against their common enemy, the Almohad dynasty, which ruled North Africa and much of al-Andalus, and Alfonso's coffers were swollen with the gold dinars given to him by his vassal every year.

By the time Alfonso VIII minted his first dinars in 1174, Ibn Mardanīsh had died and his kingdom had been conquered by the Almohads. Alfonso's dinar therefore appears shortly after he stopped receiving dinars in tribute from his vassal, and mimics their form quite closely, from the horizontal lines of Arabic text on both sides, surrounded by additional Arabic legends that wrap around the periphery of the coin, down to the band of pearls surmounted by a star and two small circles at the bottom.[11] But it is not a simple copy. Instead, Alfonso translated the Islamic messages of Ibn Mardanīsh's coin into a Christian and Castilian message in perfectly legible and grammatical Arabic. While Ibn Mardanīsh minted his dinars in his own name and that of the "Abbasid Imam" or caliph, Alfonso minted his in the name of "the Emir Alfuns ibn Sanja," and "The Imam of the Christian Church, the Pope of Rome the Most Great." Where Ibn Mardanīsh's marginal legend quotes a Qur'anic passage, ("Whoever desires a religion other than Islam, it will never be accepted from him, and in the afterlife he will be among the losers"), Alfonso's quotes the Bible ("Whoever believes and is baptized will be saved").[12] And where Ibn Mardanīsh's dinar is minted "In the name of God," Alfonso's is minted "In the name of the Father, the Son and the Holy Ghost." Alfonso's dinar shows that the coins he received in tribute from his Muslim vassal Ibn Mardanīsh were not just pleasing chunks of gold – he also understood their message and prestige and wanted a similar (but Christianized) version for himself.

Alfonso's dinars advance the same kinds of claims both political and religious that appeared on Ibn Mardanīsh's dinars. Ibn Mardanīsh's coins rejected Almohad visions of authority, and Alfonso's coins continued this legacy even as they also advanced a Christian vision of authority.[13] While the two rulers saw the relationship of religious and political power in distinct ways, with one rooted in God's revelation to the Prophet Muhammad and overseen by the caliph in Baghdad, and the other based in a tripartite God mediated through the pope in Rome, both systems oppose Almohad power. In his choice to imitate Ibn Mardanīsh's dinars, Alfonso claimed the mantle of leadership from the anti-Almohad Andalusī ruler.

Gold arrived in the Iberian peninsula via the Islamic world, most commonly via the westerly trans-Saharan trade route that terminated in Sijilmasa, called by Arab historians "the Gate of Gold." When Spanish Christians wanted gold in the period before the thirteenth century, their best bet was to get it from Spanish Muslims, whose trading networks and linguistic competence gained them easier access to North African markets.[14] After the fall of the Almohads in the thirteenth century, multiple sources of gold opened up to Mediterranean merchants directly, and the role of al-Andalus as a center of gold redistribution declined, however, Islamic territories remained a coveted source of finished gold products. Alfonso's dinars were likely made by reminting Ibn Mardanīsh's dinars, which were in turn made from West African gold. Al-Andalus served as a vector for transmitting goods and materials from Africa and the Middle East, as the linguistic competence and cultural know-how of its traders offered them broad access to regions beyond Europe.

But, as Alfonso's dinar demonstrates, the Christians of the Iberian peninsula were far from passive recipients of materials, techniques, iconography and objects from al-Andalus. They translated and recast these objects, whether materially, as Alfonso did, or by using them in new contexts. These objects, moving through geography and time, transformed what courtliness looked like. As María Judith Feliciano has shown regarding thirteenth-century textiles woven with Arabic inscriptions in al-Andalus and used throughout the Iberian peninsula, such objects became signs of respectability and even of "Castilian monarchic grandeur and cultural legitimacy."[15]

This adoption of forms and materials from Muslim neighbors had no bearing on Christians' attitudes toward Muslims more generally. Alfonso VIII was a great hero of the so-called Reconquista, known by his sobriquet "el de Las Navas" for the crushing defeat he inflicted upon the Almohads at the battle in 1212 that was officially termed a Crusade. But he was also enmeshed in an imbricated culture in which articulating one's authority as a Castilian king involved adapting and transforming materials, languages, and techniques from neighbors in al-Andalus. Like the textiles studied by Feliciano, which she argues would have been seen as sartorially correct for an elite Castilian noble or royal, this coin modeled on that of Alfonso's erstwhile vassal would have looked right for an audience accustomed to Arabic-language dinars.[16]

Alfonso's choice to mint his dinar on the model of Ibn Mardanīsh's was not haphazard or inevitable. His rival Fernando II of Leon (r. 1157-1188) minted gold coins shortly after him, modeled on an ancient Roman denarius, with a portrait of the king wearing a toga. Ibn Mardanīsh's ubiquitous dinars, which simultaneously enriched Alfonso and served as a symbol of their alliance against the Almohads, were an appropriate model for the Castilian king, echoing the coinage of other powerful Mediterranean rulers and proclaiming his continuation of their fight against the Almohads. That is, Alfonso's dinar was not a contradiction of his crusading bona fides, but a confirmation of them. Using language and forms that now seem "Islamic," but with Christian messages, was part of a fight against the territorial expansion of the Almohads. Fighting the Almohads was not coterminous with fighting Islam, and vowing to fight Islam on the battlefield did not preclude using or producing objects modeled on those made by Muslims. Alfonso doubtless would have been puzzled by the contradiction the use of these objects and the pursuit of crusade poses to modern scholars.

A "Nasrid" Golden Helmet

In 1417, Alfonso V (the Magnanimous) of Aragon sent his mudejar "cadi," Ali de Bellvís, to Granada with a letter to the Nasrid king Yusuf, asking for "morisco" weapons and horse trappings all adorned with gold, and promising Yusuf whatever he wanted from his kingdom in return.[17] With the fall of the Almohads in the thirteenth century, as Olivia Remie Constable has shown, Christian Mediterranean merchants gained direct access to the gold sold in North Africa, and Andalusīs lost their role as crucial intermediaries for access to gold. Nevertheless, the Nasrids, the last remaining Muslim kingdom of al-Andalus, continued to provide gold coins as *parias* to the Castilians, and the fame of their goldsmiths, who fashioned bridles, harnesses, weapons, armor and jewelry adorned with gold and enamels, was unrivaled in the Iberian peninsula in the fifteenth century. Roser Salicrú has noted that *mudejares*, or Muslims living under Christian rule, long served as intermediaries for Christian kings and noblemen in the north, bringing them back gold objects, fine textiles, and horses from Granada and North Africa.[18]

Although we have no record of what the objects Ali de Bellvís brought back to Alfonso the Magnanimous looked like, many Nasrid weapons, horse trappings and pieces of armor adorned with gold survive. Inlaid cloisonné enamels on gold or gilt silver became a hallmark of Nasrid metalwork, in jewelry (as we will see below) as well as weaponry and armor. Ibn al-Khaṭīb, the Nasrid historian, described how Andalusīs' weapons and armor had shifted over time, from metal lances, heavy chainmail, and unadorned helmets like their Christian neighbors to light lances, short chainmail, and gilded helmets (*al-bayḍāt al-mudhahhaba*).[19] These new forms reflected shifts in weaponry and armor adapted from North African and European models. Alfonso the Magnanimous's desire for gold horse trappings and weapons suggests that these objects were different enough from those produced in his kingdom to justify a journey to acquire them, but that they were still appropriate for Christian kingly use. The records of other kings suggest that they also had collections of gilded weapons and armor. Pedro I of Castile (r. 1350–69) included in his will four gold "gineta" swords, a style with a round pommel at the top associated with North Africa and the Nasrids, as well as his "espada castellana," or Castilian sword, all to be given to his son Don Juan.[20] The profusion of these objects across kingdoms reflects what Feliciano, working on similarly widely diffused textiles, has called a "pan-Iberian aesthetic vocabulary," but as is indicated by the names Alfonso and Pedro used ("morisca," "gineta"), golden weapons and armor could also carry a strong association with Muslims, especially with the Nasrids.[21]

An unusual gilded helmet attributed to a Nasrid workshop is on display at the Metropolitan Museum of Art (fig. 3).[22] The helmet is in a form known in European arms and armor as a "sallet," with a curving edge that extended over the neck, but also incorporates semi-circular cut-outs above the eyes like

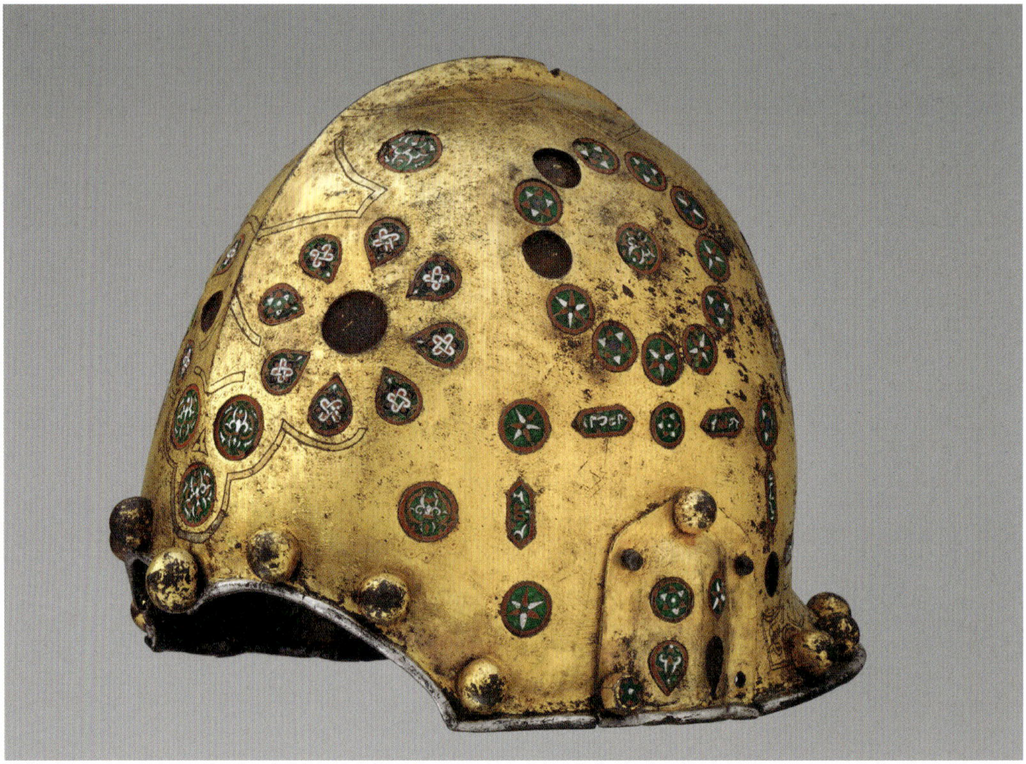

Fig. 3. Gilded sallet, gilt on steel with cloisonné enamel inlays, 20 × 20.6 cm, diameter 26.7 cm. New York, The Metropolitan Museum of Art, accession no. 1983.413

many Islamic helmets. It is covered with a series of inlaid enamels arranged to form six circles, with additional enamels creating a line along the bottom and around the ears. Engraved double lines curve under the cluster of enamels above the eyes and trace curves around the comb of the helmet along the top. On the back, an engraved double line demarcates a cartouche between the enamels and the large gilded rivets that surround the base, within which a pseudo inscription in Arabic script hovers. The enamels themselves, made using the cloisonné technique, are circular, elongated hexagons, or teardrop in shape, and use the standard Nasrid colors of green, red, turquoise, blue and white. They contain six pointed stars, "Solomonic" knots made of two intersecting elongated loops, palmettes, and illegible cursive inscriptions. Each enamel is embedded in the gold helmet and is surrounded by a light punchwork border (fig. 4).

No other Nasrid helmets survive, so scholars do not know whether the form or decoration of this object were typical. The vast majority of textual and

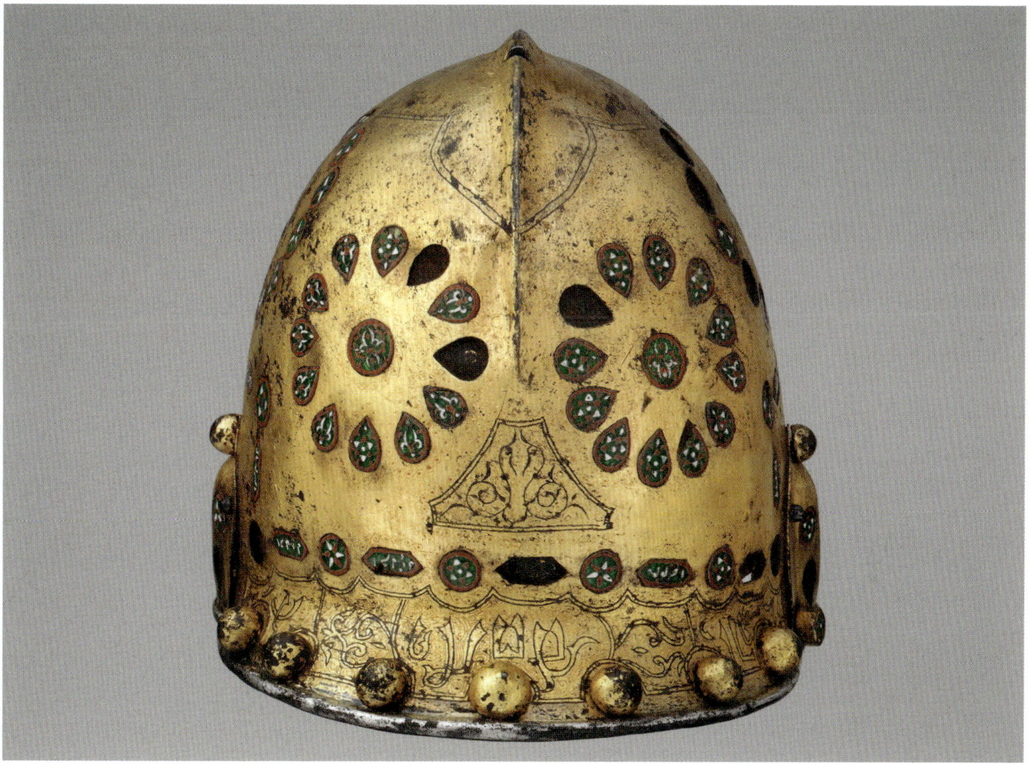

Fig. 4. Back of gilded sallet, gilt on steel with cloisonné enamel inlays, 20 × 20.6 cm, diameter 26.7 cm. New York, The Metropolitan Museum of Art, accession no. 1983.413

visual representations of Andalusī warriors depicts them wearing turbans, in distinction to Christian knights wearing helmets, but, as Ibn al-Khaṭīb noted, this seemed to change in the fourteenth century, as the Nasrids imported new forms of weaponry and armor from the Islamic east, including gilded helmets.[23] It may have been, as Teresa Pérez Higuera suggests, that important leaders wore such helmets all the time, or that gilded helmets only appeared beginning in the fourteenth century.[24]

Whether destined for Nasrid use or for a powerful patron to the north, the combination of strong steel, gilded surface and colorful enamels would have made the wearer awe inspiring. Yet the construction of the helmet indicates it likely had a use off of the battlefield rather than on it – the holes into which the enamels have been laid puncture the steel substructure of the helmet, rendering it weak and susceptible to damage. The helmet itself suggests a multistage production that likely incorporated both Muslim and Christian craftsmen and required the movement of people and materials across substantial distances.

The interior form of the helmet seems to have been produced in Calatayud, where thirteenth-century texts indicate that gilded helmets were frequently manufactured.[25] As Alvaro Soler suggests in his *Al-Andalus* catalog entry, the placement of some of the cloisonné plaques so that the inscriptions are inverted and the use of pseudo-inscriptions may indicate that the helmet was a work of Christian artisanry based on Nasrid forms.[26] As we know from other objects, however, enamels were closely associated with Nasrid Granada and were also in great demand in the Christian kingdoms of the Iberian peninsula.[27]

The particular pseudo-Arabic inscription on the body of the helmet suggests intriguing possibilities for understanding its production or destined audience. The form of the engraved inscription along the curved edge of the back of the helmet echoes letters without forming any. Nasrid art and architecture are defined by the use of inscriptions, in every script, across surfaces so distant from the viewer they would be impossible to read. But even when the letters grow into leaves and niches, and even when words are highly stylized, they maintain the edge of legibility. This inscription, however, shares formal qualities with the pseudo-Arabic used in paintings executed by Christians in fifteenth- and sixteenth-century Spain. In Bartolomé Bermejo's Saint Engracia retable (likely produced in Daroca between 1472 and 1477), the turban worn by the villain Dacianus, who watches as the saint is flayed to death, is bordered with a gold pseudo-Arabic inscription that echoes the one along the neck of our sallet (fig. 5).[28] Despite the fact that Dacianus was a fourth-century Roman governor, he is depicted sitting on an inlaid wooden chair that mirrors Nasrid furniture. Whether this is intended, as Joan Molina suggests, to equate the pagan Romans with the Muslim Nasrids, or simply as an expression of the governor's wealth and status, the use of this pseudo-inscription powerfully indicates an association with Nasrid forms.[29]

Other surviving objects with the same pseudo-inscription seem to have been copied from one another or from a common source. The leather shield (*adarga,* from the Arabic *daraqa*) at the Armería del Palacio Real in Madrid that has the characteristic shape known from images of Almoravid, Almohad, and Nasrid warriors, has bands of inscription that include oval cartouches with near duplicates of the same inscription as the helmet.[30] So, too, does a tiny plaque of gilded bronze adorned with a champlevé enamel knot of Solomon, perhaps once a fitting for a horse, at the Instituto Valencia de Don Juan in Madrid.[31] The

Fig. 5. Bartolomé Bermejo, *Flagellation of Saint Engracia*, ca. 1474–77, oil on panel, 92.5 × 52 cm. Bilbao, Museo de Bellas Artes de Bilbao

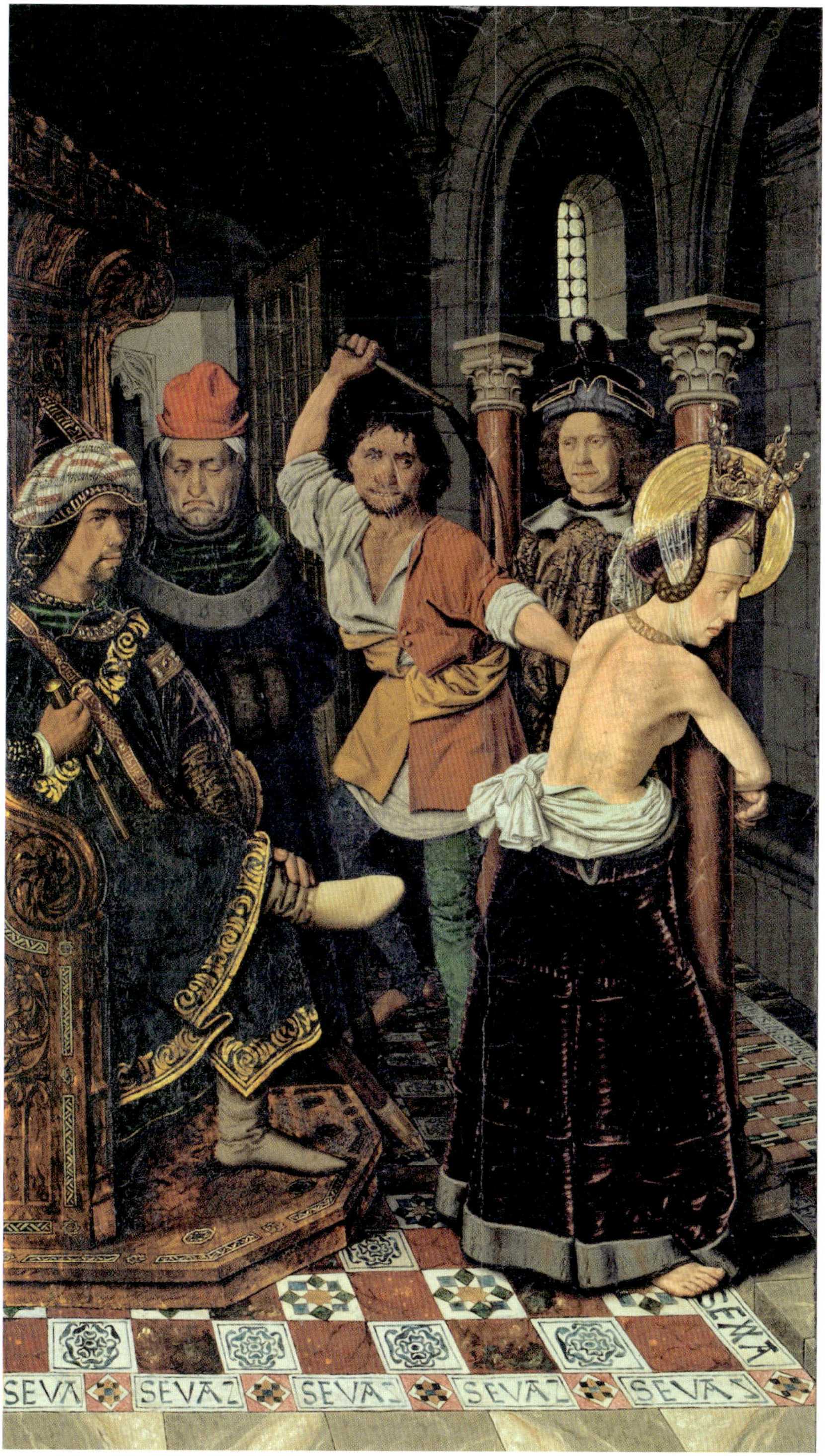
SEVA
SEVAZ
SEVAS
SEVAZ
SEVAS

two bands of pseudo-inscription, along the top and the bottom, follow exactly the same form as the inscription on the back of the golden sallet. Similarly, swords, like the one in the Cabinet des Medailles Luynes at the Bibliothèque nationale de France, have inscriptions inside tiny shields that evoke the Nasrid motto *Lā ghālib illā Allāh* (there is no victor but God) but are illegible.[32]

Other Nasrid weapons and armor, like the so-called Sword of Boabdil, which was passed through generations of Castilian kings until its placement, in the twentieth century, in the Museo del Ejercito in Madrid, have legible Qur'anic inscriptions, which suggests their production by Nasrid craftsmen for elite Nasrid use. Made of gilt silver, cloisonné enamel, and carved ivory, with patterns of eight-pointed stars and crosses surrounded by delicate strapwork, this sword's tiny inscriptions are from Surah 112 of the Qur'an. This surah, focused on the oneness of God, was traditionally inscribed on amulets and talismans as well as in architectural contexts. It appears frequently on weaponry and armor from the Islamic world, and was particularly prevalent in Nasrid architecture. Cynthia Robinson has argued that this inscription, asserting that God does not beget and was not begotten, carried special urgency in the context of the Nasrid fight against Christian hegemony.[33]

Such potent inscriptions, seen as apotropaic in battle and beyond, may have militated against its production by Muslims for Christian use. Many objects destined for general consumption had Arabic inscriptions with generic well wishes, while elite Nasrid objects also included specific, often Qur'anic, inscriptions. It is possible that Muslim or Morisco craftsmen commissioned to make a martial object for a Christian patron who, unlike Alfonso VIII, would not notice how legible the script was, made enamel plaques with illegible inscriptions. It is also possible that they were produced by Christian craftsmen in imitation of Nasrid style. Inventories and orders from Christian royalty in the late fifteenth and early sixteenth centuries indicate that enamel pieces with *cifras moriscas* (morisco letters) were in high demand: Isabella "the Catholic" ordered eighty-four gold pieces thus decorated for a belt from her silversmith Fernando Bernal in 1490, and in 1515 Isabella of Aragon purchased thirty-seven enameled gold pieces for the decoration of a collar.[34] Whether the gilded helmet itself was produced in Granada or elsewhere on the peninsula, the similarities of its pseudo-inscription to other sixteenth-century evocations of Arabic suggests production outside of Granada, or for an explicitly Christian audience.

These "morisco"-style pieces were clearly in great demand in fifteenth- and sixteenth-century Spain, where they were valued for their fine technique and materials, and the artistry of their craftsmanship. They were also crucial for the performance of elite status known as the *juego de cañas* or game of canes, in which costumed noblemen dressed as "moros" and Christians fought each other in a stylized battle. In the case of clothing, as Javier Irigoyen-García argues, "morisco" clothing should not be seen as distinct from "Christian" clothing but rather as a category within "Christian" clothing—worn and largely produced by "Old Christian" tailors.[35] Throughout the sixteenth century, tailors in Toledo, Granada, Lisbon, and Madrid were tested on "Moorish craft," ensuring that they were able to make appropriate clothing for use in the game of canes.[36] After the conversion of the Muslims, royal decrees like that of Philip II in 1567 banned clothing and adornments that looked "morisco," and yet Philip II himself wore clothing *a la morisca* to participate in games of canes. Wearing such clothing, which was often made of silk and elaborately embroidered, was thus a signifier of elite status, not of religion. Like this clothing, "morisco"-style arms and armor may well have been produced by Christian craftsmen for those Christians elite enough to dress *a la morisca* without risking investigation by the Inquisition.

In the fifteenth century, nobles and royalty commissioned or purchased gold arms and armor from Nasrid Granada via Muslim intermediaries. By the sixteenth century, such objects had become crucial signifiers of nobility, produced under Christian rule for Christian audiences alone. It is hard to know when and where, precisely, this helmet was produced. But its form suggests that it was meant to evoke the highest standards of Nasrid craftsmanship and that it was destined for an explicitly Christian audience.

The "Hail Mary" Necklace

Another gold object at the Metropolitan Museum merges Nasrid techniques and Christian forms in a way that makes classifying it similarly difficult (fig. 6). The "Elements of a Necklace" held in the medieval galleries include a large round medallion (7.6 cm diameter, 0.5 cm thickness), made using filigree and granulation, with a central panel incised with delicate foliate patterns and an inscription that reads AVE MARIA GRACIA PLEN[A] ("Hail Mary full of grace") (fig. 7).[37] The remaining elements—four stylized hand shaped pendants (8.4 × 5.2 × 0.5 cm), and five cylindrical beads of varying sizes—highlight the consummate skill in gilt filigree and enamel production commonly associated with Nasrid workshops. Here, however, the tiny enamel plaques embedded in all of the necklace elements use the colors and forms of Nasrid cloisonné (green, red, turquoise, blue and white) to make red crosses and gold pseudo inscriptions that evoke the word "Allah."

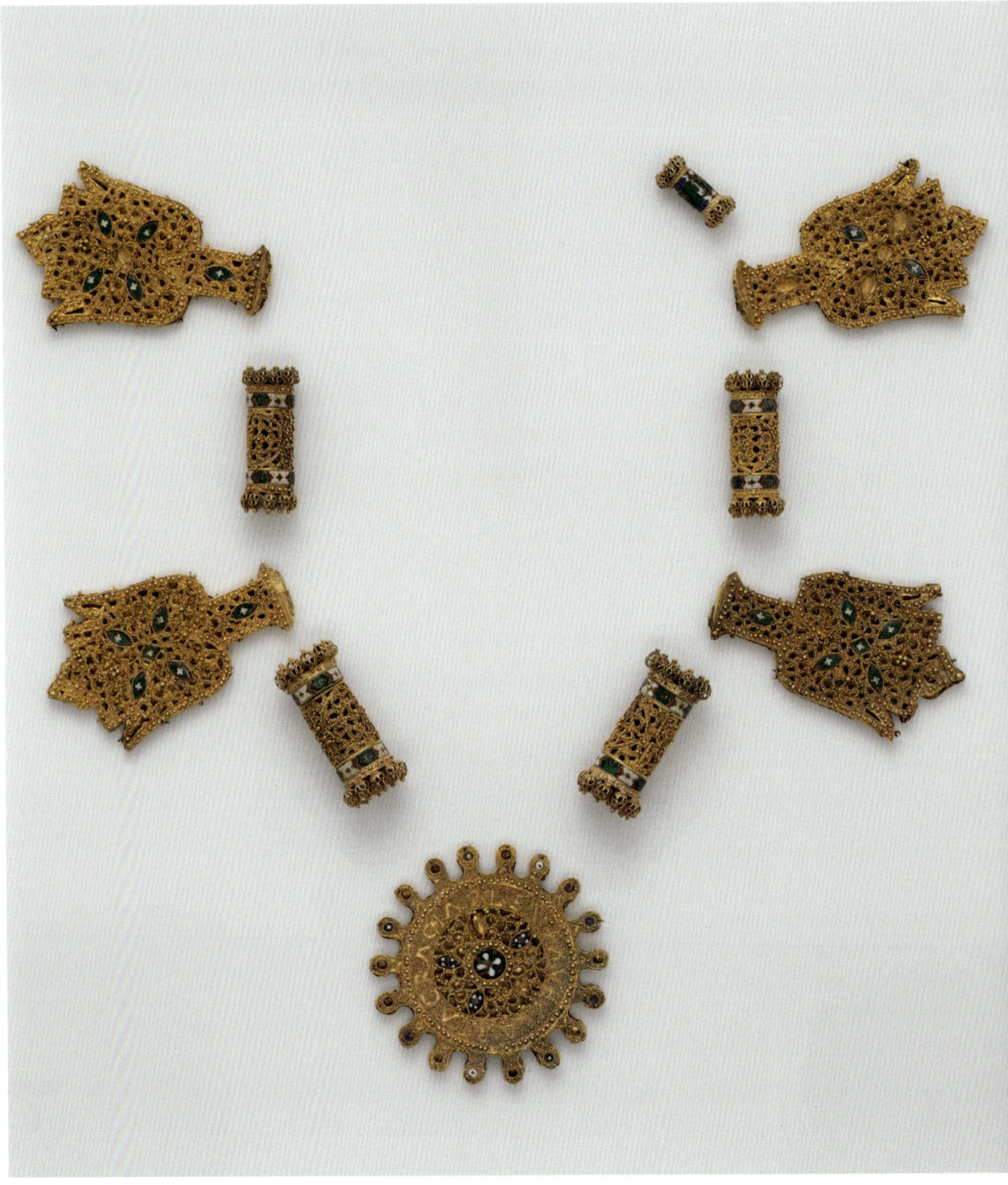

Fig. 6. Elements from a Necklace, gold and cloisonné enamel, Granada,15th-16th century; wheel shaped medallion: 7.6 × 0.5 cm, 4 lotus bud plaques: 8.4 × 5.2 × 0.5 cm, largest cylindrical beads: 5.1 × 1.9 cm, smaller cylindrical beads: 4.8 × 1.7 cm, smallest cylindrical bead: 2.5 × 1.3 cm. New York, The Metropolitan Museum of Art, accession no. 17.190.161a-j

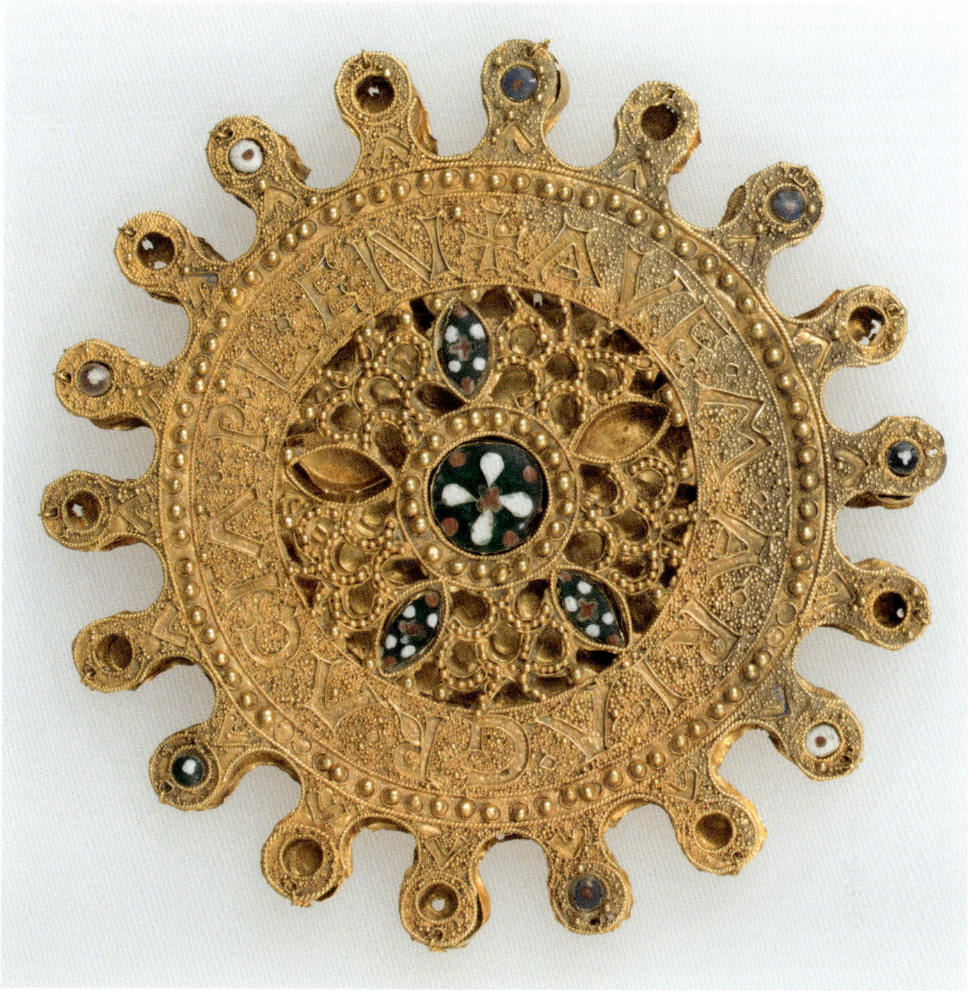

Fig. 7. Central medallion, elements from a necklace, Granada, 15th-16th century, gold and cloisonné enamel, 7.6 × 0.5 cm. New York, The Metropolitan Museum of Art, accession no. 17.190.161f

The slightly incomplete Latin inscription, with "grace" spelled according to the Castilian rather than traditional Latin form and the final "a" missing, reflects the Castilian fascination with the Virgin that Cynthia Robinson sees as a response to the Nasrid emphasis on God not begetting or being begotten.[38] The combination of reference to Mary and the use of apotropaic hand forms brings together two of the most common themes of sixteenth-century Spanish jewelry.[39] Like the dinar of Alfonso VIII, this necklace uses the forms and techniques developed to their peak by Muslim patrons and craftsmen to articulate a Christian claim—but this time with an inscription in Latin instead of Arabic.

Likely produced in the late fifteenth or early sixteenth century in Granada, this necklace captures the aesthetic of the moment of transition from Islamic to Christian Granada.

Gold jewelry made using filigree and granulation was an ancient technique, employed by the Etruscans, Greeks, and Romans, and finds from Necropolis of Tútugi at Galera in the province of Granada show that items made using granulation were produced on the Iberian peninsula as early as the fourth century BCE.[40] This technique also flourished in North Africa and al-Andalus, beginning in the caliphal period. Excavations at Madinat al-Zahra, the caliphal palace city outside Cordoba, show that enameled gold jewelry was being produced in al-Andalus as early as the tenth century.[41] At roughly the same time, the Fatimids produced vast quantities of jewelry that circulated in al-Andalus, using hollow, box-like forms that were covered with strips and openwork designs made up of twisted filigree. Polychrome cloisonné enamels in green, white, and red were often glued on after the rest of the object was constructed. In al-Andalus, these techniques were used to create forms that included figural elements as well as inscriptions. The Nasrids developed this style to its peak, producing enormous quantities of filigreed jewelry that have been discovered in caches across the Iberian peninsula.[42]

Ibn al-Khaṭīb described how completely the elite of the Nasrid kingdom covered themselves in gold jewelry in the fourteenth century:

> They adorn themselves with necklaces, bracelets, bangles (*khalākhīl*) and pendants (*shunūf*) of the purest gold, down to this day, among those who are wealthy, and of silver, including adornments (*ālāt*) of the feet, among those who are not rich.[43]

The jewelry that survives gives a taste of what this might have looked like. Nasrid jewelry often included enameled plaques with Arabic inscriptions, so-called knots of Solomon, palmettes and tracery, much like the plaques used in the sallet discussed above. A typical set of beads at The Metropolitan Museum of Art, likely from fifteenth century Granada, are made using filigree and granulation as well as green, white and red cloisonné enamels. The cylindrical beads include tiny Arabic inscriptions evoking God's glory.[44]

After the Castilian conquest of Granada in 1492, many of the military and leading elite of the Nasrids left for North Africa, by September or October 1493.[45] But many of the craftsmen remained, organized in guilds, each run by an *amīn* or syndic, according to earlier Islamic forms. As L.P. Harvey notes, the guilds under Nasrid rule had spiritual dimensions and would likely have remained inaccessible to the Christian immigrants who entered Granada after its conquest. Two separate and parallel systems of craftsmen would therefore have existed alongside each other, one Granadan and with Andalusī roots, the other immigrant and Christian.[46] The long-term survival of Nasrid-era guilds offers intriguing possibilities for understanding the continued production of objects that use the same techniques and materials after the Castilian conquest of Granada.

The "Hail Mary" necklace, with its gold filigree and granulation and its use of cloisonné enamel plaques, alongside its Latin Christian inscription, embodies this moment of transition. Like the other luxury goods produced in this time of great change, it reflects the myriad networks that linked the Catholic Monarchs to the cultural centers north of the Pyrenees and to Granada, their newest and most prized territory, incorporating Nasrid techniques and materials alongside motifs and forms from the north.[47] Inventories of Isabella's jewelry from 1504 indicate she had many "morisco" jewels similar to this necklace, including ones made with enamels and of gold filigree and granulation.[48]

The necklace suggests more than a simple appropriation or "dressing up," however. Its use of forms indelibly associated with the richest and most elite workshops of Nasrid Granada, incorporating tiny inscriptions suggesting the name of God and the hand-shaped forms used to ward off the evil eye within and beyond Islamic contexts, to surround a central medallion asserting the holiness of Mary, carries particular weight. The inscription of "Ave Maria," like the tripartite God on Alfonso's dinar, counters Islamic visions of piety with a Christian one, even while using the forms, techniques and materials of Muslim workshops. When she was dying, Isabella indicated that she should be buried in the Franciscan convent in the confines of the Alhambra, in a tiny domed pavilion with a muqarnas ceiling that echoed Islamic funerary *qubba*s, a space explicitly Christian in function though maintaining the same form it had when it was a Nasrid palace.[49] Like her funerary chapel in the Alhambra, the "Hail Mary" necklace's inscription proclaims a dominant Christian meaning, even as its filigreed and enameled form harnesses the spiritual power of Nasrid aesthetics. In the moment of the capture of Granada and in the generation that followed, Nasrid-style forms were de rigueur, symbols of power and ostentation and also potent forms of protection. Two generations later, in the time of the Catholic Monarch's grandson Charles V, who would move Isabella's body to a newly constructed royal chapel next to the cathedral of Granada, this had begun to change.

"Morisco" Gold in the Spanish Imaginary

In 1502, the Catholic Monarchs issued an order demanding the Muslims of Castile convert to Christianity or leave. Although the population of Granada became exclusively Christian, clear distinctions remained between the "Old Christians," immigrants from the north, and the "New Christians," or Moriscos, who according to critics continued to speak, dress, act and live like Muslims. They were accused of perfidious loyalty to Islam, of secret treachery, even as Old Christians continued to covet the goods they produced in the old style, especially their rich silks, lustered ceramics and fine gold work. Over time, Moriscos' possession of gold, and their facility in working it, came to be associated with this treachery.

The Ordinances of Granada, repeatedly cried in the streets around the Alcaicería, and the Zacatín, and near the Puerta del Carbón, all centers of the manufacture and sale of silver and gold goods between 1529 and 1538, accused the city's goldsmiths of using impure gold and required that all their gold be of 20-karat quality.[50] In 1532, the goldsmiths responded to King Charles V in a petition that denied any wrongdoing and pointed out that the gold they used was as pure as that used in Toledo, Seville, and Cordoba. Forcing them to use purer gold than their rivals in these other cities put them at a disadvantage, they argued.[51] The ordinances mentioned several different kinds of jewelry produced by these craftsmen, including stamped or *albordado* bracelets with designs in relief.[52]

One of the ordinances specifically criticized the manufacture of large gold bangles, called *axorcas Moriscas* (fig. 8), which were made by placing a thin layer of gold over a base of chalk or mastic. These bracelets, according to the city ordinances, purported to be of pure gold but were in fact made with very little, and could only be made pure by placing them in a fire, which nevertheless blackened the gold.[53] After decades of trying to regulate the production of "morisco" jewelry, with increasing anxiety about its authenticity and purity, the rulers of Castile began trying to stop people from wearing it.

In 1600, Philip III of Spain promulgated sumptuary laws that allowed women to wear pearls and simple jewelry adorned with a single precious stone, but banned jewelry "in relief" for any non-liturgical use. The specific list of prohibited forms and materials reflects the standard styles of "morisco" jewelry:

> "We order that from here forward one cannot make nor obtain in these our kingdoms, nor bring in from outside of them, any jewelry of gold that has relief, nor enamels, nor points with pearls, nor stones, nor [may they wear] small

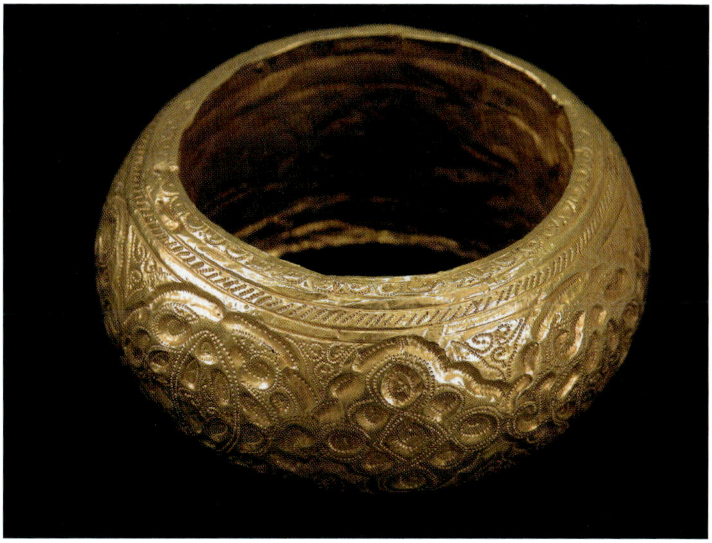

Fig. 8. Axorca or gold bangle, Granada, Nasrid period, 14th-15th century, thin gold layer formerly over chalk or mastic filling. New York, The Metropolitan Museum of Art, accession no. 17.190.157

> pieces of jewelry or decorative pins (*brincos*) that contain enamels or reliefs, and that they may only wear small pieces of jewelry and decorative pins (*brincos*) that have a stone with pendants of pearls, and we also permit women to wear any strands and threads of pearls freely."[54]

The same sumptuary laws also outlawed silks adorned with gold or silver, a form that was also produced under the Nasrids and continued by the Moriscos, often for royal Christian patrons.

This attempt to regulate signs that seem to refer to Arabo-Islamic culture was a major project of Philip III. It followed on earlier attempts by religious and royal authorities to make Moriscos dress, speak, and act more like "Old Christians," and to eliminate material traces of earlier cultures and craft traditions, like his predecessor Philip II's destruction of Arabic inscriptions throughout Spain.[55] Nevertheless, the banning of "morisco" clothes and jewelry did not detract in the slightest from their appeal for the most elite segments of society.[56] Nobility staged events that showcased Moriscos or "old Christians" wearing "morisco" garb: in 1601 the Marqués de Mondéjar held a nocturnal procession in honor of the birth of an infanta that featured forty Moriscos wearing traditional clothing, playing morisco instruments, and dancing the (long since outlawed) morisco dance, the *zambra*.[57]

Barbara Fuchs has advanced the concept of a "moorish habitus," within which sixteenth-century literary maurophile and maurophobe discourses operated, and she argues that Moorishness was "vivid presence in quotidian

Spanish culture."[58] As she and Javier Irigoyen-García have shown, dressing *a la morisca* was widespread among elite Christians throughout the Iberian peninsula, and became a visual sign of Spanishness beyond the Pyrenees. This, in turn, led to the exotic othering of Spain itself by northern Europeans, who saw in Spain's "morisco"-style embroidered silks, enameled gold helmets and carved stucco architecture exoticism and miscegenation.

Purifying Spain

Philip III went further in this project of eliminating the traces of Islam on the peninsula than his father had, by eventually commanding the expulsion of all of the Moriscos—those who those whose ancestors had been forced generations earlier to convert to Christianity. Even supporters of this action acknowledged the enormous cost to the kingdoms affected, as they lost a large proportion of their tax base, their craftsmen and their agricultural workers. Yet an examination of the texts written after the expulsion justifying and celebrating Philip III's order shows that treachery—and gold—continued to operate as leitmotifs in the narrative of the creation of a purely Christian Spain.

A number of churchmen in southern Spain began campaigns urging Philip III to expel the Moriscos, writing letters and petitions that characterized them as crypto-Muslims without hope for redemption, and as hoarders of gold. In 1602, the Valencian Archbishop Juan de Ribera wrote a petition that described the Moriscos as "the sponge of all the wealth of Spain," and that declared "without a doubt there is a great quantity of gold and silver in their power."[59] The suggestion that the expulsion would bring hoards of Morisco wealth to the kingdom has had a long afterlife, as even nineteenth century writers like Washington Irving imagined hidden caches of Morisco treasure that could be found in Granada. But these masses of treasure never appeared after the expulsion, and apologists sought to explain the absence of great wealth by accusing the Moriscos of theft.

After Philip enacted the expulsion in 1609, a number of observers wrote to the king, describing how Moriscos stole Spanish wealth as they departed. They claimed that the Moriscos exchanged counterfeit currency for goods before their departure, and that they also left with innumerable treasures taken from faithful Christians and from churches. One Christian writer reported that Moriscos departed with much silver and gold, though they were forbidden to do so, with women sewing it into their clothes (fig. 9).[60] This led to disadvantages for "Old Christians," who were faced with a dearth of precious metals.[61] Another observer, the Marqués of Vélez, wrote to Philip III in November 1609 from Mula that "Now, a Real [silver coin] cannot be found in all of these places,

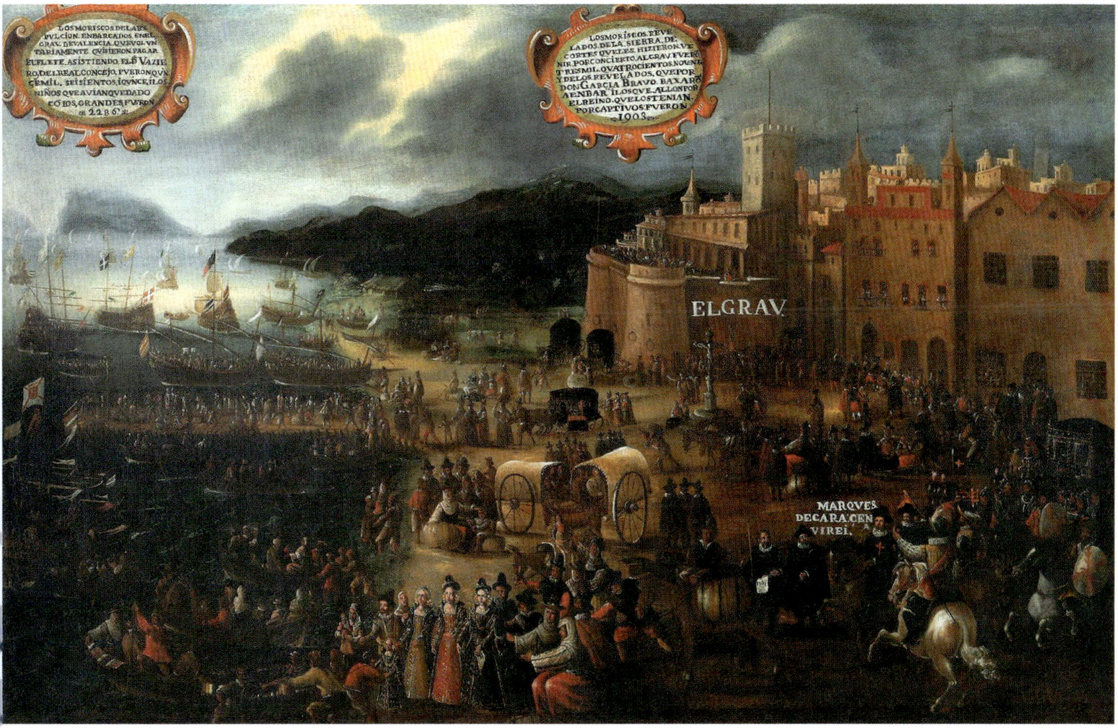

Fig. 9. Pere Oromig, *Embarco Moriscos en el Grao de Valencia*, from the series "La expulsión de los moriscos," 1616, oil on canvas, 110 × 174 cm. Valencia, Fundación Bancaja, Colección de arte

except in the hands of Moriscos who have extracted all of the treasure."[62] While continuing the association of Islam, gold, and deceit discussed earlier, these accounts also reflected the very real costs of the expulsion for the "Old Christians" who were left behind. Tax revenue dropped dramatically, especially in the regions that had contained substantial Morisco populations, and cities lost craftsmen, farmers and others who produced important goods that were also sources of trade.

For this reason, many opposed the expulsion. Pedro Aznar Cardona wrote his *Justification of the Expulsion of the Spanish Moriscos and Summary of the Excellences of Our King Don Philip*, in 1612, to persuade those hostile to the expulsion to support it.[63] He criticized the Moriscos for their continued adherence to Islamic cultural customs, accused them of continuing to follow their "lord" Muhammad, and decried their eating, drinking, and social behaviors. According to Aznar, the Moriscos would never have become true Christians, and the expulsion was the only option to make Spain into a truly Christian nation. In language that would have been immediately legible to his contemporaries as a reference to the debate about Morisco wealth, he wrote that their forced departure purified the Church "like gold in a crucible."[64] Thus, even if their departure did not reveal storehouses full of treasure, and even if it led to a dearth in precious metals, the "gold" of Spain and its Church would now be free of deceit.

Aznar's argument reflects the broader movement, over the course of the sixteenth and seventeenth centuries, from appropriation of "Islamic" forms to their rejection and eventual erasure. Gold—which had once been indelibly associated with the mines of Africa, the Muslim traders who brought it to Christian markets, and the Andalusī craftsmen who transformed it into jewelry, now became the material with which to construct a new, unsullied, Christian kingdom. Gold as material was transfigured into gold as metaphor for purity – losing Morisco gold did not matter, for it would be replaced with the authentic and immaculate gold of Christian Spain. This transformation was facilitated by the emergence of new sources of gold in the Americas, which could bypass West African gold and its associations with Islam.

While, in the fifteenth century, rulers like Alfonso the Magnanimous of Aragon specifically sought "morisco" horse trappings and jewelry adorned with gold and enamels, by the early seventeenth century other rulers sought to ban such goods entirely. Instead, Philip III encouraged men and women to wear gold jewelry with single precious stones, and strings of pearls, mirroring the jewelry en vogue on the other side of the Pyrenees. But this was not a simple shift in taste. It was part of the broader ideological project of erasing evidence of an Islamic presence on the Iberian peninsula, a project that included the banning of speaking or writing in Arabic, the destruction of inscriptions and structures, and the prohibition of wearing clothing or jewelry that seemed related to Islamic culture. Eventually, this process resulted in the expulsion of the Moriscos themselves, justified by contemporaries through their literal contamination of Christian gold and their metaphorical contamination of the Christian Church. Purifying the blood of the Spanish people by expelling those of Muslim ancestry went along with purifying the gold of Spain, and by extension, the Church itself.

Conclusion: Religion, Nationalism and Objects on the Move

In the fall of 1887, a peasant discovered a buried treasure in the Alpujarras Mountains outside of Granada. The Treasure of Berchules, or "El Tesoro de la Reina Mora" (the treasure of the Moorish queen), as it became known in news reports, included both the "Hail Mary" necklace and some *axorcas*, alongside enameled Nasrid beads with tiny Arabic inscriptions that read "Glory belongs to God." Like Washington Irving, who imagined he would discover hidden Moorish treasure in the hills outside Granada, the nineteenth-century champions of this cache of jewelry saw it as proof of the wealth and luxury of the Nasrids, and imagined that the collection had belonged to an important Moorish queen who had hidden it in the hills at the time of the Christian conquest. The treasure is recorded to have included two silver coins of the Catholic Monarchs. Following its discovery in 1887, the contents of the treasure were photographed and published as "joyas moriscas" in the *Ilustración Española y Americana*, and then lost, only to reappear in the gift of J. Pierpont Morgan to the Metropolitan Museum in 1917 (fig. 10).[65]

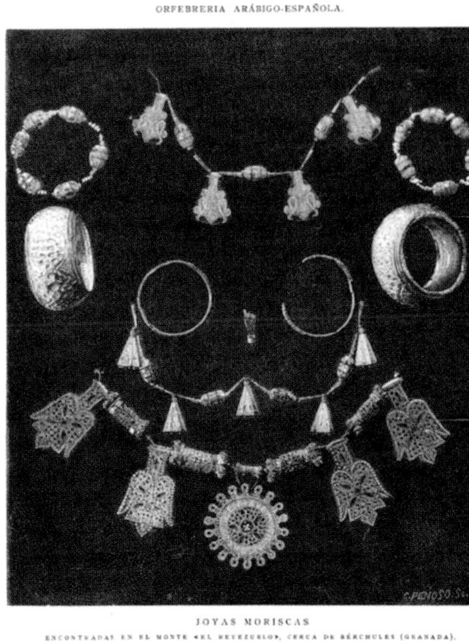

Fig. 10. Bérchules treasure, discovered in the hills outside Granada in 1887, Photographed as "joyas moriscas" in the *Ilustración Española y Americana* 46, Madrid, 13 December 1887, p. 365

Pierpont Morgan was also, briefly, the owner of the sallet discussed above, buying it from the French antique arms dealer Bachereau in the first years of the twentieth century for 250,000 francs and then returning it. In the publication of the proceedings of museum professionals in Amsterdam in 1905, Gaston Migeon brought up this sale and suggested that the helmet was a modern forgery of a Nasrid helmet, made using enamels taken out of a sword, since, as he noted, the only other surviving objects that use similar enamel plaques are late Nasrid swords, and the enamels were clearly placed on the helmet after its production.[66] The swords he mentioned as comparanda are the sword in the Bibliothèque nationale de France, mentioned above, and another in the collection of the Marquis de Viana, with similar tiny pseudo-script and star enamels. His observation that this helmet looks more like these swords than anything else is striking, though it does not indicate that it was a nineteenth century forgery, but rather that these objects were likely all produced in a similar post-Nasrid context for Christian use. Nevertheless, many of these objects, including the sallet and the sword in the Bibliothèque nationale de France, became associated in the late nineteenth century with Boabdil, the last Nasrid ruler. Even the Italian sallet produced by the Milanese Negroli family for the Spanish court around 1500, now in the Palacio Real de Madrid, was imagined by nineteenth-century viewers to have belonged to Boabdil![67] Like the "treasure of the Moorish queen," these objects gained value and appeal through their association with Iberia's last Muslims, and their Christian roots and meanings were obscured.

The scholarly fixation in the nineteenth and twentieth centuries with the religion of craftsmen as the key to understanding the religious "identity" of objects and their cultural meaning has made objects like these almost impossible to understand.[68] Whether the sallet and necklace discussed above were made by Muslims or Moriscos, whether in Granada or in Castile, has little bearing on their meanings as objects. What the forms of these two objects reveal, like the dinar of Alfonso VIII, is that elite Iberian aesthetics, whether in the thirteenth or the sixteenth century, relied upon gold worked according to Andalusī methods. What makes these objects different from similar Andalusī ones is simply that their form highlights their transculturality. Many other objects understood unproblematically as "Andalusī" would also have circulated widely in Christian contexts. In the thirteenth century, Alfonso's dinar marshaled the language and design of Andalusī coinage to express a Christian message. In the transition from the fifteenth to the sixteenth century, the helmet and the necklace were both made using Nasrid-style gold-working and enamel techniques for a Christian audience. The helmet's shape, its pseudo-script, and its use of upside-down enamels, all suggest that it was designed to look "morisco" for an audience that saw wearing such objects as a sign of unassailably Christian noble blood. The gold filigreed and granulated necklace, like the dinar, expressed a Christian message through a form developed in al-Andalus, bringing Marian devotion, apotropaic hands, crosses and enamel evocations of Allah together into a spectacular protective ornament. Each of these objects were made for Christian use, and each includes forms, techniques and languages associated today with Islam. As we have seen, many such objects were called "morisco" in their own day. But the thousands of objects and spaces that navigated between the cultural terrains of Muslims and Christians did not follow a single script. They did not function as icons of coexistence or as symbols of dominance. They, like the people who manufactured and used them, made meaning contextually, transforming and being transformed by the spheres they moved through.

While, in the medieval period, such objects carried multiple and layered meanings that rarely mapped onto religion alone, in the early modern period, anxieties about Morisco cultural power meant that objects understood as "morisco" in form were reserved for the use of elite Christians, who would not be contaminated by them. Later, as the elimination of the traces of Islam became an ecclesiastical and national priority, advocates of the expulsion couched their rhetoric in metaphors about redeeming the purity of the Church and recapturing the gold of the Moriscos. Some of these objects survived buried, like the so-called treasure of the Moorish queen, only to be rediscovered at a time of Romantic fascination with Spain's Islamic past. Others were kept as curios in Christian contexts, first valued for the richness of their material and the fineness of their technique, and later, as in the case of the helmet, explicitly valued as a symbol of the Christian conquest of Granada. Ironically, the specific meanings of these gold objects in the Christian contexts in which they were produced or circulated was effaced in favor of a vision of a totalizing Islamic identity. Like Don Quixote's transformation of a brass barber's bowl into a magical Moorish helmet, the objects considered here were reimagined in the aftermath of the conquest, expulsion and Inquisition. Goods that were at one point quotidian, at least for the elite, became, in the absence of Muslims and the destruction of their traces, imbued with foreignness and otherworldly power.

Notes

1. This story appears in Miguel de Cervantes, *Don Quixote*, First Part, Chapter XXI. In the translation by Edith Grossman (New York: Harper Collins, 2003), this corresponds to pp. 152-55; in the Spanish edition published in Leipzig in 1818: First Part, Vol. 2, pp. 198-204. I use the word "Moor" here because that is the term typically applied to Mambrino in the chivalric romances in which he appears and the scholarly literature discussing him. Generally, however, I do not use "Moor" to describe the people of al-Andalus or the period, since its usage in English has unnecessary racial connotations and since it reifies the distinction of Andalusī Muslims from those of other regions.

2. Cervantes, *Don Quixote,* trans. Grossman, p. 155.

3. Ibid.

4. Throughout this chapter, I will use terms such as "morisco" (applied to people and to objects) as contemporary sources did, and will occasionally discuss the concept of "Moorishness," following the work of Barbara Fuchs and others. The problems of using terms like "Moorish" or "morisco" when applied to objects have been elucidated by Javier Irigoyen-García, *Moors Dressed as Moors: Clothing, Social Distinction and Ethnicity in Early Modern Iberia* (Toronto: University of Toronto Press, 2017), pp. 21-23.

5. Morisco, as used by modern scholars, means "New Christian," or Muslims forcibly converted to Christianity in the first half of the sixteenth century. They were not consistently known as such in this period, and as we will see, the word "morisco" was most commonly used in the fifteenth-sixteenth centuries as an adjectival form of "moro" or Muslim. There is great scholarly debate about the extent to which the people known as Moriscos maintained their Islamic beliefs and practices, but they were seen as suspicious, and the majority were expelled from the Iberian peninsula between 1609 and 1614. For more, see L.P. Harvey, *Muslims in Spain, 1500-1614* (Chicago: University of Chicago Press, 2005).

6. On how "Moorishness" became associated with "Spanishness," see Barbara Fuchs, *Exotic Nation: Maurophilia and the Construction of Early Modern Spain,* Philadelphia: University of Pennsylvania Press, 2009; on the particular case of the development of Granada's communal identity, see A. Katie Harris, *From Muslim to Christian Granada: Inventing a City's Past in Early Modern Spain,* Baltimore: The Johns Hopkins University Press, 2009.

7. Mary Douglas, *Purity and Danger: An Analysis of the Concepts of Pollution and Taboo,* London and New York: Routledge, 1966, p. 4.

8. The term "Reconquista" is a historiographic construct that emerged between the sixteenth and nineteenth centuries, and the piecemeal Christian conquests of Islamic Iberia were rarely seen in totalizing terms before the modern period. See Martín Ríos Saloma, *La reconquista: Una construcción historiográfica (siglos XVI-XIX)* (Madrid: Marcial Pons Ediciones de Historia, 2011), as well as the work of Alejandro García-Sanjuan and Carlos Ayala, among others. I use the term here because the same historiographic construct that imagines the piecemeal Christian conquests of Islamic territories on the Iberian peninsula as a singular ideological mission also promoted the association of gold and Islam.

9. On Alfonso VIII's dinars or *morabetinos,* see Antonio Vives y Escudero, *Monedas de las dinastías Arábigo Españolas,* (Madrid: Juan R. Cayón, 1893), no. 2022; Antonio Medina Gómez, *Monedas hispano-musulmanas: Manual de lectura y clasificación,* Instituto Provincial de Investigaciones y Estudios Toledanos, 1992, p. 380-86; *al-Andalus,* cat. 133, p. 390.

10. When the Genoese agreed to sell their third of the city of Tortosa back to Ramon Berenguer in 1153 (which they had won through helping him conquer the city in 1148), they set the cost in *morabetinos lupinos,* or those of Ibn Mardanīsh, Rex Lupus. J.J. Todesca, "What Touches All: Coinage and Monetary Policy in Leon-Castile to 1230," PhD Dissertation, Fordham University, 1996, p. 264.

11. On Ibn Mardanīsh's coinage, see Vives y Escudero, *Monedas de las dinastías Arábigo Españolas,* numbers 1931-1968; Hanna Kassis, "The coinage of Muḥammad ibn Sa'd (Ibn Mardanīsh) of Mursiya: An attempt at Iberian Islamic Autonomy," in *Problems of medieval coinage in the Iberian area,* ed. Mário Gomes Marques, Santarém, Portugal: Instituto Politécnico, 1988, 3:209-29; Juan José Rodriguez Lorente, *Numismática de la Murcia Musulmana,* (Madrid: Juan J. Rodriguez Lorente, 1984), 59-79; José Ferrandis Torres' "Tesorillo de dīnāres almorávides hallado en la Alcazaba de Almería," *al-Andalus* 11 (1946): 389-94.

12. Ibn Mardanīsh's dinars' marginal legend is Quran 3:85 and represents a continuation from earlier Almoravid coinage. Alfonso VIII's dinar's marginal legend is the first part of Mark 16:16. The latter part of this Biblical verse, which does not appear on his coinage, reflects an even closer parallel to Quran 3:85: "Whoever believes and is baptized will be saved, *but whoever does not believe will be condemned."* (Emphasis added)

13. On the political program of Ibn Mardanīsh's coinage, see my article, "Political and Religious Authority in the Coinage of Ibn Mardanīsh," in Sergio Carro Martín et al., eds., *Mediterráneos: An Interdisciplinary Approach to the Cultures of the Mediterranean Sea* (Newcastle upon Tyne: Cambridge Scholars Publishing, 2013), pp. 303-318.

14. Although gold was not an Andalusī product, Constable has noted that it can be seen as an Andalusī export, since it was redistributed by Andalusīs (and Berbers) to the Mediterranean world and beyond. O.R. Constable, *Trade and Traders in Muslim Spain: The Commercial Realignment of the Iberian Peninsula, 900-1500* (Cambridge: Cambridge University Press, 1994), p. 212.

15. María Judith Feliciano, "Muslim Shrouds for Christian Kings? A Reassessment of Andalusi Textiles in Thirteenth-Century Castilian Life and Ritual" in Cynthia Robinson and Leyla Rouhi, eds., *Under the Influence: Questioning the Comparative in Medieval Castile* (Leiden: Brill, 2005), pp. 101-131, here p. 105.

16. Feliciano, p. 118.

17. Roser Salicrú i Lluch, *Documents per a la història de Granada del regnat d'Alfons el Magnànim, 1416-1458* (CSIC Press, 1999), no. 9, 31-32 (ACA C, reg. 2410, fol. 136 v).

18. Roser Salicrú i Lluch, "Mudéjares y cristianos en el comercio con Berbería: Quejas sobre favoritismo fiscal y acusaciones de colaboracionismo mudéjar, una reacción cristiana a la defensiva," in *De mudéjares a moriscos: una conversión forzada. VIII Simposio Internacional de Mudejarismo.* Teruel, 15-17 de septiembre de 1999 (2002), 1: 283-301, at 286-87.

19. Ibn al-Khaṭīb, *al-Lamḥa al-Badriyya fī al-Dawla al-Naṣriyya*. 2nd ed. (Beirut: Dār al-Āfāq al-Jadīdah, 1978), p. 39.

20. Ada Bruhn de Hoffmeyer, *Arms and Armour in Spain: A Short Survey* (Madrid: CSIC, 1982), Vol. 1, p. 47. For more on the term "gineta" and its variants, and their derivation from the Berber tribal name Zanata, see Hussein Fancy, *The Mercenary Mediterranean: Sovereignty, Religion, and Violence in the Medieval Crown of Aragon* (Chicago: University of Chicago Press, 2016), pp. 16-21.

21. Feliciano, "Muslim Shrouds for Christian Kings?" p. 105.

22. The Metropolitan Museum of Art Inv. 1983.413. This object has been published in David Alexander, Stuart Pyrrh and Will Kwiatkowski, *Islamic Arms and Armor in the Metropolitan Museum of Art* (Metropolitan Museum of Art, 2015), pp. 119-21, cat. No. 43, Jerrilynn D. Dodds, ed., *Al-Andalus: The Art of Islamic Spain* (Metropolitan Museum of Art, 1992), pp. 294-95, no. 65; Valérie Gonzalez, "Les collections d'oeuvres d'art du metaille emaillé hispano-musulman dans les musées hors d'Espagne," *Sharq al-Andalus* 7 (1990): 195-202; Valérie Gonzalez, *Émaux d'al-Andalus et du Maghreb* (Aix-en-Provence: Edisud, 1994), pp. 140-143; Teresa Pérez Higuera, *Objetos e imagenes de al-Andalus* (Barcelona: Lunwerg Editores, 1994), pp. 119-122.

23. Images of Christian and Muslim warriors in the thirteenth-century *Cantigas de Santa María* show most Muslims in turbans and most Christians in helmets, as do the paintings in the Sala de los Reyes of the Alhambra, whereas some wall paintings in the Partal palace of the Alhambra seem to show Nasrid soldiers in gilded helmets. Pérez Higuera, pp. 119-120, 126.

24. Pérez Higuera, p. 119.

25. David Alexander, *Islamic Arms and Armor in the Metropolitan Museum of Art* (New York: Metropolitan Museum of Art, 2015), 120-21.

26. Alvaro Soler, in Dodds, *Al-Andalus,* p. 295, cat. no. 65.

27. Valérie Gonzalez, *Emaux d'al-Andalus et du Maghreb;* Francisco Hernández Sánchez, "Una obra excepcional de la platería castellana bajomedieval con esmaltes nazaríes: el exvoto de don Juan de Zúñiga," *Goya* 355 (2016): 108-25.

28. Joan Molina Figueras, ed., *Bartolomé Bermejo* (Madrid: Museo Nacional del Prado, 2018), pp. 153-164.

29. Molina, *Bartolomé Bermejo,* p. 162.

30. Pérez Higuera, p. 124.

31. Valerie Gonzalez, *Émaux d'al-Andalus et du Maghreb,* p. 117, figure 81. The plaque to which I am referring is the one in the top left of the image.

32. Dodds, *Al-Andalus,* 284-86 (cat. no. 59). I disagree with the reading of these inscriptions as the Nasrid motto and instead see stylized pseudo-inscriptions meant to evoke the Nasrid shield.

33. Cynthia Robinson, "Towers, Birds and Divine Light: The Contested Territory of Nasrid and 'Mudéjar' Ornament," *Medieval Encounters 17* (2011): pp. 27-79, here p. 56.

34. Priscilla E. Muller, *Jewels in Spain, 1500-1800* (New York: Hispanic Society of America, 1972), p. 23.

35. Irigoyen-García, *Moors Dressed as Moors,* p. 13.

36. Ibid., pp. 13-14.

37. Dodds, ed., *Al-Andalus: The Art of Islamic Spain*, no. 73, pp. 302–3; Gonzalez, *Emaux d'al-Andalus et du Maghreb*, pp. 124–25, 129, fig. 90; Marilyn Jenkins-Madina and Manuel Keene, *Islamic Jewelry in The Metropolitan Museum of Art* (New York: The Metropolitan Museum of Art, 1983), no. 52, pp. 92–93.

38. Robinson, "Towers, Birds and Divine Light," pp. 67ff.

39. Natalia Horcajo Palomero, "La sociedad española del siglo XVI y las joyas," in Miguel Cabañas Bravos, et al., eds., *Arte, Poder y Sociedad en la España de los siglos XV a XX* (Madrid: CSIC, 2008), pp. 485-495.

40. See, for example, the earring excavated from tomb 118 at Galera held in the Museo Arqueológico Nacional, Madrid, inv. 28522, as well as inv. nos. 28531 and 28532.

41. Gonzalez, *Émaux d'al-Andalus,* p. 80.

42. See, for example, the treasures of Nasrid/Morisco jewelry found at Charrilla (Jaén), Garrucha (Almería), Loja (Granada), Bentarique (Almería), Mondújar (Granada), Mallorca, Ermita Nueva in Alcalá la Real (Jaén).

43. Ibn al-Khaṭīb. *al-Lamḥa al-Badriyya,* p. 40.

44. Metropolitan Museum of Art, inv. no. 17.190.159 and 17.190.160

45. Harvey, *Muslims in Spain,* p. 327.

46. L.P. Harvey, *Islamic Spain 1250-1500* (University of Chicago Press, 1990), 328

47. The ex voto of Juan de Zúñiga, probably produced in Castile in 1476-77, incorporates Nasrid-style cloisonné enamel plaques around the halo and base of a sculpture of Saint Vincent Ferrer. See Francisco Hernández Sánchez, "Una obra excepcional de la platería castellana bajomedieval con esmaltes nazaríes: el exvoto de don Juan de Zúñiga," *Goya* 355 (2016): 108-125.

48. Manuel Gómez-Moreno, "Joyas Árabes de la Reina Católica," *Al-Andalus* 8: 2 (1943): 473-475.

49. Isabel's body was later moved to the Royal Chapel of Granada by her grandson Charles V.

50. "Titulo de las Ordenanças que los muy Illustres y muy magnificos Señores [de] Granada mandan que le guarden para la buena governacion de su Republica. Las quales mandaron imprimir para que todos las sepan y las guarden." Granada, 1552. 50.clxix v. - 50.clxxvii r. Biblioteca Nacional de España, R/2118.

51. "Titulo de las Ordenanças," 50.clxix v.

52. "Titulo de las Ordenanças," 50.clxx v. - 50.clxxi r.

53. "Titulo de las Ordenanças," 50.clxxii v. - 50.clxxiii r.

54. "Otrosi, mandamos, que de aqui adelante no se puedan hazer, ni hagan en estos nuestros Reynos, ni traer de fuera dellos joyas algunas de oro que tengan relieves, ni esmaltes, ni puntas con perlas, ni piedras, ni joyeles, ni brincos que las lleven, ni que tengan esmaltes, ni relieves, y que solo puedan llevar los joyeles, y brincos una piedra con suspendientes de perlas; aunque permitimos, que las mugeres puedan traer libremente qualesquier hilos, y sartas de ellas." *Libro de las leyes del reyno,* (Madrid: Imprenta de Juan de Ariztia, 1723); 1 Libro septimo, titulo XII, 240.

55. This order resulted in the destruction of 100 Arabic language tombstones in 1574 in Toledo alone. E. Lévi-Provençal, *Inscriptions arabes d'Espagne* (Leiden-Paris, 1931), p. xi.

56. Juan Martínez Ruiz, "Joyas y ropas de moriscos granadinos en un proceso inquisitorial (años 1577-1580)," *Revista de dialectología y tradiciones populares* 43 (1988): 385-395, esp. 387.

57. Martínez, 387.

58. Fuchs, *Exotic Nation*, p. 5.

59. Cited in Benjamin Ehlers, *Between Christians and Moriscos: Juan de Ribera and Religious Reform in Valencia, 1568-1614* (Baltimore: Johns Hopkins University Press, 2006), 130.

60. Damian Fonseca, *Justa expulsión de los moriscos de España* (Rome: Jacomo Mascardo, 1612), p. 273.

61. Chapters X and XI of book five of Fonseca's *Justa expulsión* focused on the harm caused by the Moriscos' expulsion to the Christians left behind. See pp. 322-342.

62. Archivo General de Simancas, Simancas, Estado, legajo 214, letter dated November 30, 1609, n.p., as cited in Mary Elizabeth Perry, *The Handless Maiden: Moriscos and the Politics of Religion in Early Modern Spain* (Princeton: Princeton University Press, 2013), 134. ("... y no se halla un Real que todo lo tienen los moriscos y lo mismo es en todos los lugares que sacan todo el tesoro de ellos.")

63. Pedro Aznar Cardona, *Expulsión justificada de los moriscos españoles y suma de las excellentias Christianas del nuestro Rey Don Felipe* (1612).

64. Aznar, *Expulsión justificada*, 191.

65. *La Ilustración Española y Americana,* year 31, number 46, Madrid, 13 December 1887, discussion of the treasure on pp. 358-359, and illustration on p. 365.

66. *Verhandlungen der achten Versammlung des Verbandes von Museums - Beamten zur Abwehr von Fälschungen und unlauterem Geschäftsgebaren* (Amsterdam: 1905), p. 25. Interestingly, this theory of reuse of Nasrid enamels from a sword in an object of Christian manufacture is also proposed by Francisco Hernández Sánchez in his discussion of the ex voto of Juan de Zúñiga, which is adorned with similar Nasrid-style enamel plaques. See "Una obra excepcional de la platería castellana bajomedieval," 123.

67. Palacio Real de Madrid, Inv. no. 19000003, cat. D. 12. See https://www.patrimonionacional.es/colecciones-reales/real-armeria/celada-de-felipe-i-de-castilla-el-hermoso

68. On this issue, see, in addition to the works by Robinson and Feliciano cited above, Jerrilynn D. Dodds, "Islam, Christianity, and the Problem of Religious Art," in *The Art of Medieval Spain AD 500-1200* (New York: Metropolitan Museumo of Art, 1993), pp. 27-37.

Bibliography

Alexander, David, Stuart Pyrrh, and Will Kwiatkowski. *Islamic Arms and Armor in the Metropolitan Museum of Art*. New York, Metropolitan Museum of Art, 2015.

Aznar Cardona, Pedro. *Expulsión justificada de los moriscos españoles y suma de las excellentias Christianas del nuestro rey Don Felipe*. Huesca: P. Cabarte, 1612.

Balbale, Abigail Krasner. "Political and Religious Authority in the Coinage of Ibn Mardanīsh." In *Mediterráneos: An Interdisciplinary Approach to the Cultures of the Mediterranean Sea*, edited by Sergio Carro Martín, Arturo Echavarren, Esther Fernández Medina, Daniel Riaño Rufílanchas, Katja Šmid, Jesús Téllez Rubio, and David Torollo Sánchez, 303–18. Newcastle upon Tyne: Cambridge Scholars Publishing, 2013.

Cervantes, Miguel de. *Don Quixote*. Leipzig, 1818.

Cervantes, Miguel de. *Don Quixote*. Translated by Edith Grossman. New York: HarperCollins, 2003.

Constable, O. R. *Trade and Traders in Muslim Spain: The Commercial Realignment of the Iberian Peninsula, 900–1500*. Cambridge: Cambridge University Press, 1994.

Dodds, Jerrilynn D., ed. *Al-Andalus: The Art of Islamic Spain*. New York, Metropolitan Museum of Art, 1992.

Dodds, Jerrilynn D. "Islam, Christianity, and the Problem of Religious Art." In *The Art of Medieval Spain AD 500–1200*, 27–37. New York: Metropolitan Museum of Art, 1993.

Douglas, Mary. *Purity and Danger: An Analysis of the Concepts of Pollution and Taboo*. London: Routledge, 1966.

Ehlers, Benjamin. *Between Christians and Moriscos: Juan de Ribera and Religious Reform in Valencia, 1568–1614*. Baltimore: Johns Hopkins University Press, 2006.

Fancy, Hussein. *The Mercenary Mediterranean: Sovereignty, Religion, and Violence in the Medieval Crown of Aragon*. Chicago: University of Chicago Press, 2016.

Feliciano, María Judith. "Muslim Shrouds for Christian Kings? A Reassessment of Andalusi Textiles in Thirteenth-Century Castilian Life and Ritual." In *Under the Influence: Questioning the Comparative in Medieval Castile*, edited by Cynthia Robinson and Leyla Rouhi, 101–31. Leiden: Brill, 2005.

Ferrandis Torres, José. "Tesorillo de dīnāres almorávides hallado en la Alcazaba de Almería." *Al-Andalus* 11 (1946): 389–94.

Fonseca, Damian. *Justa expulsión de los moriscos de España*. Rome: Jacomo Mascardo, 1612.

Fuchs, Barbara. *Exotic Nation: Maurophilia and the Construction of Early Modern Spain*. Philadelphia: University of Pennsylvania Press, 2009.

Gómez-Moreno, Manuel. "Joyas Árabes de la Reina Católica." *Al-Andalus* 8, no. 2 (1943): 473–75.

Gonzalez, Valérie. "Les collections d'oeuvres d'art du metaille emaillé hispano-musulman dans les musées hors d'Espagne." *Sharq al-Andalus* 7 (1990): 195–202.

Gonzalez, Valérie. *Émaux d'al-Andalus et du Maghreb*. Aix-en-Provence: Edisud, 1994.

Harris, A. Katie. *From Muslim to Christian Granada: Inventing a City's Past in Early Modern Spain*. Baltimore: Johns Hopkins University Press, 2009.

Harvey, L. P. *Islamic Spain 1250–1500*. Chicago: University of Chicago Press, 1990.

Harvey, L. P. *Muslims in Spain, 1500–1614*. Chicago: University of Chicago Press, 2005.

Hernández Sánchez, Francisco. "Una obra excepcional de la platería castellana bajomedieval con esmaltes nazaríes: el exvoto de don Juan de Zúñiga." *Goya* 355 (2016): 108–25.

Hoffmeyer, Ada Bruhn de. *Arms and Armour in Spain: A Short Survey*. 2 vols. Madrid: CSIC, 1982.

Horcajo Palomero, Natalia. "La sociedad española del siglo XVI y las joyas." In *Arte, poder y sociedad en la España de los siglos XV a XX*, edited by Miguel Cabañas Bravos, Amelia López-Yarto Elizalde, and Wifredo Rincón García, 485–95. Madrid: CSIC, 2008.

Ibn al-Khaṭīb, *al-Lamḥa al-Badriyya fī al-Dawla al-Naṣriyya*. 2nd ed. Beirut: Dār al-Āfāq al-Jadīdah, 1978.

Ilustración Española y Americana, year 31, no. 46. Madrid, 13 December 1887.

Irigoyen-García, Javier. *Moors Dressed as Moors: Clothing, Social Distinction and Ethnicity in Early Modern Iberia*. Toronto: University of Toronto Press, 2017.

Jenkins-Madina, Marilyn, and Manuel Keene. *Islamic Jewelry in the Metropolitan Museum of Art*. New York: Metropolitan Museum of Art, 1983.

Kassis, Hanna. "The Coinage of Muḥammad ibn Sa'd (Ibn Mardanīsh) of Mursiya: An Attempt at Iberian Islamic Autonomy." In *Problems of Medieval Coinage in the Iberian Area*, vol. 3, edited by Mário Gomes Marques, 209–29. Santarém: Instituto Politécnico, 1988.
Lévi-Provençal, E. *Inscriptions arabes d'Espagne*. Leiden: Brill, 1931.
Libro de las leyes del reyno. Madrid: Imprenta de Juan de Ariztia, 1723.
Martínez Ruiz, Juan. "Joyas y ropas de moriscos granadinos en un proceso inquisitorial (años 1577–1580)." *Revista de dialectología y tradiciones populares* 43 (1988): 385–95.
Medina Gómez, Antonio. *Monedas hispano-musulmanas. Manual de lectura y clasificación*. Toledo: Instituto Provincial de Investigaciones y Estudios Toledanos, 1992.
Molina Figueras, Joan, ed. *Bartolomé Bermejo*. Madrid: Museo Nacional del Prado, 2018.
Muller, Priscilla E. *Jewels in Spain, 1500–1800*. New York: Hispanic Society of America, 1972.
Pérez Higuera, Teresa. *Objetos e imagenes de al-Andalus*. Barcelona: Lunwerg Editores, 1994.
Perry, Mary Elizabeth. *The Handless Maiden: Moriscos and the Politics of Religion in Early Modern Spain*. Princeton: Princeton University Press, 2013.
Robinson, Cynthia. "Towers, Birds and Divine Light: The Contested Territory of Nasrid and 'Mudéjar' Ornament." *Medieval Encounters* 17 (2011): 27–79.
Rodriguez Lorente, Juan José. *Numismática de la Murcia Musulmana*. Madrid: Juan J. Rodriguez Lorente, 1984.
Salicrú i Lluch, Roser. "Mudéjares y cristianos en el comercio con Berbería: quejas sobre favoritismo fiscal y acusaciones de colaboracionismo mudéjar, una reacción cristiana a la defensive." In *De mudéjares a moriscos. Una conversión forzada. VIII Simposio Internacional de Mudejarismo. Teruel, 15–17 de septiembre de 1999*, 1.283–301. 2 vols. Teruel: Centro de Estudios Mudéjares, Instituto de Estudios Turolenses, 2002.
Salicrú i Lluch, Roser. *Documents per a la història de Granada del regnat d'Alfons el Magnànim, 1416–1458*. Barcelona: CSIC Press, 1999.
"Titulo de las Ordenanças que los muy Illustres y muy magnificos Señores [de] Granada mandan que le guarden para la buena governacion de su Republica. Las quales mandaron imprimir para que todos las sepan y las guarden." Granada, 1552.
Todesca, J. J. "What Touches All: Coinage and Monetary Policy in Leon-Castile to 1230." PhD diss., Fordham University, 1996.
Verhandlungen der achten Versammlung des Verbandes von Museums. Beamten zur Abwehr von Fälschungen und unlauterem Geschäftsgebaren. Amsterdam, 1905.
Vives y Escudero, Antonio. *Monedas de las dinastías Arábigo Españolas*. Madrid: Juan R. Cayón, 1893.

In the Shadow of Silver: The Gold of New Granada under the Habsburgs

Kris Lane

Introduction

Amid hundreds of pre-Columbian gold objects in New York's Metropolitan Museum of Art sits the so-called Crown of the Andes, installed in 2015 (fig. 1). It is a large and finely wrought colonial masterwork surrounded by similarly impressive *pre*-colonial masterworks. The average viewer of this resplendent gold-and-emerald artifact may not notice the temporal and cultural disjuncture: an early modern Catholic devotional object set among ancient Indigenous diadems, shamanistic animal deities, and coca dippers.

As a product of colonialism, the Crown of the Andes, over a foot (34 cm) tall, more than a foot (33.4 cm) in diameter, containing nearly five pounds (2.2 kg) of high-karat gold, and encrusted with 850 carats of top-grade emeralds, represents an over-the-top baroque aesthetic. As a statement, it symbolizes the triumph of the conquistadors' faith in the Americas. Still, its imposing size and opulence are perplexing—more so when one learns that it sat upon the head of a sculpted Virgin Mary in the tiny Colombian city of Popayán, an old colonial capital in the Andean foothills southeast of Cali. This was a crown fit for the Vatican Treasury, yet here it lay tucked away for centuries, unpacked, dusted off, and paraded only once each year in a solemn procession.

Another mystery regards how the Crown of the Andes made its way to New York. The story goes as follows. Having fallen on hard times in the early twentieth century, members of Popayán's Immaculate Conception confraternity elected to sell the crown to raise funds to build an old folks' home. Astonishing as this may sound, such were the needs of the day. Although the Colombian government would love nothing more than to "repatriate" the Crown of the Andes, the story of its sale already challenges value assumptions. Was the confraternity's choice stupid or righteous? Details remain elusive. Some say that the crown was coveted by Russia's doomed Czar Nicholas II.[1] Whoever sought it, the Popayán confraternity won a dispensation to sell from Pope Pius X in 1914, and the Crown of the Andes was subsequently displayed at the

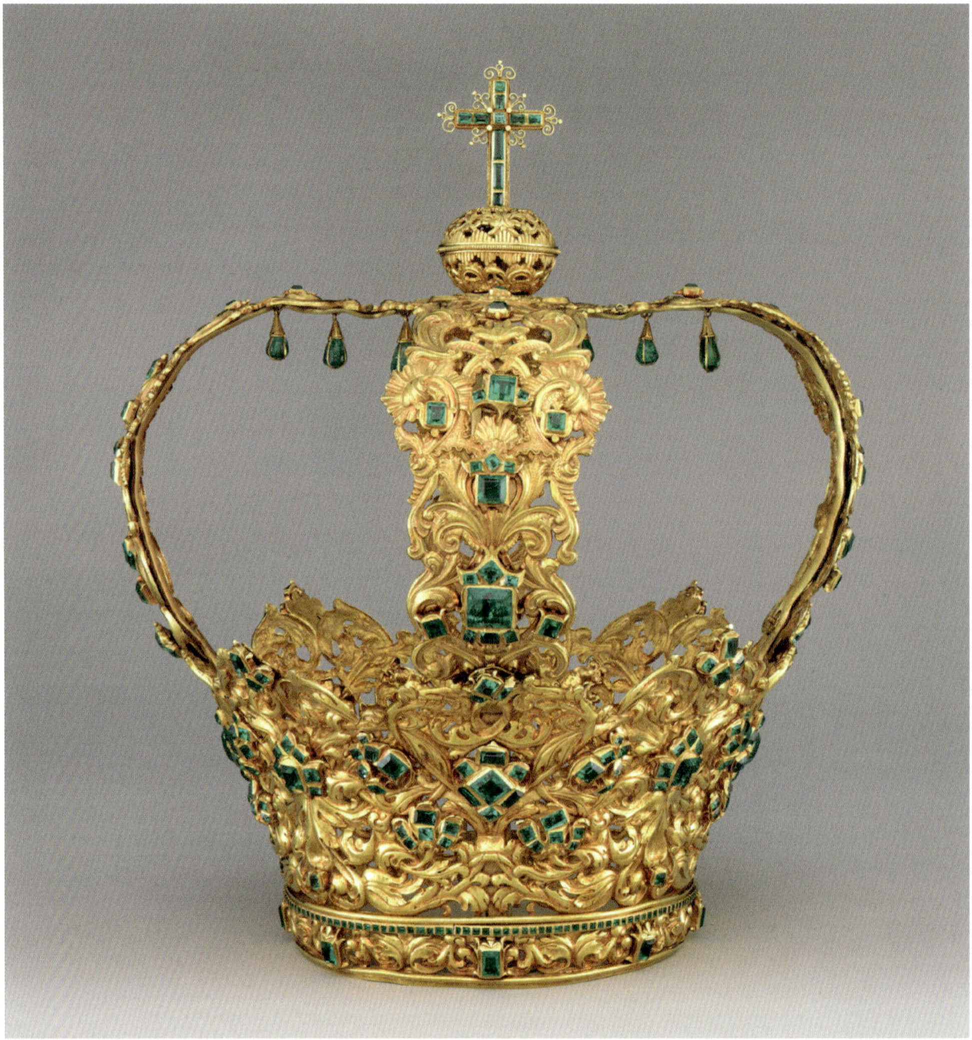

Fig. 1. "The Crown of the Andes," Popayán, Colombia, seventeenth or eighteenth century, 34 × 33.4 cm, 2.2 kg. New York, The Metropolitan Museum of Art, accession no. 2015.437

Panama-Pacific International Exposition in San Francisco in 1915, drawing the attention of the Chicago-based jeweler Warren Piper. World War I intervened. In 1925, a group of European jewelers tendered a bid but failed to produce cash, after which Piper assembled a syndicate to buy the crown in 1928. Cursed by history, the purchase was interrupted by the stock market crash of 1929. Undeterred, by 1935 Piper had managed to raise the funds—some US$ 125,000—by partnering with Oscar Heyman Bros. of New York. To avoid customs officials and thieves, a courier spirited the crown out of Colombia in a top hat. Arriving by steamer in 1936, the Crown of the Andes was handed off at Manhattan's Waldorf Astoria Hotel, the final transfer brokered by a trust.

Meanwhile, back in Colombia, the Archbishop of Popayán, Maximiliano Crespo Rivera, cursed the sellers. The prominent Olano family, trusted heads of the Confraternity of the Immaculate Conception, had kept the dangerously large gold crown in their home for safekeeping since the wars of independence. Devout Catholics ever fearful of anticlerical Liberals, they did not apparently profit from the sale. As originally planned, the Olanos and their confreres simply wanted to build a nursing home to be run by a local charity, the Sisters of the Poor (Hermanitas de los Pobres).

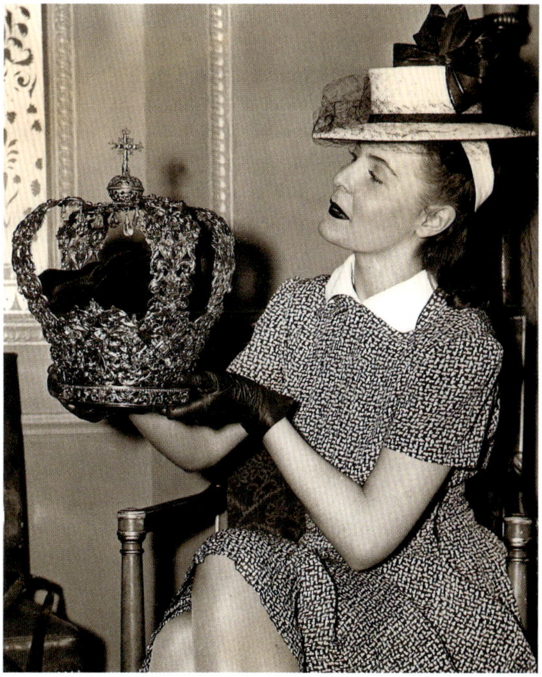

Fig. 2. Model Jane Charlton with the Crown of the Andes, 1939. After reaching New York City in 1936, the crown appeared at numerous fairs and jewelry expositions before World War II

Amid legal wrangling, a representative of the New York trust, which took its cut, transferred interest-bearing notes worth some $US 85,000 to the curia and archbishopric of Popayán. Rather than use the resulting revenue to care for his archdiocese's needy seniors, as the confraternity members had wanted, Archbishop Crespo set about rebuilding the archepiscopal palace on Popayán's main square. The colonial structure had been leveled by a 1906 earthquake and the new, "crown-funded" one would be severely damaged by another massive quake in 1983, possibly indicating the Virgin's displeasure.

After the 1936 expatriation, the Crown of the Andes toured several U.S. and Canadian fairs, museums, and even jewelry stores before disappearing from view at the onset of World War II (fig. 2). There were select appearances in the late 1950s, after which it came up for auction at Sotheby's in 1963, only to end up back in the hands of the New York jeweler Oscar Heyman.[2] The crown disappeared yet again amid concerns that it had been improperly wrested from the Piper interest, a dispute later settled in court. Due to a high reserve price, it failed to sell at a 1995 Christie's auction (Oscar Heyman had died in 1970, leaving the crown to his heirs). But at last, the resplendent, inimitable, and massive gold-and-emerald Crown of the Andes was sold directly to the Metropolitan Museum of Art by Heyman's daughter, Alice, in 2014 for an undisclosed sum. A century had passed since Pope Pius's dispensation, freeing the Virgin's crown from Church control and rendering it a secular object—which is to say, divorcing it from its sacred and social context.

Much has been written about the Crown of the Andes, both true and false, but nothing has been said about the enslaved Africans and forced Indigenous workers who mined the gold and emeralds, or about the colonial lapidaries, often men of African or Indigenous descent, who prepared the stones. Only wild speculation has been offered regarding the goldsmiths who fashioned the crown itself in two parts (a Habsburg base, it is said, with Bourbon arches). And nothing is known of the elite women of Popayán whose deathbed bequests likely supplied the eye-popping emeralds. Most post-1914 observers have helped fetishize the crown by tying it to the fates of those who have obsessed over it or lost it, from czars to stars. It has also been falsely linked to the Incas, Caribbean pirates, and Simón Bolívar.

The Crown of the Andes might seem a perfect fetish, fashioned from some of the world's most fetishized commodities.[3] Yet it is a genuine expression of religious devotion. It is an object of unbridled greed, to be sure, but it is also a priceless emblem of sacrifice, humility, and painstaking workmanship in the penumbra of divine power and grace. In this sense the colonial crown is not unlike the many gold objects that surround it in the Met's pre-Columbian gold collection. Most of these objects are looted grave goods that originally accompanied revered or feared personages to the afterworld: a helmet, a staff, an elaborate nose ornament, a necklace of cast-gold frogs.

For the purposes of this chapter, the fabled Crown of the Andes spurs us to de-fetishize gold in greater New Granada under the Habsburgs by digging into its troubled history. Under the Habsburgs' successors, the Bourbons, New Granada expanded to encompass Venezuela, Panama, and Ecuador, in addition to Colombia. In the eighteenth century, north Andean gold production soared, in direct relation to the expansion of slavery.[4] This chapter backs up and focuses entirely on Colombia and Ecuador, as these were the principal gold-producing regions of Spanish America from conquest to 1700 (see Map 1), the year of Bourbon succession. Like the fabled silver mines of Mexico and Upper Peru (which includes Bolivia and thus Potosí), New Granada's and Quito's gold mines articulated regional as well as global patterns of production and trade. They also articulated the new and complex social world that produced the Crown of the Andes.

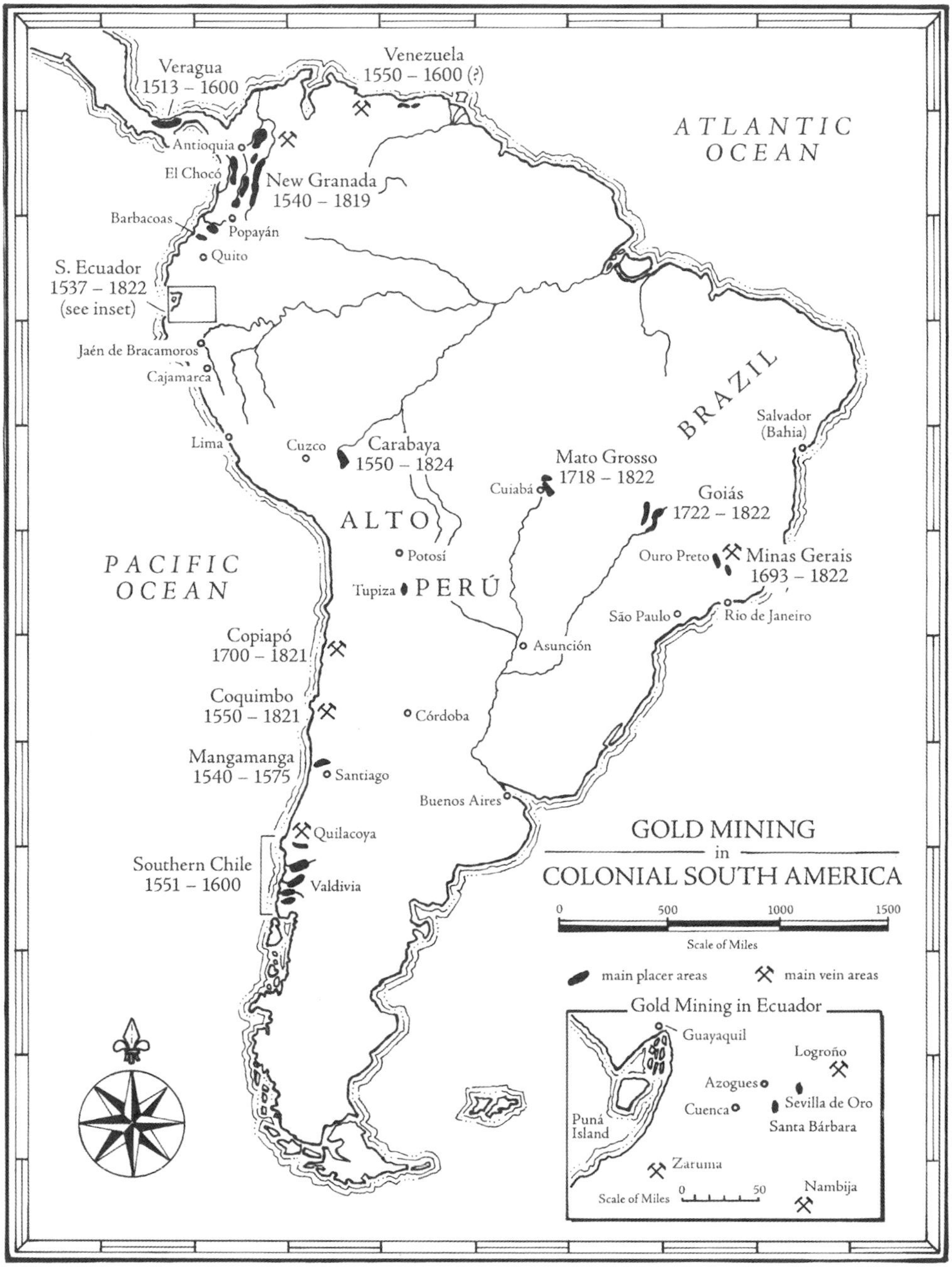

Map 1. Gold mining in colonial South America. By R. Britton after R. C. West

Plunder

On June 3, 1535, the Spanish conquistador Sebastián de Benalcázar (or Belalcázar, as he is known in Colombia) paid about 3,000 pesos in *quintos* (royal fifths) on over 15,000 pesos' worth of *oro bajo y joyas* (gold alloy and jewelry). Thus opened the era of European exploitation of precious metals in Quito. As in Peru just a few years earlier, the first metal treasure to be taxed was entirely comprised of stolen Indigenous artwork, mostly personal and religious objects. Some plundered items merited cursory description prior to destruction. The conquistador Pedro Martín Montanero paid half the value of "a globe and disk of gold said to have been taken from a grave."[5] Since under crown law funerary regalia was treated like war booty and taxed at up to 50 percent, Spanish plunderers learned to melt plundered items and present royal officials with the resulting "scrap" bullion in order to pay only the fifth, or 20 percent (still a high royalty).

Plunder persisted, but mining soon commenced.[6] In these same royal foundry books or *libros de fundición*, the first entry of taxes paid on *oro de minas* (mined gold) in Quito came on March 12, 1537, about two years after the conquest of the highlands. The crown encouraged mining by lowering the gold tax in Quito to 10 percent, the *diezmo*, a concession initially intended to last five years. Similar breaks were granted to miners in other parts of Spanish America, renewed until the mid-seventeenth century, when gold taxes were universally lowered to the *veintavo*, or 5 percent. (The Bourbons would drop it to 3 percent in 1777.)

After leading the conquest of Quito, Belalcázar drove north beyond the Inca frontier to lay claim to Popayán and Cali, before crossing the central Andes to rendezvous with other conquistadors in Bogotá, in the heart of Muisca territory. He joined Niklaus Federmann of Ulm, who had just arrived from Venezuela, and also Gonzalo Jiménez de Quesada, who had climbed up into the Andes from the Caribbean coast via the Magdalena River. Federmann was sponsored by the German Welser family, bankers to Spain's king, the Holy Roman Emperor Charles V. Despite the Welsers' desire for north Andean treasure, Jiménez de Quesada possessed the strongest legal claim to Muisca booty. Not only had Jiménez arrived first, but he also revealed a royal concession signed in Madrid in 1535 that ended (somewhat confusingly) as follows:

> In accordance with the rights and laws of our kingdoms, when our subjects and the captains of our armies happen to capture some prince or lord from the lands where, under our orders, they are at war, the ransom collected from that lord or *cacique*, as well as all his private possessions, belong to us. However, in consideration of the great hardships and difficulties that our subjects endure in the

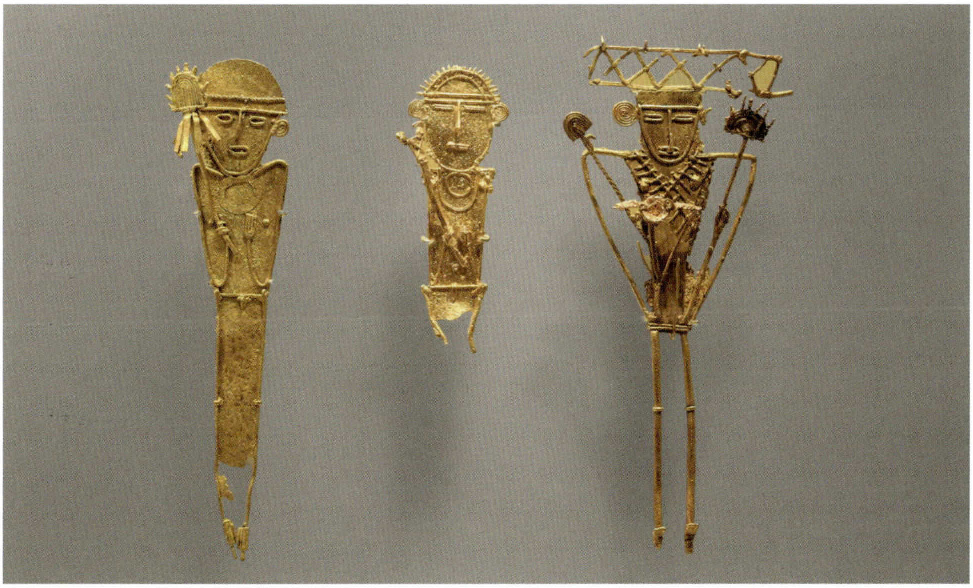

Fig. 3. *Tunjos*, Muisca funerary objects, ca. 1500, gold copper alloy. Largest figure 8.3 cm, Bogotá, Museo de Oro. Muisca goldwork has a whimsical, stick-figure quality, quite unlike the more elaborate pieces found in the hot lowlands of the Upper and Lower Cauca, Colombia

> conquests of the Indies, and in order to reward them for their services and offer them some compensation, we declare and order that should you happen to take some *cacique* or lord captive, then his treasures of gold, silver, precious stones, and pearls that you acquire, either through ransom or in any other manner, that you give us a share of one sixth. The remainder should be divided among the conquistadors, having first paid the royal fifth. In the event that the said *cacique* or principal lord should die in battle, or later through the legal process, that we be given half of his belongings. This payment shall be issued before any of the costs incurred by our royal officials are reimbursed. The other half shall be divided [among the conquistadors], once again after the royal fifth is paid.[7]

The rules of spoil were ambiguous in part because Charles V had just received his portion of the massive ransom of Atahualpa, the Inca emperor throttled by the Pizarro brothers in 1533 after a drumhead trial in Cajamarca, Peru.[8] The Muisca caciques Bogotá and his successor Sagipa soon met a similar end, jailed and tortured as the conquistadors competed for mineral treasure, a mix of grave goods and personal adornments (fig. 3). There was no time to waste. Jiménez de Quesada's men had in fact tortured and killed Sagipa in early 1539, just before Federmann and Belalcázar reached what became known as the

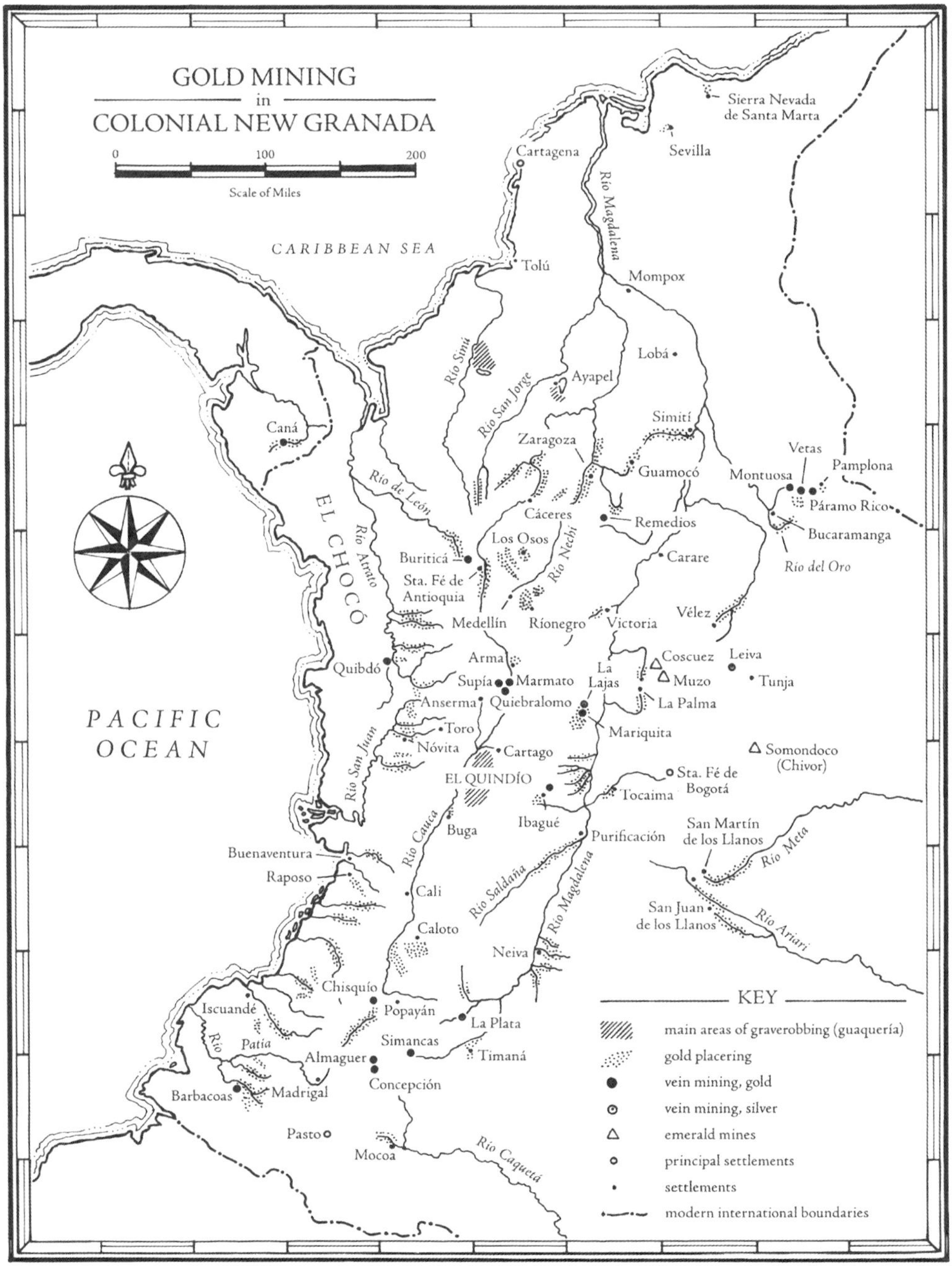

Map 2: Gold mining in colonial New Granada. By R. Britton after R. C. West

Sabana de Bogotá, future site of Colombia's capital. What had happened in Quito (and Cajamarca) would happen again: torture, drumhead trial, execution, plunder.

The Spanish had also been led to the Muisca emerald mines of Somondoco (today Chivor), but their main interest was gold, most of it in the form of ritual objects.[9] According to an official accounting, the booty taken from Sagipa, Bogotá, and neighboring Indigenous lords totaled 191,294 pesos of "fine gold" (*oro fino*), 37,388 pesos in gold alloy (*oro bajo*), and 18,390 pesos in "metal trinkets" (*chafalonía*). The booty was shared out among the conquistadors, along with 1,815 emeralds of varying size and color.[10] As far as we know, no sacred crowns were yet commissioned.

Although ransom, theft, and tomb robbing continued in New Granada throughout the colonial period, as it did in Ecuador and Peru (to say nothing of Mexico and Central America), the triumphant conquerors did not hesitate to leap from plunder to production (Map 2), or rather, to force native Andeans and enslaved Africans to mine gold and emeralds wherever they might be found. This quick transition from theft to mining happened all over the Andes, despite the lure of El Dorado, the persistent belief in a hidden golden kingdom ruled by a "gilded man."[11] We may consider the recurrent El Dorado expeditions that followed conquest foolish, but they were no joke. Belief in the gilt cacique led many Spaniards and thousands of forced Andean porters (plus enslaved Africans and mixed camp followers) to their deaths in the Pacific lowlands, along the upper Amazon, and throughout the Orinoco basin to the end of Habsburg times. Even New Granada's famed conqueror Gonzalo Jiménez de Quesada squandered his stolen Muisca fortune on this chimera, to be followed by the likes of Walter Raleigh.

The Placer Mines of Greater Quito

As the Spanish penetrated the greater Quito region—the north Andean extension of the Inca Empire or Tawantinsuyu—they discovered that the Incas had incorporated pre-existing gold-mining and refining cultures. For example, significant gold was found in the vicinity of Tomebamba, renamed Cuenca by the conquistadors (Map 1, inset). Just north of Cuenca were the highland placer or alluvial mines of Sangurima, near the modern towns of Sigsig and Gualaceo. This was the heartland of the Cañaris, who had resisted the Incas and who also joined the Spanish as allies. The conquerors plundered Cañari graves near Sigsig and Gualaceo, but a few tombs survived to be excavated in the nineteenth and twentieth centuries.[12]

Early foundry records confirm that hundreds of native Andean workers washed placer gold at Santa Bárbara (near Sangurima) soon after conquest. Forced but not enslaved, most were held in so-called *encomienda*, a quasi-feudal "entrustee-ship." In the north Andes, conquerors like Belalcázar and Jiménez de Quesada doled out Indigenous subjects to favored soldiers, "entrusting" (*encomiendo*) them as wards requiring protection and conversion to Christianity in exchange for tribute in goods and labor. In many places, Indigenous tribute requirements were commuted to quotas of gold dust and, in some cases, grave goods.

Quito's earliest *encomenderos* were predictably rapacious. A common dream was that of the *perulero*, to get rich quick in "The Indies" and return to Spain to set up like a gentleman. The Quito district's Santa Bárbara placers were seen as an early means to this end. Abuses suffered by Andean *encomienda* subjects working in these mines (and in nearby Sangurima and Shingata) included forced marches, exhaustion, drowning, sickness, and starvation. Only after over a decade of unbridled exploitation did the town council of Quito (precursor to the *audiencia*, or royal circuit court, established in 1563) see fit to curb abuses. The Quito mining ordinances of 1549 did not seek worker protection for humanity's sake, but rather to slow exhaustion of the labor pool.[13] The rules were spurred by Charles V's New Laws of 1542, drafted at the urging of Bartolomé de Las Casas.

The 1549 Quito mining mandates stated that Indigenous wards should not be moved from hot country to cold, or vice versa, a common stricture in tropical Spanish America's first labor codes. Instead of the previously customary eight months, mine work was to be limited to the six-month period of heavy rains, and hence high-water volume for washing gravels, beginning in August and ending in February. Mine overseers or owners (*mineros*) were to provide Indigenous workers with a sleeping platform (*barbacoa*), a blanket, and a shirt at the beginning of the mining season, and with more bedclothes should they become ill. The *minero* was also to provide each worker with two *almudes* (ca. 12.5 kg or 27.5 lb.) of maize, along with a small supply of capsicum peppers and coca leaves, a swine every fifteen days, and a pouch of salt each month. As outside merchants were already pumping the captives for gold dust, another rule outlawed private truck in maize within ten leagues of the mines.

Indigenous mineworkers tending canals and other water works during the night were to be relieved of daytime duties and allowed to rest. Ordinary work hours were said to stretch from sunup to sunset (always twelve hours at the equator) with some unspecified break for eating and resting. Mine laborers were not to be forced to bear burdens before or after their own mining shift. At the end of their six-month obligation, workers were to be freed for the remaining six months to tend subsistence farms. Pregnant Indigenous women or those who had recently given birth were to be relieved of carrying duties altogether.

The maximum cargo for men and women alike was set at the equivalent of four *almudes* of maize (ca. 25kg or 55 lb.), and no mine owner or overseer was to keep more than two Indigenous women and two boys in personal service. Scale was key in alluvial mining, but no work gang (*cuadrilla*) was to exceed eighty Andeans, including hired peons (*concertados*). Documents suggest that these latter individuals were not free wageworkers but rather laborers rented from other *encomenderos*, a direct violation of the New Laws.

In sum, the 1549 ordinances reveal that, even by law, Andeans held in *encomienda* in Quito's first colonial gold mines were treated much like slaves. They were moved around at their *encomenderos*' will, and they worked incessantly, even at night. Coerced Andeans of both sexes and all ages worked in mines, on farms, and in carrying cargo, and they were rented and otherwise exchanged against their will. It appears that right after the 1549 rules were issued, some 2,165 Andeans taken from twenty-five villages between Quito and Cuenca worked the Santa Bárbara placers. Twenty-odd *encomenderos* benefited from their labors, receiving steady rents in high-karat gold dust.

Such late-coming and loosely enforced controls as the 1549 ordinances did little to slow the destruction of Indigenous communities, and those who did not die in the mines or on the way to them fled to regions where gold deposits were unknown. As Karen Vieira Powers found, migration in response to mine labor abuses in the southern Ecuadorian highlands contributed to Quito's seemingly anomalous demographic curve.[14]

Many minor placers were exploited in the hinterland of Cuenca, and before long durable gold mines were developed in and around Zaruma, in Ecuador's southwest highlands (discussed further below). But the most exciting gold frontier for the Spanish in what became the Audiencia of Quito appeared in the upper Amazon rainforest east of Cuenca and Loja.[15] Aided by highland auxiliaries, conquistadors and merchants advanced this rugged gold frontier, provoking attacks by the Shuar and other forest dwellers that led to near-total Spanish evacuation by around the year 1600. Still, as Linda Newson demonstrated, overall population figures for the southern Ecuadorian region suggest nothing short of a general demographic collapse.[16] As elsewhere in early Spanish America, forced mine labor coupled with so-called virgin soil epidemics devastated

Indigenous communities in nearly every ecological zone, but especially in the warmer and more humid lowlands.

Unfortunately, the *encomienda* survived despite these population crashes; in search of gold, colonists steadily advanced into unconquered lowland regions, mostly at the Audiencia of Quito's margins, where "second sons" revived the semi-feudal institution for at least another century, frequently petitioning the Spanish crown for exemption and extension despite the New Laws. An example of a region in which the *encomienda* survived and was repeatedly revived to support gold-mining operations was the Pasto district, politically part of the Governorship of Popayán, but subject to both the Audiencia and the Bishopric of Quito (Map 2, lower left). As Luis Calero demonstrated, *encomienda* subjects from Pasto's various altitude zones were made to work in gold mines from conquest until the late seventeenth century, in some cases to the point of extinction. Of the three major ethnic groups in the district, known loosely as Pastos, Quillacingas, and Abades, the last appear to have suffered most in the mines during the sixteenth-century boom. In the three decades between 1558 and 1590, the number of Abad tributaries dropped from 2,772 to 357.[17]

Demographic catastrophe notwithstanding, several thousand Andeans held in *encomienda* were drawn from these three groups annually to work in the placer mines of the Sibundoy Valley and the vein mines of Almaguer, some as tributary "gold specialists" (*curicamayos*) and others as *mita* laborers allotted by crown officials. The *mita*, as will be seen later in this chapter, was another means to force Indigenous workers into the gold mines. Furthermore, though *encomienda* abuses in the hot Mocoa lowlands to the east of Pasto led to violent uprisings similar to those experienced in Ecuador's Amazonian mines, the *encomienda* was revived by Pasto's elites in the seventeenth century, during the conquest of the gold-rich Pacific lowlands of Barbacoas to the west. As will be seen, these were among the north Andes' richest gold placers.

The Placer Mines of New Granada

By comparison with the geographically compact Quito district, gold mining proved more sustainable in New Granada's extensive intermontane valleys, far away to the north (Map 2). Beyond the Inca border at Rumichaca lay a territory much richer in gold than Tomebamba or any other part of Tawantinsuyu (including the famed placer mines of Carabaya, in eastern Peru). It took great effort to extract it, but gold was everywhere. As in the Muisca highlands and other parts north, early Spanish invaders demanded to be led to grave goods before turning to mines. The grave mounds of the Quindío region north of

Cali and those of the middle Sinú River southwest of Cartagena were famous for their golden plunder (source of many of the Metropolitan Museum of Art's finest pieces). As in the greater Quito region, mines soon followed.

Placer gold mining was fairly straightforward thanks to the nature of the metal. At almost any time of year, one could pan a bit of gold dust from streams using gravity and water, a labor-intensive and skilled process but not a terribly complex one. Larger placer mines were by contrast seasonal, requiring more effort and investment in ground sluices, canals, dams, aqueducts, and other devices and earthworks to wash gravels and sands more efficiently. Even so, all work ended with concentration in the gold pan or *batea*. At times miners used mercury to separate fine gold-dust particles from black sand and other dense detritus, but this could also be done with plant resins or simply great patience.

Gold deposits of all sorts and grades peppered the extensive Cauca River drainage, starting near Popayán in the south and ending near the town of Mompóx (on the Magdalena River) in the north. Among the earliest mines to be exploited by native Andeans held in *encomienda* were those near Cartago (today Pereira), Anserma, Quiebralomo, and Arma, near modern Colombia's famous Coffee Belt. Less-concentrated placers were discovered (or, rather, revealed to the Spanish) in the mountains north and east of Medellín on the margins of the Antioquia Batholith. Low-karat gold is still mined in the cool heights of Los Osos and Rionegro.

As seen in the highlands of southern Ecuador, *encomenderos* abused Indigenous gold miners all over New Granada. A 1550 denunciation paints a portrait of cruelty meted out to the cacique Bosa and his subjects around the village of Fontibón, near Bogotá.[18] Amid proclamation of the New Laws, *encomenderos* were said to be torturing caciques and others to make them dig for gold, partly in tombs and partly in mines. The 1550 document describes widespread enslavement of native Andeans to further spite the New Laws. According to witnesses, Bosa was chained to two enslaved Africans and later tortured and killed for not yielding enough gold.

Another extreme abuse case from 1559 regards an *encomendero* who shows up in one record only as "Rodríguez Juárez." Crown officials jailed the rogue conquistador on charges of burning native Andeans alive in their dwellings in the Sierra Nevada de Santa Marta, not far from the Caribbean coast, while searching for gold. Rodríguez also allegedly fed captured Indigenous men to dogs, ordered soldiers to rape women, especially virgins, and had them impale men on stakes. Survivors were forced to mine gold in 1557 near Pamplona on the Río del Oro (Map 2, upper right). This was part of a larger district, with earlier

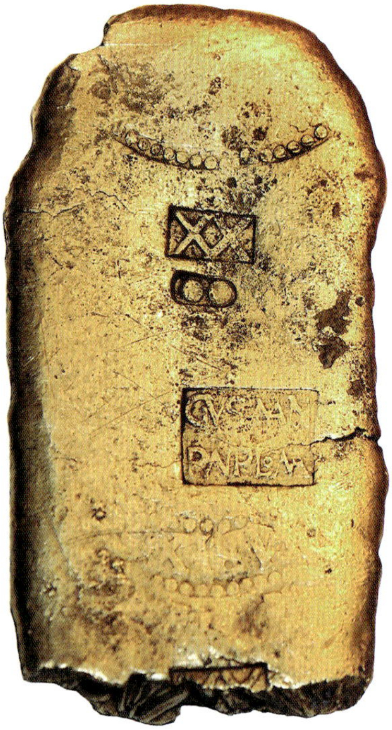

Fig. 4. Gold bar tip from Pamplona mines stamped 20 karats, 2 grains, ca. 1620. Daniel Frank Sedwick LLC, Auction #11, lot 206. This portion of a gold bar would have circulated as quasi-currency in New Granada, ultimately shipped abroad for foreign exchange. Merchants would determine its value by weight plus purity, here 20 karats, 2 grains, against the royal standard for coin metal: 22.5 karats. According to the stamp, the bar was founded and taxed in Pamplona's royal smeltery, presumably overseen by an assayer named Gusmán. It survives thanks only to shipwreck

placer mines exploited at nearby San Gil; Pamplona gold could be as high as 20-karat (83.33 percent) purity or more (fig. 4). Following Rodríguez's arrest, his goods were confiscated, including thirty-five *almocafres* (a hoe-like mining tool), five crowbars, six mattocks, and an enslaved African named Juan Zape who served as overseer for a team of Indigenous (Batagua and Cathagua) gold panners (such blending of Indigenous and African mineworkers was first developed on Hispaniola). Prosecuted under the New Laws, the *encomendero* was sentenced by Bogotá's circuit court to be drawn and quartered. No such punishment took place. Rodríguez escaped, passing through Pamplona on his way to Venezuela.[19]

Another site of chronic Indigenous abuse was Mariquita, on the middle Magdalena River (Map 2, near center), where food shortages were said to have been common. A 1559 general inspection or *visita* revealed that several Indigenous groups held in *encomienda* were forced to provide food for their own sustenance, as well as for their *encomenderos* and for the larger colonial market.[20] The inspection record (though long) is incomplete, and what is most striking about it is how little is said of gold, the region's mainstay at this time. Suspiciously, all of Mariquita's *encomenderos* were said to be strictly abiding by the New Laws. We know from other sources that the placers around Mariquita were mined heavily after 1551, and substantial "oro de Mariquita" shows up regularly in Bogotá treasury records. The *encomienda* killed thousands of Indigenous miners, virtually wiping out entire linguistic groups such as the Guali here along the middle Magdalena. Enslaved Africans helped shoulder the burden, and they would likely have replaced Indigenous workers entirely were it not for the discovery ca. 1580 of lode deposits and substantial silver. As described further below, Spanish settlers and officials demanded a Potosí-like *mita* draft to pull highland Indigenous workers from the more populous Sabana de Bogotá into the hot lowlands around Mariquita.[21] Thousands more would die.

Unlike in most of Peru and Greater Mexico, the *encomienda* persisted in New Granada and Quito long after the 1542 New Laws, frequently tied to placer gold mining. As an institution it was exhaustive, which is to say genocidal. In part for this reason it kept replicating itself at the outer edge of empire, moving along like a slow fire. The Dominican firebrand Bartolomé de Las Casas had goaded Charles V to curb the *encomienda*, in large part because of gold-mining abuses, but Charles's Habsburg heirs, beginning with Philip II (r. 1556–98), proved morally flexible when offered gold. They compromised with local elites, allowing new generations of frontier settlers to win the concession of native tributaries in exchange for expanding the realm and extracting ever more mineral wealth.

In geologically complex New Granada, it seemed there was always more mineral wealth to be had. Near where the Cauca River meets the Magdalena lay the placer mines of Cáceres (Map 2, upper middle), exploited by the ancient Sinú cultures of Colombia's north coastal plain. Many of these swampy lower Cauca sites were difficult to reach, and transport costs soared. A 1590 request for permission to bring supplies to the Cáceres diggings by poling upriver noted that in the mines salt cost seven times what it did downstream near the Cauca–Magdalena confluence. Worse, prospectors were killing and eating their precious mules on the way to the goldfields for lack of food.[22]

Richer still were the mines of Zaragoza, not far to the east of Cáceres on the Nechí River, a Cauca tributary. Located in the hot lowlands and within striking distance of Cartagena de Indias, the Zaragoza mines were soon populated by enslaved Africans. An old pirate fighter calling himself Captain Martín Camacho claimed he had brought ninety "slave mariners" and three boats from Panama's Chagres River to ascend the Cauca and Nechí, establishing a supply network stretching all the way to the Caribbean coast. Upriver from the Zaragoza diggings were the still more remote mines of Remedios and Guamocó (described in further detail below).[23]

Smaller placers were exploited far away to the south, on the upper Magdalena River near Timaná and Neiva, and also along the course of the Saldaña, a Magdalena tributary (Map 2, bottom center). Other short-lived washings sprouted in the hills around Ibagué, southwest of Bogotá, some of them overrun by Indigenous rebels, including the famous Paez and Pijao of the Central Cordillera. Paez and Pijao resistance was in no small part the result of their refusal to mine gold and silver for Popayán elites and other would-be conquerors. Survivors of Spanish punitive raids did not escape this fate. After 1600, conquered and resettled Pijaos reduced to *encomienda* status joined neighboring Coyaimas and Natagaimas near Ibagué to pay tribute in gold dust panned from the Saldaña River.[24]

Placer gold mining continued all around the edges of New Granada's extensive and deep intermontane valleys—the greater Cauca and Madgalena basins—in many places (like Saldaña, and even Pamplona) petering out in the last years of Habsburg rule as easy diggings and Indigenous workers grew scarce. Some highland settlers made forays into the upper Amazon and Orinoco drainages in search of gold and *encomienda* subjects, but few of these attempted conquests lasted, or yielded profit. Other settlers turned to Colombia's last and richest gold-mining frontier: the Pacific lowlands.

The Pacific Lowlands

By most accounts, the north Andes' richest placer mining district abutted the Pacific Ocean, an ecological zone geographers call the Greater Chocó (Map 2, left side). Renowned for unmatched biodiversity thanks to Colombia's Western Cordillera, the warm El Niño current, and the phenomenon of inter-tropical convergence, the Greater Chocó stretches north to eastern Panama from Esmeraldas, Ecuador. The region's many and diverse Indigenous peoples remained unconquered at the turn of the seventeenth century, prompting highland settlers to seek *encomiendas* and gold yet again, a continuation of the conquest cycle. Gold-rich sub-districts included Raposo, west of Cali, and greater Barbacoas, a zone encompassing several Pacific coast river valleys south of Buenaventura (port of Cali) all the way to Tumaco (port of Pasto). *Barbacoa* was a Caribbean term for stilts, grills, and elevated bedframes—incorporated into English as "barbecue." Here in Colombia's Pacific lowlands, "Las Barbacoas" referred to houses built on wooden pilons to avoid flooding and to the people inhabiting them (fig. 5).

Most rivers flowing to the Pacific from Colombia's Western Cordillera have short courses, but they are voluminous and swift since they drain the planet's wettest rainforest. Tidal flux on this stretch of coast is also high, requiring estuarine inhabitants to seek humps of high ground, build on stilts, or retreat as far as 100 km upriver. Catastrophic tsunamis have occurred in historic times, making ports like Tumaco and Buenaventura vulnerable. Substantial placer gold is

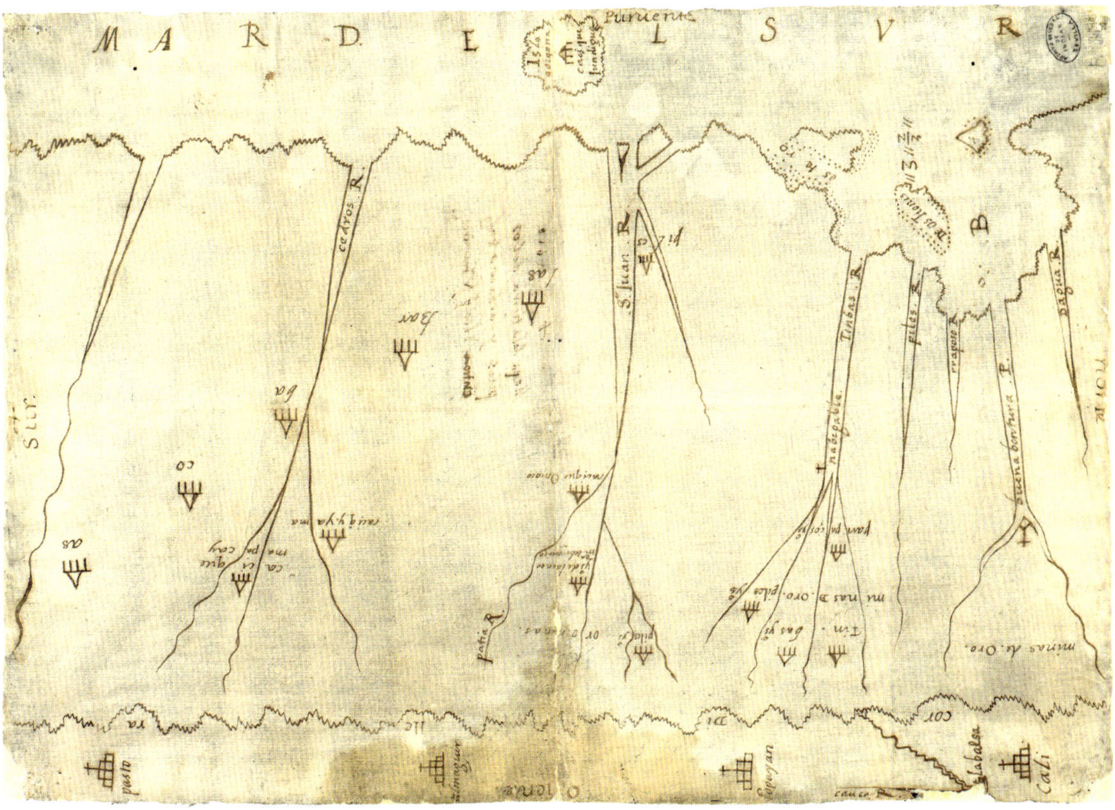

Fig. 5. The Province of Las Barbacoas, ca. 1610. Seville, Archivo General de Indias, Mapas y Planos Panamá 30. Mining camps (*minas de oro*) are located upriver near Indigenous villages, represented by triangles on stilts, the namesake *barbacoas*. Named Indigenous groups include the Timbas, Piles, and several Barbacoan bands under various caciques. On the left is Colombia's Western Cordillera, with a church-like symbol indicating the highland towns of Cali, Popayán, Almaguer (itself a gold-mining town), and Pasto. The port of Buenaventura is labeled with a small cross to the right of Cali. Gorgona Island is at center right, just off the Pacific coast

found midway along most of the greater Barbacoas region's river courses. Select deposits are located higher up, in the densest jungles.

The Barbacoas district was home to several dozen Indigenous peoples, including sub-groups such as the Sindagua rebels who violently challenged Spanish colonists throughout the 1630s. Modern linguists refer to Barbacoan languages, including that of the Chachi of northwest Ecuador, whose territory also included gold-bearing rivers. The colonial provinces of Barbacoas and Esmeraldas straddled the territory formerly inhabited by the La Tolita-Tumaco peoples, who flourished between ca. 350 BCE and 350 CE. They have become famous for fashioning items from welded platinum, but they also produced technically sophisticated filigree goldwork.[25] The province of Esmeraldas, despite its name, did not produce emeralds. They were traded into the region from northern New Granada.

The Spanish conquest of Colombia's Pacific lowlands began almost a century after highland conquest, enabled by the resilient *encomienda* system. Second (or third) sons from Cali, Popayán, and Pasto, as well as some strivers from the northern capital of Santa Fe de Antioquia (Map 2, center left) and later Medellín, vied for their share of lowland people and plunder. The only reason to seek an *encomienda* along Colombia's Pacific coast, aside from the status it conferred, was to collect tribute in gold.[26] Given the permanent wetness of the region, most highland descendants of Spaniards did not wish to settle permanently in the Pacific lowlands. An exception was the town of Barbacoas.

The *encomenderos* of Barbacoas, a district subject to Popayán (and, by extension, Quito), managed to carve out a small village in the jungle along the Telembí River by about 1615, dubbed Santa María del Puerto (today Barbacoas, Nariño: see Map 2, lower left, and fig. 6). Hard-won *encomiendas* provided the bridge to mining fortunes. Though tributary numbers were already much reduced, several Barbacoas *encomienda* titles were proudly conferred upon heirs at the close of the Habsburg era in 1700. For comparison, the several dozen *encomenderos* of the northern Chocó were slower to consolidate their gains. *Encomenderos* typically lived far from their Indigenous charges, including in the city of Popayán itself. Even so, they clung to their semi-feudal titles, passing *encomiendas* to collateral kin. As will be seen in other instances below, *encomienda* charges here and elsewhere in Colombia were made to supply food, wooden gold pans, canoes, and other necessities to an increasingly enslaved African workforce in the gold mines.

North of greater Barbacoas lay the province of Raposo, encompassing several gold-bearing rivers flowing into the Pacific from the vicinity of Cali. Climatically and geologically this region differs little from Barbacoas, although it is distinct from the more northerly Chocó, which is framed by mountains east and west and links up to the Atlantic via the Atrato River. The *encomendero* elite of Cali extracted gold from their conquered lowland Indigenous subjects beginning in the 1610s and 1620s, and some participated in the conquests of Barbacoas and the more northerly Chocó.[27] They also struggled to maintain a viable port at Buenaventura, greater Popayán's best outlet to the sea and a means to import foreign goods, including Asian textiles.

The core of the modern Department of Chocó centers on the Atrato River, which flows north to the Caribbean near the Panama border, plus the upper San Juan, which flows south and west into the Pacific not far north of Buenaventura.

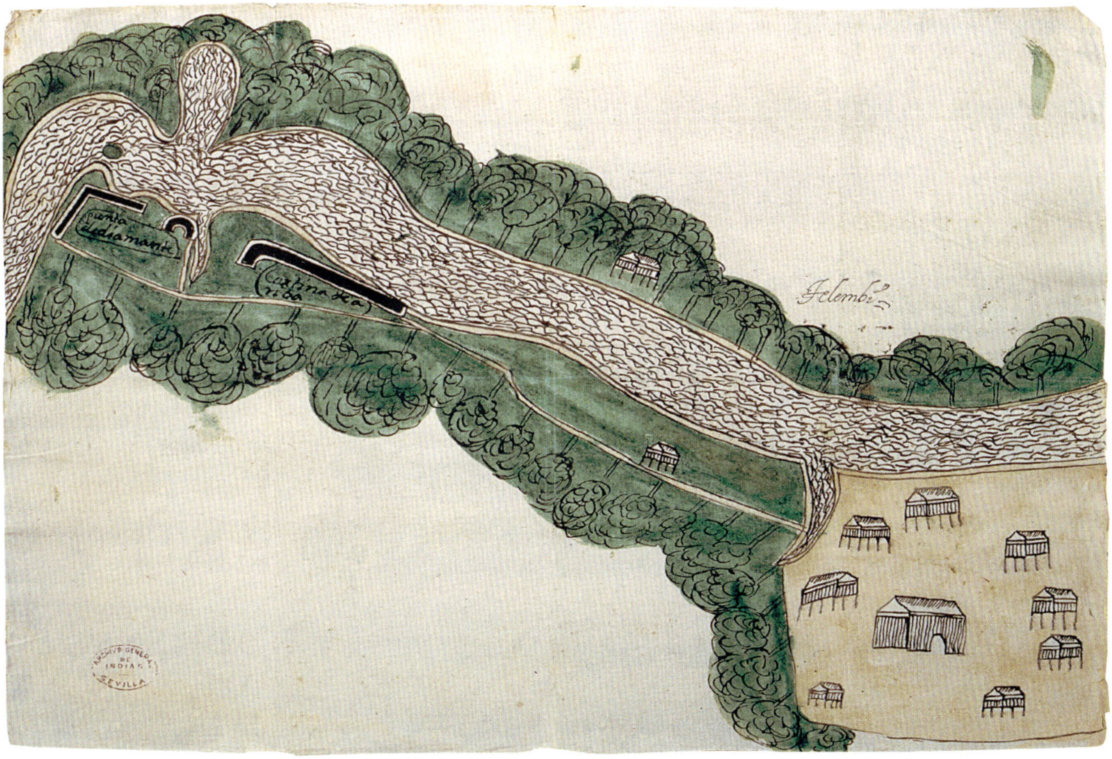

Fig. 6. Telembí River gold camp, Barbacoas, ca. 1691. Seville, Archivo General de Indias, Mapas y Planos Panamá 246. This map seems to depict a canal just below the miners' village to provide water for excavation of gold diggings downstream. Curiously, the watercolor was submitted to Spanish crown authorities as part of a report on pirates, who swarmed the Pacific coast of South America in the 1680s and early 1690s. The author of the report, a local mine owner (*encomendero*) and official named Bartolomé Estupiñán y Flores, turned the gold diggings into defensive ramparts with names like "Upper Curtain," proof that he was doing his best to defend the realm and thus deserving of royal favor. He was throttled in 1699 for tax evasion

Like the placers of greater Barbacoas and Raposo, the Chocó placers proved long-lasting because ancient gold-bearing rivers were crosscut by more recent streams. Colonial placer mining thus required considerable stream diversion, a laborious task that in the eighteenth century occupied thousands of enslaved African laborers. First, though, came *encomiendas* made up of Indigenous peoples like the Chocóes, Noanamáes, and Tootumes.[28] Placer gold mining was the only means to foreign exchange in such an isolated place, and as in Barbacoas even subsistence agriculture was made difficult due to high rainfall throughout most of the year. There was some hope for a Chocó transport corridor, even an interoceanic canal, as the watershed or continental divide between the Atrato and San Juan rivers is narrow and low.[29]

It was here that a strange metal was first discovered, or first made known to Europeans. It so happened that New Granada's most concentrated alluvial platinum deposits were clustered along the smaller tributaries of the upper San Juan River near the continental divide, although fine-grained platinum appears in many of the Greater Chocó's rivers as far south as Esmeraldas.[30] Platinum is next to gold in the periodic table of elements, and it does not easily oxidize, making it hard to separate from gold in a pan except by color. There are notable differences between the metals, however. For example, platinum melts at a much higher temperature than gold (1,774 °C versus 1,064 °C), and platinum-alloy grains found in lowland Colombia tend to be quite hard thanks to a slight iron content. All this meant that platinum—or "platina," as the raw substance found in the gold pan was called—created headaches for merchants and crown officials. For example, one could "seed" a gold ingot with platinum grains and only on cutting it open could one discover the ruse, since the metals shared such a similar specific gravity. Separating platinum from gold after it was welded into a solid bar was expensive work, and mint machinery could be damaged by platinum-rich ingots. In short, platinum was an annoyance rather than a precious metal in the colonial era. Some believed it to be unripe gold, best left in the ground.

After 1700, Chocó platinum was ordered to be publicly and ritually discarded, and traffic in it was strictly forbidden. Grains of the silvery metal were nevertheless passed off to unsuspecting foreigners, including English and Dutch contraband traders, prompting scientists in London and Leiden to learn more about it. Eventually touted as "the eighth metal," platinum became a scientific cause célèbre, convincing the King of Spain to place a premium on its collection, so that it might be studied more widely. By the end of the eighteenth century, the metal was fused by oxygen torch and also worked into fine art objects via new powder metallurgy techniques. As in the case of the Crown of the Andes, what is generally forgotten is that enslaved Africans located and extracted nearly all the platinum collected in New Granada prior to 1850. But platinum's scientific "discovery" is a Bourbon-era story. Was there a Habsburg prequel?

The absence of trusted coin in Habsburg New Granada and greater Quito made space for various cheats. The Audiencia of Quito was struck with a minor scandal in the early seventeenth century when a substance known as "John White" (*juan blanco*) appeared mixed with gold dust in Cali and Popayán.[31] Typically some form of fool's gold or pyrite, *juan blanco* was allegedly burned off in assay. Angry merchants and crown officials blamed wily Indigenous traders for debasing the gold-dust money supply with this unknown material,

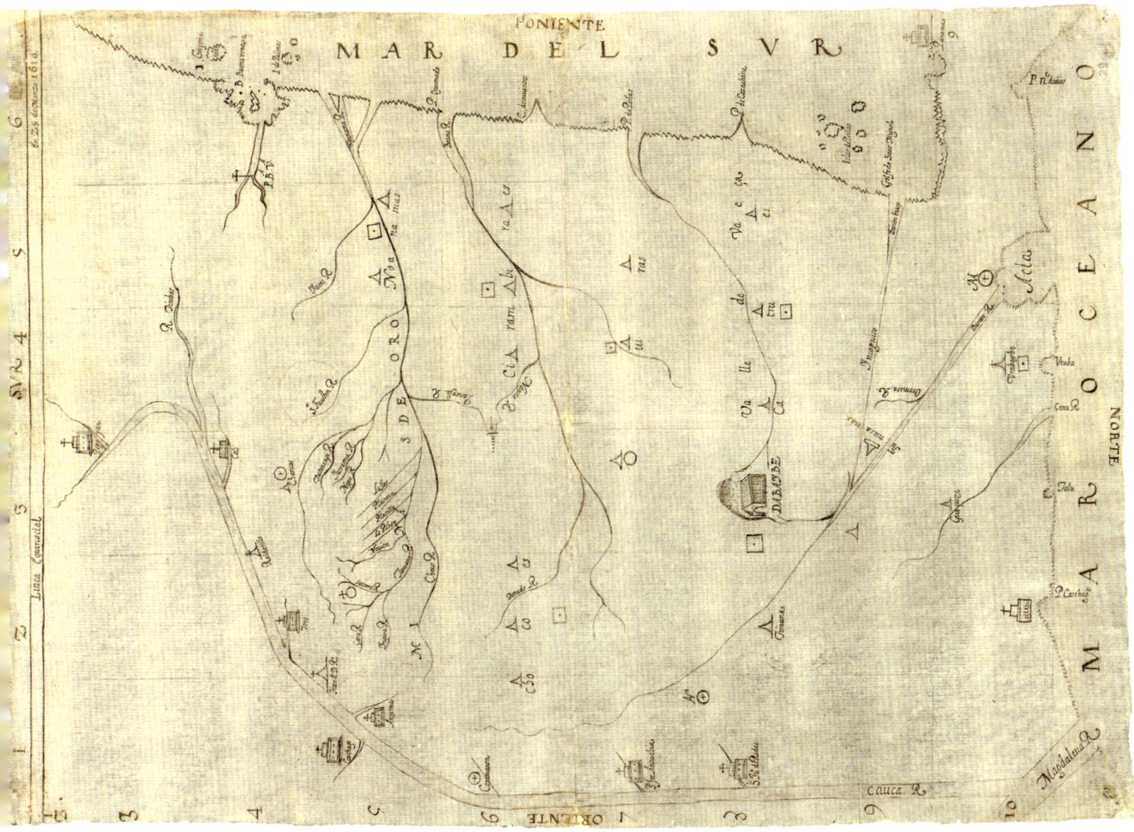

Fig. 7. Detail of Nóvita district, Colombian Chocó, ca. 1610. Seville, Archivo General de Indias, Mapas y Planos Panamá 29. This map matches the one of greater Barbacoas (Fig. 5), taking us north all the way to the Caribbean coast. It is more schematic and less accurate than the Barbacoas map, and reveals that the author knew nothing about the course of the Atrato River, for example. What is curious is the high level of detail along the course of the upper San Juan River, also not clearly understood and variously labeled. Downriver were the fearsome Noanamáes. This was a map of preliminary reconnaissance, focused on the search for gold and prospective *encomienda* conquests from the perspective of highland towns such as Cartago and Santa Fe de Antioquia

but there is no reason to believe that Spanish traders were innocent.

It could be that some of what circulated under the name *juan blanco* in the early seventeenth century was indeed Pacific lowlands platinum. I have not found clear evidence of this, but a ca. 1610 map of the central Chocó now housed in the Archive of the Indies offers tantalizing clues (fig. 7). Near where the mining town of Nóvita would be, the map depicts three small, parallel rivers: "La Plata," "La Platilla," and "La Platona."[32] There is no river called "La Platina," but the "silvery trio" comes awfully close: "Silver," "Little Silver," and "Big Silver," possibly referring to a Goldilocks array of platinum grain sizes.

This was a zone of placer mines containing no silver whatsoever; the only thing similar to "plata" here was "platina."

Placer Mining and African Slavery in Greater Quito and New Granada

In 1592, Francisco de Auncibay, a high court judge in Quito with long experience in New Granada, wrote a proposal to King Philip II. He called it: *Discourse on the blacks which it would be convenient to transport to the Governorship of Popayán, to the cities of Cali, Popayán, Almaguer, and Pasto, where there is need of up to 2,000 blacks, 1,200 males and 800 females, [all] older than seventeen, although some ought to be [about] forty, because for this colonization it is important that some be of an age the others respect.*[33] The elaborate proposal, directly inspired by Thomas More's *Utopia*, started with a beguiling description of the large and biodiverse district of Popayán, emphasizing its extensive gold deposits and generally sparse—and allegedly cannibalistic—Indigenous population. The idea, said Auncibay, was to create a chain of Black mining towns or *pueblos de negros mineros* for the good of the realm (fig. 8).

Periodically bankrupted by foreign wars, Philip II ignored this and several other such proposals, but within a few decades of Auncibay's petition the demography of Popayán's many gold mines began to resemble what the Quito judge had proposed. By about 1610, enslaved African gold miners of all ages and both sexes were the economic engines of Popayán, as they were by this time in much of lowland New Granada. The market effectively accomplished what the king did not, yet enslaved Africans were not passive victims. As the mines grew and workers became more self-sufficient, the number of runaway communities or *palenques* also soared.

Slavery overlapped with the Indigenous *encomienda*, enabling knowledge transfer and occasional alliances. Already in 1572, a description of the New Kingdom of Granada noted that "Blacks" worked alongside "Indians who go of their own free will" in the gold mines of Mariquita and Ibagué, whereas enslaved African workers in the emerald mines of Muzo still labored alongside native wards held in *encomienda*.[34] Hinting at troubles to come, a Spanish petitioner in 1575 claimed service in capturing "rebellious" slaves (*negros alzados*) in the mountains around Mariquita. Afro-New Granadan subcultures were already forming left, right, and center. As evidence, enslaved men and women with specialized herbal knowledge got swept up in a long poisoning case in Mariquita from 1583.[35]

In an early dispute from the gold washings of Río del Oro, near modern

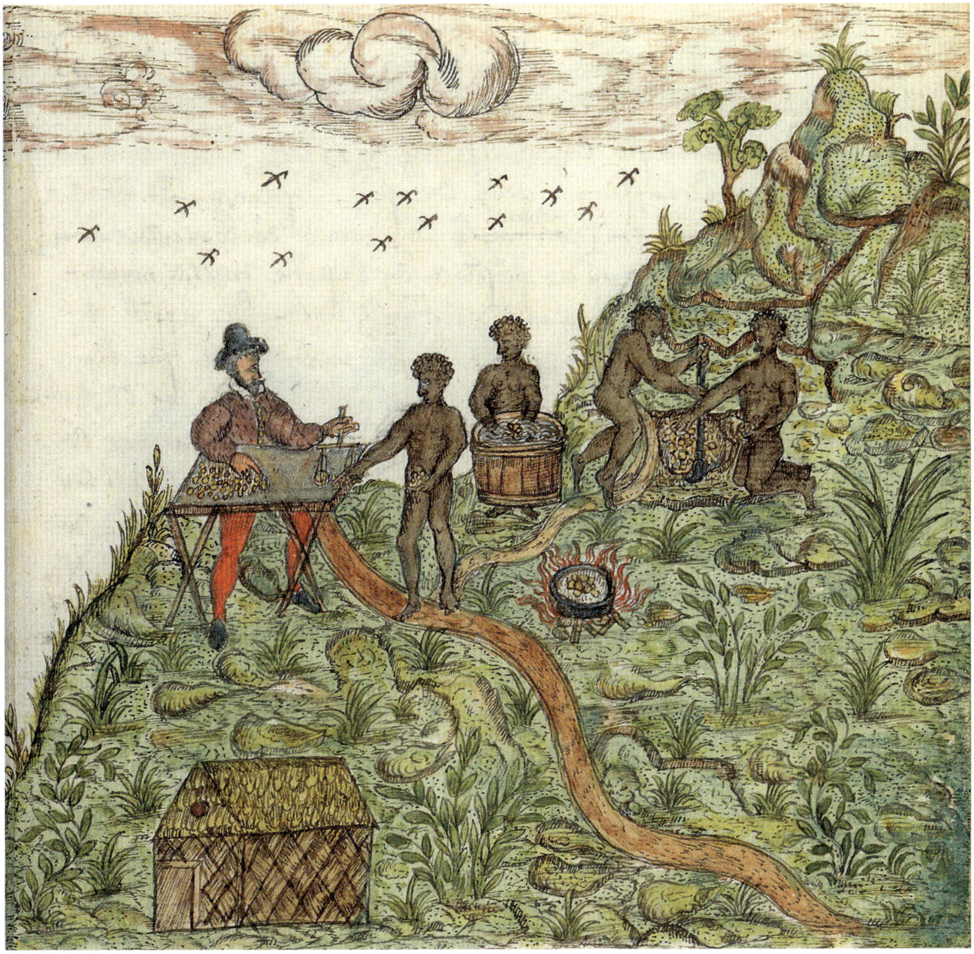

Fig. 8. Enslaved African gold panners, ca. 1590. New York, The Morgan Library & Museum, Drake Manuscript, Ma 3900, fols. 99v–100r. The anonymous French author of the so-called Drake Manuscript seems to have witnessed Spanish-run placer gold mines near Veragua, Panama. In this image, enslaved (and naked) African men excavate gravels with the hoe-like *almocafre*, scooping them into a wooden gold pan or *batea*. Another enslaved man washes paydirt in the *batea* over a water barrel, and another hands off the gold collected to a Spanish overseer, who weighs it on a folding table. A crucible bearing gold sits on a small fire, and the out-of-scale structure at lower left is apparently the dwelling of either the enslaved men or their overseer, or both

Bucaramanga, a Spanish enslaver challenged native Andean villagers. In 1564, Juan Peronegro claimed before the *audiencia* or high court in Bogotá that his enslaved African *cuadrilla* was within the law in constructing a special canal "the length of a crossbow shot" to reach gold deposits. Indigenous inhabitants of the village of Butaregua disagreed, arguing that this project was interfering with crop irrigation. It appears that the courts favored extraction over agriculture, siding with the mine owner.

Peronegro was not alone in employing enslaved Africans in canal building for gold placers at Río del Oro. Another, similar dispute arose in 1566 between two Spaniards, although the case's outcome is also uncertain. The high court's generally pro-mining stance was affirmed around 1610, when *audiencia* judges pushed for a return to Indigenous draft labor when the nearby lode mines of Pamplona faltered. Yet, as in the case of Mariquita, the mines' decadence could not be easily reversed; the "labor clock" could not be turned back to early post-conquest times when "Indians" were relatively plentiful and Africans scarce. Mineworkers had grown mixed by the time a crown investigator visited Pamplona in 1627; several laborers were referred to as *zambos* or *mulatos*, even though they were listed as *indios* on a draft roll.[36]

The lode mines of Buriticá near Santa Fe de Antioquia (Map 2, upper left) may have been the earliest to employ large numbers of enslaved Africans alongside Indigenous workers held in *encomienda*. It was said to have 300 enslaved African miners and about 1,500 native Andean laborers in 1583. The Buriticá mines fell on hard times around the turn of the seventeenth century, but small teams of enslaved men and women were still mining there in the 1620s. By the 1680s, abandonment spurred a controversial transfer of mining specialists and enslaved laborers from distant Pamplona.[37]

One of the first recorded slave rebellions or mass escapes occurred sometime around 1570 in the mines of Anserma, in the lush hills of the middle Cauca (Map 2, center left). A Spaniard who claimed he helped capture several fugitives said that the Africans working the gold mines of Quiebralomo and Mapurá rose up and fled over the mountains toward the Chocó. The documents provide minimal details, but several maroon leaders were allegedly caught on the trail waiting for other escapees.[38]

Down the Cauca River at Cáceres, Spanish prospectors embraced African slavery, with some 300 captive miners reported working in 1608. As hinted already, along the Nechí River to the east, the booming Zaragoza gold mines were almost a neo-Africa by 1595, when some 2,000 enslaved workers were counted. A 1593–96 dispute over water rights between two mine owners paints the Zaragoza goldfields as a kind of Wild West, overrun by murderous gangs.

Slavery flourished amid the violence. A pair of mine owners at Zaragoza deployed 150 workers, women and men together.[39] As Chief Justice Auncibay had pointed out in his proposal for greater Popayán, gender and age complementarity were essential to colonial placer-mining *pueblos* or slave colonies.

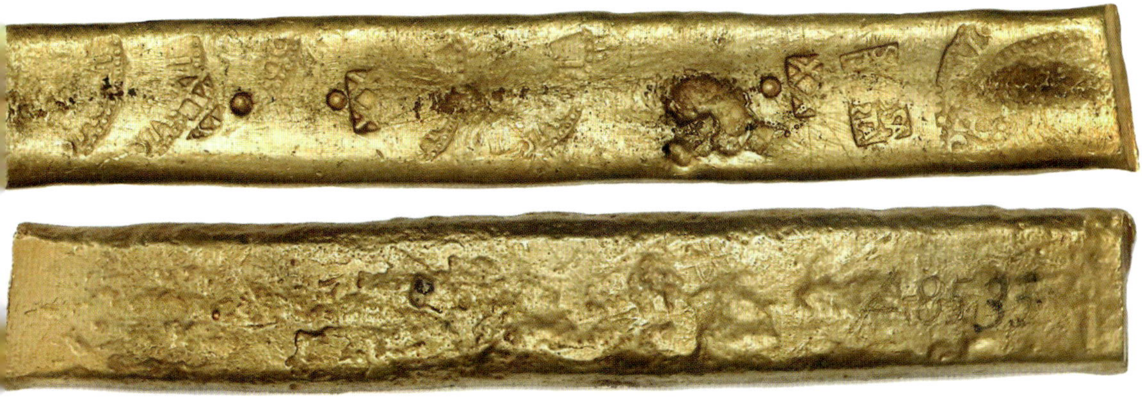

Fig. 9. Gold bar from the Zaragoza mines stamped 20 karats, 1 grain, ca. 1620. Daniel Frank Sedwick LLC, Auction #25, lot 196. Gold bars of this type have only survived thanks to shipwrecks such as that of the galleon *Nuestra Señora de la Atocha*, which went down off the Florida Keys in the summer of 1622 while on its way to Spain. The bar's stamps identify it as being taxed in the town of Zaragoza, although the assayer's name is not clear (possibly "Puerta")

Unlike the *encomienda*, which at least theoretically exempted all but adult males, among the enslaved everyone, including children, was expected to perform work essential to the mines. The result was higher yields, with monthly quotas of gold dust cast into bars, taxed, and stamped for export. Ingots salvaged from Florida shipwrecks tell the tale (fig. 9).

A prominent Zaragoza mine owner was Vicente de Villalobos. In his 1606 merit report, he claimed to have been among the first Spanish settlers in the region, subsisting on "roots and wild herbs" while also establishing some of the first major placer diggings. He took credit, but it was of course his enslaved workers who hit paydirt. The unnamed pioneers included several African men who paddled Villalobos upriver in a canoe. Skilled miners, these enslaved men discovered deposits yielding 23-karat, or nearly 96% pure, gold. Other such workers periodically cast gold dust into bars in brick-lined foundries (fig. 10).

Unfortunately for him and his workforce, Villalobos's Zaragoza-area mining claim was high and dry. To work the deposits, enslaved miners had to build a wooden aqueduct connecting two ranges of steep-sided hills. At its highest point the aqueduct was said to have been suspended 22 *estados* or some 121 feet (37 m) "in the air" (*por el aire*) above the bottom of the canyon.[40] Witnesses testified that several enslaved workers had fallen to their deaths while building and maintaining this impressive structure, consisting of interlinked "canoes of special wood" (*canoas de madera especial*). It was the highest aqueduct or "waterworks" (*edificio de agua*) in the land.

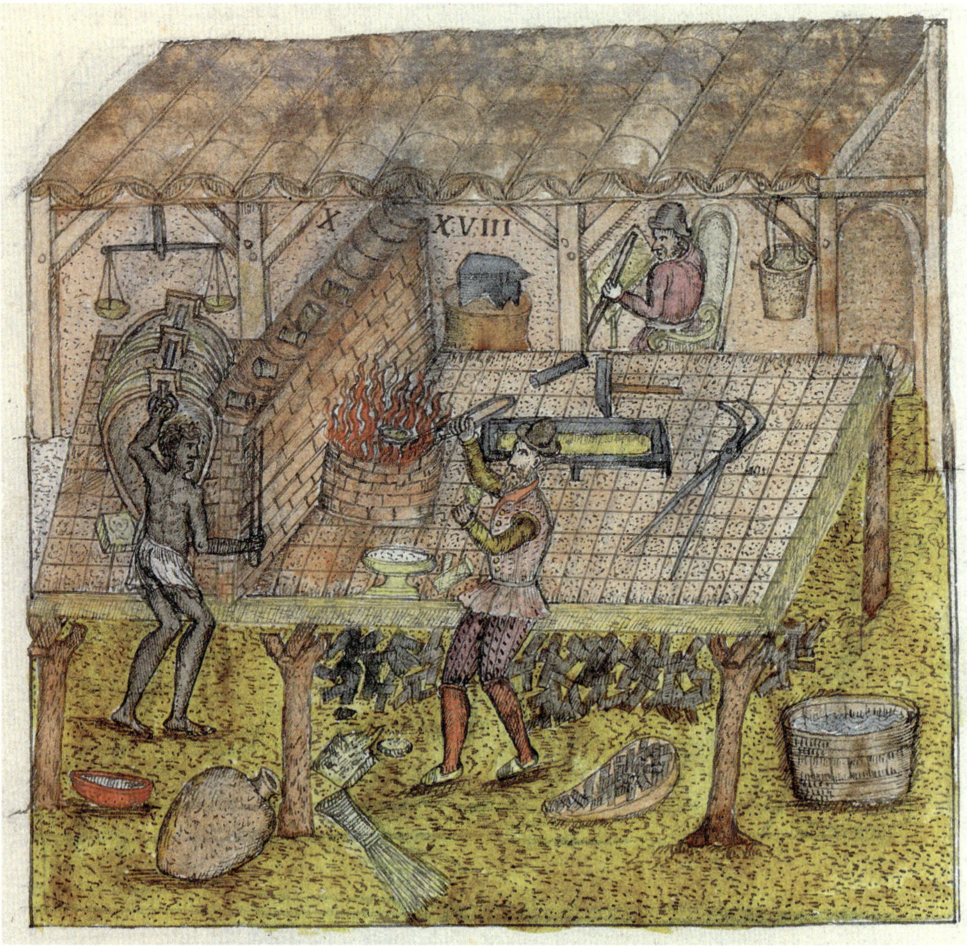

Fig. 10. Spanish American gold foundry, ca. 1590. New York, The Morgan & Museum, Drake Manuscript, Ma 3900, fols. 101v–102r. This image depicts a royal Spanish foundry (*fundición*) in either Panama or northern New Granada. Housed within regional treasury offices (*cajas reales*), such foundries typically employed a Spanish master goldsmith, an apprentice, and one or more enslaved Africans or drafted Indigenous workers. An enslaved African man (wearing only a pair of white cotton "shorts") pumps the bellows to stoke the Spanish assayer's fire. The assayer, retrieving a crucible with simple tongs, is fully clad and hatted in accordance with his status. A less elaborately clad helper sits inside, under a tiled roof, possibly rolling out gold sheets that have been hammered on the anvil. If so, the work depicted may be cementation, or gold purification using salt and brick dust. Gold was then cast into bars like the large one sitting in an iron mold right above the assayer's head, next to the large tongs and hammer. Charcoal is spread beneath the tile-covered table, presumably to keep it dry, along with a broom, wine jug (*botija*), dowsing barrel, and other utensils. At upper left is a balance

Villalobos's mines were said to be near the Amacerí River (northeast of Zaragoza), and reaching them required enslaved paddlers and miners to shoulder their canoes and supplies over several portages. In other places, prospectors crossed hanging bridges made from vines. Villalobos said that he and his enslaved workforce also prospected in the even more remote Guamocó mountain diggings to the east in the first years after their discovery, losing several miners to ambush. Others were killed by snakebite, a perennial problem throughout lowland New Granada's goldfields.

Resistance was rife, according to the documents. Dozens of Africans and their descendants fled into the hills around Zaragoza to live as maroons, surviving in part by attacking mule trains and sacking remote gold-mining camps (*rancherías de minas*). According to one Spanish bush captain, a quasi-military campaign to suppress the Zaragoza maroons provoked an organized uprising in 1599. The maroons continued to augment their numbers, capturing enslaved women gold panners in 1606 "by force or consent," according to one Spanish observer, and prompting another reprisal in 1608. Zaragoza was also home to a number of accused African witches persecuted by the Inquisition tribunal at Cartagena in the first decades of the seventeenth century.[41]

Mining camp maroons became a widespread and enduring concern for Spanish enslavers and officials all over New Granada. The *audiencia* at Bogotá granted a commission to the mine owner Juan Ruiz de Osma in 1616, as he was struggling to suppress maroons in the mountains around Remedios, to the south of Zaragoza. These maroons were said to be holding out near the sites of Matopocoro and Nitiniti, where Ruiz had staked placer gold claims and planted enslaved work gangs.[42] According to the *audiencia*, the Remedios maroons were to be offered amnesty should they turn themselves in peacefully. Otherwise they were to expect "blood and fire" (*sangre y fuego*). Ruiz evidently did not succeed, as the *audiencia* issued another commission in 1648 to one Gregorio Díaz Parladoyro to conquer "Indians and Blacks" in the Remedios area and farther inland. Díaz asked for a 100-peso bounty on any fugitive slaves captured, while promising to resettle anyone born free in the backcountry, citing their "indomitable" wills.[43]

Elite colonists in New Granada's various mining zones marked status by the size of their enslaved *cuadrillas*, much as they had done (and continued to do) by displaying *encomienda* titles. In 1631, Captain Francisco Beltrán Caicedo announced himself the boss of the mines of Remedios, effective lord of the Pocuné River. He said he had some 200 "slaves fit to work" (*esclavos útiles de trabajo*), mostly in canal construction, bringing water to remote placers.[44]

The enslaved were divided into three *cuadrillas*, and several of their likewise enslaved bosses (*capitanes*) testified on their master's behalf. Rewards and status divisions within working groups sometimes dampened the possibility of rebellion or flight and occasionally enabled negotiation.

Caicedo had begun as an *encomendero*, transitioning to slave labor beginning in around 1590. A 1611 commission from the *audiencia* at Bogotá gave Caicedo permission to conquer or "punish" neighboring Indigenous groups who resisted colonization, ordering him to also "procure with all possible care your discovery of whatever type of metals there may be."[45] As we have seen throughout this chapter, Spanish conquests (and reconquests) were assumed to go hand in hand with precious minerals extraction. All that was new about these "neo-conquests" was slavery, the rapid Africanization of the north Andean backlands. By 1640 there were said to be some 21,000 enslaved African mineworkers (*negros de batea*) washing gold in northern New Granada.[46] A little later, the greater Chocó region, including Barbacoas and Raposo, would undergo a similarly radical transition, becoming a virtual neo-Africa by the early eighteenth century.

Another colonist seeking reward for employing enslaved African miners and also punishing runaways was Captain Fernando de Toro Zapata, whose 1629 petition demanded special recognition for his relentless expansion of mining frontiers. He had forced his enslaved African workers to wash gold in numerous diggings, including new discoveries on the Itiguí (Tigüi) and Bagre rivers and other Lower Cauca tributaries.[47] In 1623, Toro had marched forty leagues beyond Remedios to the Guatapé River in search of gold and silver, an expedition that finally took him west over the batholith to Santa Fe de Antioquia, his residence at the time of the petition. Toro had captured a number of "rebellious" runaway slaves and he now turned his sights on the Chocó, New Granada's last mining frontier.

Enslaved Life in the Mines

In 1614, Popayán's recently established Encarnación convent was audited by Quito's archbishop, following misconduct allegations. Donors had bequeathed the convent numerous enslaved Africans to support a few dozen nuns and novitiates, and the inquest meant that all assets had to be inventoried. Key among the convent's enslaved workforce were forty-seven women, children, and men forced to labor in two gold mines in the Popayán hinterland, also donated to the convent. The mines of San Onofre and San Lorenzo occupied thirty-three mine laborers, a mix of men and women, yielding between 1,300 and 1,400 pesos or about 13 lb. (6 kg) of fine gold a year.[48] The remaining fourteen enslaved Africans included small children and a few older individuals tasked with driving mules and cattle, cooking, and carrying out other support tasks. Nuclear family units were common, according to the inventory (there were eleven couples, seven with children), and one married man served as work-gang captain. Many adults had African surnames, among them Angola, Congo, Bañón, Folupo, and Bran.

The documents suggest formation of a small and diverse gold-mining community, a colony, but why did it exist? In short, money. The African miners of San Onofre and San Lorenzo provided Popayán's elite religious women with a vital rent stream, essentially money in the bank. Mined gold dust was lent out at interest to urban householders at 5 percent per annum, backed with liens on real estate. Mine rents for 1613 may not have been terribly high by Zaragoza standards, but gold output exceeded interest income. The cost of maintaining the enslaved workers, providing them with maize, beef, dairy products, and clothing, was said to total 400 pesos yearly. Mining tools were rudimentary: hoe-like *almocafres*, heavy iron bars, and wooden *bateas*. The thirty-three core mineworkers themselves were referred to as *bateas*, or as so many "working pans." A Spanish majordomo received 50 pesos a year to visit the mines to collect gold dust from the enslaved captain. Gold collected from enslaved Africans in this way likely made it into the base of the Crown of the Andes.

Other documents suggest that the Popayán convent's gold mines were atypical only in belonging to a religious organization. The social composition of the workers roughly matches elite-owned work gangs planted in the goldfields. As in greater Zaragoza, such *cuadrillas* constituted a kind of rural extractive colony, largely overseen by their own headman and other leaders. This is not to say that Africans and their descendants had nothing to fear from owners or overseers, some of whom lived permanently on site or who visited frequently. Some were sadists; others, misers.

A court case from 1634–36 involving the Remedios gold mines in what is today the northeast of the Antioquia Department includes a rare account book with details on everyday life and labor for enslaved African workers. Here an absentee owner in Tunja (Map 2, center right), Juan de Ossa, sued his hired administrator for mishandling funds. The account book lists 109 enslaved Africans, many with names hinting at their places of origin (e.g., Luis Biafara, Antonico Ñenguele, Juan Casangue, Juan Galumbo).[49] Most interesting perhaps is the appearance of two entirely female *cuadrillas*, one headed by "capitana" Elvira Biafara and the other by a woman known only as Ysabel. Elvira Biafara was responsible for collecting gold panned by nearly forty women (with names such as Ynés Mandinga, Juana Conga, Francisca Bran, and Leonora Zape).[50]

By contrast, it appears that Capitana Ysabel oversaw only four women, whose main job was planting, weeding, and harvesting maize. They also looked after seventeen children, mostly under the age of ten.

All the enslaved workforce together produced about 200–300 pesos' worth of "milled and washed" gold each month, with a weekly or biweekly handoff from the *capitán* or *capitana* to the administrator. The demands and pace of production appear much higher than in the Popayán case above, and mine work appears to have gone on year-round, even in dry spells (when it was possible to excavate normally flooded riverbeds). One account entry mentions a fee paid to a sexton for a "sung mass" requesting rain. Gold placering, like farming, demanded water—just not too much.

Maize was the enslaved workforce's staple food, often purchased by the administrator, according to the account book, but also grown near the mine property on the special plot (*rosa*) tended by Capitana Ysabel and her crew. There were other receipts for imported ham, salt fish, rice, beans, cheese, flour, wine, salt, and tobacco—all trucked in from Cartagena or other distant markets. Only the last two items were shared with the enslaved; the rest were consumed by the administrator himself (with some items possibly sold to others off the books). An occasional exception was wine, used in curing illnesses. The master also got a supply of wax and candles.

Other ledger entries reveal steady payments for manatee oil, mostly used for lighting underground mines. The document mentions some vein mines (*vetas*) lit with *candiles* or lamps, but the scribe added that manatee oil was also used to cure mules and to light the slave quarters when women were giving birth or when someone was ill. The Remedios mines were just close enough to the Caribbean coast via the Magdalena River that manatee oil was available, although other documents show that manatees were being hunted to extinction, forcing a turn to caiman or "gator" oil.[51]

Mining tools inventoried included the familiar *barras* (long iron crowbars) and *almocafres*, along with picks, mattocks, chisels, and the like. Wooden *bateas* are not inventoried, but every mineworker undoubtedly had one. The enslaved women planting corn mostly worked with machetes and hatchets, all counted on the list. Eleven pack mules bore loads of various sorts, and maize for enslaved workers was stored in a thatch-roofed structure (*bohío*). All the enslaved, plus mules, tools, and mines together, were appraised at 31,500 pesos in 20-karat gold (worth ca. 50,000 pesos in silver—a considerable sum). The value of the enslaved workforce alone constituted the lion's share of this figure, as labor was everything.

Although the mine administrator, Álvaro de Losa, was charged with unnecessary maize purchases and coming up short in gold rents for his boss, local witnesses testified that drought and famine in 1631 had forced Losa and his mine overseer, twenty-four-year-old Laureano de Miranda, to order enslaved women to plant more maize. Many workers were dying of malnutrition even as maize prices shot up from 6 pesos to 18–20 pesos a basket (*fanega*). Extra corn was produced by unnamed Amerindians held in *encomienda*, but witnesses also mentioned itinerant *indios forasteros* (foreign Indians) selling maize to miners. We do not know if these enslaved Africans understood nixtmalization or alkaline pre-cooking to prevent pellagra (niacin deficiency), but the fact that many corn sellers were native Colombians may have enabled such knowledge transfer.

The absentee owner questioned Losa's purchase of tobacco as irrelevant to subsistence, but witnesses argued that it was necessary ("es fuerza") to supply enslaved mineworkers with this modest vice. The same witnesses said it was also customary to provide the mine administrator with a pound of lard and a cheese each week, more if he had an assistant (which Losa did, the *minero* Miranda). Slave rations were far more significant, of course, and witnesses said their most important allowances were fresh meat and salt. Most meat arrived as *tasajo* or chipped beef, much of it reserved for the sick.

Although we long to hear directly from any these 109 enslaved African mineworkers, the 1630s Remedios account books do at least provide a rare snapshot of their hardscrabble lives. Clearly, the African miners and their children were suffering from overwork and malnutrition, but there was more to the story. Losa was found to be using his position (and income) to import more African captives from Cartagena, along with large quantities of merchandise. Witnesses said that he brought twenty enslaved individuals at a time to Remedios, putting them to work in the mines as they awaited sale.

Many of the captives—and not only the newcomers—suffered from severe and chronic medical conditions, including "ulcerated sores, buboes, foot pains, and bone spurs" (*dolores y clavos en los pies*). Others had "pinta on the whole body" (*carate* [treponema carateum] *por todo el cuerpo*). Some of these skin ailments may have been symptoms of pellagra from overdependence on untreated maize, but there were plenty of other potential causes. Still other enslaved workers were said to suffer from asthma, stomach pains, fevers, and "throat secretions," plus chronic back and shoulder pain (*corrimientos en la garganta y umbrago [lumbago] o en las espaldas*). Several women also suffered problem pregnancies, no doubt exacerbated by malnutrition and work demands.

These many ills in turn required purchase of numerous and often caustic medicines, including copper carbonate (*cardenillo*), mercury chloride (*solimán*), copper sulfate (*piedra alipe*), sulfur, and "pitch for unguents" (*brea para unguentos*). Also mentioned was the purgative *cañafístula* or American senna, a reminder of the galenic or humoral medical theory dominant among Europeans.[52] Purging may have been necessary at times, but it could only exacerbate malnutrition—hence the reserve of chipped beef as medicine. The documents tell us nothing of African and Indigenous therapies, but non-Western medicines and treatments were undoubtedly applied.

According to witnesses, pregnant women were supplied with modest rations of chicken and bread, plus sugar for syrups and honey for porridges. The great famine of 1631 had made it impossible for many enslaved miners to produce even a peso of gold per week "due to their illnesses" (*por sus indisposiciones*). Their weekly ration consisted of only four pieces of manioc and two small loaves of bread (presumably corn bread) per week. Harvesting, grating, detoxifying, and toasting manioc were not small chores, performed by African women who learned from Indigenous women. The mines were nevertheless in such crisis that the overseer stopped work between November 19 and December 31, 1631, as nearly every enslaved miner was suffering from a respiratory ailment or "catarrh" (*catarro*).

From this unusually detailed case we gain a small glimpse of enslaved life under the Habsburgs in the gold mines of New Granada. The work was hard, constant, and dangerous—more so when mines dove underground. Swift rivers were also a perennial killer, as were venomous snakes. Indigenous knowledge was likely required to treat snakebites, a reminder of the all-important transition from *encomienda* to slavery. Enslaved workers' subsistence and general health remained precarious as masters tried to minimize rations, medicines, and other necessities while insisting on steady rents in gold dust. Yet documents also show that masters could ill afford total neglect; enslaved Africans were, even individually, much more valuable than any gold mine.

The Remedios ledger makes no mention of clothing or shelter for these enslaved workers and their families, as if such basic necessities were beneath consideration. The Popayán documents similarly say nothing about slave quarters or clothing. From other documents we know that the usual dress of enslaved Africans in New Granada's hot low-country mines consisted of minimal swaths of cotton cloth (*cotones*), typically breechclouts for men and a kind of wraparound skirt for women. Children were often naked. Shelter most often consisted of wattle-and-daub barracks thatched with palm fronds. These were the so-called *rancherías*, or clusters of huts. The "neo-African" utopia imagined by Chief Justice Auncibay in 1592 bore little resemblance to the mining camps described in documents only about a generation or two later.

One strains to imagine a recently arrived African woman's experience panning gold in the midday heat of the lower Cauca or an African teenager's experience chipping away at rocks by the light of a manatee-oil lamp—to say nothing of children's agonies while dying of malnutrition amid drought and famine. But only by doing so may we begin to contemplate the true price of New Granada gold under the Habsburgs. The goldfields of Popayán, which produced the raw material for the Crown of the Andes, were virtually identical, as were the fabled emerald mines of Muzo.[53]

Lode Mines

In what is today southwestern Ecuador, in the mountains above the vast banana plantations of Machala, lay the lode mines of Zaruma (fig. 11). For a time, Zaruma was considered the most promising gold source in all of Spanish America, a golden Potosí. The great bonanza never materialized despite creation of a *mita* or draft labor system in the last decade of the sixteenth century, yet Zaruma produced a steady stream of gold after discovery in the mid-1550s, and it continues today. Mines all over Zaruma's main hill are still producing gold as of this writing, and those of Portovelo near the base of the same mountain have also been periodically revived after being abandoned in the second quarter of the twentieth century by a New York-based American company.

Perhaps the most dramatic story of gold mining in early colonial Ecuador regards the lode mines of Nambija, high in the hilly jungles east of Loja. These and the mines of Sevilla de Oro and Logroño, east of Cuenca, retain a mythical character, since they were established by Spanish conquistadors in the 1550s, only to be snuffed out by Indigenous rebels by ca. 1600.[54] After centuries of abandonment, prospectors rediscovered the mines of Nambija in the 1980s after scouring colonial records for clues. The lost lodes of Sevilla de Oro and Logroño have been reopened by more organized drillers.[55] But these were isolated jungle mines, atypical of colonial lode extraction.

As has been seen, Indigenous workers not subject to the *encomienda* were often forced to mine gold via the *mita*, a royally administered labor draft based partly on Inca precedent. *Mita* conscripts labored in all kinds of colonial projects, from sewer maintenance to church building, but mining entailed demands of a different order of magnitude. Mine *mitas* were common in greater Quito and New Granada under the Habsburgs, and the longest-running drafts of this type were found in the mines of Mariquita (on the middle Magdalena), Chisquío (outside Popayán), and Zaruma (in southern Ecuador).[56]

The Mariquita mines, particularly the diggings known as Las Lajas and Santa Ana, were first famous for placer gold. When miners went underground in around 1580, they discovered silver—mixed with gold. This was cause for celebration, as if yet another Potosí had been found, but Mariquita's silver ores proved refractory, or difficult to refine due to their complex chemistry. Developing New Granada's silver industry, totally overshadowed by gold, became a Habsburg obsession. For decades it drank up mercury imported from Almadén, Spain, as entrepreneurs experimented with amalgamation formulas. The Mariquita mines were also the destination of thousands of unlucky highland Muisca men in the decades after 1600, when the crown copied the infamous Potosí *mita*.[57]

Like other imports, Spanish mercury had to be poled up the Magdalena River in cargo canoes from Cartagena, then transported by mule to the mines. A major mercury spill was reported in 1606, when a canoe capsized on the Magdalena near the site of Puerto Real del Carare (famous for attacks by the Indigenous Carare rebels; Map 2, center).[58] The loss was significant, some 2,600 lb. (ca. 1,200 kg), but three divers hired from another canoe—aided by nearly 200 enslaved polers, presumably using ropes, rafts, and the like—were able to recover 2,300 lb. or some 88 percent of the total. The high recovery rate suggests that the mercury had been well packaged and "lost" in relatively shallow water, as the Magdalena is a fast and muddy river, often quite deep. We know about the 1606 spill only because the Spaniard in charge of transport failed to get properly reimbursed. Strangely, the three divers (*buzos*) turned out to be foreigners, although their nationality is not given in their testimonies. The two names recorded, Miguel Rato and Geronimo Verdino, suggest that they were Italians.

Unlike the Mariquita *mita*, the gold mine draft at Chisquío, nestled in the Munchique mountains west of Popayán, was a peculiar hybrid: a crown-owned *encomienda* administered by a majordomo. Although these mines yielded only low-karat gold, they produced steady rents. According to a 1631 treasurer's audit, a few dozen Indigenous men staffed the mines plus a small, adjacent

Fig. 11. View of the town and mines of Zaruma, ca. 1817. Seville, Archivo General de Indias, Mapas y Planos Panamá 232. In this image the old gold-mining town of Zaruma ("A") sits on the flank of a steep hill, the Cerro del Sesmo ("C"), pocked with mines and crosscut with gold-bearing vein systems, each numbered. Near the Amarillo River at lower right is "Portobelo," surrounded by the "Royal Veins of Our Lady." At bottom are three types of ore-crushing mills, including a water-powered stamp mill, plus a smelting furnace and a calcination oven

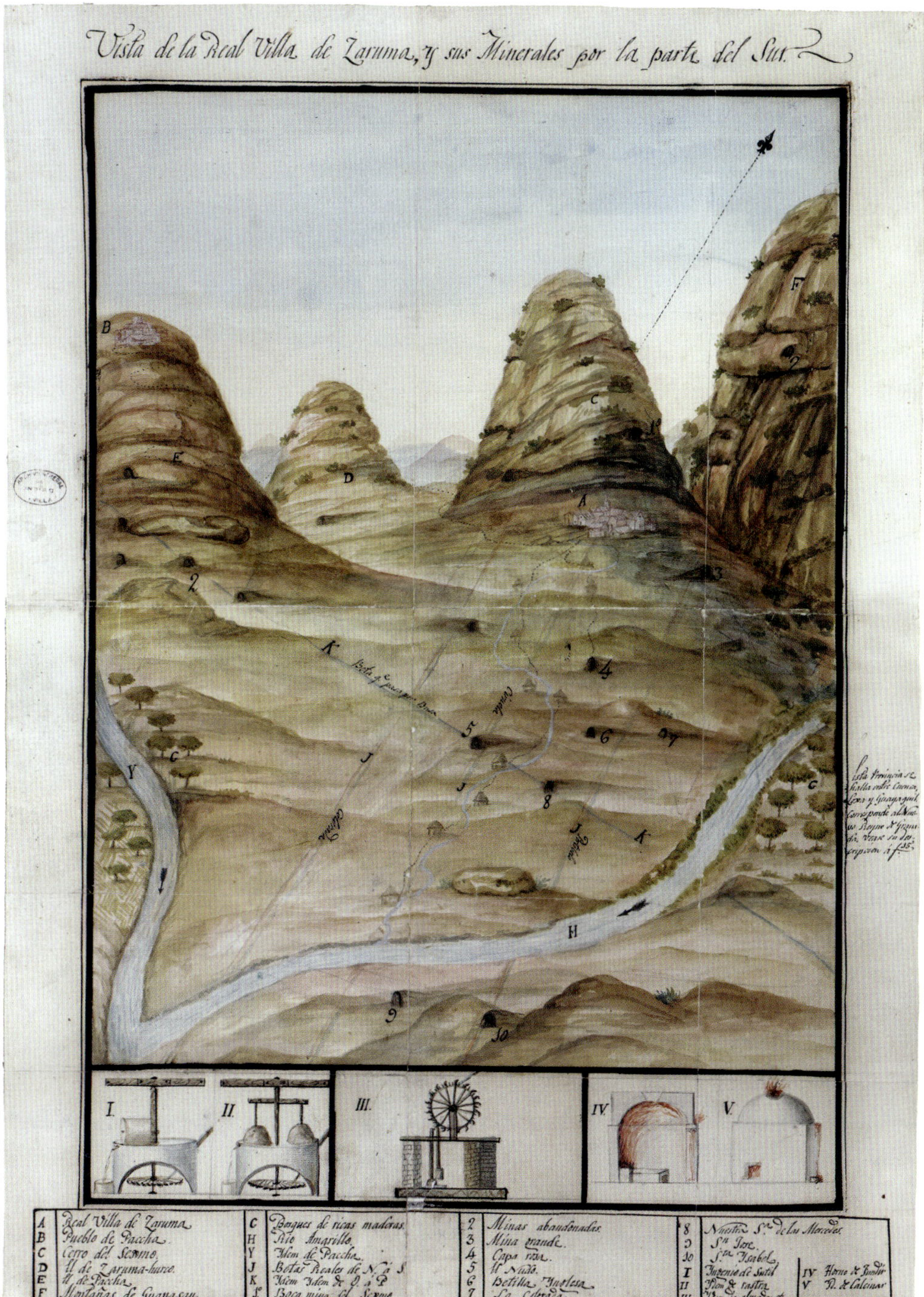
Vista de la Real Villa de Zaruma, y sus Minerales por la parte del Sur.
A Real Villa de Zaruma
B Pueblo de Paccha
C Cerro del Sexmo
F Montañas de Guanasan
C Bosques de ricas maderas
H Rio Amarillo
Y Idem de Paccha
1º Boca mina del Sexmo
2 Minas abandonadas
3 Mina grande
4 Capa rica
6 Betilla Inglesa
7 La Colorada
8 Nuestra Sra. de las Mercedes
9 Sn. Jose
10 Sta. Ysabel
I Ingenio de Sutil
III Idem de almadaneta
IV Horno de fundir
V Id. de Calcinar

refinery in the 1610s and 1620s, yielding a little over 1,000 pesos a year, similar to the output of the nearby Popayán Encarnación convent's placer mine output noted above.[59] Rather like the enslaved miners of Zaragoza and Remedios, Chisquío's Indigenous workers received rations of maize, beef, and salt, plus a wage paid in cotton cloth. The majordomo took home 10 percent of gross output. As with the Mariquita mines, Indigenous draftees were sent to their deaths on the crown's orders, but like the enslaved Encarnación miners they did so to benefit the elites of Popayán. "Oro de Chisquío" circulated as currency in Popayán into the mid-seventeenth century. Some of this gold, too, may have made its way into the Crown of the Andes.

The southern Quito district's more familiar-looking Zaruma mine *mita* was formalized in 1579, also an attempt to copy the Potosí *mita* with its vast catchment zone. It met stiff resistance. As happened in nearly all districts subject to mining corvées, the Zaruma *mita* was slowed by Indigenous flight and pushback from *encomenderos* who wanted "their" workers to be spared for other tasks, mostly in agriculture, livestock raising, and textile manufacture—but also, in some cases, private gold mining.

All told, there was never a north Andean *mita* as widespread or as punishing as those of Potosí (Bolivia) or Huancavelica (Peru, site of mercury mines). Even so, the Zaruma draft shared the ill fame of Mariquita's. Both killed highland Andeans not accustomed to hot country disease and diet regimes, not to mention brutally hard, underground work. There was also chronic silica dust and mercury exposure in the refining mills. As happened in the placer districts, hard-rock mine owners increasingly looked to Africa for gold mine labor.

In addition to the famous diggings of Mariquita and Chisquío, underground gold mines were scattered all over New Granada, some worked in pre-Columbian times. Even if only a few were supplied with *mita* labor, all were greatly expanded with the introduction of iron and steel tools, plus mercury amalgamation. In the Western Cordillera of the Andes not far from Santa Fe de Antioquia (Map 2, center left) lay the lode mines of Buriticá, which according to early Spanish visitors had gone deep underground prior to Spanish arrival. Indigenous miners using fire-hardened sticks had managed to pry friable ores from weathered quartz veins, later grinding them with rocking stones to recover gold dust in the *batea*. Other lodes were pursued (as they are today) in other corners of the Antioquia Department, from Guamocó south to Segovia, Los Osos, and beyond. More gold lodes were exploited in the mountains on either side of the middle Cauca, including the venerable mines of Marmato.

Still more lode mines were discovered in the southern mountains east and

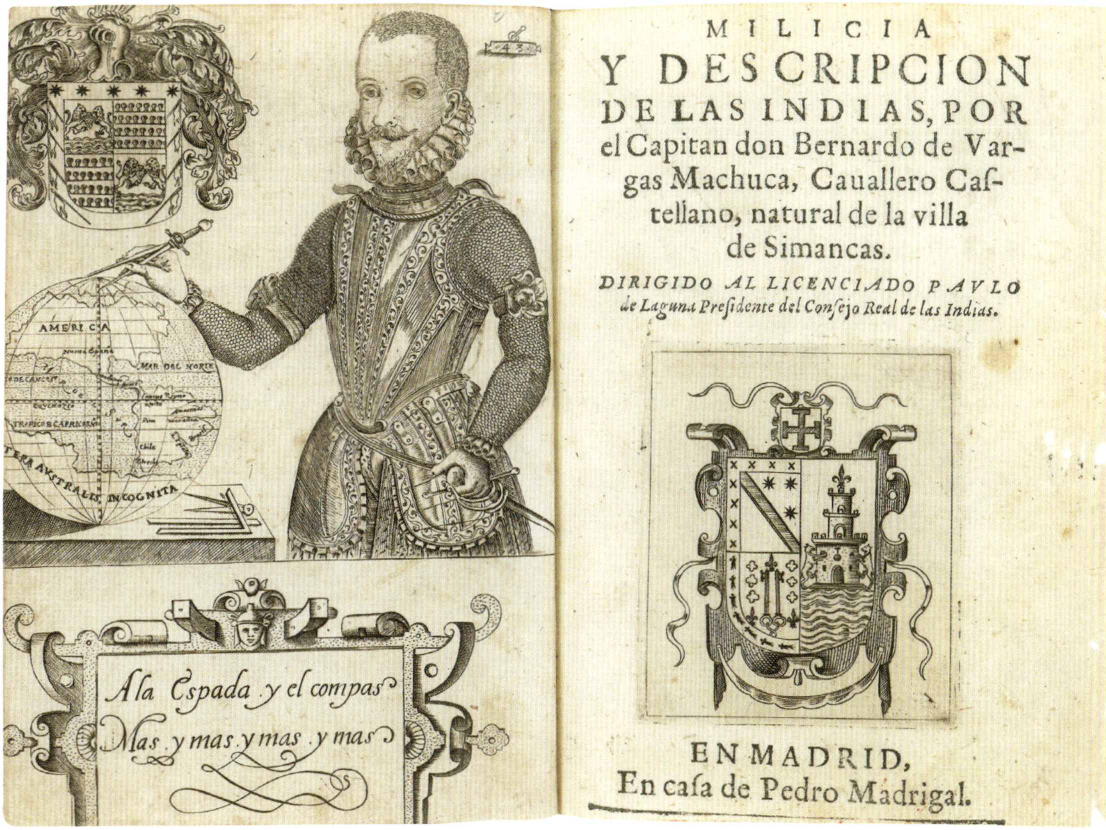

Fig. 12. Frontispiece to Bernardo de Vargas Machuca, *Milicia y descripcion de las Indias* (Madrid, 1599). A Spanish subject with global ambitions, bush captain Vargas Machuca holds a compass over a globe depicting the western hemisphere. In the cartouche is the motto "By sword and compass, more and more, and more and more"

west of the Patía River, between Popayán and Pasto. To the east—in the Central Cordillera—were the hard-rock mines of Almaguer; to the west, on the Pacific slope, were the legendary lodes of Madrigal, abandoned after a series of Indigenous uprisings in the late sixteenth century.[60] Almaguer, too, abutted an Indigenous frontier, and it is important to note that in Habsburg times much of New Granada, greater Popayán, and Quito remained "Indian Country" despite the conquistadors' and their descendants' best efforts. As in the deserts of northern Mexico, the Spanish barely controlled a string of towns, mines, farms, and pastures, linked by exposed and extremely rugged mule paths grandly known as the Camino Real. Fears, rumors, and memories of "Indian" attacks filled settlers' minds, governors' reports, and preachers' sermons.

Not far from Almaguer was the ill-fated town of Simancas on the upper

Iscancé, founded by a well-known Indian fighter, Bernardo de Vargas Machuca (fig. 12). Vargas Machuca, who hailed from the Castilian archive town of Simancas, spent many years "punishing" Indigenous rebels and hunting escaped African captives all over New Granada. He is best known for publishing a manual for neo-conquistadors in 1599 called *The Indian Militia and Description of the Indies*. Vargas Machuca also penned a rejoinder to Bartolomé de Las Casas's famous *Brief Account of the Destruction of the Indies*, but its publication was suppressed. The town he founded was destroyed by Indigenous "rebels," the Andakí, dashing his dream of another north Andean frontier gold-mining colony.

In all of his work, Vargas Machuca embodied the spirit of the Spanish colonizer as gold seeker but also as seeker of Amerindian labor, of *encomiendas*. As he put it, "the Spaniard does not settle or inhabit deserted lands, however healthy and rich they may be in gold and silver; he inhabits and settles where he finds Indians, though they may be poor and sickly, for without Indians for tribute, one cannot enjoy the fruits of the land."[61] In lieu of this, as we have seen, New Granada's conquistadors and their descendants increasingly imported enslaved Africans to dig for treasure in order to "enjoy the fruits of the land."

Making Money

How did all this gold circulate, and where did it go? As noted above, gold dust circulated as currency throughout greater Quito and much of New Granada in Habsburg times, yet neither gold dust nor ingots cast from it were convenient forms of money. Mined gold varied considerably in purity, although placer gold tended to be above about 18-karat (75 percent) fineness. The balance was usually a mix of copper and silver. As is common today, the Spanish used the karat (*quilate*) as a fraction of 24 to indicate purity (not to be confused with the weight measure for gemstones). Since pure gold is 24-karat (100 percent), casting gold bars of lesser purity meant assaying them and appraising them according to a standard measurement for purposes of trade and taxation. Under the Habsburgs, the royal gold standard, used for coin metal as well, was 22.5 karat (0.9375 fine). Assayers purified gold by cementation, but this process was known only to a few specialists.

After fineness or *ley* came weight. A *peso de oro de minas* or *castellano* was by law one-hundredth of a Castilian pound, or 4.6 g, set at the royal standard of 22.5-karat purity. All taxed gold had to be converted to this standard for accounting purposes, but gold in circulation was rarely refined above its original purity. That is, a given ingot's weight and purity could be translated mathematically to its equivalent in 22.5-karat gold in order to pay the king his

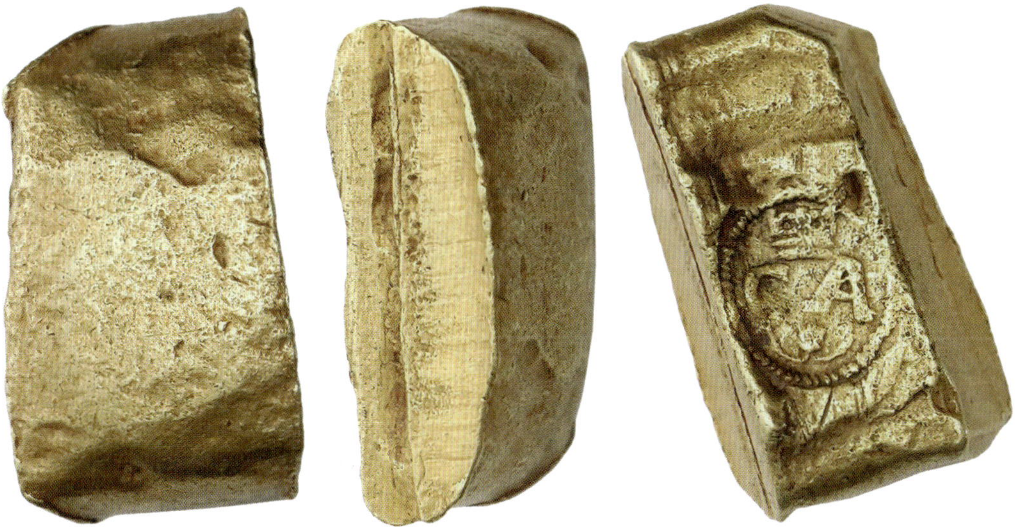

Fig. 13. Taxed New Granada *oro corriente* (gold currency). Daniel Frank Sedwick LLC, Auction #25, lot 195. In the absence of coin, traders sometimes chopped gold bars and ingots into coin-like chunks, ideally stamped to show they had been taxed; otherwise, they would have been subject to confiscation by royal authorities. New Granadan *oro corriente*, like gold bars, was a cumbersome form of money, and it has only survived thanks to shipwrecks

tax without going through the hassle of refining. It was simply too onerous and expensive to do so on a regular basis (except when minting coins).

"Oro de Mariquita," for example, was especially low-karat (usually 13-karat or so) since it came from a polymetallic deposit heavy in silver, copper, and other metals.[62] The same was true of "oro de Chisquío," the coin of the realm in parts of Popayán. "Oro de Quito" was higher-grade at 19 or 19.5 karats, but unless one had a keen eye it was difficult to know where exactly gold dust, bars, bar slices (fig. 13), or cakes (*tejos*) came from, and thus how pure they might be. Occasionally, as seen above (figs. 4 and 9), gold disks and bars were stamped with a place name and even the assayer's or owner's name, but this was rare. Fraud or at least dissimulation tempted gold's handlers, especially since different royal foundries and treasury offices (*cajas reales*) offered different tax rates based on gold origins. Quito's royal foundry offered a discount on Popayán gold, for example, drawing it south for taxation and away from the Popayán office.

Gold coins were distinct from the "mine peso" in that they were based on the *escudo*, a dime-sized 22.5-karat disk weighing about 3.38 g (fig. 14). Royal assayers, usually hired goldsmiths, purified gold submitted by merchants for coining via the cementation process, yet coin color still varied due to remaining admixtures of copper and silver. Determining purity was more art than

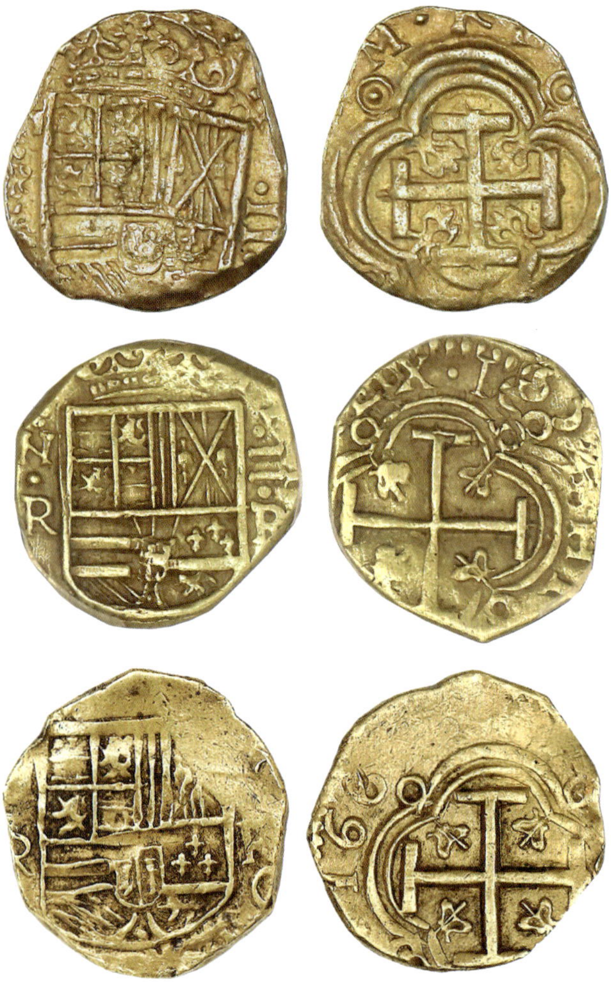

Fig. 14. Gold "doubloons," or two-escudo coins, minted in Bogotá, ca. 1636, 1659, and 1669. Daniel Frank Sedwick LLC, Auction #25, lots, 30, 33; Auction #26, lot 49. Gold escudos and larger denominations were minted in fairly limited quantities in New Granada under the Habsburgs, intended only to lubricate regional commerce. Documents suggest that most of this money was sucked out of circulation and into the global economy due to the growing value of gold against silver, which was far more abundant thanks largely to the Potosí bonanza

science, and coins, bars, and even gold jewelry were tested for fineness using a dark touchstone (*piedra de toque*) and an array of touch needles of pre-determined karat in copper/silver/gold alloy. One could also bite or bounce a coin, or try to determine specific gravity, but true assays required the use of *agua fuerte* (hydrochloric acid), usually reserved for identifying counterfeits or other scams. Although it was a capital offense, royal insignia and tax stamps could be faked, and some folks trusted gold dust more than coins or bars.

It was not until the 1620s that mints began to operate at Cartagena de Indias and Bogotá, and these remained too small and inconsistent in Habsburg times to supply the realm with adequate coinage.[63] Even the smallest gold coins were of relatively high denomination, worth between one and two silver pesos. The mint at Cartagena was closed by royal order in 1630 (to be sporadically reopened in later decades), and the Bogotá mint remained a small franchise until the eighteenth-century Bourbon reforms. Doubloons were hammered out by hand (in part by enslaved Africans), but much of what the Bogotá mint produced was shipped to Spain or traded away to foreigners for contraband merchandise. Some Mariquita silver was coined in Bogotá as well, but far less than was needed to enable fluid exchanges. It appears that silver coin was more available in the Audiencia of Quito in mid-Habsburg times, due to the textile trade to the central Andes, specifically to Potosí, but people still complained that royally sanctioned cash was always in short supply, especially small change. Small change had a way of concentrating in church coffers as alms, the kinds of funds that over time may have helped finance fabrication of the Crown of the Andes.

Conclusion

Though largely overshadowed by the huge silver bonanzas of Upper Peru and Mexico, substantial gold was found in many sites all over Habsburg New Granada and Quito. Placer mines tended to play out faster than lode mines, sometimes within a decade or two, but there were many exceptions. The placers of Colombia's wet Pacific lowlands are still mined extensively today, for example, as are many other alluvial and hard-rock deposits throughout the interior, including the Lower Cauca basin of northeast Antioquia.[64] As another example of revival, several "lost" colonial lode mines in southeastern Ecuador are again booming, driven by high gold prices, lax laws, and a mix of folk and high technology.

Most of Quito's and New Granada's gold mines had been discovered and worked for many years by Indigenous peoples when the Spanish conquistadors arrived in the 1530s. Gold objects were the first sign of hope for these desperate men, to which were added emeralds and, in a few places, silver. Native Andeans were thus immediately thrust into mine labor, and many were marched into hostile territories and worked to death. Others were sent off to the eastern lowlands in search of El Dorado, never to return. The conquerors mostly exploited native Andeans by way of the so-called *encomienda* system, which spurred further conquests and searches for mineral wealth.

Exploitation produced a raft of Spanish laws to limit native abuse, promoting importation of enslaved Africans to search for gold instead, prompting a transition from *encomienda* to slavery. Some Africans arrived in New Granada and Quito with previous mining and metallurgical experience, including gold, iron, and copper alloys. Technologies were exchanged, not only in mining but also in woodworking, foraging, farming, and medicine. In several gold-mining enclaves such as Zaragoza, inland from Cartagena, Africans vastly outnumbered Indigenous peoples within a few generations of settlement, yet dwindling Indigenous communities still supplied essential items. The cycle was repeated on other mining frontiers, as evidenced by the demography of the Pacific lowlands today. By contrast, in southern Ecuador Indigenous draftees remained the dominant labor force, but the scale of mining in greater Quito dropped precipitously after 1600, when many Andeans were forced to work in textile mills (which in turn supplied cloth to Andean mines north and south).

Environmental costs of gold mining during the "low-tech" Habsburg era are difficult to calculate but they were manifold. Colonial placer mining denuded landscapes and sped stream sedimentation. Deforestation was significant, and many square miles of fragile tropical lands were rendered sterile. There is even evidence of overhunting of manatees to render their fat for fuel oil in the Lower Cauca. Far more insidious were the refineries found around hard-rock gold mines in places such as Mariquita, Marmato, Chisquío, and Zaruma. Like the silver refineries of the same period in Potosí (Bolivia) or Zacatecas (Mexico), most of these mills relied on mercury amalgamation, which fouled air, water, and soil with crippling toxins. I have also noted a mercury spill on the Middle Magdalena in 1606. Lead, zinc, arsenic, and other metals were added to the mix in hard-rock camps. Lode mines bled acidic water, which disrupted pH levels in streams and rivers to the detriment of fish and many other organisms. Mine-worker health was universally deplorable as a result of these and other factors.

For all its ills, gold lubricated the north Andean economy and tied distant fringes to tenuous cores, including Quito, Popayán, Cali, Medellín, and Bogotá, sites of major religious as well as administrative building projects. Cartagena was a rare Atlantic port sustained by New Granada's repeated gold cycles, and gold paid for its massive fortifications. Gold was from the start a global commodity as well. Most of the gold of New Granada and Quito was exported to Europe, and a considerable amount went on to purchase exotic commodities in the Middle East and India, both of which had huge absorptive capacity for gold as well as silver in the seventeenth century.

Yet gold working was also a locally appreciated art. Colombian and Quito gold went into jewelry, particularly as a form of portable wealth for women, or into religious objects such as the Crown of the Andes, monstrances, chalices, and patens. The great Popayán crown stands out only for its size and opulence. Notary records suggest that, by the early seventeenth century, many north Andean goldsmiths were men of color, referred to as *indios*, *mestizos*, *mulattos*, and even enslaved "Blacks." Emeralds proved a fine complement to gold, yet both gold and emeralds were so abundant in New Granada—in relative terms—that objects like the Crown of the Andes were undervalued. How else to explain this massive religious artifact from a tiny colonial town? The same was true of platinum, which for colonial miners was an accidental byproduct of placer gold mining that throughout the period under consideration was entirely unwanted, a nuisance to be cast away.

Fetishism of these mostly slave-produced mineral commodities hardened when they were exported from Spanish South America. Bogotá's gold *escudos* might be remade into Ottoman *sultanis*, and faceted Muzo emeralds could be refashioned or carved to adorn Mughal turbans. The farther these precious commodities got from home, the easier it was to forget who produced them, and under what circumstances. A more delayed, south-to-north path of expatriation was taken by the long-hidden but now publicly exhibited Crown of the Andes. Its material integrity, despite some lost stones, makes it a fitting symbol if not the perfect physical manifestation of the congealed labor and suffering of so many thousands of coerced and enslaved Indigenous and African mineworkers and artisans. It is also the distilled product of a despoiled and intoxicated landscape. And perhaps it is a fitting symbol of a heartfelt baroque-to-modern Catholic religious longing, even if its sale never supported the poor elderly residents of twentieth-century Popayán. Perhaps when she passes the archbishop's palace on her feast day or during Easter week, the Virgin of the Immaculate Conception ponders the strange journey taken by her crown.

Thumbnail Historiography

The history of gold mining in Habsburg Colombia has not been neglected, although the same is not true of Ecuador. New Granada's national identity was closely tied to gold production, and the "peso de oro" was Colombia's currency until recently. Ecuador, by contrast, had only a few mining enclaves after independence, mostly in the far south. Early students of gold mining in Colombia included Alexander von Humboldt, who visited around 1800, but the first synthetic study using colonial records was that of Vicente Restrepo. Restrepo's work was complemented by regional studies until the historical geographer Robert C. West published a thorough synthetic study in 1952, a major inspiration for my own work and source for the maps I had commissioned for this chapter. After West, historians returned to regional studies, led by Germán Colmenares and several of his students, including Guido Barona, Zamira Díaz, and Mario Diego Romero. The ex-Peace Corps volunteer William Sharp examined slavery and gold mining in the Chocó, focused mostly on the Bourbon era. More recently, the historian Heraclio Bonilla has revived interest in the mines of Mariquita, among others. Sherwin Bryant and Claudia Leal have returned our attention to greater Popayán and the Chocó, as have Juan David Montoya and the geographer Marta Herrera. Most recently, Lorena Campuzano Duque has revived interest in the venerable and highly productive gold mines of northeast Antioquia.

The history of gold mining in Ecuador has drawn the interest of few scholars, but a key figure was the Jesuit historian José María Vargas, who wrote on this and other aspects of colonial political economy in the mid-twentieth century. Quito's legendary gold mines and lost Inca treasures were also treated by the eighteenth-century Jesuit historian Juan de Velasco, repeated by the turn-of-the-century historian Federico González Suárez. These seductive "myth-histories" have required some unwinding. Writing in the 1980s, the regional historian Juan Chacón outlined the geography and cycles of mining in the Cuenca area, and others produced articles about the hard-rock mines of Zaruma. All told, the history of gold mining in colonial Spanish America remains hidden in the shadow of silver.

Glossary of Spanish Gold Terms

After Juan de Arfe y Villafañe, *Quilatador de la plata, el oro y de las piedras* (Valladolid, 1572).

castellano.................... Spanish raw gold unit of 4.6 g, 22.5 karats
doblón......................... doubloon or "doubled" gold coin of 2, 4, or 8 *escudos*
escudo......................... Spanish gold coin of 3.38 g, 22.5 karats
grano .... a fraction of a karat based on wheat grains
juan blanco .... "John White" or fool's gold
peso de oro de minas ... "gold mine peso"; see *castellano*
quilate......................... karat, or gold fineness, as a fraction of 24

Notes

1. Franklin Stewart, *Crown of the Andes: A History of the Oldest and Largest Collection of Emeralds in the World* (Chicago: Crown of the Andes Company, 1936). This brief history is to be taken with a large grain of salt, but it makes for fascinating reading. My reconstruction of the crown's past draws from reporting in various Colombian newspapers and magazines, especially the Bogotá weekly *Semana*.

2. "The Crown of the Andes: A Magnificent Devotional Crown in Gold and Emeralds to be sold by auction on the order of an American syndicate, 21 Nov. 1963" (London: Sotheby's, 1963).

3. Michael Taussig, *My Cocaine Museum* (Chicago: University of Chicago Press, 2004). Despite the title, Taussig's focus is Colombian gold.

4. New work on this later era includes Yesenia Barragán, *Freedom's Captives: Slavery and Gradual Emancipation on the Colombian Black Pacific* (New York: Cambridge University Press, 2021). On gold circulation on either side of Independence, see James V. Torres, "Trade in a Changing World: Gold, Silver, and Commodity Flows in the Northern Andes, 1780–1840" (PhD diss. Georgetown University, 2021).

5. Archivo General de Indias, Seville (hereafter AGI), Contaduría 1536, Quito quintos fol. 28, March 13, 1539. The terms were *coco*, *tejuelo*, and *sepultura*.

6. See, for example, Jorge Garcés G., ed., *Testamento del Señor Capitán Don Sebastián de Benalcázar (1551)* (Quito: Archivo Municipal, 1935), 24. Among Benalcázar's belongings were six disk-shaped ingots (*tejuelos*) of gold of various karats weighing almost 1,500 pesos, some labeled "oro de minas."

7. J. Michael Francis, ed., *Invading Colombia: Spanish Accounts of the Gonzalo Jiménez de Quesada Expedition of Conquest* (University Park: Penn State University Press, 2007), 32–33.

8. John J. TePaske, *A New World of Gold and Silver*, ed. by Kendall Brown (Leiden: Brill, 2010), 141–43. See also Alan Covey, *Inca Apocalypse: The Spanish Conquest and the Transformation of the Andean World* (New York: Oxford University Press, 2020).

9. Francis, *Invading Colombia*, 62, 71. See also Kris Lane, *Colour of Paradise: The Emerald in the Age of Gunpowder Empires* (New Haven: Yale University Press, 2010), 50–52.

10. Francis, *Invading Colombia*, 86.

11. John Hemming, *The Search for Eldorado* (New York: E.P. Dutton, 1978).

12. Marshall Saville, *The Gold Treasure of Sigsig, Ecuador* (New York: Heye Foundation, 1924). See also the Cañari or Sigsig diadem in the British royal collection sent to Queen Victoria by President Gabriel García Moreno.

13. The 1549 ordinances are summarized in José María Vargas, *La economía política del Ecuador durante la Colonia* (Quito: Banco Central, 1981; first published 1957), 190–91.

14. Karen V. Powers, *Andean Journeys: Migration, Ethnogenesis, and the State in Colonial Ecuador* (Albuquerque: University of New Mexico Press, 1995), 45. In short, the Indigenous population of the central highlands does not appear to have declined as precipitously nor rebounded as slowly as in Mexico, Peru, or the Caribbean. Powers gives the example of two towns subject to mine labor at Zaruma in the 1570s and 1580s, Cañaribamba and Garrochamba. The former had declined in population from 2,100 to 500 in six years, and the latter from 2,000 to 183 in the same period. The local residents explained that those Andeans not working in the mines already had chosen to flee in order to avoid this work (38).

15. Kris Lane, *Quito 1599: City and Colony in Transition* (Albuquerque: University of New Mexico Press, 2002), 120–45. For transcribed documents describing Spanish expeditions, see Ann Christine Taylor and Cristóbal Landázuri, eds., *Conquista de la región jívaro (1550–1650). Relación documental* (Quito: IFEA/Abya-Yala, 1994).

16. Linda A. Newson, *Life and Death in Early Colonial Ecuador* (Norman: University of Oklahoma Press, 1995), 347. Newson estimates that declines between conquest (1535) and 1600 ranged from ca. 80 percent in the Quito Basin to ca. 90 percent in the Corregimiento of Loja to a staggering 99 percent in the area around Guayaquil (here due largely to new diseases rather than labor exploitation).

17. Luis F. Calero, *Chiefdoms under Siege: Spain's Rule and Native Adaptation in the Southern Colombian Andes, 1535–1700* (Albuquerque: University of New Mexico Press, 1997), 186.

18. Hermes Tovar Pinzón, ed., *Relaciones y visitas a los Andes, siglo XVI. Tomo III. Región Centro-Oriental* (Bogotá: Instituto Colombiano de Cultura Hispánica, 1996), 147–61. See also new work by Santiago Muñoz Arbeláez, "The New Kingdom of Granada: The Making and Unmaking of Spain's Atlantic Empire, 1530–1620" (PhD diss., Yale University, 2018).

19. Archivo General de la Nación de Colombia, Bogotá (hereafter AGN), Historia Civil, 17.7, 18.2. The Bishop of Bogotá allegedly called for mercy and church sanctuary. Rodríguez's henchman Juan Esteban testified that the cruel acts were retribution for an Indigenous attack.

20. Hermes Tovar Pinzón, ed., *Relaciones y visitas a los Andes, siglo XVI. Tomo IV. Región del Alto Magdalena* (Bogotá: Instituto Colombiano de Cultura Hispánica, 1996), 73–388.

21. See, for example, AGN, Minas de Tolima, 1.7, 3.1, 4.10, 4.12.

22. AGN, Historia Civil, 9.9.

23. Captain Camacho's 1616–21 service report is in AGN, Historia Civil, 7.2. Archivo Histórico de Antioquia, Medellín, Minas de Guamocó, foundry books (doc. 1659) reveal a boom in the 1620–1640s. Gold was taxed at one-twentieth or 5 percent to stimulate production and it seems to have worked. In eight months (April 23 December 14, 1623) nearly 33,000 pesos in gold (adjusted to 22.5-karat standard) were taxed. Another book (doc. 1669) shows registered production dropping off somewhat by 1641–42, but the mines paid considerable taxes into the 1670s.

24. AGN, Historia Civil, 6.18. This document from 1621 suggests that gold income was falling, but that local Indigenous parishioners and penitents offered gold dust wrapped in paper to support a new church.

25. For a sense of the cultural diversity of contact-era Barbacoas, see Marta Herrera Ángel, *El conquistador conquistado. Awás, Cuayquer y Sindaguas en el Pacífico colombiano, siglos XVI–XVIII* (Bogotá: Universidad de los Andes, 2016). For pre-Columbian Esmeraldas, see Warren DeBoer, *Traces Behind the Esmeraldas Shore: Prehistory of the Santiago-Cayapas Region* (Tuscaloosa: University of Alabama Press, 1996). On Tolita-Tumaco gold and platinum, see Paul Bergsøe, *The Metallurgy and Technology of Gold and Platinum among the Pre-Columbian Indians* (Copenhagen: DNSS, 1937), discussed below.

26. Kris Lane, "The Transition from Encomienda to Slavery in 17th-Century Barbacoas (Colombia)," *Slavery & Abolition* 21, no. 1 (2000): 73–95. For the Chocó proper, see Caroline A. Williams, *Between*

Resistance and Adaptation: Indigenous Peoples and the Colonisation of the Chocó, 1510–1753 (Liverpool: University of Liverpool Press, 2005).

27. Mario Diego Romero Vergara, *Poblamiento y sociedad en el Pacífico colombiano, siglos XVI al XVIII*, 2nd ed. (Cali: Universidad del Valle, 2017). See also Juliet Wiersema, *The History of a Periphery: Spanish Colonial Cartography from Colombia's Pacific Lowlands (1720–1820)*, (Austin: University of Texas Press, 2023).

28. Williams, *Between Resistance and Adaptation*.

29. For a superb history of this region, see Claudia Leal, *Landscapes of Freedom: Building a Postemancipation Society in the Rainforests of Western Colombia* (Tucson: University of Arizona, 2018). The classic geographical overview is Robert C. West, *The Pacific Lowlands of Colombia* (Baton Rouge: Louisiana State University Press, 1957).

30. Kris Lane, "Gone Platinum: Contraband and Chemistry in Eighteenth-Century Colombia," *Colonial Latin American Review* 20, no. 1 (2011): 61–79; Bergsøe, *Metallurgy and Technology of Gold and Platinum*.

31. Lane, *Quito 1599*, 169–72.

32. AGI Mapas y Planos 29, map of the Chocó sent by the Popayán Governor Don Francisco Sarmiento de Sotomayor, dated Cali, April 14, 1610 (document/letter in Quito 16). Both are on PARES (Portal de Archivos Españoles); the letter is Quito,16,R.12,N.36. The letter refers to the abandoned town of Toro, the legendary Dabaybe, and various Indigenous groups, but not specifically to Nóvita or any other mining sites. Who named the Plata, Platilla, and Platona rivers? Does not this writer also denounce *juan blanco*? There may be more details on Nóvita in other letters from 1607 (May 28).

33. The transcribed Spanish text is in Pilar Ponce Leiva, ed., *Relaciones historico-geográficas de la Audiencia de Quito, siglos XVI–XIX*, 2 vols. (Madrid: CSIC, 1992–93), 1.518–26. The original manuscript is in the AGI, Patronato 240, ramo 6. See also Lane, *Quito 1599*, 76.

34. Tovar Pinzón, *Relaciones y visitas a los Andes, siglo XVI. Tomo III. Región Centro-Oriental*, 305–6.

35. AGN, Historia Civil, 16.20. The petition mentions Guasquí and Guali provinces. The long and convoluted poisoning case, which may have inspired a tale in Rodriguez Freyle's *El carnero*, is in AGN, Historia Civil, 21.1. For the broader phenomenon, see Pablo Gómez, *The Experiential Caribbean: Creating Knowledge and Healing in the Early Modern Atlantic* (Chapel Hill: University of North Carolina Press, 2017).

36. AGN, Minas de Santander (unico), no. 1, fols. 1–53; no. 9; no. 21. On *mestizaje* in early New Granada, see Joanne Rappaport, *The Disappearing Mestizo: Configuring Difference in the Colonial New Kingdom of Granada* (Durham, NC: Duke University Press, 2014).

37. Archivo Histórico de Antioquia, Medellín, Minas T.351, docs. 6609, 6610.

38. AGN, Historia Civil, 11.33. The petitioner Martín de Vargas of Tunja filed his report from Cartago.

39. Robert C. West, *Colonial Placer Mining in Colombia* (Baton Rouge: Louisiana State University Press, 1952), 13–14, 22, 25–27. The long 1593–96 case is in AGN, Minas de Antioquia, 4.1, fols. 1–673.

40. AGN, Historia Civil, 10.10, 11.16. Villalobos, described as "persona muy abil y experto en el arte de minas" (an individual quite handy and expert in the art of mining), was the royal comptroller in Zaragoza's new treasury, which assayed and stamped gold bars. He also claimed to have fought maroons (*negros alzados*) and the rebellious Comocoy Indians, and that three of his "best miners" drowned in the course of exploration.

41. On the anti-maroon campaign, see AGN, Historia Civil, 1, fols. 83–130. The literature on the alleged witches of Zaragoza is growing. A recent treatment is Nicole von Germeten, *Violent Delights, Violent Ends: Sex, Race, and Honor in Colonial Cartagena de Indias* (Albuquerque: University of New Mexico Press, 2013), 125–43. More in tune with regional geography is Luz Adriana Maya Restrepo, *Brujería y reconstrucción de identidades entre los Africanos en la Nueva Granada, siglo XVII* (Bogotá: Ministerio de Cultura, 2005).

42. AGN, Historia Civil, 6.15.

43. AGN, Historia Civil, 9.2.

44. AGN, Minas de Antioquia, 2.1, fols. 1–611.

45. AGN, Historia Civil, 4.36.

46. Enriqueta Vila Vilar, "La sublevación de Portgual y la trata de negros," *Ibero-Amerikanische Archiv*, new series, 2, no. 3 (1976): 171–92, esp. 176.

47. AGN, Historia Civil, 12.4.

48. I discuss the case in Lane, *Quito 1599*, 79–81. The documents are in the Archivo Nacional del Ecuador, Quito, Religiosos, caja 1.

49. See David Wheat, "The First Great Waves: African Provenance Zones for the Transatlantic Slave Trade to Cartagena de Indias, 1570–1640," *Journal of African History* 52, no. 1 (2011): 1–22; David Wheat, *Atlantic Africa and the Spanish Caribbean, 1570–1640* (Chapel Hill: University of North Carolina Press, 2016).

50. AGN, Minas de Antioquia, 5.1, fols. 1–306. The original owner was Captain Geronimo de Quesada. Most enslaved worked in mines called Oca and La Loma, plus a hard-rock mine called La Paloma.

51. AGN, Historia Civil, 20.32. In 1630 a cacique called Don Gerónimo of Jegua, a village somewhere near the confluence of the Cauca and Magdalena rivers, filed a complaint against the *encomendero* Martín de Zabaleta. Zabaleta, who had possessed the *encomienda* for two decades, was allegedly forcing the cacique and his subjects to hunt manatees and caimans constantly, demanding 100 jugs of their rendered fat each year. Some thirty-five men were dedicated to this job, using their own canoes, knives, and so on, forced to buy village-produced maize back from their own *encomendero* at extortionate prices. Village women produced hammocks, baskets, and other items, but these were simply taken from them for resale. Some payments were made in worthless swaths of cotton cloth. The *encomendero* was also charged with keeping young indigenous females (*chinas*) serving in his house in Mompóx, with no days off and round-the-clock tasks. The *encomendero* was getting rich by abusing his "entrusted" charges, stripping them even of their Saturdays, normally reserved for subsistence farming: "Con el trabajo y fuerzas de los dichos indios se ha hecho rico el encomendero, entablando hatos y compro 15 o 16 esclavos." The Indians, according to the cacique, lived "in greater slavery than the blacks." Of special interest is the testimony of a roughly thirty-year-old Indian pilot, Gonzalo, who said "today it is all caiman for there are no manatees." The usual hunting method was for the Indian men to go out in pairs in six or seven shallow boats (*barquetas*) corralling caimans during dry spells. They then speared the reptiles with harpoons (which they supplied) and gutted them immediately. The carcasses were handled by women, who rendered the fat on the spot by cooking in cazuelas. The Indians received 3 reales' worth of unwanted cotton cloth in exchange for each jug of fat. Other village men were sent to Zaragoza poling canoes to run the oil, maize, and meat to the mines. Women planted maize twice a year in plots cleared by men, but everyone was starving. Many children died very young. The *audiencia* in Bogotá reprimanded the *encomendero* and asked Cartagena's Indian Protector to look into the charges, but mostly Zabaleta was asked to provide his wards with better clothing, which was specified.

52. On these medicines, see Linda Newson, *Making Medicines in Early Colonial Lima, Peru: Apothecaries, Science and Society* (Leiden: Brill, 2017), esp. chap. 6; on slave diet and health in these years in the slave trade, see Linda A. Newson and Susie Minchin, *From Capture to Sale: The Portuguese Slave Trade to Spanish South America in the Early Seventeenth Century* (Leiden: Brill, 2007), esp. chap. 8.

53. For a comparable case from Popayán a few decades earlier (ca. 1614), see Lane, *Quito 1599*, 79–81.

54. Ibid., 136–45.

55. The Canadian mine entrepreneur Keith Barron runs the so-called Lost Cities-Cutucu Project: see http://www.aurania.com.

56. Heraclio Bonilla, *Las minas de Mariquita en el Nuevo Reino de Granada. Minería, mano de obra y circulación monetaria en los Andes del siglo XVII* (Bogotá: Doce Calles, 2015), 41–71; Guido Barona, "Estructura de la producción de oro en las minas de la Real Corona: Chisquío (Cauca) en el siglo XVII," *Anuario colombiano de historia social y de la cultura* 11 (1983): 5–42; Kris Lane, "Unlucky Strike: Gold and Labor in Zaruma, Ecuador, 1699–1820," *Colonial Latin American Review* 13, no. 1 (2004): 65–84.

57. Bonilla, *Las minas de Mariquita*.

58. AGN, Real Hacienda, T.23, fols. 68–74. On the structure of the *boga* or cargo canoe economy, see Thomas Gomez, *L'envers de l'Eldorado. Economie coloniale et travail indigene dans la Colombie du XVIeme siècle* (Toulouse: Université de Toulouse, 1984).

59. Peter Marzahl, *Town in the Empire: Government, Politics, and Society in Seventeenth-Century Popayán* (Austin: University of Texas Press, 1978), 24–25.

60. Herrera Ángel, *El conquistador conquistado*, 120–24.

61. Bernardo Vargas Machuca, *Defending the Conquest: Bernardo de Vargas Machuca's Defense of the Western Conquests*, ed. by Kris Lane, trans. by Timothy F. Johnson (University Park: Penn State University Press, 2010), 61. See also Bernardo Vargas Machuca, *The Indian Militia and Description of the Indies*, ed. by Kris Lane, trans. by Timothy F. Johnson (Durham, NC: Duke University Press, 2008). Vargas Machuca laments his lost town amid "gold and silver mines" in *Defending the Conquest*, 138.

62. AGN, Historia Civil, 15.32. Low-karat *oro de Mariquita* was used to pay wages in the late 1580s to carpenters and stonemasons building the town's new church.

63. A. M. Barriga Villalba, *Historia de la Casa de la Moneda*. 3 vols. (Bogotá: Banco de la República, 1969).

64. See Lorena Campuzano Duque, "'The People's Gold': Race and Vernacular Mining in the 'Ailing' Landscapes of Antioquia, Colombia, 1540–1958" (PhD diss., SUNY Binghamton, 2021).

Bibliography

Archivo General de Indias, Seville, Contaduría 1536

Archivo General de Indias, Seville, Mapas y Planos 29

Archivo General de Indias, Seville, Patronato 240

Archivo General de la Nación de Colombia, Bogotà, Historia Civil

Archivo General de la Nación de Colombia, Bogotà, Minas de Antioquia

Archivo General de la Nación de Colombia, Bogotà, Minas de Santander

Archivo General de la Nación de Colombia, Bogotà, Minas de Tolima

Archivo General de la Nación de Colombia, Bogotà, Real Hacienda, T.23

Archivo Histórico de Antioquia, Medellín, Minas T.351

Archivo Histórico de Antioquia, Medellín, Minas de Guamocó, foundry books

Archivo Nacional del Ecuador, Quito, Religiosos

Arfe y Villafañe, Juan de. *Quilatador de la plata, oro y de las piedras*. Valladolid, 1572.

Barona, Guido. "Estructura de la producción de oro en las minas de la Real Corona: Chisquío (Cauca) en el siglo XVII." *Anuario colombiano de historia social y de la cultura* 11 (1983): 5–42.

Barragán, Yesenia. *Freedom's Captives: Slavery and Gradual Emancipation on the Colombian Black Pacific*. New York: Cambridge University Press, 2021.

Barriga Villalba, A. M. *Historia de la Casa de la Moneda*. 3 vols. Bogotá: Banco de la República, 1969.

Bergsøe, Paul. *The Metallurgy and Technology of Gold and Platinum among the Pre-Columbian Indians*. Copenhagen: DNSS, 1937.

Bonilla, Heraclio. *Las minas de Mariquita en el Nuevo Reino de Granada. Minería, mano de obra y circulación monetaria en los Andes del siglo XVII*. Bogotá: Doce Calles, 2015.

Bryant, Sherwin K. *Rivers of Gold, Lives of Bondage: Governing through Slavery in Colonial Quito*. Chapel Hill: University of North Carolina Press, 2014.

Calero, Luis F. *Chiefdoms under Siege: Spain's Rule and Native Adaptation in the Southern Colombian Andes, 1535–1700*. Albuquerque: University of New Mexico Press, 1997.

Campuzano Duque, Lorena. "'The People's Gold': Race and Vernacular Mining in the 'Ailing' Landscapes of Antioquia, Colombia, 1540–1958." PhD diss., SUNY Binghamton, 2021.

Covey, Alan. *Inca Apocalypse: The Spanish Conquest and the Transformation of the Andean World*. New York: Oxford University Press, 2020.

"The Crown of the Andes: A Magnificent Devotional Crown in Gold and Emeralds to be sold by auction on the order of an American syndicate, 21 Nov. 1963." London: Sotheby's, 1963.

Cummins, Thomas B.F. "'They esteem emeralds even more than gold': Muiscas, Spaniards, and Objects of Value." In *Portable Universe/El universo en tus manos: Thought and Splendor from Indigenous Colombia*, 168–79. Los Angeles: LACMA, 2022.

DeBoer, Warren. *Traces Behind the Esmeraldas Shore: Prehistory of the Santiago-Cayapas Region*. Tuscaloosa: University of Alabama Press, 1996.

Díaz, Zamira. *Oro, sociedad y economía. El sistema colonial en la Gobernación de Popayán, 1533–1733*. Bogotá: Banco de la República, 1994.

Francis, J. Michael, ed. *Invading Colombia: Spanish Accounts of the Gonzalo Jiménez de Quesada Expedition of Conquest*. University Park: Penn State University Press, 2007.
Friede, Juan, ed. *Documentos sobre la fundación de la Casa de la Moneda en Santa Fé de Bogotá*. Bogotá: Banco de la República, 1963.
Garcés G., Jorge, ed. *Testamento del Señor Capitán Don Sebastián de Benalcázar (1551)*. Quito: Archivo Municipal, 1935.
Germeten, Nicole von. *Violent Delights, Violent Ends: Sex, Race, and Honor in Colonial Cartagena de Indias*. Albuquerque: University of New Mexico Press, 2013.
Gómez, Pablo. *The Experiential Caribbean: Creating Knowledge and Healing in the Early Modern Atlantic*. Chapel Hill: University of North Carolina Press, 2017.
Gomez, Thomas. *L'envers de l'Eldorado. Economie coloniale et travail indigene dans la Colombie du XVIeme siècle*. Toulouse: Université de Toulouse, 1984.
Hemming, John, *The Search for Eldorado*. New York: E.P. Dutton, 1978.
Herrera Ángel, Marta. *El conquistador conquistado. Awás, Cuayquer y Sindaguas en el Paciífico colombiano, siglos XVI–XVIII*. Bogotá: UniAndes, 2016.
Lane, Kris. *Colour of Paradise: The Emerald in the Age of Gunpowder Empires*. New Haven: Yale University Press, 2010.
Lane, Kris. "Gone Platinum: Contraband and Chemistry in Eighteenth-Century Colombia." *Colonial Latin American Review* 20, no. 1 (2011): 61–79.
Lane, Kris. "Mining the Margins: Precious Metals Extraction and Forced Labor Regimes in the Audiencia of Quito, 1534–1821." PhD diss., University of Minnesota, 1996.
Lane, Kris. *Potosí: The Silver City that Changed the World*. Oakland: University of California Press, 2019.
Lane, Kris. *Quito 1599: City and Colony in Transition*. Albuquerque: University of New Mexico Press, 2002.
Lane, Kris. "The Transition from Encomienda to Slavery in 17th-Century Barbacoas (Colombia)." *Slavery & Abolition* 21, no. 1 (2000): 73–95.
Lane, Kris. "Unlucky Strike: Gold and Labor in Zaruma, Ecuador, 1699–1820." *Colonial Latin American Review* 13, no. 1 (2004): 65–84.
Leal, Claudia. *Landscapes of Freedom: Building a Postemancipation Society in the Rainforests of Western Colombia*. Tucson: University of Arizona Press, 2018.
Lenis Ballesteros, César Augusto. "Oro y fomento minero en la Antioquia del siglo XVIII." *Historia y sociedad* (Medellín) 18 (2010): 213–57.
Lenis Ballesteros, César Augusto. *"Una tierra de oro." Minería y sociedad en el Nordeste de Antioquia, siglos XVI–XIX*. Medellín: Instituto para el Desarollo de Antioquia, 2007.
Marzahl, Peter. *Town in the Empire: Government, Politics, and Society in Seventeenth-Century Popayán*. Austin: University of Texas Press, 1978.
Montoya Guzmán, Juan Davíd. "Las mas remotas tierras del mundo: historia de la frontera del Pacífico, 1573–1687." PhD diss., Universidad Pablo Olavide, 2014.
Moreno Sandoval, Armando. *Minería y sociedad en la jurisdicción de Mariquita. Reales de minas de Las Lajas y Santa Ana, 1543–1651*. Ibagué: Universidad de Tolima, 2006.
Muñoz Arbeláez, Santiago. "The New Kingdom of Granada: The Making and Unmaking of Spain's Atlantic Empire, 1530–1620." PhD diss., Yale University, 2018.
Newson, Linda A. *Life and Death in Early Colonial Ecuador*. Norman: University of Oklahoma Press, 1995.
Newson, Linda A. *Making Medicines in Early Colonial Lima, Peru: Apothecaries, Science and Society*. Leiden: Brill, 2017.
Newson, Linda A., and Susie Minchin. *From Capture to Sale: The Portuguese Slave Trade to Spanish South America in the Early Seventeenth Century*. Leiden: Brill, 2007.
Ponce Leiva, Pilar, ed. *Relaciones histórico-geográficas de la Audiencia de Quito (siglo XVI–XIX)*. 2 vols. Quito: Abya-yala, 1992.
Powers, Karen V. *Andean Journeys: Migration, Ethnogenesis, and the State in Colonial Ecuador*. Albuquerque: University of New Mexico Press, 1995.
Rappaport, Joanne. *The Disappearing Mestizo: Configuring Difference in the Colonial New Kingdom of Granada*. Durham, NC: Duke University Press, 2014.
Restrepo, Luz Adriana Maya. *Brujería y reconstrucción de identidades entre los Africanos en la Nueva*

Granada, siglo XVII. Bogotá: Ministerio de Cultura, 2005.
Restrepo, Vicente. *Estudio sobre las minas de oro y plata de Colombia*. 2nd ed. Bogotá, 1888.
Romero Vergara, Mario Diego. *Poblamiento y sociedad en el Pacífico colombiano, siglos XVI al XVIII*. 2nd ed. Cali: Universidad del Valle, 2017.
Ruiz Rivera, Julián Bautista. *La plata de Mariquita en el siglo XVII. Mita y producción*. Bogotá: Ediciones Nuestra América, 1979.
Saville, Marshall. *The Gold Treasure of Sigsig, Ecuador*. New York: Heye Foundation, 1924.
Sharp, William F. *Slavery on the Spanish Frontier: The Colombian Chocó, 1680–1810*. Norman: University of Oklahoma Press, 1976.
Stewart, Franklin. *Crown of the Andes: A History of the Oldest and Largest Collection of Emeralds in the World*. Chicago: Crown of the Andes Company, 1936.
Taussig, Michael. *My Cocaine Museum*. Chicago: University of Chicago Press, 2004.
Taylor, Ann Christine, and Cristóbal Landázuri, eds. *Conquista de la región jívaro (1550–1650). Relación documental*. Quito: IFEA/Abya-Yala, 1994.
TePaske, John. *A New World of Gold and Silver*. Edited by Kendall Brown. Leiden: Brill, 2010.
Torres, James V. "Trade in a Changing World: Gold, Silver, and Commodity Flows in the Northern Andes, 1780-1840." PhD diss., Georgetown University, 2021.
Tovar Pinzón, Hermes, ed. *Relaciones y visitas a los Andes, siglo XVI. Tomo III. Región Centro-Oriental*. Bogotá: Instituto Colombiano de Cultura Hispánica, 1996.
Tovar Pinzón, Hermes, ed. *Relaciones y visitas a los Andes, siglo XVI. Tomo IV. Región del Alto Magdalena*. Bogotá: Instituto Colombiano de Cultura Hispánica, 1996.
Vargas, José María. *La economía política del Ecuador durante la Colonia*. Quito: Banco Central, 1981 (first published 1957).
Vargas Machuca, Bernardo. *Defending the Conquest: Bernardo de Vargas Machuca's Defense of the Western Conquests*. Edited by Kris Lane, translated by Timothy F. Johnson. University Park: Penn State University Press, 2010.
Vargas Machuca, Bernardo. *The Indian Militia and Description of the Indies*. Edited by Kris Lane, translated by Timothy F. Johnson. Durham, NC: Duke University Press, 2008.
Vila Vilar, Enriqueta. "La sublevación de Portgual y la trata de negros." *Ibero-Amerikanische Archiv*, new series, 2, no. 3 (1976): 171–92.
Webster, Susan V. *Lettered Artists and the Language of Empire: Painters and the Profession in Early Colonial Quito*. Austin: University of Texas Press, 2017.
West, Robert C. *Colonial Placer Mining in Colombia*. Baton Rouge: Louisiana State University Press, 1952.
West, Robert C. *The Pacific Lowlands of Colombia*. Baton Rouge: Louisiana State University Press, 1957.
Wheat, David. *Atlantic Africa and the Spanish Caribbean, 1570–1640*. Chapel Hill: University of North Carolina Press, 2016.
Wheat, David. "The First Great Waves: African Provenance Zones for the Transatlantic Slave Trade to Cartagena de Indias, 1570–1640." *Journal of African History* 52, no. 1 (2011): 1–22.
Wiersema, Juliet. *The History of a Periphery: Spanish Colonial Cartography from Colombia's Pacific Lowlands (1720–1820)*. Austin: University of Texas Press, 2023.
Williams, Caroline A. *Between Resistance and Adaptation: Indigenous Peoples and the Colonisation of the Chocó, 1510–1753*. Liverpool: University of Liverpool Press, 2005.

CONTRIBUTORS

Thomas B.F. Cummins is the Dumbarton Oaks Professor of the History of Pre-Columbian and Colonial Art in the Department of the History of Art and Architecture, Harvard University and Director of Dumbarton Oaks. His most recent book is a co-edited *Sacred Matters: Animism and Authority in the Pre-Columbian Americas* (Dumbarton Oaks, 2020); he is a Fellow of the Academy of Arts and Science and is the co-director of the Getty Foundation Connecting Art History Grant: *Afro-Latin American Art: Building the Field.*

Chiara Crisciani is Professor of Medieval Science and History in the Department of Humanistic Studies in the Universiity of Pavia. She is a member of the Société Internationale pour l'Étude de la Philosophie Médiévale, the Académie internationale d'Histoire des Sciences, and the Società italiana di Storia della filosofia. Among more than one-hundred publications she is the co-editor of the volume *Michele Savonarola, Medicina e cultura di corte* (Sismel, 2011).

Anne Dunlop, FAHA, is the Herald Chair of Fine Arts at The University of Melbourne. She works on medieval and Renaissance art in Europe, on the materials of early art, and on the cultural links between Europe and Asia at the time of the Mongol Empires. Dunlop's book publications include *Andrea del Castagno and the Limits of Painting* (Brepols, 2015), *Antipodean Early Modern* (Amsterdam University Press, 2018); and, as co-editor, *The Matter of Art: Materials, Practices, Cultural Logics* (Manchester University Press, 2014, 2015). She has been an invited Visiting Professor at Peking University in Beijing and at Zhejiang University in Hangzhou; and in 2022 she served Krautheimer Guest Professor at the Bibliotheca Hertziana Max-Planck-Institut in Rome.

Cecilia Frosinini, an Art Historian, served in several positions at the Opificio delle Pietre Dure and Laboratori di Restauro (OPD), Florence, Ministry of Culture, from 1990 to 2021.
She is presently a member of the Gallerie degli Uffizi Advisory Board.
At the Opificio, she was member of the Scientific Research Commitee and member of the OPD Managing Committee. She served as Director of the Panel and Canvas Paintings Department, Director of the Wall Paintings Department, Director of the Paper and Parchment Department, Deputy Director of the Polychrome Wood Sculpture Department.
She has published more than two-hundred scholarly articles on medieval and Renaissance art, and has authored or co-edited twenty books and catalogues, including *Masolino and Masaccio Panel Paintings: The Role of Technique*. She has been Ailsa Bruce Mellon Fellow and E. J. Safra Visiting Professor at CASVA, National Gallery of Art, Washington D.C., in 2012 and 2013. She is Member (Accademico d'Onore) of the historic Accademia delle Arti del Disegno, Florence.
She has taught as Adjunct Professor at the University of Florence, University of Pisa, and Catholic University in Milan.
She lectures widely in Europe and the United States, and has presented at international conferences, including at I Tatti, The Harvard University Center for Italian Renaissance Studies, The Metropolitan Museum of Art (NYC), the Virginia University, the Musée du Louvre, the National Gallery in London, the Leonardo Society in London, the Kunsthistorisches Institut in Florenz.

Abigail Krasner Balbale is Associate Professor in the Departments of Middle Eastern and Islamic Studies and History at New York University. Her research focuses on the Islamic west in the medieval period, with a particular interest in comparing written sources and material culture. Her prize-winning book, *The Wolf King: Ibn Mardanīsh and the Construction of Power in al-Andalus,* was published by Cornell University Press in 2022.

Kris Lane holds the France V. Scholes Chair in Colonial Latin American History at Tulane University, specializing in the history of the Andean region of South America. His most recent publications include *Potosí: The Silver City that Changed the World* (University of California Press, 2019) and *Pandemic in Potosí: Fear, Loathing, and Public Piety in a Colonial Mining Metropolis* (Penn State, 2021).

Yukio Lippit is Jeffrey T. Chambers and Andrea Okamura Professor of the History of Art and Architecture at Harvard University. He specializes in Japanese painting. His book *Painting of the Realm: The Kano House of Painters in Seventeenth-Century Japan* (University of Washington Press, 2012) was awarded the Charles Rufus Morey Book Award by the College Art Association and the John Whitney Hall Book Prize by the Association of Asian Studies. Recent publications include *Japanese Zen Buddhism and the Impossible Painting* (Getty Research Institute, 2017), *The Artist in Edo* (National Gallery of Art, 2018), and *Shukei: A Zen Monk-Painter in Medieval Japan* (Hirmer, 2022).

Suzanne Preston Blier, Allen Whitehill Clowes Professor of Fine Arts and of African and African American Studies, Harvard University, is an historian of African art and architecture in both the History of Art and Architecture and African and African American Studies Departments. Her most recent book projects include the forthcoming *1325: How Medieval Africa Made the World Modern* (Yale University Press, 2024), and *Picasso's Demoiselles: The True Origins of a Modern Art Masterpiece* (Duke University Press. 2019).

Carlo Taviani teaches at the University of Teramo (Italy). He was a research fellow of the Deutsches Historisches Institut in Rome, fellow and research associate at I Tatti. He taught at the University of Cape Town and Bologna. His last book is titled *The Making of the Business Corporation:. The Casa di San Giorgio and its Legacy* (Routledge, 2022) and he is currently working on Genoese merchant networks in Africa and across the Atlantic Ocean (ca. 1450–1530).

PHOTO CREDITS

Bergamo
Accademia Carrara: p. 40

Bilbao
Museo de Bellas Artes de Bilbao: p. 225 fig. 5

Bogotá
Museo de Oro: p. 251 fig. 3

Cambridge (Massachusetts)
Harvard University, Houghton Library: p. 112 fig. 1, pp. 114–115 fig. 2a–b

Copenhagen
Courtesy of the Nationalmuseet, Copenhagen: pp. 14–15 figs. 3–4

Florence
Berenson Collection, Villa I Tatti: p. 25 fig. 3
Biblioteca Medicea Laurenziana: p. 118 fig. 5 (World Digital Library)
Biblioteca Nazionale Centrale: p. 31 fig. 5
Church of Ognissanti: pp. 46–47 figs. 2–3

Glasgow
University Library, Special Collections: p. 132 fig 13-a–b

Grand Rapids (Michigan)
Gerald R. Ford Presidential Museum, gift of S. E. Quarm, Ambassador of Ghana: p. 163 fig. 4

Key West (Florida)
Mel Fisher Museum: p. 133 fig. 14ab

Kyoto
Kyōto Shi Rekishi Shiryōkan (Kyoto City Fire Department Historical Archive): p. 72 fig. 2
Lippit Yukio: p. 71 fig. 1, p. 77 fig. 4, p. 80 figs. 5–6

London
The British Museum: p. 143, fig. 20a–b

Madrid
Tonegawa Collection: p. 218 fig. 2

Mexico City
Archivo General de la Nación de México, Inquisición: p. 125 fig. 8, p. 125 fig. 9a
Museo Nacional de Antropología: p. 117 fig. 4

New York
American Numismatic Society: p. 218 fig. 1
Brooklyn Museum, Carll H. de Silver Fund, 45.11.5, Brooklyn Museum: p. 176 fig. 8
The Metropolitan Museum of Art: p. 126 fig. 9b (Purchase, 2015 Benefit Fund and Lila Acheson Wallace Gift, 2016 Accession Number: 2016.64), p. 161 fig. 1 (1978.412.384ab; gift of Nelson A. Rockefeller, 1964), p. 166 fig. 5 (L.1982.92; lent by the estate of Christian Humann, 1982), p. 222 fig. 3 (1983.413), p. 228 fig. 6 (17.190.161a-j), p. 229 fig. 7 (17.190.161f), p. 233 fig. 8 (17.190.157), p. 246, fig. 1 (Purchase, Lila Acheson Wallace Gift, Acquisitions Fund and Mary Trumbull Adams Fund, 2015, 2015.437)
The Morgan Library & Museum: p. 267 fig. 8

Paris
Bibliothèque nationale de France: p. 28, fig, 4
Musée du Louvre, Département des Peintures: p. 51 fig. 4

Rignano sull'Arno (Florence)
Abbey of Santa Maria di Rosano: p. 43 fig. 1

Rome
Museo delle Civiltà—Museo Nazionale Preistorico Etnografico Luigi Pigorini, su concessione del MIC, item no. 4190

San Lorenzo de El Escorial
Monasterio de San Lorenzo, photo by Felipe Pereda: p. 141, fig. 19

Seville
Archivo General de Indias: p. 261 fig. 5, p. 263 fig. 6, p. 265 fig. 7, p. 278 fig. 11

The Hague
Paleis Huis ten Bosch: p. 12 fig. 2
Thomas Lurie collection: p. 11 fig. 1

Tokyo
The Asahi Shimbun: p. 73 fig. 3

Toulouse
Muséum de Toulouse, donated in 2010, photo Roger Culos, 21.11.2014: p. 175 fig. 7

Urbino
Galleria Nazionale delle Marche: p. 55 fig. 5

Valencia
Fundación Bancaja, Colección de arte: p. 235 fig. 9

Veracruz
Secretaría de Cultura—INAH, Museo Baluarte de Santiago: p. 120 fig. 6

Washington, D.C.
Library of Congress, Manuscript Division, Harkness Collection: p. 122 fig. 7

Wikimedia Commons: p. 22 fig. 1, p. 23 fig. 2, p. 22 fig. 6, p. 23 fig. 7, p. 162 fig. 2 (United Kingdom Government, National Archives, public domain)
Winter Park (Florida)
Daniel Frank Sedwick LLC: p. 258 fig. 4, p. 269 fig. 9, p. 283 fig. 13, p. 284 fig. 14

INDEX OF NAMES

Page numbers in *italics* refer to illustrations

Printed in the month of January 2024 on the presses of Esperia, Lavis (Trento).

PEFC
PEFC/18-31-390

PEFC Certified

This product is from sustainably managed forests and controlled sources

www.pefc.it

Ex Officina Libraria Jellinek et Gallerani